after effects
in PRODUCTION

2nd Edition for After Effects 6.5

A tutorial companion from the authors of

Creating Motion Graphics with After Effects

Trish & Chris Meyer

CMP **Books**

San Francisco, CA

DEDICATED

To the memory of **Kevin McGrath** (1921–2001)
You loved to learn new things, and we loved you for it. Braithimid uainn thú. – Trish

Published by CMP Books
An imprint of CMP Media LLC
CMP Books, 600 Harrison St., San Francisco, California 94107 USA
Tel: 415-947-6615; Fax: 415-947-6015
www.cmpbooks.com
Email: books@cmp.com

For individual orders, and for information on special discounts for quantity orders, please contact:
    CMP Books Distribution Center, 6600 Silacci Way, Gilroy, CA 95020
    Tel: 1-800-500-6875 or 408-848-3854; Fax: 408-848-5784
    Email: bookorders@cmp.com; Web: www.cmpbooks.com

Distributed to the book trade in the U.S. by: Publishers Group West, 1700 Fourth Street, Berkeley, California 94710

Distributed in Canada by: Jaguar Book Group, 100 Armstrong Avenue, Georgetown, Ontario M6K 3E7 Canada

Library of Congress Cataloging-in-Publication Data

Meyer, Trish
    After effects in production : a tutorial companion from the authors of creating motion graphics with after effects
    / Trish & Chris Meyer. -- 2nd ed.
        p. cm. -- (DV expert series)
    ISBN 1-57820-264-7 (alk. paper)
1. Cinematography–Special effects–Data processing. 2. Computer animation. 3. Computer graphics. 4. Adobe After Effects.
I. Meyer, Chris II. Title. III. Series.
    TR858.M4897 2004
    778.5'235'0285536–dc22   2004026758

ISBN: 1-57820-264-7

Printed in the United States of America

05 06 07 08 09   5 4 3 2 1

Table of Contents

PART 1 // TUTORIALS

PART 2 // CASE STUDIES

Learning by Doing

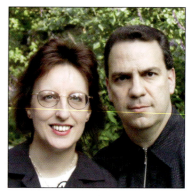

Different people learn differently. Some prefer to study the theory behind a task so that they have an idea of what's possible with a particular tool, and with that knowledge in hand, then go about solving their current challenge. Others prefer to dig in, getting their feet wet and hands dirty doing real work from the start, and sit back later to take in what they've learned.

That's why we've written two different types of books. Our *Creating Motion Graphics* series is a reference for the many different things After Effects can do, broken down by sections of the program or specific tools. *After Effects in Production* is by contrast a collection of in-depth tutorials, where a variety of tricks and tools are employed in concert to create a final work. The two are in fact companions for each other; at the end of each chapter in this book, we cross-reference chapters in *Creating Motion Graphics* where you can learn more.

All of these tutorials are based on artistic ideas and technical concepts that we've employed in our own design and production work for video and film. In addition to giving you the steps necessary to achieve a particular end, you will also find we take numerous detours explaining the "why" behind a particular approach, as well as detailing all of the little tweaks that go into creating finished work. Where we feel a subject is deep enough that it requires us to spend time covering more fundamental concepts, you will find a companion bonus tutorial on the DVD-ROM that presents a more complex project that builds on the concepts you've learned.

The second part of this book is devoted to case studies of broadcast spots created by leading studios such as ATTIK, Belief, Curious Pictures, The Diecks Group, and Fido, as well as our own studio, CyberMotion. These demonstrate different ways that After Effects has been used to combine film and video, 3D models, and elements as organic as water and wooden puppets, to realize a client's goal. Taken as a whole, we hope this book helps you realize your own creativity in using After Effects on the projects that may come your way.

Trish and Chris Meyer

CyberMotion

December 2004

How to Use This Book

This book was designed for people who already have some experience using Adobe After Effects. Its goal is to help you build on that experience by sharing a number of tricks and techniques in an artistic context.

That said, we've endeavored to make the instructions for each tutorial easy to follow, without assuming too much. The first tutorial in particular – *Atomic Café* – is a good starting point for beginners. You can then fill in the information behind a feature by referring to the manual, online Help, or our companion book series *Creating Motion Graphics with After Effects*.

Each tutorial follows its own path. Some feature step-by-step instructions for how to build a project from scratch; others begin with several elements already in place, then show you how to put them to work. Some provide exercises on general concepts, then walk you through a more complex project that uses those same concepts; a couple encourage you to build on our base and customize the project on your own. There are a handful of two-part tutorials, which either are continued on a PDF file on the DVD-ROM, or which form the base for the next tutorial in the book. There are even occasions when we purposely lead you down the most common blind alleys, just to make sure you know how to find your way back out.

The case studies should be of value to any motion graphics artist or producer, even if you don't use After Effects for your own work.

The Ground Rules

Before you start each tutorial, we recommend you copy its folder from the DVD to your hard drive. This will speed up file access and allow you to save your own intermediate versions of the project as you work – something we suggest you do often. The QuickTime movies of the finished pieces will also play back more smoothly.

If files become "unlinked" for some reason, they will appear in *italics* in the Project window. Simply double-click the first missing item: This will bring up a standard file navigation dialog where you can locate that item. Select it and click OK. Provided the folder relationship between the project and its sources has not changed, After Effects will now search all folders for any other missing items and link them in as well.

You should read the Overview box on the first page of each tutorial: It will alert you to any free third-party effects you need to have installed before you open After Effects, and to the project files you should load. If you open a project and After Effects warns you that some effects are missing, you either forgot to install one of these plug-ins, or the project requires a Professional edition effect while you're running the Standard edition.

Each tutorial is broken down into a number of Parts, which cover certain features or building blocks in the final project. Inside these Parts are numbered Steps. Our definition of what fits into a Step is pretty loose; in general, you will find that Steps in a tutorial start out short and easy and become more involved as you proceed.

There is no set amount of time that it should take to finish a tutorial: Some are very long and involved, and might take several hours and more than one session to finish; others are relatively quick and breezy.

Therefore, each tutorial project typically contains a folder of prebuilt compositions that represent where your progress should be at the end of Parts or after significant Steps. Feel free to use these to compare against your own work to make sure you understood a section. If you want to pick up a tutorial from the middle, you can also use one of these prebuilt comps as your starting place.

What's in a Name?

There are so many different elements in an After Effects project, we've tried to establish a set of typographic conventions that we hope will make it easier to understand what we are talking about and when:

• **Words in bold** refer to the specific names of folders, files, or layers you are using, or an effect that you should apply.

• [**Words in bold and in brackets**] are the names of compositions, as opposed to layers in a composition.

• "**Words in bold and in quotes**" are text you should enter – such as the name for a new composition or solid.

• **Words in bold and in this alternate font** are pieces of code used in Expressions.

• Most figures start with a number that tells you which Step they are referring to. Keep a lookout for the After Effects selection arrow shown in these figures: It often points to the values or switches being discussed. Red circles and arrows also help.

• When there is a chain of folders or effects you have to navigate through, we separate links in the chain with a > symbol: For example: **Project>Sources>Proxies**.

• We use keyboard shortcuts extensively throughout this book. The Macintosh shortcut is presented first (followed by the Windows keystrokes in parenthesis).

• "Context click" means to hold down the Control key while clicking on the Macintosh, and to right-mouse click on Windows.

Iconography

The content inside each chapter is usually presented in a linear fashion. However, you will find numerous asides throughout. In addition to sidebars, which focus on specific ideas or techniques, you will also see:

Tips: Useful tricks and shortcuts, or info on optional third-party effects we recommend.

Factoids: Tweaky bits of specific information that might help demystify some subjects (or at least provide interesting party gossip among your tweaky friends).

Gotchas: Important rocks you might trip over, such as special cases in which a feature might not work.

Connects: If you want more background information on a subject or section of the program used in the tutorial, these refer you back to chapters in *Creating Motion Graphics* where you can read more.

Professional edition: After Effects comes in two flavors: Standard and Professional editions. Whenever a chapter or section of a tutorial *requires* the Professional edition, you will see this icon.

In many cases where we designate you need the Professional edition, we provide workarounds or otherwise suggest you could perhaps skip a section, using one of our prebuilt compositions that already includes the steps that otherwise would have required a Professional edition feature to execute. In other words, if you have just the Standard edition, read on a little bit before giving up. And there's always the free Tryout version on the DVD.

The tutorials are also color-coded based on which version is recommended: Red means After Effects 6.5 or later Standard edition is fine, while Purple means the 6.5 or later Professional edition is required. The latter also have **Pro** added to their After Effects project names.

System Requirements

We assume you already have a copy of After Effects 6.5 or later installed – if not, a free Tryout copy of the version 6.5 Professional edition is included on this book's DVD. Our requirements are not that much different from what Adobe recommends for installing After Effects.

If you already have a full version of After Effects, then you have already installed QuickTime, which is required to run the program. If you are using the Tryout version and don't already have QuickTime installed, download it from Apple's web site (www.apple.com/quicktime/).

The rule of thumb with After Effects is that the more layers and compositions you are using, and the bigger those layers and comps are, the more RAM you need available. Also, the amount of RAM you have has a direct relationship to how long of a segment of time you can RAM Preview in a composition.

After Effects takes up a lot of screen real estate. In a pinch, most of these tutorials should work okay at a screen resolution of 832×624 pixels, although you will be happier if you can work at 1024×768 pixels.

We assume you are using an extended keyboard, as many great time-saving shortcuts take advantage of the function keys and numeric keypad. The Macintosh operating system may try to steal the use of some of the function keys away from you; in System Preferences, choose Exposé, and reassign any keys that are using the F1-F12 function keys.

As for the speed of the computer, faster is always better – it results in less time wasted waiting to see the results of your work. Most of the projects have been built at smaller frame sizes to reduce the rendering time needed. If they are still too slow, consider using a lower Resolution – such as Half – which will greatly reduce your rendering time while still letting you see what's going on.

Installation

Many of the free After Effects plug-ins on this DVD don't require an installer: Just drag them into the After Effects Plug-ins folder. If the Windows version ends in .aex, you can drag it directly (although if an effect fails to serialize you may need to unlock it on your disk). If it ends in .zip, it needs to be uncompressed first; if it ends in .exe, then it is an installer that you need to run. A summary of the free plug-ins with a guide to their installation is included in the Free Plug-ins folder as a PDF.

If you do not already have a copy of After Effects 6.5 or later, we have included a free 30-day Tryout version of After Effects on the DVD, courtesy of Adobe Systems. Copy the folder with the version for your operating system to your hard drive, decompress the archive, and then run the installer. More recent versions may be downloaded as they become available from Adobe's web site (www.adobe.com/products/tryadobe/main.jsp).

This Tryout contains all of the features of the Professional edition, except for the free Adobe

fonts, the Cycore FX plug-ins, and MPEG-3 encoder. It does expire after 30 days, so if you need to use it, make sure you set aside a block of time where you can work through the maximum number of tutorials in this book. Note that Chapter 8's Bonus Tutorial (*Postcards from Earth*) requires the CC Sphere effect from the Cycore FX set.

Many of the additional files on this book's DVD are in PDF format and require Adobe Acrobat Reader. If you don't already have a copy of Acrobat Reader, an installer is included on your After Effects disc; you can also download the latest version for a variety of platforms from Adobe's web site (www.adobe.com/products/acrobat/readermain.html).

Since we have tried to focus on artistic concepts as much as version-specific tricks, we hope this book earns a place on your bookshelf for years to come. You should be able to open all of these projects in future versions of After Effects; just click OK when it tells you it is converting the project from an earlier version.

The Point

We imagine you've heard the saying that if you give a person a fish, you've fed a person for a day, but if you teach a person how to fish, you've fed them for the rest of their lives. As a result, you will find this book short on tables of numbers to enter, and long on explanations of *why* you might enter a certain range of numbers. Without this background information, we fear tutorials turn into magic incantations: You may know how to repeat them to reproduce a specific effect, but are left not knowing how to apply them to your own projects. We want you to come away from *After Effects in Production* with a better understanding of how to efficiently realize the original ideas in your head.

Even More…

www.cybmotion.com/sharing

The above web page is the central hub of our web site, linking you to articles we've written, books we recommend, classes we're teaching, seminars where we're speaking, online forums where we hang out, and so on. It also includes a link to our Books page, where you can keep track of version updates to our books. You can also read about our books and videos at **www.cybmotion.com/training**.

We love to hear from our readers as to what they enjoyed – and didn't enjoy. Please email your feedback to: books@cybmotion.com. Please note that we cannot answer technical questions unrelated to the content of the books.

For Instructors

If you are an instructor, we hope that you will adapt this book to your specific needs and find it useful in teaching After Effects. Many of the concepts in this book are modeled on the advanced After Effects classes Trish teaches, as well as sessions we've both delivered at numerous conferences and trade shows.

Recognizing the budgets and time constraints of most instructional situations, we've built most of the tutorials using 320×240 comps and similar low-resolution sources. This requires less memory all around and results in faster demonstrations and previewing. However, the concepts are certainly from the real world, and should adapt directly to full-frame video projects.

For copyright reasons, each student must own their own copy of this book. This also allows them to review the material covered after class – without wasting valuable class time writing reams of notes. Students can open the tutorials from the DVD, make changes to it as they practice, and save the edited project to their own folders on a hard disk or removable media. At the next class, if they mount the DVD *before* opening their modified projects, the sources should relink properly.

If your school has the available disk space, students may copy contents from the DVD to their computers, or you may place the files on a server, but again only as long as each student owns their own copy of this book. Provided each student owns the book, you are free to modify the tutorials and adapt them to your specific teaching situation without infringing copyright.

As an instructor, you no doubt appreciate how much time and effort it takes to prepare class materials that both teach and inspire. If a school, company, or instructor distributes copies of the sources, plug-ins, projects, or PDFs to any person who has not purchased the book, that constitutes copyright infringement. Also, reproducing pages of this book, or any material included on the DVD (including derivative works), is also a copyright no-no. Thank you for protecting our copyrights, and those of the many vendors and studios who contributed sources – your cooperation enables us to write new books and obtain great source materials for your students to learn with.

Qualified teaching professionals can acquire evaluation copies of this book as well as our companion series, *Creating Motion Graphics with After Effects*, by submitting the request form provided on the CMP Books web site (www.cmpbooks.com) – look under Order Info>Classroom Resources.

DVD ROADMAP

The enclosed DVD-ROM contains all of the tutorials and case studies discussed in the book, plus a number of other useful resources. Here's what is in each folder:

1_Tutorials

The project and source files for each of the 12 tutorials, along with a movie of the final animation. Several tutorials include bonus projects and supplemental PDF files, which are also contained in these folders.

2_Case Studies

The project and source files for each of the six case studies, including QuickTime movies of the spots being discussed; you can play these or step through them frame by frame. Some of these also include demo reels from the studios who created the projects, giving you more "eye candy" to study for inspiration!

Also from CMP

Free chapters from new titles in the DV Expert series from CMP Books – the same folks who publish our books.

Credits and Info

Information about the guest artists, stock footage houses, and audio sample sources you will see and hear throughout this book. Also contains the End User License Agreements that you agree to when using the media and software provided on the DVD.

Goodies

Contains a pair of articles on timing video to audio, which are relevant to several of the tutorials; a series of Illustrator film and video templates, which will come in handy when you're designing your own titles; and other items we thought you would find useful.

Free Plug-ins

Boris Effects, Red Giant Software, and The Foundry have generously provided a set of free plug-ins which are used throughout this book:

• **Boris Continuum Complete Color Palette, Mosaic** and **Tritone:** Color Palette provides a good way for you to store commonly-used colors; Mosaic is an enhancement on the stock effect; Tritone is one of our favorite tools for colorizing footage.

• **Knoll Light Factory LE:** This very useful lens flare and "scratch" effect is featured in several tutorials. Thanks to Red Giant Software, its distributor, for making this possible.

• **The Foundry T_LensBlur:** A blur that more naturally mimics the "blooming" effect of an out-of-focus camera. You'll use this on everything…

Free Footage

This folder contains over 2 gigabytes of full-size NTSC and PAL footage for you to use in your own projects, courtesy of Artbeats and 12 Inch Design.

Tryout Version

Contains a 30-day Tryout version of After Effects 6.5 Professional edition for Macintosh or Windows. If you don't already have After Effects, decompress these archives and run the installer so you can load the projects! This Tryout contains all of the features of the Professional edition, except for the free Adobe fonts, Cycore FX plug-ins, and MPEG-3 encoder.

DVD Technical Support

If your DVD becomes damaged or won't load for any reason, please email CMP Books at books@cmp.com to arrange for a replacement.

After Effects Overview

If you are new to After Effects, these first few pages will give you a quick overview of the "lay of the land" inside the program – namely, what happens in what window.

Elements are organized in the Project window. This is where you keep your source material (*footage*), and well as your compositions (*comps*). When you import a footage item into a project, After Effects points to the file on your drives; it does not copy the footage into your project file – so you need to make sure that a project's sources are always available to it.

The main work happens inside the Comp and Timeline windows, which act as a pair. When a footage item is added to a comp, it becomes a *layer* in these windows. The Comp window is your canvas, where you get to see how your sources combine. The Timeline window shows how these sources appear and animate over time. Occasionally you will also access the Layer window, which allows you to focus on modifications to an individual layer.

Helping you as you work are a series of floating palettes. The main hub is the Tools palette, which allows you to quickly switch between tools and editing modes. The Time Controls palette helps you step through time and preview your work. The Character and Paragraph palettes are essential when using the Type tool to create text. The Effect Controls window displays the parameters specific to plug-in effects applied to a layer. These palettes and windows – as well as others – are opened and closed using the Window menu.

The **Project window** is where you organize your comps and sources. When an item is selected, a thumbnail and various specifications appear at the top of the window.

The **Time Controls** pallete. The RAM Preview shortcut is the 0 key on the keypad.

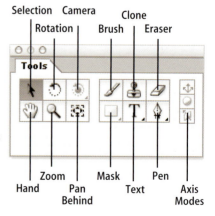

The **Tools** palette. The Selection tool (shortcut = V) is the one you will use most often. Hover the cursor over each tool to see its name and shortcut key.

Comp Icon & Tab | Close (this tab only) | Comp Name | Options menu for Comp window

Overview Comp 1

Overview Comp 1

Title Safe
Action Safe

100% | 0:00:00:00 | Full | Active Camera

Always Preview This View | Safe Areas | Toggle View Masks | Snapshot | Resolution | Toggle Transparency Grid | Comp Flowchart view

Bring Timeline forward

Magnification | Time Display | View RGBA | Region of Interest | 3D View | Fast Previews menu | Pixel Aspect Ratio correction

Composition & Timeline windows: The Comp window (above) is where you arrange your source material. Companion to the Comp window is the Timeline window (below), where you navigate and arrange your sources in time. Because these windows work as a pair, when you close one, by default the other will also close. Background movie courtesy 12 Inch Design.

Comp Tab | Time Display | Frame Rate | Close (this tab only) | Comp Name | Time Marker | Layer bars

Overview Comp 1 • Timeline

Overview Comp 1

0:00:00:00 (29.97 fps) | M

| | # | Source Name | | | | | :00s | | 05s |

▷ □	1	CM_AtomicMusic.mov
▷ □	2	aF_ML_BasicGlobe.tif
▷ □	3	Title.ai
▷ □	4	12_U02_B26_NTSC.m...

Switches / Modes

Timeline window Options

Comp Markers

Bring Comp window forward

Twirly | Layer Info (Label/#/Icon/Name) | Show/Hide Switches | Switches | A/V Features | In/Out/ Duration/Stretch | Zoom (in time)

Layer Icon & Tab   Layer Name   Close (Layer window only)   Options menu for Layer window

Set in point   Set out point

Always Preview This View   Safe Areas   Snapshot   In/Out/Duration Time Displays   View menu   Toggle Render (of current view)   Bring Comp window forward

Magnification   Time Display   View RGBA   Region of Interest   Toggle Transparency Grid   Pixel Aspect Ratio correction

Layer window: Double-click a layer to open it in its own Layer window (above). You'll use this window to create masks, adjust a layer's anchor point, and to paint on layers. If you have the Professional edition, the motion tracking controls also appear here.

Eyedropper   (black/white swatches)   Options menu

Font Family
Font Style
Font Size — Leading
Kerning — Tracking
Stroke Width — Stroke Style
Vertical Scale — Horizontal Scale
Baseline Shift — Tsume (for setting Asian type)

Fill Color (swap colors)
Stroke Color (no fill/stroke color)

Faux Bold   Faux Italic   All Caps   Small Caps   Subscript Superscript

Type Palettes The Character and Paragraph palettes are active when the Type tool is selected. You can also make changes to these palettes when a Text layer is selected (regardless of which tool is active) in which case any changes will apply to the entire layer.

Alignment
Indent Left Margin — Indent Right Margin
Indent First Line
Add Space Before Paragraph — Add Space After Paragraph
Options menu

Effects & Presets

The Effects & Presets palette stores and sorts available effects and Animation Presets. At its simplest, it provides an alternative to the Effects menu to find and apply plug-in effects to layers. You can double-click an effect to apply it to a selected layer, or drag it from the palette to the layer. The palette's Options menu (under the arrow in its upper right corner) gives you several choices on which effects you see and how they are sorted. You can search for effects by typing a few characters of their name into the Contains box (see figure to the right).

Animation Presets can contain any combination of parameters you can copy and paste in a comp, including mask shapes, transform properties (Position, Scale, Rotation and so on), text animators, and effects settings – including keyframed animation for any of these. After Effects ships with hundreds of presets with Text layer animations; you can also save your own presets. Several of the tutorials in this book provide you with presets of trickier animations or effect settings.

If the Preset has been saved or copied to the **Presets** folder inside the main **Adobe After Effects** folder, it will appear in the Effects & Presets palette under the "* Animation Presets" category, and can be applied to any layer in the same way as an effect (see above). If a Preset uses a selected effect, it will also appear in a popup along the top of an effect's settings in the Effect Controls window (see the figure to the right showing the Radio Waves effect). Finally, you can use the Animation menu and select Apply Animation Preset, and then find the Preset you want to apply anywhere on your computer's drives (not just in the Presets folder).

To save your own Preset, select the parameters and keyframes you want to remember, and select Save Animation Preset either from the Animation menu or the Effects & Presets palette's Options menu; you can also click on the Create New Animation Preset button in the lower right corner of the Effects & Presets palette. Settings for a selected effect may also be saved using its Animation Presets popup along the top of the parameters for that effect in the Effect Controls Window.

To save a preset, select a set of properties and keyframes (left), then click on the Create New Animation Preset button (circled above) at the bottom of the palette, or select Save Animation Preset from the Options menu.

6.5	6.5Pro
✓	✓

Atomic Café

Creating energy through the use of Time Remapping, Blending Modes, stock footage, and a pair of plug-ins.

In this tutorial, you will create a fun video intro that draws on retro themes from the '50s and '60s such as atomic power and psychedelic light shows. Underlying this goal are several important tricks: using the Sequence Layers keyframe assistant to auto-edit a large number of sources at once; Time Remapping to create a dramatic speedup; and using Blending Modes and Opacity to layer stock footage of various graphics with your own elements created using plug-in effects.

If you're the type who likes to peek ahead before you get started, go ahead and explore the various compositions in the project's folder **_Atomic Cafe * prebuilt** to get an idea of where you will be going.

OVERVIEW

Main Concepts:

These are the features and concepts we will be focusing on in this project:

- Importing Photoshop and Illustrator files as Comps
- Sequence Layers keyframe assistant
- Time Remapping
- Compositing with Blending Modes
- Nesting a composition
- Precomposing
- Animating Scale and Opacity
- The Wiggler *(optional)*
- Motion Blur
- Using "pyro" special effects movies
- Knoll Light Factory LE effect*
- Radio Waves effect

Requirements:

After Effects 6.5 or later standard version; Professional edition is optional (it's only necessary for the step using the keyframe assistant The Wiggler).

Third party effects: Knoll Light Factory LE effect (included on this book's DVD).

Getting Started:

* Be sure to install the Knoll Light Factory LE effect (distributed by Red Giant Software, www.redgiantsoftware.com) included on the accompanying DVD in the **Free Plug-ins** folder.

Inside the **Tutorials** master folder on the accompanying DVD, locate and copy the folder **01_Atomic Cafe** to your hard drive.

In the folder **Final Movie**, double-click on and play **AtomicCafe.mov** in QuickTime Player. Inside the **Project** folder you'll find the finished After Effects project file.

Open the project **AtomicCafe.aep**. This is your starting point; we suggest you save under a new name after each major section.

This folder contains copies of the compositions you will be building, saved after significant step numbers or at the end of whole parts. These should make it easier for you to make sure you're still on the right track. As this is a long tutorial, these prebuilt comps will also make it easier for you to jump into the middle of this tutorial later: Just find a prebuilt comp close to the step number where you want to jump in, duplicate it, rename it as if it was your own, and continue with the next step.

When you're finished exploring, close all the Comp and Timeline windows (Window>Close All) before you dive in below. As noted in the Getting Started box, this tutorial can be done in After Effects 6.5 standard. There are also some optional steps exploring The Wiggler keyframe assistant, available only with the Professional edition.

A frame from the final Atomic Café animation. The background uses movies from Artbeats/Soap Film CD and Bestshot/Retrocities CD, while the Radio Waves effect adds more radiating circles.

The Tasks

This is what you will be doing in the various parts of this tutorial. Since this is a fairly long tutorial, feel free to take breaks between parts:

PART 1: Import a layered Photoshop file of atomic icons and spread them across time using the keyframe assistant Sequence Layers.

PART 2: Import the soundtrack, alter the playback speed of the atomic icons using Time Remapping and have them scale over time, altering their speed by manipulating keyframe velocity curves.

PART 3: Mix stock movies using blending modes to create an interesting background, and precompose them.

PART 4: Import the layered Illustrator file containing the title, and animate it using Scale, Opacity, and Motion Blur. An optional section uses The Wiggler from the Professional edition to add further bounce to one of the words, or you can wiggle values using an expression.

PART 5: Create additional lighting effects using stock footage and the Knoll Light Factory LE effect.

PART 6: An optional section using the Radio Waves effect to further enhance the background; the effect controls are manipulated carefully so that the animated circles are timed to beats in the music.

Sources Diversion

Newly imported sources are automatically directed to whatever folder is currently selected in the Project window, or the folder where a selected source resides. After Effects can help you stay organized: Select the **My_Sources** folder in the Project window before you import a new source – that way you'll always know where it went!

Part 1: Getting Some Assistance

One of the central elements of this animation will be a series of stylized atomic symbols that accelerate as they play back. Oh, and the client wants short crossfades to occur between each symbol; no simple sequence or hard cuts. Your first thought might be "Well, *this* is going to be a lot of keyframes…" and you'd be right. However, After Effects features a Keyframe Assistant called Sequence Layers that will create those keyframes for you automatically.

Sequence Layers has a couple of advantages over just bringing in a series of images as a sequence. First, you can have the images cross-fade, or even leave gaps between them, rather than just switch at a speed determined by the sequence's frame rate. Second, it works with moving footage as well as still images (you can't import a set of movies as a sequence, but you can use Sequence Layers to create a video montage).

Sequencing Layers

STEP 1: We've created a layered Photoshop file for you, with one symbol per layer. You need to get these layers into After Effects, separated into individual footage items. You'll do this by importing the Photoshop file as a Composition:

• Select the folder **My_Sources** in the Project window, select File>Import>File, and locate the file **AtomSymbols.psd** from the **01_Atomic Cafe> Project>Sources** folder.

• Choose Composition from the Import As popup at the bottom of the Import dialog, and click Open. After Effects will create a folder and a composition – both named **AtomSymbols Comp 1** – for you.

1 In the Import File dialog, make sure you select Composition from the Import As menu.

• Press F2 to Deselect All, and then drag the comp (not the folder) into the **My_Comps** folder (see figure).

STEP 2: Double-click the composition [**AtomSymbols Comp 1**] to open it. Resize the Comp and Timeline windows as needed for your monitor; you should be viewing the Comp window at 100% Magnification (see readout in bottom left corner). There are a total of 30 layers in this comp, but if your comp's background color is black, you won't be able to see them! Change the color to white (Composition> Background Color).

STEP 3: You should now see a huge blob! Remember that the 30 layers are on top of each other, because each starts at the beginning of the comp – but they will play one after the other in a moment…

Double-click individual layers to view them in the Layer window, or turn on their Solo switch in the Timeline. Option+click on Mac (Alt+click on Windows) the Solo switch to turn off any other Solo switches. Close the Layer window or toggle off all Solo switches when you're done.

When you import a layered Photoshop or Illustrator file as a comp, you can choose whether or not each layer is automatically cropped to the exact size of the image portion of the *layer* (Import As: Composition – Cropped Layers) or whether each layer is the same size as the *composition* (Import As: Composition). The size of the resulting comp is determined by the Canvas Size in Photoshop. With Illustrator files, you can control the comp size in After Effects: If you don't do anything special, the sum of all the layers will determine the size of the composition. We prefer to either use the Artboard size (in Illustrator CS, with nothing selected, choose Object>Crop Area>Make), or to specify an area by first creating a rectangle the size we would like the comp to be and then selecting Object>Crop Area>Make.

3 At first, the comp looks like a blob (above), because you're seeing all the symbols at once. Open a few individually (below). These symbols were created by the Atomica illustration font from P22 (www.p22.com).

STEP 4: The duration of your comp will depend on the settings you last used to make a new comp. To adjust these settings, select Composition>Composition Settings or use the shortcut Command+K (Control+K). Rename the comp "**My_Atoms_precomp**", set the Frame Rate to 29.97 frames per second (fps) and change the Duration to 40:00 (40 seconds). (The width and height of 300×300 and the pixel aspect ratio are set automatically by the size of the Photoshop file, and are fine as is.) Click OK.

• The timecode base we prefer for NTSC production – namely 30 fps, Non-Drop Frame – has been saved with this project. You can verify this by opening File>Project Settings; close the dialog when you're done.

4 Edit the Composition Settings to give this comp a new name, a duration of 40:00, and a frame rate of 29.97 fps.

• If the original comp was shorter than 40:00 in duration, the timeline will be zoomed in, showing a smaller segment of time. If that's the case, zoom out in the timeline by hitting – (the minus key on the normal keyboard, not the numeric keypad) as many times as necessary until you're viewing the entire forty seconds.

You can view layer names as Source Name or Layer Name by clicking on the Layer Name column heading. Layers originating in Photoshop and Illustrator are shorter and easier to read if they are viewed as Layer Name. (However, some of our figures appear viewed as Source to reflect their origins.)

STEP 5: The plan is to trim each layer to 1:10 in duration, then stagger them in the timeline so they fade up and down over ten frames. Go to time 01:09, Select All using the shortcut Command+A (Control+A), and press Option+] (Alt+]) to trim all selected layer out points to 1:09.

5 To trim all of the layers at once, select them all, move the time marker to 01:09, and use the shortcut Option+] on Mac (Alt+] on Windows) to trim their out points to the current time.

If we wanted a duration of 01:10, why did we trim the out points to be at 01:09? Because all the layers currently start at 00:00, which counts as one frame of their duration. After trimming the layers at 01:09, they will play until just before 01:10, for a total duration of 01:10.

6 Set the Sequence Layers options to be Overlap, Duration 10 frames, Cross Dissolve Front and Back Layers.

STEP 6: With all the layers still selected, context+click (Control+click on Mac, right-mouse click on Windows) on any layer in the Timeline window and select Keyframe Assistant>Sequence Layers from the context-sensitive menu.

• The Sequence Layers dialog defaults to having the Overlap option unchecked, which means that the layers will sequence end to end. Since you want to soften the transitions between symbols by crossfading between each layer, turn on Overlap, and set the Duration to 00:10 (10 frames).

• Our Photoshop layers all have alpha channels, so it's important that one image fades out as the next fades in. To achieve this, set the Transition popup to Cross Dissolve Front and Back Layers. Click OK.

The layers should now rearrange themselves along the timeline from 00:00 to about 30:00, with a little overlap. If they don't, use Undo and apply Sequence layers again, double-checking your settings as you go.

> If the layers we were sequencing were simple full-frame images or movies, you would use the Transition>Dissolve Front Layer option in the Sequence Layers dialog. This is recommended for images that are full frame, as it avoids having two semitransparent layers in the middle of the crossfade. Depending on how they were stacked (top to bottom, or bottom to top), the frontmost layer would either fade out (Opacity keyframes 100–0%) to reveal the layer below, or fade in (Opacity keyframes 0–100%) to hide the layer below.

STEP 7: With the layers still selected, twirl down their Opacity property by hitting T. Notice that each layer fades in and out, with the exception of the first layer (which only fades out) and the last layer (which only fades in). Press T again to twirl up Opacity, and Deselect All (shortcut: F2).

6 *complete:* After you've executed Sequence Layers, each trimmed layer will be offset in time with a ten-frame overlap. The Opacity keyframes show each layer fades during these overlaps.

STEP 8: Move to time 30:00 and make a note of the last image in the sequence, layer **Atom_V**. You want this layer to hold at the end of the sequence. Extend the out point of this layer to the last frame of the comp by dragging the gray end of the layer bar to the right.

STEP 9: Making sure the time marker is at 30:00, hit N to end the work area at 30:00, and RAM Preview (0 on the keypad). When the preview plays back, you'll see each image for approximately one second. Note that this timing is fairly arbitrary: We chose 1:10 duration with a 10-frame overlap so that we could RAM Preview each image for a second, which is enough time to see who's who and whether the sequence is nicely balanced for variety and size (you could rearrange or resize individual layers if not). We also liked the balance of 10 frames of fade up, 20 frames for the image fully on, and 10 frames to fade down.

Save your project now – and often! If you got lost along the way, check out our prebuilt comp [**Atoms_after Step 09**]*; you'll find it in the* **Atomic Cafe * prebuilt>_compare comps_after Step ##** *folder.*

8 Extend the out point for the last layer – **Atom_V** – to the end of the comp. (Note that a layer that extends past the end of the timeline is automatically trimmed off, so you don't have to carefully drag the out point to the last frame of the comp.)

11 To automatically create a new comp the same duration as a footage file, drag the file to the Create a New Composition icon at the bottom of the Project window (where the cursor is pointing).

Part 2: Remapping Atoms

The design calls for the images to play back slowly, then get faster and faster until they culminate in a big bang as the title explodes onto the scene six seconds in. No, really…

To accomplish this, you're going to use the Time Remapping feature, timing the speedup to the soundtrack we've also provided. The atoms will also scale up over time to emphasize the gathering-energy feel. First, you need to create a new composition to hold this action, and to become familiar with the music.

Starting the Assembly Comp

STEP 10: Import the file **CM_AtomicMusic.mov** in this tutorial's **Project>Sources** folder. Make sure it ends up in the project's **My_Sources** folder. Note its duration in the Project window: 10:16.

STEP 11: You want to create a composition that is the same length as this soundtrack – this is where you will be building the main parts of this tutorial. You could remember the duration, press Command+N (Control+N) to create a new composition, and type it in, but we're going to use a handy shortcut instead.

Select **CM_AtomicMusic.mov** and drag it down to the Create a New Composition icon at the bottom of the Project window. This will automatically create a new comp with the duration of the footage file you dragged to it, and open its associated windows.

STEP 12: Open the Composition Settings (under the Composition menu), and rename this comp "**My_Atomic Cafe**". Set the Width to 320 and Height to 240. Verify that the Pixel Aspect Ratio is Square and the Frame Rate is 29.97. Click OK.

In the Project window, drag this new comp to the **My_Comps** folder. (Yes, we're sticklers for organization.)

STEP 13: RAM Preview the comp to hear the music, or press . (period on the keypad) to preview the audio from the current time. You can also twirl down the soundtrack's audio waveform (shortcut: select the layer and type LL – two Ls in quick succession), to get visual reinforcement for where the loud sections and other beats land in time.

12 Give this new comp an appropriate name, and set its size to 320×240.

If the audio cuts out before the end, set the duration of Audio Preview to 12:00 in Preferences>Previews.

The music has seven measures overall, with a major downbeat hitting at 06:00 at the start of the fifth measure. Move to this time, and type Shift+6 (on the keyboard, not the keypad) to create a comp marker at this frame. Now whenever you need to return to 06:00, just hit 6 on the keyboard. Go ahead and twirl up the waveform display – it takes up a lot of room, and needs time to redraw.

> The position of the music layer in the layer stack in the Timeline window is irrelevant, since it does not appear in the Comp window. However, we usually position the music layer at the top of the layer stack so that when the waveform is twirled down, chances are good you won't also need to scroll the Timeline window to see it.

13 After adding the audio track, either twirl down the Waveform property, or use the shortcut LL (two Ls). Move to 06:00 and create a comp marker so that you can easily locate back to this major beat in the music in the future.

Speeding Up Atoms

Truth be told, we didn't fancy trying to work out some tricky timing of how the Atoms sequence would speed up over time – for instance, Image #1 gets 20 frames, Image #2 gets 19 frames, and so on hoping that somehow it will magically all add up to Image #30 hitting exactly at 06:00 – and then calculating faster transitions as the images speed up… You get the idea of what a headache that would have been. Instead, now that you've sequenced the images to play back one every second or so, we'll use Time Remapping to create the speedup trick.

> Time Remapping is a powerful feature that allows you to keyframe time: a pretty strange concept at first. The advantage of Time Remapping over a layer's normal Time Stretch parameter is that you can change the time-stretch percentage of a layer over time – even make a layer pause by adding Hold keyframes. Another advantage is that After Effects calculates the results of Time Remapping before looking at the other animation keyframes, so you don't have to worry about other keyframes shifting in time just because you changed the speed. It's the perfect tool for the accelerating playback trick we want here.

Music Credits

The music for this tutorial was arranged by co-author Chris Meyer, using copyright-cleared samples from Keith LeBlanc's *Drum & Bass Carnage*, Zero-G's *Malice in Wonderland* (both available from Sounds Online: www.soundsonline.com) and Spectrasonics' *Distorted Reality 2* (available from Ilio Entertainment: www.ilio.com). Its tempo is 160 beats per minute, which works out to 1.5 seconds per measure. You'll notice a lot of the keyframes you create in this tutorial will be set to multiples of this duration.

14 Nest **[My_Atoms_precomp]** into **[My_Atomic Cafe]** starting at 00:00. Now you can treat the sequence of atomic symbols as just one piece of media (above and right).

Where's the Tab?

When a layer in your comp is a precomp, but its tab is not currently displayed in the Timeline window, double-clicking the layer opens its Layer window, not the precomp itself. Instead, Option (Alt) + double-click the layer to open the precomp and add its tab to the list of open comps.

15 Enable Time Remapping, type RR (two Rs) to reveal this property in the Timeline window, and twirl it down to further reveal its velocity graph. The current speed is 100%.

STEP 14: With the **[My_Atomic Cafe]** comp forward, press Home to return the time marker to 00:00. Select the **[My_Atoms_precomp]** comp from the Project window and nest it into **[My_Atomic Cafe]** by dragging it to the left side of the Timeline window below the audio layer (note that if you release the mouse in the timeline area on the right, the layer might not start at 00:00).

You can also use the shortcut Command+/ (Control+/) to add it without dragging. Another way to nest is to drag the precomp icon to the **[My_Atomic Cafe]** comp icon directly in the Project window. Both options place the precomp at the top of the layer stack.

The **[My_Atoms_precomp]** now appears as a single layer in **[My_Atomic Cafe]**, and can be manipulated as a group. However, any individual atom symbol can still be edited back in the precomp, and any changes made will ripple up through the second comp. This is the beauty of nesting: Think of it as a way to "group" multiple layers together so they can be effected or transformed easily.

STEP 15: Select the **My_Atom_precomp** layer and apply Layer> Enable Time Remapping. Type RR (two Rs in quick succession) to twirl down just the Time Remapping property. You'll notice one Time Remap keyframe is assigned automatically to the first frame of the layer (time 00:00), and the keyframe navigator indicates a second keyframe that you can't see. That's because it was assigned to the last frame of the layer (time 40:00). We'll deal with it later.

Twirl down the Time Remap velocity graph and note that the speed is running at 100%, which is realtime (one second in the precomp is one second in this comp).

STEP 16: Hit 6 on the keyboard (not the numeric keypad) to jump to comp marker 6 at 06:00. Click on the Time Remap property value in the Timeline window and change its value from 06:00 to 30:00. This tells the layer to play back thirty seconds of the precomp by the time it reaches 06:00 in this comp's timeline. The result is the equivalent of time-stretching the layer about 500% (thirty seconds now plays over six); because the keyframes are currently Linear, the speed change is consistent.

16 Locate the time marker to 06:00, click on the Time Remap property (where the top red arrow is pointing), and enter 30:00. Notice that the velocity curve now has a steeper slope, and that the Velocity values indicate the layer is playing back at 500% normal speed from 00:00 to 06:00, and at 29.41% from 6:00 to the end.

STEP 17: Remember back in Step 8 when you extended the last atom layer to play back from 30:00 through the end of [**My_Atoms_precomp**]? The result of this, plus the time remap you performed above, means that as of 06:00 in [**My_Atomic Cafe**], that last atom image will hold until the end of the comp – even though the time remap keyframes are interpolating between a value of 30:00 at time 06:00 (the new second keyframe) and a value of 40:00 at time 40:00 (that last, hidden keyframe). Even though the image is by all intents and purposes a "freeze frame" from time 06:00 to the end of the comp, it's still taking rendering time to calculate. This is because the precomp needs to be sampled at each frame to see what's going on.

To change this to a more efficient freeze frame, locate to the last Time Remap keyframe at 40:00 by clicking on the right arrow in the keyframe navigator, then delete the keyframe by unchecking the keyframe checkbox. Note that the speed after 06:00 now reads 0% per second (not 29.41%), indicating a true freeze frame. Return to time 00:00 (hit the Home key).

17 Use the navigation arrow to move the current time-marker to the last keyframe at 40:00 (which is otherwise past the end of the comp), and uncheck it to remove it. When you check and uncheck the keyframe box, you're affecting the keyframe at the current time (40:00); the second keyframe selected at 06:00 is not affected by this action.

Since no other keyframe follows the one at 06:00, the source image at 06:00 will be cached in RAM, and the precomp will be ignored from that point on. As a general tip, enabling Time Remapping for a precomp and then freezing on the last moving frame is a great way to optimize rendering when the precomp has lots of layers, but has otherwise stopped moving early on in the timeline. An example of this would be a precomp with a multi-layered title that animates on with slow-to-render effects before resolving to a final resting place – but the effects are still being "polled." Time Remap can freeze this last frame for a faster render.

Even Easier!

If you're easing the first or last keyframe of an animation, you don't need to be particular about applying Easy Ease Out and Easy Ease In – just hit F9 for Easy Ease. (Note that OS X users may need to override the Exposé shortcuts to use F9.)

STEP 18: Set the work area from 00:00 to 07:00 and RAM Preview. All 30 atom images will now play back faster over six seconds – albeit at a consistent pace. It's now time to match the action of the images to the music, which builds in intensity until the downbeat at 06:00.

*If you've had trouble following the use of Time Remapping, compare your result with the prebuilt comp, [**AtomicCafe_after Step 18**]. You can rename and continue with our comp, if you wish.*

Tweaking Speed

STEP 19: To add a speedup, the general idea is to ease out of the first keyframe, and speed up into the second keyframe. The first part is easy: Select the first Time Remap keyframe and apply the Animation> Keyframe Assistant>Easy Ease Out. (You can also context-click on the layer bar and select it from the popup menu.)

STEP 20: Move to time 05:00, and read the Velocity percentage value at this point in the animation – it should read somewhere between 600% and 700% (it's a little faster than the original 500%, because you slowed down the beginning – and that delay has to be made up later).

20 You need to reshape the velocity curve so that instead of having a slowdown right before the second keyframe, it will now be constantly increasing in speed. The cursor points to the velocity handle you need to grab and move up.

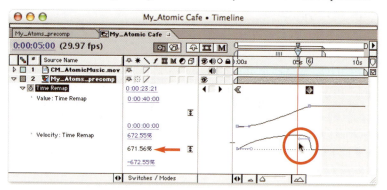

You will also notice a hump in the velocity curve, indicating that it speeds up but then slows down again slightly before reaching the second keyframe.

Drag the velocity handle for the second keyframe upward until the speed reads around 900% at time 05:00 (see figure on the next page). It's okay if you drag beyond the area (or "cell") where the velocity curve is visible; it will redraw correctly when you let go of the mouse. While you're doing so, be careful not to drag the influence handle too far to the left or right, or you will unduly increase or decrease the amount of influence this new keyframe value has. Keeping the handle end right around the 05:00 mark works well. The result will speed up the playback of the atoms as it interpolates into the second keyframe. RAM Preview and see how you like it.

Velocity Dip

When you're editing the velocity or value graph, holding down the Shift key restrains the velocity curve from dipping below the center line to a negative value. In the case of Time Remapping, that means time would run backward…

You might think you could apply Easy Ease In to the second keyframe, but that would be the opposite of what you need. Instead of slowing down to zero speed, you want it to speed up.

20 *complete:* Drag the handle for the second keyframe upwards until it reaches a velocity of 900% at time 05:00. It's okay to drag above the "cell" area – after you've released the mouse, the velocity curve will rescale itself to fit into the display area again.

STEP 21: When you preview the result of your velocity edit, if you were to find fault, it would be that the start of the animation is now too slow. Scrub the first two seconds of the timeline, and notice that the second atom image (at 1:10 in the precomp) doesn't appear until about 1:13 – which means that the beginning is playing slower than realtime. Let's speed up the takeoff by modifying the ease out values precisely, rather than just dragging the handles.

All the Easy Ease keyframe assistant does is plug in a default velocity and influence for a keyframe. You then have free rein to go in and edit what it did. Option+double-click (Alt+double-click) the first Time Remapping keyframe at 00:00 or select the keyframe and then select Animation>Keyframe Velocity. The Keyframe Velocity dialog shows the values that the Easy Ease assistant produced, namely: Outgoing Velocity = 0 seconds per second; Influence = 33.33%.

21 The Keyframe Velocity dialog lets you precisely edit the speed of parameter change at a keyframe, and how much influence that speed has before and after the keyframe. The Keyframe Velocity dialog is context sensitive, which means the configuration of the Velocity parameter display depends on the type of keyframe selected. The Continuous checkbox indicates whether or not the incoming velocity matches the outgoing velocity. In this case, the Incoming values are irrelevant, since this is the first keyframe.

Under the Influence

The amount of influence assigned to a keyframe decides how strongly it affects the velocity curve coming into or going out of that keyframe. You could think of the length of the influence handles as deciding when the speed change begins to take place. (Note that a linear keyframe has zero influence, meaning only the keyframe value matters; the incoming and outgoing velocity values for the keyframe are meaningless.)

You can roughly tell the amount of influence a keyframe has by the length of the influence handles in the velocity graph. Influence of 100% means the keyframe affects the rate of parameter change all the way to halfway between the current keyframe and the one before or after (depending on whether you are editing incoming or outgoing velocity, respectively). Seeing how far the keyframe handles reach to this halfway point, tells you how much influence it has. Easy Ease keyframes change the velocity to 0 and apply a 33.33% influence, meaning the parameter eases into and out of stopping at its keyframed value.

In Step 20, there are six seconds between keyframes. A three-second-long influence handle would be 100% influence. In this case, you want about a 33% influence (the classic "easy ease" value), so you would try to keep the influence handle roughly one second long (one-third of three seconds). That's why we instructed you to keep it around the 05:00 mark – one second before the keyframe you were editing.

My_Atomic Cafe • Timeline

My_Atoms_precomp | My_Atomic Cafe

0:00:00:00 (29.97 fps)

#	Source Name
▷ 1	CM_AtomicMusic.mov
▽ 2	My_Atoms_precomp
▽	Time Remap	0:00:00:00
	Value : Time Remap	0:00:40:00
		0:00:00:00
	Velocity : Time Remap	1279.16%
		100.00%
		-1279.16%

Switches / Modes

21 *complete:* The final velocity curve. The cursor is pointing to the fact that the velocity is now above the centerline, as it now starts at 1 second per second (100%) and only gets faster from there.

• Change the Outgoing Velocity value from 0 to 1 second per second, and click OK. The result will be that the layer will start playing back in realtime (one second per second), and get only faster from that point on. Look closely at the velocity graph: It should be raised a little off the centerline now, indicating that the speed is faster than before.

RAM Preview again and Save your project. If you need to, compare your result with prebuilt comp [**AtomicCafe_after Step 21**].

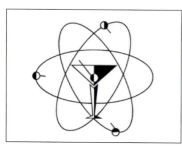

22 The atom sequence scales from 15% (above) to 75% (below) over time, to add further excitement.

Scaling Atoms

You now have the speed portion of the animation down. Next is re-inforcing the impression of gathering energy by scaling the atom sequence up in size.

Step 22: You want the atom sequence to scale up as it plays back, continuing to scale a little past 06:00. By going a little past the downbeat at 06:00, the atoms will continue scaling as the main title builds on, adding more interest. This also gives you a bit of "handle" to fade the atoms out. (On a real job, you might think of little touches like that later. But we thought we'd save you some work now.)

• Make sure the **My_Atoms_precomp** layer is still selected. Press Home to return to time 00:00, press S to twirl down Scale, and turn on the keyframe stopwatch for Scale. Enter (or scrub to) a value of around 15% so the first symbol is small but still readable.

• Move to time 06:10 and scale up to around 75%, which will confine the last atom image to roughly the Title Safe area (use the ' apostrophe key to toggle these guides on and off). RAM Preview.

It's never a bad idea to create elements at a larger size than you'll end up using later (within reason, of course; we consider about twice as big as you think you'll need it to be the edge of reason). Having some headroom to scale from 75% to 100% offers you more options when you're animating — especially when you're using pixel-based sources such as those from Photoshop, where scaling above 100% will soften and degrade the image.

23 The first Scale keyframe eases out, and the handles are adjusted to accelerate into the second keyframe. The layer is set to Best Quality (red circle) so that it antialiases nicely.

STEP 23: To make the atoms scale up more slowly at the start, select the first Scale keyframe and apply Keyframe Assistant>Easy Ease Out. Once you do this, you'll notice that the scaling now slows down a touch right before the second keyframe. Tweak the velocity of the second keyframe to that it continues to accelerate: At 06:10, twirl down the velocity graph and drag the second keyframe's handle up until its speed is about 22% per second.

> Note that as of version 6.5, layers default to Best Quality, not Draft. Best Quality ensures that layers are antialiased as they are transformed (rotated, scaled, and so on) and move with subpixel positioning. In addition, any effects applied that create new pixels (such as warping effects), will render more smoothly than in Draft.

RAM Preview and tweak the scale graph to taste. When you're done, twirl up the Scale property to clean up the Timeline, and return to time 00:00.

You know the routine: If you want to compare your version with ours, or pick up this tutorial in the middle, check out [**AtomicCafe_after Step 23**]. *And don't forget to Save your project…*

Scaling Back Your Expectations

The way we perceive the scaling of an object differs from its keyframe velocity. If an object scales up at a linear rate of speed, this scaling will appear to slow down as it reaches its final, larger size. (This makes sense when you think it through: A 10% difference in Scale means a lot if you're increasing from 0% to 10%, but it means much less if you're increasing from 90% to 100%.)

The Professional edition contains a Keyframe Assistant called Exponential Scale which can correct this perceived slowdown and make it appear that the layer is scaling at a constant rate. Although it is mathematically the most precise approach, it has the downside of creating a keyframe on every frame in the timeline, making further adjustments to Scale difficult. We try to use Exponential Scale only when the animation is locked down, and when manipulating the velocity curve doesn't produce a satisfactory result.

24 Two movies you will be using to create your background: The first is a movie of graphical circles from the Bestshot/Retrocities CD (top), which is looped two times in the Interpret Footage dialog (above); The second movie from the Artbeats/Soap Film CD is then added to the comp (below).

Part 3: Get Back!

In this section, you will build the background for the overall piece. While you're at it, you'll have a little fun combining different layers with blending modes to create a melded '60s flashback look. You'll start out building this background in the same comp as you've been speeding up the atoms, then move it to its own comp later.

STEP 24: Select the **My_Sources** folder and import **BS_Retrocities.mov** – it should be in the same folder as the soundtrack and atoms. While it's selected in the Project window, observe that it's only 7:06 in duration – too short for your 10:16 final comp. Fortunately, it was created as a seamless loop, so you can repeat it as often as necessary. With it selected, open the Interpret Footage dialog (File>Interpret Footage>Main) and set its Looping parameter to Loop 2 Times. Click OK, and note that its new duration is 14:12. (You can also change these settings after you add a source to a comp.)

STEP 25: Add **BS_Retrocities.mov** to [**My_Atomic Cafe**], starting at time 00:00, and drag it to the bottom of the stack in the Timeline window. Scrub the timeline, and notice there is no jump at 07:06 as the movie loops back to the first frame.

STEP 26: Import **AB_SoapFilm.mov**, which has a longer duration of 16:01. Add this movie to your comp, also at time 00:00, and place it just above the **BS_Retrocities.mov** layer. Scrub the timeline to see the multicolored liquid flow (see the sidebar *Soap Film* to learn how this was made). We'll use this second movie to add some texture and color to the underlying yellow movie.

STEP 27: Double-click the **AB_SoapFilm.mov** to open it in its own Layer window, and scrub along the timeline to check out the entire movie (16:01 duration). The movie is longer than the comp's duration of 10:16, and the second half of the movie is more turbulent than the beginning. Since we like the more turbulent look, trim the layer so the 10:16 portion you need comes from the later portion:

• In the Layer window, drag the layer's in point to around 05:00 until the duration reads about 11 seconds. You can also trim the in point by moving the time marker to 05:00 and clicking the In switch (which looks like an open squiggly bracket). By trimming the clip in the Layer window, the layer's in point in the timeline (00:00) is maintained. Close the Layer window when you're done trimming.

27 The **AB_Soap Film.mov** layer starts off with larger shapes (above left), and progresses over 16 seconds to more interesting shapes near the end of the movie (above right). To include more of the turbulent section, you can trim out the first five seconds. In the Layer window, drag the in point (where the red arrow is pointing) to around 5:00. You can also move to 05:00 and click the Set In Point button (circled in red) to set the in point to the current time.

Soap Film

The Soap Film collection from Artbeats (produced and directed by Ted Kinsman of Kinsman's Physics Productions) contains an explanation of the physics behind soap film images. In short:

"The brilliant displays of color are created by the wave nature of light as revealed in a thin sheet of soap. This same effect is often seen in a wet parking lot where a few drops of oil spilled on the pavement and a rainbow is seen in the water. The clips show optical interference of light waves as they reflect from a very thin moving sheet of soap. The colors are linked to varying thicknesses in the sheet of soap. As rocks in a stream create eddies in the water, obstructions placed in the flowing sheet of soap are transformed into infinitely complex changes in color and pattern."

And you thought it was just another pretty background…

Open GL issues

If the Fast Previews popup at the bottom of the Comp window is set to OpenGL, select Preferences>Previews>Fast Previews>OpenGL Info and set the Quality to More Accurate. Provided your video card supports it, you should now see the result of blending modes as you scrub the timeline.

STEP 28: We often combine multiple layers of imagery using Blending Modes to create a new image. Your goal here is to end up with a bright, colorful background that shows the twirling lines in the **BS_Retrocities** movie, but also blends in some of the flowing nature and the bright color of the **AB_SoapFilm** movie. You don't want to make it so busy that the atoms sequence in front is overshadowed; you also need to keep it light and bright so that the black atoms continue to stand out well against this background. Here's how we achieved a blend that we liked (by all means experiment to arrive at a mix that suits your own tastes):

• If the Modes column is not already visible in the Timeline window, expose it by pressing F4. Set the mode for the **AB_SoapFilm.mov** layer to Overlay. This is going in the right direction, but now the soap layer is not showing up as well as we'd like…

28 To create different looks, try using different combinations of blending modes. The first image (left) shows one copy of **AB_SoapFilm** in Overlay mode on top of the **BS_Retrocities** layer; the second (center) shows a second copy of **AB_SoapFilm** in Overlay mode with 50% opacity; the third (right) shows a third copy of **AB_SoapFilm** on top in Color mode. The Timeline window (below) illustrates this layer stack.

• Duplicate the **AB_SoapFilm.mov**. This duplicate retains the same mode, so it is also set to Overlay. The blend is getting more intense… perhaps too intense. Press T to reveal the Opacity of the duplicate, and blend it down to about 50% Opacity. You now have a nice blend of texture between the flowing liquid and the swirling lines.

• To add more color, select the duplicated **AB_SoapFilm.mov** layer, and duplicate it again. This time, set its blending mode to Color. This maintains the luminance values of the layers below, but mixes in the Hue and Saturation of this third soap-film layer. Scrub the Opacity value and set to taste (we used 50% again).

Note that when you duplicate a layer, the copy always goes above the source. Go ahead and play around with changing the order of these three copies of the soap film movie – note that when the Overlay layers are on top, the result is more intense colors. We personally left the Color version on top, going for a more pastel look.

*Save your project. Compare your version with our [**AtomicCafe_after Step 28**]. As this section was more "to taste," don't be too concerned if yours looks different. But if you want to make sure your results match the illustrations from here on, duplicate ours, rename it "My_Atomic Cafe_28", and continue.*

Precomposing the Background

Once you've finalized your mix of the background layers, it's time to give them their own composition. This will tidy up the timeline by consolidating (or "grouping") the four layers down to one, and make it easy to turn the background on and off as a group.

STEP 29: Select the four background layers – they should be the four bottom layers in the Timeline window – and Layer>Pre-compose them, or use the shortcut: Command+Shift+C (Control+Shift+C). Be sure to give the precomp a useful name, such as "**My_Background_precomp**," and click OK.

> The Pre-compose dialog usually offers more than one option of which details to send back to the precomp along with the layer. Because you've selected multiple layers, the only option available is to precompose using the Move All Attributes option. This creates a precomp based on the size and duration of the current comp, and moves all the attributes (for example, the trim points, blending modes, and Opacity values) back to the precomp.

The four background movie layers will now appear as one layer: a nested comp called **My_Background_precomp**. You can bring this precomp forward for editing at any time by Option+double-clicking (Alt+double-clicking) the nested comp layer. You can also open it by double-clicking it from the Project window, just like any other comp.

*RAM Preview or scrub through the comp, and then Save your project. You've now completed Part 3 of this tutorial. Compare your version with our [**AtomicCafe_after Step 29**]. To pick up this tutorial at Part 4, rename this comp to [**My_Atomic Cafe_29**] and continue from here.*

Blending Layers

Combining multiple layers with Blending Modes works best if the sources are not super busy. If one layer is dominating the balance of the mix, don't be afraid to reduce its opacity or desaturate its color.

29 To reduce clutter in your comp, select the four layers that make up the background and Layer>Pre-compose them (above). The result is one layer in [**My_Atomic Cafe**] (below). We unchecked the Open New Composition box (circled in red) as we didn't intend to edit these layers further. (If you check this option, the precomp will appear as a tabbed item after you click the OK button, and the precomp will be forward, not the current comp.)

Part 4: Atomic Café Title

The stage is now set for you to add the main title. As we've been alluding, the intention is for it to make an impact around 06:00 in the timeline to match the explosion and change in the music.

There are three sections to this animation: bringing on the word "Atomic," bringing on the word "Café" and making it animate, and fading out the atom symbols that got us to this point.

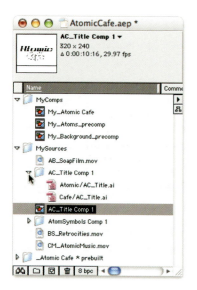

30 The Project window after importing the Illustrator layered file as a Composition.

STEP 30: Import the layered Illustrator file **AC_Title.ai**. Since you want to access its individual layers, you'll need to import it as a composition, as you did earlier with the layered Photoshop file:

• Select the folder **My_Sources** in the Project window, select File> Import>File, and locate the file **AC_Title.ai** from the **Project>Sources** folder. Be sure to choose Composition from the Import As popup at the bottom of the import dialog. Click Import (Open).

• After Effects will create a folder and a composition, both named **AC_Title Comp 1**.

Note that the individual Illustrator layers reside in the **AC_Title Comp 1** folder in the Project window (see figure). While you can drag these layers directly to any composition, opening the accompanying comp (selected in the figure), copying the layers, and then pasting the layers to another comp guarantees that any compatible *attributes* are retained. Attributes that are honored include position (crucial if you imported the file using the Composition – Cropped Layers option), opacity, and in the case of Photoshop files, also include blending modes, layer effects, adjustment layers, vector shapes, and so on.

31 The title was created in Illustrator. Atomic uses the font Axiom from T.26 (www.t26.com); Café was created with the font Telegram Plain from Fontek (www.letraset.com).

STEP 31: Open this comp [AC_Title Comp 1], and change the background color (Composition> Background color) to something other than black so you can see the text clearly. (You could also click the Toggle Transparency Grid at the bottom of the Comp window.)

• This comp contains two layers of interest: **Atomic** and **Cafe**. Best Quality should be set for both layers so that the vector text appears antialiased.

• Deselect all layers (shortcut: F2) to ensure that no properties are selected, then select both the **Atomic** and **Cafe** layers, and Edit>Copy.

STEP 32: Bring the [My_Atomic Cafe] comp forward, press Home to return to time 00:00, and Edit>Paste the layers. Press F2 to Deselect All.

• Turn on the Solo switch for the **Atomic** title as you'll be animating this layer first.

```
●●●              My_Atomic Cafe • Timeline
My_Atoms_precomp    🔲My_Atomic Cafe    AC_Title Comp 1
0:00:00:00  (29.97 fps)         ⊠ ⊡   ⊕ Ⅲ M        ):00s      05s ⑥    10s
   🔳 #  Source Name        Mode    T  TrkMat    👁◀)○🔒
 ▷ □ 1  Atomic/AC_Title.ai  Normal ▼              👁   ⚲
 ▷ □ 2  Cafe/AC_Title.ai    Normal ▼    None  ▼   👁
 ▷ □ 3  CM_AtomicMusic.mov                        ◀)
 ▷ □ 4  My_Atoms_precomp    Normal ▼              👁
 ▷ □ 5  My_Background_precomp Normal ▼  None  ▼   👁
          ◀▶  Switches / Modes            ◀▶ ⌂ △     △
```

Animating the Atomic Title

Step 33: First, you're going to animate the Scale of the **Atomic** layer to make it spring on the scene. It will have a primary action, where it first appears, and a secondary action, where it drifts a bit to keep the viewer's attention.

• Move to time 05:25, select the **Atomic** layer, and press [(left bracket) to move the layer's in point to the current time. Make sure the layer extends to the end of the comp – if not, drag the out point to the end.

• With the **Atomic** layer still selected, press S for Scale, turn on the animation stopwatch for this property, and set its value to 15%.

• If you like, zoom into the timeline by pressing + (the plus key on the regular keyboard) or drag the slider along the bottom of the timeline.

• Press 6 to move to the comp marker at 06:00 – where the downbeat of the music hits – and scale the layer up to 70%. This zooms the type quickly toward the viewer in five frames.

• Move to time 07:00 and hit Shift+7 (on the regular keyboard, not the keypad) to set comp marker #7 at this time. This will make it easy to return later to this point.

32 Import the Illustrator artwork as a comp, copy the two layers **Atomic** and **Cafe**, and paste them into [**My_Atomic Cafe**]. Solo the **Atomic** layer to remove distractions.

33 The Atomic title scales quickly from 15% to 70%, then drifts slowly to 100% scale.

```
●●●              My_Atomic Cafe • Timeline
My_Atoms_precomp    🔲My_Atomic Cafe    AC_Title Comp 1
0:00:07:00  (29.97 fps)         ⊠ ⊡   ⊕ Ⅲ M                 ⑥    ⑦    0
   🔳 #  Source Name        Mode    T  TrkMat    👁◀)○🔒
 ▽ □ 1  Atomic/AC_Title.ai  Normal ▼              👁   ○
    ▷ ⏱ Scale              ⊠ 100.0 , 100.0 %    ◀ ✓        ◆◇      ◆
 ▷ □ 2  Cafe/AC_Title.ai    Normal ▼    None  ▼   👁
 ▷ □ 3  CM_AtomicMusic.mov                        ◀)
 ▷ □ 4  My_Atoms_precomp    Normal ▼              👁
 ▷ □ 5  My_Background_precomp Normal ▼  None  ▼   👁
          ◀▶  Switches / Modes            ◀▶ ⌂ △  △ ◀      ⬭ ▶
```

- Set the Scale value to 100%. The title will continue to "drift" for another second, adding interest while the viewer digests the meaning of the word.

- Set the work area to extend from around 05:00 to 08:00. You can either drag the work area handles directly (keeping an eye on the Info palette), or move to 05:00 and press B to set the beginning of the work area, then move to 08:00 and hit N to set the end.

- RAM Preview this section. You should notice that by using the Linear interpolation method (denoted by diamond-shaped keyframe icons), there will be a hitch in the speed as it reaches each keyframe.

My_Atomic Cafe • Timeline

33 *complete:* The interpolation for **Atomic**'s second Scale keyframe is smoothed to Auto Bezier; the layer then eases into the third keyframe thanks to the Easy Ease In assistant.

Diamonds Aren't Forever

To return a temporal keyframe back to Linear after applying Easy Ease or otherwise changing it, Command+click (Control+click) on the keyframe until it reverts back to the familiar diamond icon.

Twirl down the Velocity graph for Scale so you can view how the shape of the graph changes as you make the following edits:

- To refine the Scale keyframe interpolation, select the third keyframe (at 07:00) and apply Animation>Keyframe Assistant>Easy Ease In. This will create a gradual slowdown as the title interpolates from 70% to 100%. RAM Preview and note the result.

There's still a slight hitch to the animation as it abruptly changes from one speed to another at the second keyframe. A good keyframe interpolation type to use in cases like this is Auto Bezier, which smoothes the transition through a keyframe by averaging the incoming and outgoing velocities:

- Command+click (Control+click) on the second keyframe in the Timeline to change its interpolation type from Linear (the diamond icon) to Auto Bezier (circle icon). RAM Preview again, and see if you like the smoother result. Twirl up the Velocity and Value graphs when you're done.

Depending on the placement of the Anchor Point for a layer, scaling can cause a layer to appear to drift in position as it scales away from the center point defined by the anchor. In this case, we already centered the word Atomic in the Illustrator file, using our center guides for placement, so its anchor would end up centered in the word in After Effects. However, you can change the position of a layer's Anchor Point in After Effects if necessary.

	#	Source Name	Mode	T	TrkMat				05s				07s	08s	

My_Atomic Cafe • Timeline

My_Atoms_precomp **My_Atomic Cafe** AC_Title Comp 1

0:00:06:00 **(29.97 fps)**

▽	1	Atomic/AC_Title.ai	Normal ▼			
		▷ Scale	70.0 , 70.0 %	◀ ✓ ▶	
		▷ Opacity	100 %	◀ ✓	
▷	2	Cafe/AC_Title.ai	Normal ▼		None	
▷	3	CM_AtomicMusic.mov				
▷	4	My_Atoms_precomp	Normal ▼			
▷	5	My_Background_prec...	Normal ▼		None	

Switches / Modes

STEP 34: There is a slight visual "pop" when the word Atomic comes on, because it is starting at a Scale larger than 0%. This can be smoothed over with some quick Opacity keyframing:

• Make sure the **Atomic** layer is still selected, and press I to move back to the layer's in point at 05:25.

• Press Shift+T to twirl down Opacity while keeping the Scale property open as well. Turn on the animation stopwatch for Opacity, and set its initial value to 0%.

• Press 6 to move to 06:00, and set the Opacity back to 100%. Editing its value will automatically create the second keyframe.

• Turn off the layer's Solo switch so you can see all the other layers again.

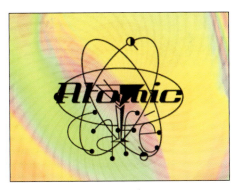

34 To smooth over the visual pop when Atomic comes on, quickly fade up its opacity. However, having both the atomic symbols and the word Atomic on at the same time is visually messy; you'll straighten that out in the next step.

Atoms Be Gone

STEP 35: As the Atomic title is zooming up, you want the atoms behind it to quickly fade down. Simple enough; just add some more Opacity keyframes.

• Select the **Atoms_precomp** layer. If the layer's keyframes are not already visible, hit U to show animated properties.

• Move to time 05:25, press Shift+T to also view Opacity, and turn on its animation stopwatch to create a keyframe at 100%.

• Note the position of the Scale keyframe at 06:10. Click on the keyframe navigator right arrow for the Scale property to jump to 06:10, and scrub the Opacity value down to 0% (see figure on next page).

> When you're synchronizing keyframes, use the keyframe navigator arrows to jump to certain keyframes — that way you can be sure that new keyframes created for another property synchronize exactly with the existing keyframe(s). It also avoids errors where extra keyframes are created one frame to the left or right of a keyframe you were trying to edit.

The Show Me Shortcuts

Pressing U (known as the Über key) for a selected layer will twirl down animated properties only. To see what parameters have changed from their default values, type UU (two Us in quick succession).

36 The **My_Atoms_precomp** layer fades down to 0% as the title builds on, and is trimmed out at 06:10.

STEP 36: Even though the layer is at 0% Opacity and therefore is taking no rendering time, it's still a good idea to trim layers that have faded out – this will help you know who is playing at what point in time just by glancing at the Timeline window.

• With **My_Atoms_precomp** still selected and with the time marker at 06:10, press Option+] (Alt+]) to trim out the end of this layer.

Save the project and twirl up the **My_Atoms_precomp** *layer. Compare your version with our* **[AtomicCafe_after Step 36]**.

Animating the Café Title

The word Café will get a different treatment. It will scale and fade up after the word Atomic, stretching from the center of the frame rather than its own center. If you have the Professional edition, you'll also take advantage of the keyframe assistant The Wiggler to make it continue to bounce around to attract attention, and to follow the talking, bouncy nature of the music after the big hit at 06:00. The last step in this part of the tutorial will then be adding a drop shadow to both words in the title.

If you have a large computer monitor, drag the Timeline window larger so you can see the timing interplay between layers. On the other hand, if you're short on screen real estate, feel free to twirl up the animating properties for the other layers.

STEP 37: Select the **Cafe** layer and press 7 (on the keyboard) to jump to comp marker #7 at 07:00. Press [to move this layer's in point to the current time. Check to make sure that the layer extends to the end of the comp – if not, drag the out point to the end.

Note that the [and] keys *move* selected layers' in and out points respectively, while adding the Option/Alt key *trims* selected layers' in and out points to the current time.

More on Music

There is an article in the **Goodies** folder on the DVD that came with this book – *Timing Video to Audio* – which goes into greater detail about matching animation moves to music.

STEP 38: With the **Cafe** layer selected, notice in the Comp window that its Anchor Point – the circle with an X through it – defaults to the center of the layer (which also happens to coincide with the center of the **Atomic** layer). If you have trouble seeing this, double-click on the layer to open it in its own Layer window, and set the View menu to either Masks or Anchor Point Path. Any scale or rotation applied will originate from this Anchor Point. Press / (backslash) to bring the Comp window forward again.

- With the **Cafe** layer still selected, press S to twirl down Scale, turn on its animation stopwatch, and set the Scale value to 0%.

- Move to 07:15, and set the Scale to 90%.

STEP 39: Next you'll add a fade-up that syncs with the Scale keyframes – but let's do it in reverse, to reduce the amount of parameter entry you have to do:

- With **Cafe** still selected, press Shift+T to also twirl down its Opacity property in the Timeline window.

- Still at time 07:15, turn on the animation stopwatch for Opacity. This will set a keyframe value of 100%, its final value.

- Hit I to return to the layer's in point at 07:00, and change the Opacity to 0%.

- Set the work area around these two keyframes and RAM Preview. The Café title will stretch out from the center of the comp.

- Save your project!

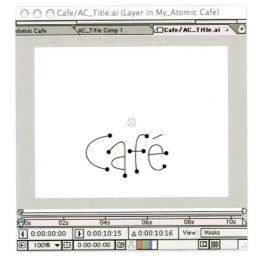

38 Any scale or rotation a layer undergoes is centered around its Anchor Point – the icon of a circle with an X inside. It is often easiest to view it in the Layer window. (If you animate the Anchor Point, its motion path is editable only in the Layer window.)

39 The Café title animates on after the word Atomic. Since its Anchor Point is set to the middle of the overall frame instead of the word Café, it seems to stretch out from the center of the comp.

Motion Blur

When objects move quickly in the digital world, they can seem to strobe as they jump from one position to another, frame to frame. In the film world, the same objects appear more as streaks, because the shutter of the camera is open and still exposing film while they move. This latter look is considered more natural.

STEP 40: After Effects can simulate the open shutter streaking effect through its Motion Blur feature. When an object is animated by After Effects, it can calculate a streak along the path the object is traveling between frames. Let's employ this feature to improve the look of the title animation.

40 To enable motion blur calculations for a layer, set its M switch in the Timeline window (top). To preview the results in the Comp window, enable the larger M switch along the top of the Timeline window. The result will be a zoom blur on the titles as they scale up (above).

• Check that the Timeline window is displaying the Switches column; press F4 if it's currently displaying Modes. In the Switches column, turn on the M (Motion Blur) switch in the Timeline window for both the **Atomic** and **Cafe** layers. This enables motion blur to be calculated for these layers during final rendering.

• To see this blur in the Comp window, turn on the Enable Motion Blur switch (the large M button along the top of the timeline), and either RAM Preview or set the time marker to a point where the title layers are animating (such as 07:15 for the **Cafe** layer).

• You can optionally turn on the Motion Blur switch for the **Atoms_precomp** layer that's scaling up. Understand that the blur effect will be less on this layer since it is scaling at a much slower rate, and the motion blur effect adds considerably to your rendering time – it's a tradeoff you'll have to make a decision about.

• Change the Motion Blur amount to 360° for longer streaks and more impact. To do this, press Command+K (Control+K) to open the Composition Settings dialog (or select Composition>Composition Settings). Click on the Advanced tab, and enter "**360**" for Shutter Angle. You can set this value between 0 and 720 on a per-composition basis; the Shutter Angle can also be overridden on a project-wide basis when you render (Render Settings>Time Sampling section).

40 *complete:* You can set different Motion Blur Shutter Angle values per composition. This parameter is hiding under the Advanced tab in the Composition Settings window.

Wiggle Expression

If you don't have the Professional edition, there is a simple expression that creates a result similar to The Wiggler in Step 41 below:

• Select the **Cafe.ai** layer and hit S to reveal its Scale keyframes.

• Option+click (Alt+click) on the animation stopwatch for Scale – this enables expressions, and enters the word "scale" in the expression field to the right.

• Replace the word "scale" by typing

   wiggle(5.333,15)

and hit Enter (not Return). To see a visual representation of the wiggle values, click on the Show Post-Expression button (circled in red in figure).

• Set the work area the same length as **Cafe.ai**, and RAM Preview.

Where did those numbers come from? The first is how many wiggles per second. As noted earlier, our music takes 1.5 seconds per measure. To make Café dance eight times per measure, you need to wiggle 8 ÷ 1.5 = 5.333 times per second.

The second value is how many units to wiggle by. Since our starting Scale is 90%, a value of 15 means the layer's Scale will bounce around between 75% and 105%.

(Note: Expressions are covered in more detail in Tutorial 11, *Just an Expression*.)

The Wiggler *(Professional edition)*

This next part is optional, as it requires that you have the Professional edition version of After Effects. You'll be using a keyframe assistant in it called The Wiggler.

Cute name, but what does it do? The Wiggler takes previously existing property values and offsets them randomly. You can decide how often it does this (e.g. every five frames), and what is the maximum amount the parameter will be offset (e.g. ±10 pixels). It works between the keyframes you select. As a result, you need to select at least two keyframes for a property – even if there is no change in value between those keyframes – to use The Wiggler.

In this tutorial, you're going to use The Wiggler to randomize the Scale of the Café title. This will make it dance around during the last few seconds of this clip.

Step 41: Press 7 to jump to 07:00 and press B to set the beginning of the work area. Hit End to go to the last frame of the comp (10:15) and press N to end the work area here.

• Select the **Cafe** layer. Its Scale property should be visible (if not, type S to twirl it down).

• Check the keyframe box for the Scale property to add another Scale keyframe at this time (10:15). It should have the same value as the previous keyframe: 90%.

Forced Motion Blur

After Effects can add motion blur only to objects it animates – not to footage of moving objects. To add blur to footage, use a third-party plug-in like ReelSmart Motion Blur from RE:Vision Effects (www.revisionfx.com).

Click the keyframe box for the Scale property to create a new keyframe at the current time (10:15).

41 Set a third Scale keyframe at 10:15 and select the last two keyframes before you apply The Wiggler.

41 *continued:* The parameters for The Wiggler. These settings mean a new keyframe will be created 5.333 times a second, randomizing the X and Y scale independently by up to ±15%.

41 *continued:* The Wiggler creates new keyframes between the ones you selected (below). Note the Scale parameter (where the cursor is pointing): the X and Y dimensions were randomized separately. Zoom into the timeline to get a better view of the individual keyframes.

• This new keyframe will automatically be selected when you created it. Shift+click on the second keyframe back at 07:15 so that both the second and third Scale keyframes are highlighted. *Remember that you can use The Wiggler only when two or more keyframes are selected.*

• Select Window>The Wiggler to open its floating palette. Some of the default settings – namely, Apply To>Temporal Graph, with Noise Type>Smooth, and All Dimensions Independently – are fine. The All Dimensions Independently setting is of particular interest: This means the X and Y scale randomizations will be independent of each other, which should result in some fun stretch and squash movements.

• To make the title dance in time to the music, you need to pick a Frequency that matches the tempo of the soundtrack. As noted earlier, our music takes 1.5 seconds per measure. To make Café dance eight times per measure, you need a Frequency parameter of 8 ÷ 1.5 = 5.333 wiggles per second. Go ahead and enter **"5.333"** for Frequency.

• In the Magnitude field, enter **"15"**. This will keep the new scale keyframes created by The Wiggler confined to a range of ±15% from the current value (90%), or in a range from 75% to 105%. (Yes, any value over 100% will soften the type, but sometimes you have to live dangerously…and in reality, this is the outer limit; most keyframes will be well inside the maximum values of 75% to 105%.)

- Click Apply. Keyframes will be added along the timeline at a spacing decided by the Frequency parameter, with values randomly determined by the Magnitude parameter. RAM Preview.

- Remember that the Wiggler values are truly random! If you don't like the result – too subtle or too boingy – Undo until the extra keyframes disappear but the two Scale keyframes are still selected, then hit the Wiggler's Apply button again. You don't need to adjust any other Wiggler parameters. Feel free to RAM Preview, Undo, and Apply again until you arrive at a bounce pattern you find pleasing. Don't be surprised if it takes a few tries.

> If you find the RAM Previews are taking too long, turn off the Enable Motion Blur switch for this comp (the big M switch along the top of the Timeline window) – this will speed things up considerably. Remember to keep the individual layer M switches on, so motion blur will still be calculated during your final render.

- Close The Wiggler palette when you're done, and twirl up the layer properties for the **Atomic** and **Cafe** layers.

Compare your version with our [**AtomicCafe_after Step 41**]. *If you don't have the Professional edition, you can use this comp – which already has Wiggler-generated keyframes – for the remaining steps.*

41 *complete:* The Professional edition's keyframe assistant The Wiggler creates a fun stretch/squash animation for Café.

Drop Shadows

STEP 42: For the last step in this part, lift the title layers off the background using drop shadows.

- Select the **Atomic** layer, and apply Effect>Perspective>**Drop Shadow**. In the Effect Controls window, set the shadow parameters to taste. We created a dark diffuse glow by changing the shadow's Opacity value to 100%, Distance to 0.0, and Softness to taste (around 20 should work).

- Once you're happy with your settings, select the name of the effect in the Effect Controls window, Copy it, select the **Cafe** layer, and Paste.

42 Apply a dark diffuse glow with the Drop Shadow effect to finish off the title layers at the end of Part 4.

End of Part 4! RAM Preview, Save your project, and close the Effect Controls window. Compare your comp with our [**AtomicCafe_after Step 42**] *if you got lost.*

Part 5: Sparks and Flares

The basic animation is now finished. For the remaining steps, you'll be spicing up this spot. First, to further emphasize the "energized" feeling of the piece, you'll be adding various lighting effects such as sparks and lens flares. Two different approaches will be employed: using stock footage elements, and applying plug-in effects. (That plug-in effect will be Knoll Light Factory LE which we suggested you install back in the Overview box at the beginning of this tutorial. If you haven't installed it yet, save, quit, install, restart After Effects, and reload your project.)

Particle Movies

STEP 43: First, let's light the fuse that will lead up to the big hit at 06:00:

- Import **BS_Particulars2.mov** from the **Project>Sources** folder.

- Add it to [**My_Atomic Cafe**] and set it to start at 01:15 (remember that you can also move to 01:15 and hit [to move its in point to this time). Position it directly above **Atoms_precomp** in the layer stack.

43 The **BS_Particulars2.mov** file (courtesy of Bestshots/Particulars 2 CD) is a set of particles swirling in a figure-eight pattern (above). When applied in Add mode, the black background drops out, and the particles illuminate the layers behind (below).

Note that you can drag a footage item to a specific time and layer stack position in the Timeline window. To do this, drag the movie to the right side of the Timeline window, watching for the black insertion bar within the layer stack for positioning. The current time (top left of Timeline window) will display the layer's in point until you release the mouse.

- Scrub the timeline and you'll see particles swirling around in a figure-eight pattern. The problem is that it obscures all that's behind it. You need to drop out its black background, and keep just the particles.

- Make sure the Modes column is exposed in the Timeline window (shortcut: F4 to toggle between Switches and Modes), and select the Add blending mode for the **BS_Particulars2.mov** layer.

The Add mode reveals the layers behind, adding to them the color values of the selected layer. Since the color value of black is zero, it adds nothing to the layers behind, revealing them untouched. The bright particles will greatly brighten the background where they're swirling. If you find this effect too bright, use Screen mode – it's a tamer version of Add.

- These particles are supposed to fade away when the title comes on. Press 6 to move to time 06:00. With the **BS_Particulars2.mov** layer selected, press T to reveal its Opacity, and click on its corresponding animation stopwatch to turn on keyframing. This will create a first keyframe with a value of 100%.

- With the particles still selected, press the letter O to jump to this layer's out point, and change its Opacity to 0% to fade the movie out.

- With the **BS_Particulars2.mov** selected, press Command+Option+B (Control+Alt+B) to set the work area to the duration of the layer. RAM

○ ○ ○	My_Atomic Cafe • Timeline

My_Atoms_precomp   ⊠My_Atomic Cafe □   AC_Title Comp 1

0:00:07:02 (29.97 fps)

	#	Source Name	Mode	T TrkMat		:00s	05s	10s
▷ □	1	Atomic/AC_Title.ai	Normal ▾		👁			
▷ □	2	Cafe/AC_Title.ai	Normal ▾	None ▾	👁			
▷ □	3	CM_AtomicMusic.mov			🔊			
▽ □	4	BS_Particulars2.mov	Add ▾		👁			
▷		Opacity	0 %		◀ ✓		◆ ◆	
▷ □	5	My_Atoms_precomp	Normal ▾	None ▾	👁			
▷ □	6	My_Background_precomp	Normal ▾	None ▾	👁			

Switches / Modes

Preview and observe the result. If you feel the particles linger a little too long after the word Atomic comes up, you can move the second Opacity keyframe earlier in time, or try applying Easy Ease In to it to taper the fade. When you're done, twirl up the layer (or press T again).

> Notice how the particles appear to wrap themselves serendipitously around the atoms. This is emphasized because the particles are composited on top of the atom symbols as well as the background. To compare, drag the **BS_Particulars2.mov** layer below **Atoms_precomp** in the layer stack and you'll see that the interaction between the two is reduced. Undo to move the particles back above the atoms layer again.

Step 44: As if that wasn't enough pizzazz, we have a second particles movie for you to apply. It will be treated much like the particles in the step above, but will add spice to the Atomic Café title section.

• Import **BS_Particulars1.mov**, and add it to [**My_Atomic Cafe**].

• Position this new movie above the **Atomic** and **Cafe** title layers (at the top of the layer stack).

• Press 6 to move to 06:00 and hit [to start **BS_Particulars1.mov** at this time.

• Set its Blending Mode to Add.

• With the movie still selected, press Command+Option+B (Control+Alt+B) to set the work area to the duration of the movie, and RAM Preview. The particles build from the center out, creating a horizontal energy whorl.

Notice that this movie has a built-in "fade up" as the particles gain momentum, and a natural "fade down" as the particles dissipate, so there is no need to add Opacity keyframes.

*Save! We took some shortcuts in the explanations of the steps, as we figured you already knew the basic dance by now. If we assumed too much, compare your version with our [**AtomicCafe_after Step 44**].*

43 *complete:* The particles layer starts at 01:15, the beginning of one of the measures of the soundtrack, and fades out after the bang at 06:00 when the title starts to build.

Work Area Snap To

Use Command+Option+B (Control+Alt+B) to set the work area to the duration of the selected layer(s).

44 A second particle movie (from the Bestshots/Particulars 1 CD) adds an energy whorl around the word Atomic.

45 Create a new blank layer – a Solid – that's black, and the same size as the composition.

Light Manufacturing

To further emphasize the big musical hit at 06:00, you're going to create a flare effect to temporarily blind the viewer as the word Atomic comes up. Well, maybe not *blind*, but at least make a statement…

Like many of the other elements so far, this one will start just before the downbeat, ramp up quickly for impact, then fade down to make room for other elements. In this case, you'll be animating some of the Knoll Light Factory LE parameters to create this effect, instead of the Scale and Opacity you have been using so far.

Go ahead and close the other windows aside from [**My_Atomic Cafe**] – you're done with them, and it will reduce screen clutter as you focus on these last few effects. Rather than close windows individually, you might find it easier to use the shortcut Command+Option+W (Control+Alt+W) to Close All windows, then double-click just the [**My_Atomic Cafe**] comp again from the Project window!

STEP 45: Locate to time 05:25 in your comp, just before that downbeat. Create a new Solid by either using the shortcut Command+Y (Control+Y) or the menu item Layer>New>Solid. Give the solid a good name such as "**My Flare**", click on the Make Comp Size button, and select black as its color. Click OK. (Note that a **Solids** folder has been created in the Project window to store your solid layers.)

STEP 46: With the new layer selected, choose the plug-in Effect> Knoll Light Factory>**Light Factory LE** (provided free on this book's DVD). A nice bright spark, with a series of lens reflections, will slash across your black solid. Go ahead and try out the different Flare Types available in the Effect Controls window; we're going to stick with the Warm Sun Flare default.

• *Make sure the effect is selected in the Effect Controls window.* This will cause its control point for the Light Source Location to appear in the Comp window: It will be a circle with a + symbol in the middle, right where the sparks originate. (If you can't see it, select View Options from the Comp window's wing menu and check that the option Effect Controls is checked on.) Imagine a line that runs from this Light Source Location through the center of the layer; notice how the lens reflections are drawn along this imaginary line.

46 The default Light Factory LE lens flare. Make sure you can see the Effect Control for its Light Source Location in the Comp window; you'll be dragging this to the center of the comp to create a pure spark effect.

• In this case, you don't want all those reflections; you just want the spark. The way to make the reflections go away is to align the Light Source Location with the centerpoint of the layer. Drag it in the Comp window until they align, or set the Light Source Location value in the Effect Controls window to X = 160, Y = 120.

• Scrub the Angle parameter in the Effect Controls window. Notice how it makes the rays in the spark rotate and create new patterns. You'll be using this to create additional excitement in your flare. Undo, or set it back to 0.0 when you're done.

STEP 47: Time to animate your flare:

• You want the spark to start from nothing, so scrub its Brightness parameter down to zero.

• Still at time 05:25, turn on the keyframe animation stopwatches for the Brightness, Scale, and Angle parameters; you will be animating all of these. You can set these stopwatches directly in the Effect Controls window.

• After you've set this trio of stopwatches, press U to reveal these keyframes in the Timeline window.

• Press 6 to locate to comp marker 6 at 06:00 in the timeline.

• Increase the Brightness parameter to somewhere over 100. You want the flare to illuminate most of the frame, with just a bit of dark in the corners. We chose a value of 140.

• Increase the effect's Scale parameter. This increases the size of the center of the flare, increases the overall illumination, and makes the individual rays more pronounced. We settled on a value of 2.00.

   After this initial blow-out, you want the flare to reduce in size over the next couple of musical beats, as the word Atomic comes up underneath. (You can't see the word Atomic right now – it's obscured by the black solid you created for the flare. We'll deal with that shortly.) We mentioned earlier that one measure of the music was 1.5 seconds, which is about 45 frames; let's fade out the flare over half a measure.

• Go to time 06:23. Reduce the Scale parameter back down to 1.00, and the Brightness back down to 0.0.

• Trim the out point of this layer at 06:23 by making sure it is still selected and pressing Option+] (Alt+]).

• Press Command+Option+B (Control+Alt+B) to set the work area to equal the length of this layer, and RAM Preview. Pretty cool! But the rays aren't doing anything other than growing and contracting.

• With **My_Flare** still selected, press the letter O to locate to its out point, and increase the Angle parameter to give the rays a bit of movement. A little goes a long way; we chose to animate from 0° to 45°. RAM Preview and adjust to taste. (Figure of Timeline on next page.)

47 After you've set the Light Source Location to equal the center of the layer (X = 160, Y = 120), reduce the Brightness to zero. Next, enable keyframing for the Brightness, Scale, and Angle parameters at time 05:25.

47 *complete:* At maximum brightness, the flare should just fill the frame, with some dark falloff visible in the corners.

Flares Galore

If you like this free Light Factory LE effect, you should check out the full Knoll Light Factory (www.redgiantsoftware.com). A demo version is included in the Free Plug-ins folder on your DVD. (Yes, it was created by the same John Knoll who has supervised special effects for numerous blockbuster films.)

My_Atomic Cafe • Timeline

My_Atomic Cafe

0:00:06:00 (29.97 fps)

	#	Source Name	Mode	T	TrkMat		05:15f	06:00f	06:15f	07:00f	07
▽	1	My Flare	Normal								
		Light Factory LE	Reset								
		Brightness	140.0								
		Scale	2.00								
		Angle	0 x +8.0 °								
▷	2	BS_Particulars1.mov	Add		None						
▷	3	Atomic/AC_Title.ai	Normal		None						
▷	4	Cafe/AC_Title.ai	Normal		None						
▷	5	CM_AtomicMusic.mov									
▷	6	BS_Particulars2.mov	Add								
▷	7	My_Atoms_precomp	Normal		None						
▷	8	My_Background_precomp	Normal		None						

Switches / Modes

47 *complete:* The parameters of Light Factory LE have now been animated to make the flare grow and contract in time with the pivotal hit in the music. Pick a blending mode that works for you in Step 48.

STEP 48: Finish the effect off by using Blending Modes to composite your flare over the logo and background.

• Press 6 to locate to the point of maximum brightness. Make sure the Switches/Modes column in the Timeline window is set to Modes (press F4 if it isn't). There are a few Blending Modes which are ideally suited to blending in layers on black backgrounds: Add, Screen, Linear Dodge, and Color Dodge. (Lighten, Difference, and Exclusion also work with black backgrounds, but they give pretty weird results.)

48 Different Blending Modes create different effects. Here are Add (left), Screen (center), and Color Dodge (right).

Screen is the most middle-of-the road, and it creates an easier-to-watch effect. Add mode is the one that will temporarily blind your viewer. Color Dodge is psychedelic. Go ahead and experiment with various modes, and choose the one you like the best. We personally took the safest route and chose Screen: It did the best job of preserving our original colors, while still adding a lot of light to the scene.

Save, twirl up all layers, and RAM Preview. Compare your version against [AtomicCafe_after Step 48]. *If you had trouble animating the flare, you can cheat: At Step 46, select the solid, choose Animation> Apply Animation Preset, and use our preset* **Atomic Cafe>_Presets> LightFactory.ffx.** *Just add the Mode in Step 48.*

Part 6: Radio Waves *(optional)*

You could end this tutorial at this point, and be very happy with the result. Make sure you either RAM Preview or render the whole thing, so you can see all the parts strung together. However, if you want to push on and add one more layer of interest to the piece, we've got one more effect to add: Radio Waves.

Radio Waves generates geometric patterns that can animate. The most common use for it is to create a series of concentric circles that expand from a central point, yielding the common graphical representation of radio waves emanating from an antenna. That's what we'll use it for here – but as you learn the basics, keep in mind it's a very flexible plug-in that can be used to create a wide variety of shapes.

STEP 49: Just like Light Factory LE in Steps 45 through 48, the Radio Waves effect will be applied to a solid layer, and tweaked to taste. The idea is to complement the circles that appear throughout the background thanks to the **BS_Retrocities.mov** layer you added back in Steps 24 and 25.

• Hit 6 to move to time 06:00. Create a new Solid (Layer>New>Solid) just as you did back in Step 45 (same size as the comp, black in color), and name it "**RadioWaves_solid.**"

• Drag this new Solid down the layer stack in the Timeline window so that it sits directly above the **Background_precomp** layer.

• Apply Effect>Render>**Radio Waves**. Rather than compositing on top of the black solid as Light Factory LE did, Radio Waves defaults to creating its own alpha channel, so you see only the effect, and not the solid it's applied to. The waves draw on over time, so they are not yet visible at 06:00.

• Solo the **RadioWaves_solid** layer so that previews are fast, and you can see more clearly what you are doing. At this point, all you should see is the comp's white background.

• Press Command+Option+B (Control+Alt+B) to set the work area to match the duration of the solid (06:00 to the end of the comp), and RAM Preview. The default settings produce a thin, fast-moving blue wave pattern. You'll need to change some settings to create thick, slow-moving, light-colored waves.

STEP 50: You'll start by tweaking the frequency and speed of the waves. In the Effect Controls window, twirl down the Wave Motion section of the effect. The Frequency parameter sets how often a new wave is "born," while the Expansion value sets how fast it moves. Remember that the speed dictates how long each wave will be onscreen before it moves outside the edges of the comp. This in turn defines how long of

49 The idea is to use the Radio Waves effect to create additional animating circles, which will serve to reinforce the circles that appear in the background you built earlier.

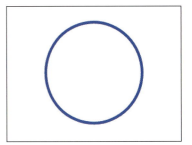

49 *complete:* Apply Radio Waves to the new solid layer and Solo the layer. When you first apply Radio Waves, the default settings create a thin blue wave, which you can see if you advance a few frames or RAM Preview.

My_Atomic Cafe • Timeline

50 The **Radio Waves_solid** layer sits above the background layer and is set to Solo. To help time out where you want new waves to appear, set layer markers at 07:15 and 09:00. Also place comp marker 9 at 09:00 by pressing Shift+F9.

50 *complete:* To generate a new wave every 1.5 seconds, set the Wave Motion>Frequency parameter to 0.67.

a "life" each wave appears to have (though we'll change the Lifespan to match the apparent life span of the wave in a moment).

• Since a measure of music is 1.5 seconds or 45 frames long, it would work well to create a new wave every measure. And because a downbeat falls at the start of the layer at 06:00, you will want a second wave to start at 07:15, and a third one to start at 09:00. Move to time 07:15, and with **Radio Waves_solid** still selected, hit the asterisk key on the extended keypad to add a layer marker (or select Layer>Add Marker if you don't have an extended keyboard). Create another layer marker at time 09:00.

• Press Shift+9 (on the keyboard) to also set a comp marker at 09:00.

• Scrub the timeline, starting at 06:00, and you'll notice that waves are being generated starting every second (at 07:00, 08:00, 09:00 and so on). This confirms that the waves are being produced too often.

• Hit 9 to jump to 09:00. Press Command (Control) and slowly scrub the Frequency value from 1.0 to a lower value – notice how the third wave moves back toward the center. A value of 0.67 should place the beginning of the third wave at exactly 09:00. RAM Preview, and see how the waves are now timed to start on beats of the music.

Why 0.67? If you want one wave to start every 1.5 seconds, that means the frequency at which the waves should be generated is 1 wave ÷ 1.5 seconds = 0.67 waves per second.

STEP 51: The speed at which the waves travel from the center is controlled by the Expansion value, which defaults to 5. This pacing is so fast that the first wave is completely off screen before the second one even starts. To create more overlap, slow down the wave Expansion value to 2. (Remember that when scrubbing values, press Command (Control) to scrub in fine increments.) RAM Preview to confirm that this new Expansion rate works better, and that altering it did not affect the Frequency (how often they trigger) – the waves still sync to the music.

STEP 52: Scrub the timeline and you'll notice that the first wave, which started at 06:00, exits the comp at around 09:10. This tells you that each wave has an "onscreen time" of about 03:10. You might consider this to be the lifespan of the layer, but the actual default for the Lifespan parameter – how long the Radio Waves plug-in considers a wave to be around, whether you can see it or not – is 10 seconds. Change Wave Motion>Lifespan to 3.5 seconds so it more closely matches the timing of your waves. This will make the effect more intuitive to deal with when you're setting values that defer to Lifespan. For instance, the Fade-in and -out parameters, as well as the Start and End Width values, take their cues from Lifespan – they don't look at your animation, decide what point the wave moves outside the comp area, then consider that to be the "end" or "out" point!

STEP 53: The waves will now appear faded, due to the default settings in the Stroke section. Twirl down Stroke in the Effect Controls window, and change the Fade-out Time from 5 seconds to 1 second. This will make the wave fade out between 2.5 and 3.5 seconds in its lifespan, or just when it reaches the edges of the comp. Since the wave is outside the comp when it's 03:10 old, it will never fade completely to 0% even as it moves outside the frame.

The Fade-in Time fades up the wave as it starts to move out from the center – it can remain at 0 (no fade in) for this project since the title and particles will obscure the center of the Radio Waves layer.

53 To reduce the amount of fading you saw in the previous figure, reduce the Stroke>Fade-out Time (where the arrow is pointing) to 1.000 seconds.

51–52 The Expansion rate has been slowed down so more waves appear onscreen at the same time, and the Lifespan parameter has been reduced to roughly the length of time one wave is visible – note how it fades out as it gets close to the edge.

54–55 By setting a larger End Width than Start Width, the waves grow in thickness as they expand. The Stroke Color is then set to a soft yellow.

55 This soft yellow color (below left) blends well with the background. To blend it in even more, choose a blending mode such as Soft Light, and reduce the Opacity a touch (below right).

STEP 54: There are also settings for the Start Width and End Width. These defer to the duration of the Lifespan, with the Start Width interpolating to the End Width over the course of 3.5 seconds. Leave the Start Width at 5, but change the End Width to 25, or to taste. RAM Preview again, and tweak the fades and width settings until you're happy with the general look. As you can see, it's important to set the Lifespan value first, as it has an impact on other parameters.

STEP 55: All that's left is to set the color and the layer's blending mode:

• Under the Stroke section, change the effect's Color to a soft yellow that you think will blend well with the background.

• Verify that **Radio Waves_solid** is set to Best Quality so that the waves are smoothly antialiased, and turn off its Solo switch in the Timeline window so that you can view the waves in context with the other layers.

• Experiment with the blending mode for this layer. We used Soft Light, as it blended the yellow waves in a way that they rendered subtly in the background. Adjust the Stroke Color if necessary.

• If the waves are still too prominent, set the Opacity of the Radio Waves layer to taste. Somewhere around 75% will help them sit more into the background. You can either use the regular Opacity, or set Radio Waves' own Stroke>Opacity parameter to 0.75, if you prefer.

• And now, the moment of truth: Do a RAM Preview with all layers on from 06:00 to the end, and see if the Radio Waves perform their function (adding interest without overwhelming anyone else).

My_Atomic Cafe • Timeline

	#	Source Name	Mode	T	TrkMat		
▽	1	**My Flare**	Screen ▾			👁	
▷	2	BS_Particulars1.mov	Add ▾		None ▾	👁	
▷	3	Atomic/AC_Title.ai	Normal ▾		None ▾	👁	
▷	4	Cafe/AC_Title.ai	Normal ▾		None ▾	👁	
▷	5	CM_AtomicMusic.mov				🔊	
▷	6	BS_Particulars2.mov	Add ▾			👁	
▷	7	My_Atoms_precomp	Normal ▾		None ▾	👁	
▽	8	**RadioWaves_solid**	Soft Light ▾		None ▾	👁	
		⏱ Opacity	75 %				
▷	9	My_Background_pre...	Normal ▾		None ▾	👁	

0:00:09:00 (29.97 fps)

Switches / Modes

STEP 56: There's just one problem with our well-planned wave element: the timing. Although each new wave starts on a downbeat, you don't *see* each wave until it's about 20 frames old because the waves are partially hidden behind the title.

Yes, what you did above is technically correct, but now it's time to cheat to make it visually correct as well. To make the waves hit the beats of music as far as our final composite is concerned, you'll need to slide the layer back in time by about 20 frames:

• Hit 9 to move to time 09:00, where the third wave starts to trigger. Slowly drag the layer bar for **Radio Waves_solid** to the left (earlier in time) until you see the wave appear over the top of the Atomic title. Watch the Info palette as you drag (if it's not visible, open it by pressing Command+3 on Mac, Control+3 on Windows); the in point for the layer should end up around 05:10 (20 frames earlier).

• RAM Preview again, and adjust the in point to taste.

When you're timing to music, don't be afraid to slip and slide elements so they work better visually, even if they don't precisely hit the beats of music when you refer to the audio's waveform. Sometimes there's a cue in the instrumentation or vocal track, or an accent drum beat, that is more fun to hit. Just listen, look, and tweak.

Save your project and RAM Preview the entire comp one last time with motion blur on. If you got lost, compare your settings with those saved in the prebuilt comp, [**Atomic Cafe_final**].

The Radio Waves settings are also saved as an Animation Preset in the **Atomic Cafe>_Presets** *folder.*

Feel free to render your movie to disk (Composition>Make Movie); name your movie, select the Render Settings>Best Settings template, and set the Output Module appropriately for your hardware.

56 Project complete: The final Timeline window. The Radio Waves solid is reduced in Opacity and moved earlier in time to start at 05:10.

Connect

For more information on topics covered in this tutorial, check out the following volumes of *Creating Motion Graphics:*

Volume 1:

The Sequence Layers keyframe assistant

Keyframe velocity manipulation

Animating Scale and Opacity

Blending Modes

Motion Blur

Nesting and Precomposing compositions

That Ol' Black Solid chapter (lens flare)

Importing and interpreting footage

Rendering

Volume 2:

Importing Photoshop files as Comp

Importing Illustrator files as Comp

Time Remapping

The Wiggler keyframe assistant

Expressions

RoboTV

Employing Parenting to animate a multi-segment robot arm, and editing a video montage for the inset screen.

One of the most significant features in After Effects is Parenting, which lets you attach one object to another and animate both while they remain linked. This feature is particularly useful for character-style animation, as it makes anthropomorphic chains of objects much easier to manage.

In this tutorial you will employ Parenting to control a robot arm to use as a pointing device in a bumper for a hypothetical sports program. You will link the different segments of the arm and animate it to point at different places in the frame. We'll lead you through the first set of keyframes; you can animate the rest on your own if you like.

OVERVIEW

Main Concepts:

These are the features and concepts we will be focusing on in this project:

- Importing Photoshop as Comp
- Anchor Point and Rotation
- Parenting
- Guide Layers
- Trim Comp to Work Area
- Slip Editing, Overlay Edit
- Vignetting the background
- Mask Feather and Mask Expansion
- Importing Illustrator as Comp
- Motion Blur and Shutter Angle
- Animating with the Type tool
- Boris Mosaic effect* *(optional)*
- Fractal Noise effect (Pro) *(optional)*
- Boris Tritone effect* *(optional)*

Requirements:

After Effects 6.5 or later standard version.

Third party effects: Boris Mosaic, Boris Tritone (included free on this book's DVD in the **Free Plug-ins** folder).

A bonus tutorial on the DVD requires the effect Fractal Noise, which is available in the version 6.5 Professional edition.

Getting Started:

* *If you don't already own the third-party effect set Boris BCC3 (www.borisfx.com), be sure to install the Boris Tritone and Mosaic effects included on the accompanying DVD in the* **Free Plug-ins** *folder.*

Inside the **Tutorials** master folder on the accompanying DVD, locate and copy the folder **02_RoboTV** to your hard drive.

In the folder **Final Movie** which is inside this main folder, open **RoboTV.mov** in the QuickTime Player and preview it.

Inside the **Project** folder you'll find the finished project file **RoboTV.aep**. Open this project file: This is your starting point; we suggest you save under a new name after each major section.

You will also learn different approaches to editing a sequence of shots in After Effects. Of course, we'll be throwing in a few design tips along the way, including a guided tour of the finishing touches we applied. An optional bonus tutorial on this book's DVD demonstrates using the Fractal Noise effect to create abstract backgrounds.

A frame from the final *RoboTV* animation. Footage from the Artbeats volume Skydiving.

The Tasks

This is what you will be doing in the various parts of this tutorial. Since this is a fairly lengthy project, feel free to take breaks between major sections:

PART 1: Import the layered Photoshop file containing the robot arm, set anchor points for correct rotation, and build the parent/child hierarchy.

PART 2: Import the soundtrack and turn it into a guide layer, perform edits on an existing video sequence, nest this video edit comp into your main comp, and position it inside the robot's frame.

PART 3: Composite the background plate out of a combination of three layers using various faux-lighting tricks.

PART 4: Add text from a layered Illustrator file and slide it in time to match the video edits, animate the robot arm using different interpolation types, and render the final.

PART 5: Take a guided tour of additional touches we added to the finished project, including color correction, adding shadows, tweaking the timing, animating the Type tool to create an additional subtitle, and using Boris Mosaic to transition into the first piece of video.

CD BONUS TUTORIAL: A bonus step-by-step tutorial showing how we created the fractal noise elements used in Part 3 with the Fractal Noise plug-in included in the Professional edition.

Part 1: Building the Robot

Your first task will be building the robot arm, including creating a parent/child chain for it.

By now you should have the project **RoboTV.aep** open. In its Project window you will find folders named **My_Comps** and **My_Sources** to keep your own work organized. There is also a folder called **_RoboTV** * **prebuilt** which contains this project paused at various steps so you can compare your own work. Feel free to explore some of the comps in it ahead of time if you like, but make sure you close all windows except for the Project window before starting in below.

Importing the RoboBody

STEP 1: Select the **My_Sources** folder in the Project window, then select the menu command File>Import>File by typing Command+I on Mac (or Control+I on Windows). Locate the folder **02_RoboTV>Project>Sources** on your drive, and select **RoboBody.psd**: a layered Photoshop file. At the bottom of the Import dialog, be sure to set the Import As popup to Composition – Cropped Layers rather than its default of Footage. Click Open, and both a folder and composition named **RoboBody Comp 1** will be added to the **My_Sources** folder in the Project window. (If instead you got a dialog asking you to choose a layer, you missed the Import As Composition popup; cancel and try again.)

1 Import the layered Photoshop file **RoboBody.psd** as a composition. This comp will contain four pieces: the frame and three arm segments. If you want to check what each layer looks like, use the Solo switch in the Timeline window (where the cursor is pointing below).

The folder called **RoboBody Comp 1** contains the individual pieces of the robot arm. Drag the comp to the **My_Comps** folder, and double-click it to open it. This comp includes four layers: the **Frame**; plus **Big**, **Medium**, and **Small Arms**. All layers will be aligned with each other, just as they were in Photoshop. If you want, solo the individual layers to get a feel for which piece is which. Option+click (Alt+click) on a Solo switch to turn off other Solo switches.

STEP 2: Press Command+K (Control+K) to open the Composition>Composition Settings dialog, and set the following:

- Change the name of the comp to "**My_RoboTV.**"

- The width and height (640×480) and pixel aspect ratio (square) is dictated by the size of the original Photoshop file, and should not be changed.

- The frame rate should read 29.97 frames per second (fps) – the NTSC video rate.

- Set the Duration to 06:00 seconds. This is the length of the animation you'll be creating. (Photoshop and Illustrator files imported as compositions use the duration of the last comp you created or edited.)

- Make sure the Composition is in Full Resolution, and click OK.

   You can also select Full from the Resolution popup at the bottom the Comp window, or use the keyboard shortcut Command+J (Control+J).

2 Set the comp's duration to 06:00 in Composition Settings.

STEP 3: If your composition was originally shorter than 06:00 in duration, you will need to zoom out the timeline and trim all layers to last the full six seconds.

- Zoom out the timeline by pressing – (the minus key on the keyboard), dragging the right edge of the Time Navigator (the topmost brackets above the timeline's ruler area in the Timeline window), or using the zoom controls below the timeline in the same window.

- Hit End to move to 05:29.

- Select All layers by using the shortcut Command+A (Control+A).

- Hit Option+] (Alt+]) to trim the out point of all layers.

- Press Home to return to 00:00.

3 Make sure you can see all six seconds of your timeline. One way to set this view is to drag the Time View Brackets in the Timeline window (where the cursor is pointing).

Setting the Anchor Points

In After Effects, all the rotations and scalings a layer undergoes is centered around its Anchor Point. In order for the robot animation to work correctly, each arm must be set to rotate around a sensible point, such as where it would join to the previous robot piece, before you begin setting up the parenting hierarchy.

   When you're setting the anchors in the next step, make sure you're viewing all the pixels available. Set the comp's Resolution to Full and its Magnification to 100% — there are popups along the bottom of the Comp window where you can set these. If you're short on monitor space, resize the window to focus in on each arm as needed but still view at 100%.

When a layer is selected, its Anchor Point can be seen in the Composition window as a circle with an X in the center. This is what you will be moving:

STEP 4: To see each arm's joints more clearly, we recommend you solo each layer as you work on each arm. This temporarily turns off all other layers.

• Select the **Big Arm** layer, and solo it.

• Select the Pan Behind tool (also known to some as the Anchor Point tool) from the Tools palette; the shortcut is Y. If the Tools palette is not visible, type Command+1 (Control+1) to reveal it.

4 Solo the **Big Arm** layer, select the Pan Behind tool (above), and use it to move its anchor to the middle of its lower joint (below).

• In the Comp window, drag this layer's anchor to the center of the *lower* joint – the one you would expect it to pivot around. Zoom in to 200% or more if you need to see the area more clearly.

Any rotation will now occur around this area. If you want to verify this, select the Rotate tool (shortcut: W) and spin the layer around in the Comp window. When you're done, Undo until the arm is back to its original rotation, and press Y to re-select the Pan Behind tool.

STEP 5: Select the **Medium Arm** layer and Option+click (Alt+click) on the Solo button to solo this arm only. Repeat Step 4, moving this layer's anchor point to its lower joint.

STEP 6: Select the **Small Arm** layer and Option+click (Alt+click) on the Solo button to solo this arm only. Repeat Step 4 again, moving its anchor point to its lower joint.

The Anchor Point should now be set for all three arms. To turn on all layers again, turn off the Solo switch for the **Small Arm**. *Don't turn on all the Solo switches to see all layers again* – if you do, any new sources you add to the comp will not be visible!

STEP 7: Revert to the Selection tool (shortcut: V) when you're done. If zoomed in, return to 100% Magnification.

You do *not* want to have the Pan Behind tool selected except when it's needed. It may look like a friendly "mover" tool, but you can create a big mess by trying to move layers with it! This is even worse if the layers have masks applied, as its true purpose will reveal itself: panning an image behind a mask shape, and changing the Position value automatically.

Save your project. We've prebuilt a version with the anchor points already set up and named it [RoboTV_after Step 07]; *you can find it in the* RoboTV * prebuilt comps>_compare comps_after Step ## *folder. If you're not sure whether you've set your anchor points correctly, compare your Anchor Point and Position values with our version.*

The Parenting Chain

Parenting is the ability to link one object to another. Once this bond has been established between parent and child, the two are grouped together as one complex object – if you move, scale, or rotate the parent, the child is affected in the same way. A child can still have its own animation; if the parent happens to be animating as well, the child just follows it around while it also does its own thing.

There are two different ways to establish Parenting links between layers: a popup menu and a pick whip tool. We'll try out both.

Step 8: Spend a moment thinking through what relationship between the robot pieces would make sense: For example, what should be attached to the **Big Arm** piece? Should **Big Arm** be attached to anyone else?

• Make sure the Parent column is visible in the Timeline window. Shift+F4 is the easiest way to toggle it on and off; you can also select it from the wing menu of the Timeline window under Columns>Parent.

• In the Parent column for the **Big Arm** layer, there is a popup menu that initially says None. Click on it and you will see the names of all the other layers in the current comp. Select the **Frame** layer as the Parent. This way, you can later reposition or scale just the frame, and all of the attached arms will follow along.

• Time to try out the other tool. In the Parent column for the **Medium Arm** layer, note the spiral icon to the left of the popup menu: This is the *pick whip* tool. Click on it and drag the cursor to the name of the layer you want to be the parent – in this case, the **Big Arm** layer.

• The last step is hooking up the **Small Arm** layer to the **Medium Arm** layer. Go ahead and use the tool of your choice – menu or pick whip.

> You can reassign a layer's parent at any time. You can also reset it to None by using the popup menu or by Command+clicking (Control+clicking) on its pick whip icon. A parent can have multiple children, but each child can have no more than one parent.

Parent Column Position

It is easy to drag the Parent column to a new position in the Timeline window by dragging its column header left or right. We like to position it close to the layer names, as it makes using the pick whip more convenient.

8 To assign a parent for a layer, you can use either the popup menu under the Parent column (above), or the pick whip tool to click and drag to the parent of your choice (below).

STEP 9: The point of setting up the Parenting chain is so that you can later rotate the position of any one of the robot arms, and know that any children will follow along naturally without you having to animate their position as well. You will build an animation based on this in Part 4; for now, let's test this theory and make sure your chain works:

- Select all three arms, and hit R to twirl down just their Rotation property in the Timeline window. Deselect the layers by hitting F2.

- Scrub (click and drag) the rotation value for the **Big Arm** layer, and watch the other two arms follow in the Comp window.

- Scrub the rotation value for the **Medium Arm**, and watch the **Small Arm** also react.

- Since the **Small Arm** is the end of the chain, rotation affects only this one layer.

- If an arm seems "out of round" when you rotate it – the hole for its pivot wanders off from the pivot point underneath – you might want to re-adjust your anchor point for that layer. Return its rotation to zero, select the Pan Behind tool again, nudge the anchor, and scrub that layer's rotation again.

- Return all Rotation values to zero when you're through experimenting, and twirl them up in the Timeline window. Later on you'll animate the rotation values so that the arms will reach different words in a title, appearing to trigger different video events. But next, you're going to import the video layers that will fill that hole in the RoboTV frame, and build the background.

9 After you've correctly built the Parenting chain (top), the other two arms will automatically follow when you rotate the **Big Arm** layer (above).

Save your project. If you are completely lost, open our prebuilt comp [**RoboTV_after Step 09**] *from the* **RoboTV * prebuilt comps> _compare comps_after Step ##** *folder and compare your results. Feel free to drag this comp to the* **My_Comps** *folder, rename it "**My_RoboTV_09**", and use it to continue with the tutorial.*

Part 2: The Video Montage

If you need to work with a large number of clips or a long running time, it is often better to arrange these clips in a dedicated non-linear editing system and import the result in After Effects. However, After Effects does sport a very useful set of editing utilities which make it easy to modify a sequence of clips without a trip back to your NLE, which we'll explore in this section. But first, let's load in the groove…

The Making of RoboBody

The video frame and robot arm were much easier to build than it might seem at first glance. The original shapes were drawn in Adobe Illustrator, then swept to create an inset look using Zaxwerks Invigorator Pro (www.zaxwerks.com), with the resulting model exported for use in the 3D program Electric Image (www.electricimage.com).

The main texture for the frame and arm pieces came from the Plaid Companion library by Dedicated Digital.

The surface detail was not modeled; it's just a combination of a texture map from the Plaid Companion library by Dedicated Digital plus fractal-based procedural shaders. Shades of gray were used while in the 3D program, to maintain flexibility for tinting later on.

The camera was positioned far away, with a high amount of zoom. This reduced perspective-based distortions. Each piece was then soloed and rendered one at a time. These pieces were imported into After Effects and tinted individually using the third-party effect Boris Tritone (free on the DVD that came with the book, in the **Free Plug-ins** folder). The Professional edition's Stylize>Glow was added for warmth, and a diffuse Perspective>Drop Shadow effect was added to give the perception of depth. This shadow was centered on each object so they could be rotated freely without the shadow's direction appearing to change.

The file was exported from After Effects as a Photoshop layered file (type: PSD). We then opened the file in Photoshop and masked out some of the glow that bled into the center of each arm's pivot, to better reveal the joint of the arm piece underneath.

Adding Music

Step 10: Select the **My_Sources** folder in the Project window, and press Command+I (Control+I) to File>Import the music track **CM_RoboMusic.mov** from the **02_RoboTV>Project>Sources** folder that came with this tutorial. Double-click it in the Project window to open the QuickTime player for it, and audition it. Close the player, then drag it from the Project window into the [**My_RoboTV**] comp so that it starts at 00:00. Where it lands in the layer stack is unimportant.

Step 11: In the Project window, twirl open the folder **video sequence**. It contains a comp with a series of video clips a co-worker edited together for you earlier. Double-click [**video sequence**] to open it.

Step 12: Re-select **CM_Robomusic.mov** in the Project window, and type Command+/ to add it to [**video sequence**] starting at 00:00.

With this soundtrack still selected, choose the menu item Layer>Guide Layer. This turns it into a special layer that can only be seen or heard in the current comp, but not in any comps downstream or in the final render. This means we can audition the soundtrack in this comp to see how the video edit works, and not worry about it reappearing unwanted in our final comp later. Note the blue Guide Layer icon next to its name in the Timeline window.

12 Choosing Layer>Guide Layer means this source can only be seen or heard in this comp, and not any other comps or the final render. Note the special blue icon.

13 The Layer window indicates that the movie has been trimmed to a one-second section from 06:00 to 06:29.

13 *complete:* Placing the cursor beyond the currently used portions of a clip activates the Slip Edit tool (below), which allows you to slide the section of the clip you want to use while occupying the same slot in the overall timeline. The new in point will be the frame where the skydiver in red just starts to lift his hand (above).

Slip and Slide

As noted earlier, After Effects has several tools which make it easier to change video edit decisions after the fact. The first of these we'll explore is the Slip Edit tool.

STEP 13: The full version of **AB_Skydiving.mov** is over eight seconds long, but your animation allows for only one second to be used – from 03:00 to 03:29 in the timeline. Of course, you want to use the best one second of action.

Double-click the **AB_Skydiving.mov** layer to open the movie in the Layer window, hit Home to return to 00:00, and hit the spacebar to play the entire clip. Notice the one-second section that's currently being used (from 06:00 to 06:29)as defined by the Layer window's in and out points. Also notice that shortly after this "select," the diver on the left side raises his hand and waves at the camera. Your co-worker thought this was a bit corny, but wouldn't you know – this was your client's favorite bit of the entire shot. You've been asked to change the edit to get it back in.

- Close the Layer window. Make sure **AB_Skydiving.mov** is still selected, and type I to locate to the layer's in point.

- Place the cursor just to the left of the layer's in point, and note that the normal cursor changes to a double-arrowed icon (see figure below).

- Drag the empty layer bar area to the left. This "slides" the movie along the layer bar, while maintaining the clip's relative position in the timeline. Move it left until you reach the frame where the diver's hand just starts to break away from the group.

- Scrub the timeline from 03:00 to 03:29 and check that you selected the full hand-wave action in the space of one second.

You can also slide the layer while the time marker is parked at any point in the clip; just remember to drag the layer from the "empty bar" section – you won't be able to slide it if there is no "handle" (extra material) left in the clip. More tips on using the Slip Edit tool can be found in the sidebar *Slippery Keyframes*.

Slippery Keyframes

If the layer already has keyframes applied to it, you can choose whether or not keyframes move as well when you slide the video with the Slip Edit tool:

• If you don't want keyframes to move when you slip a layer, make sure they're deselected (shortcut: select the layer, then type Shift+F2). The keyframes will then remain attached to the same point in the overall timeline, rather than the source footage. For example, two Opacity keyframes at the head of a clip for a fade-in will remain locked to the layer's in point, regardless of what time in the clip that in point is.

• If you want keyframes to also slide along the timeline, select those keyframes first, then slip the layer.

• Only selected keyframes will slide, so you could slide some keyframes and not others. For example, if you had rotoscoped a figure by setting mask shape keyframes, these keyframes need to travel with the frames they are masking. On the other hand, you might have a fade or a special effect that's synchronized to the beginning or end of a clip or another layer in the timeline, in which case you'll want these keyframes to remain locked to the same point in time.

Before you slip a layer, we recommend you twirl down all keyframes by using the shortcut U and decide which, if any, keyframes need to be selected so they remain attached to the source frames.

• Beware of hidden selections: If you've just edited a keyframe and twirled up the layer, that keyframe will still be selected, even though you can't see it! If you then slip the layer, that hidden, selected keyframe will slide too – potentially causing much confusion later. So be sure to deselect keyframes (Shift+F2) when in doubt.

Overlay Edit

Press 0 on the numeric keypad to RAM Preview [**video sequence**]. The clients are happy with the skydiving edit now, and in particular they love the way the snowboarder takes off as the music starts up. However, they note that while they can focus on the individual athletes in most of the shots, the current skateboarding shot has a lot of distracting people in the background. They say "Do something to fix it," and cheerily wave their hands as they leave.

You go knock on the door of the co-worker who made the original edit, and ask if she has any solo skateboarding shots. She's busy editing another piece, but gives you a clip of a street-style skateboarder she thinks will work. It's up to you to edit it in.

Step 14: In the Project window, select the folder **video sequence> video clips** and type Command+I (Control+I) to import a file. Locate and import the **CL_Skateboarding_street.mov** inside the **Project> Sources>video sequence** folder.

From the Project window, Option+double-click (Alt+double-click) to open this movie in the special After Effects Footage window. In addition to previewing a clip, this window features its own trimming tools as well as Ripple Insert Edit and Overlay Edit buttons.

If you simply double-click the movie, it opens in a QuickTime Player window, with no timecode or in and out points. Another bonus to the After Effects Footage window is that it also premultiplies any alpha channel so that edges in an RGB+Alpha movie look correct.

Sliding Up Close

If you've zoomed way into the timeline to where an empty portion of the layer bar is not visible – but you still need to slip a layer – press Y to select the Pan Behind tool. The cursor will change to the Slip tool when it's placed over the layer bar in the Timeline window.

Music Credits

The music for this tutorial was arranged by Chris Meyer. Rather than the harsh guitar rock or skittering "drum & bass" dance music commonly used for extreme sports shows, we opted for something more surreal that played up the robotic angle. This soundtrack employs copyright-cleared samples from Spectrasonics' *Distorted Reality 2* (the main groove), and *Bass Legends* (the half-speed Marcus Miller bassline) plus Zero-G's *Malice in Wonderland* (the ascending hi-hat-ish riff), servo sounds from The Producers' *Science Fiction 1*, and a startup whine courtesy of sound designer Alan Howarth.

STEP 15: RAM Preview the movie. Note that the most exciting part seems to happen around the middle of the clip's duration. Pick your favorite one second of action, and trim the movie to those frames by setting the in and out points. We picked the section from 1:15 to 2:14, but you can choose a different section if you like.

You can trim footage by dragging the triangles at the left and right of the main timeline (the top timeline is just for zooming in time, which is handy for a very long clip). You can also trim by moving the time marker to a frame, and clicking the In or Out buttons (these are the { and } squiggly brackets). The Duration readout will update to reflect your changes.

STEP 16: This is a great time to take advantage of the Overlay Edit feature to add your trimmed clip directly into the video montage:

• Bring [**video sequence**] forward, and move to time 02:00 where the new skateboarding movie will begin.

• Turn off the Video switch for the old **CL_Skateboarding_ramp.mov** layer.

• Bring the Footage window for **CL_Skateboarding_street.mov** forward.

At the bottom of the Footage window it should say "Edit Target: video sequence" which means that if you use the Overlay Edit button, the trimmed clip will be added to this – the most forward – comp. If a different comp is showing up as the Edit Target comp, verify that [**video sequence**] is indeed the forward composition, and select the Footage window again.

• Click on the Overlay Edit button in the bottom right-hand corner of the Footage window. The one-second portion you trimmed this clip to will be added to the top of [**video sequence**], starting at 02:00.

There's nothing special about this clip after you've added it; the result is not unlike adding the original clip to the comp, then trimming it down to one second afterward. Overlay Edit is just another tool that can occasionally save a few clicks. The Overlay Edit tool can also be handy for pretrimming a folder of clips while you're just checking them out, without having to add them to a comp first.

16 Trim the new clip in its Footage window to use a second of material out of the middle. Click on the Overlay Edit button (where the cursor is pointing in the lower right) to add the trimmed clip to your comp. Skateboarding footage courtesy of Creative License.

video sequence • Timeline

My_RoboTV   video sequence

0:00:02:00 (29.97 fps)

	#	Source Name			:00s	02s	04s	06s
▷	1	CM_RoboMusic.mov						
▷	2	GI_MountainPursuits.mov						
▷	3	AB_Skydiving.mov						
▷	4	CL_Skateboarding_street.mov						
▷	5	CL_Skateboarding_ramp.mov						
▷	6	AB_Recreation_24.mov						

Switches / Modes

Overlay Edit also makes it easy to add the same trimmed clip to multiple comps: If you re-open the Footage window, the trimmed area will still be active but it is not "live" – changing the trim points will not update the footage already in use in a comp. This means you could retrim the layer and Overlay Edit a different section to the same – or even a different – comp. If you add the clip to a comp normally (by dragging it from the Project window rather than by using Overlay Edit), the trim information from the Footage window will be ignored.

16 *complete:* The final timeline for the video montage. Note that we've turned off the layer Video switch for the old skateboarding clip so it won't accidentally render, but have kept it around just in case we need it again.

• Drag the new clip down the layer stack so that it sits in place of the old one and Save your project. Go ahead and leave the previous skateboarding clip in the composition (just in case the clients change their mind) – since it's turned off, it won't take up additional rendering time. RAM Preview, and see if you're happy with the new montage. If you'd like to tweak the new clip's in and out points some more, practice using the Slip tool you learned back in Step 13.

Ripple Insert Edit

In addition to the Overlay button covered in Step 16, After Effects features another handy tool for adding pretrimmed source footage to a comp: Ripple Insert Edit. This tool is similar to Overlay Edit, except that when you add footage to a composition, all the other layers move down the timeline to accommodate the new footage.

To access this feature, hold down the Option (Alt) key and double-click a source from the Project window to open it in After Effects' Footage window. If necessary, trim the in and out points in the Footage window to remove unwanted frames.

In the Composition, move the time marker to where you'd like the new footage to be inserted. Back in the Footage window, click the Ripple Insert Edit button (the one immediately to the right of the Duration value). The trimmed movie will be inserted in the

timeline at the current time, and all other layers will move down the timeline. If the time marker is placed in the middle of a layer, that layer will be split and the new footage inserted in the middle. Lock any layers if you don't want them to be affected (moved or split).

Nesting the Video Montage

The video editing is done; the next step is nesting this video montage into your main composition. To remember where the video cuts were, we'll add comp markers along the timeline; these will convert to layer markers when you nest it into [**My_RoboTV**].

STEP 17: While you're still in [**video sequence**], locate to the following times and set corresponding comp markers:

- At 02:00, press Shift+2 to create comp marker #2
- At 03:00, press Shift+3 to create comp marker #3
- At 04:00, press Shift+4 to create comp marker #4

Once set, press just the number 2, 3, or 4 to jump to these markers. You can also hold down Shift while dragging the time marker along the timeline to "snap" to markers and in/out points as it gets near them. Use these features to locate easily to specific frames.

17 Set comp markers at the various video edits, to make it easier to remember their locations when you nest this comp into your main composition.

STEP 18: Time to nest the edited video sequence and place it into the TV frame. Bring the [**My_RoboTV**] comp forward. If its time marker isn't already at 00:00, hit Home to locate there.

Select [**video sequence**] from the Project window and drag it to the bottom of the layer stack in the [**My_RoboTV**] Timeline window. This will nest [**video sequence**] into [**My_RoboTV**], starting at 00:00, and sorted behind the robot body layers. The [**video sequence**] comp is now a precomp that is rendered before the current comp.

18 Nest the video montage into the [**My_RoboTV**] comp, starting at 00:00, and placed at the bottom of the layer stack. Note that the comp markers you created in Step 17 appear as layer markers here. There's no need to turn off the Audio switch for this layer as you made the audio a Guide Layer in the precomp back in Step 12.

You can drag a layer to the timeline and place it anywhere in the layer stack. If you drag and drop to the left side of the Timeline window (in the Source/Layer name column), the in point for this new layer will start at the current position of the time marker. If you drag the new layer to somewhere in the timeline area, the point at which you release the mouse determines the in point for this layer as well as its order in the layer stack. Dragging new footage to the Comp window will always start it at the current time and add it to the top of the layer stack, as will the Command+/ (Control+/) shortcut.

The entire comp [**video sequence**] will now appear as one layer, so you can manipulate the entire montage as one group. Since you made the soundtrack in the precomp a Guide Layer, you don't need to worry about hearing it in this comp, even though its Audio switch is on.

Notice how the comp markers in the precomp appear as layer markers when they're nested. These markers are not linked back to the original comp in any way, though; changing a comp marker in the precomp will not update the layer markers here.

19 The video sequence defaults to being too large and out of position (above); center it behind the opening in the robot frame, and scale it down so it just fills the hole (below).

STEP 19: You'll need to position and scale the **video sequence** layer so that it fits nicely behind the TV screen.

• In the Comp window, drag the montage layer so it's centered behind the screen. It's just a bit too large at its default size; you will have to scale this montage layer down so that you see the maximum image area inside the screen.

• Verify that the **video sequence** layer is the one selected. Drag one of its corner handles in the Comp window to scale the layer, then add the Shift key to maintain its aspect ratio. If you have the Info floating window open, it will update as you drag to display the current Scale value; about 83% should work nicely.

There are some handy shortcuts for scaling layers in small increments. You can increase the Scale amount in 1% increments by holding down the Option key (Control in Windows) and using the + or – keys on the numeric keypad. Add the Shift key for 10% increments. If you don't use the Option (Control) key, you'll rotate the layer instead of scaling it.

• Set the **video sequence** layer's Parent popup to Frame, so it becomes part of the RoboBody group.

• Save the project. As a final reminder that **Frame** is the main parent of all the visible layers in this comp, try moving or scaling the **Frame** layer and notice how the entire RoboTV – frame, three arms, and the inset movie – are treated as a group. Be sure to Undo any changes.

Synching Comps

The option "Synchronize time of all related events" in Preferences>General means that the time marker will be synchronized across nested comps. This option is on by default as of version 6.5.

19 *complete:* Make the **video sequence** layer a child of the **Frame** layer.

Part 3: Background Noise

The background consists of two movies, both previously created with the Fractal Noise effect (included in the Professional edition). One instance of the effect created a blocky pattern, while a second layer rendered a soft blurry pattern that will serve as a subtle lighting effect. These effects have been prerendered as movies because (a) you may not have the Professional edition, and (b) using live effects for the background slows down the previews.

Go Home!

To force selected layers to start at 00:00, select them and hit Option+Home (Alt+Home).

This tutorial's folder on the DVD contains a copy of the project that was used to create these layers, along with a PDF bonus tutorial on how they were created. In the meantime, take advantage of the pre-rendered movies:

Step 20: Select the **My_Sources** folder and Command+I (Control+I) to import a file, locate to the **Project>Sources** folder for this tutorial, and import the movie **FractalNoise_blocky.mov**.

• Open it in its Footage window and scrub through it to become familiar with it. It consists of an abstract, randomized series of blocks that seem to zoom slowly toward you. Close the Footage window when you're done.

• Add the movie to your [**My_RoboTV**] comp and drag it to the bottom of the layer stack, starting at 00:00.

20 Add **FractalNoise_blocky.mov** behind all of the other layers in [**My_RoboTV**].

Step 21: Select the **My_Sources** folder again and this time import the movie **FractalNoise_soft.mov**.

• If you like, open it in its Footage window and scrub through it to become familiar with it. This movie contains a hazy, cloudy pattern that you will use to add a lighting effect to the blocky background above. Close the Footage window when you're done.

• Add this movie as well to your [**My_RoboTV**] comp, also at time 00:00, and drag it down the layer stack so that it sits above the FractalNoise_blocky.mov layer.

21 The **FractalNoise_soft.mov** will provide a lighting effect for the blocky pattern background.

Step 22: All that's left for your lighting trick to work is to change the blending mode for the **FractalNoise_soft.mov** layer to Overlay. Toggle the Switches/Modes column to Modes (shortcut: F4) and change its mode from the default Normal to Overlay.

To get a feel for what effect this is having, turn the Video switch for **FractalNoise_soft.mov** on and off, and observe the changes in the Comp window. Leave it switched on when you're done, and Save the project.

	#	Layer Name	Parent	Mode	T	TrkMat		:00s	05s
▷ ■	1	[CM_RoboMusic.mov]	None						
▷ ■	2	Small Arm	3. Medium Arm	Normal					
▷ ■	3	Medium Arm	4. Big Arm	Normal		None			
▷ ■	4	Big Arm	5. Frame	Normal		None			
▷ ■	5	Frame	None	Normal		None			
▷ ■	6	[video sequence]	5. Frame	Normal		None		2 3 4	
▷ □	7	[FractalNoise_soft.mov]	None	Overlay		None			
▷ □	8	[FractalNoise_blocky.mov]	None	Normal		None			

My_RoboTV · Timeline

My_RoboTV · video sequence

0:00:00:00 (29.97 fps)

Switches / Modes

Overlay is a useful mode for boosting the contrast and apparent saturation of a composite. If the source layer has 50% gray, these areas will have no effect on the layers underneath. Where the source layer is brighter, it will brighten the underlying layers akin to Screen mode; where the source is darker, it will darken the underlying layers akin to Multiply mode. It works great with grayscale sources; interesting hue shifts occur if the source has color in it as well.

Expanding Masks

STEP 23: To finish off our background, add a "vignette" effect by using a black solid with a soft-edged mask to darken the corners:

• With the time marker still located at 00:00, press Command+Y (Control+Y) to create a new Solid layer. Name it "**Vignette solid**," click the Make Comp Size button, set its color to black, and click OK.

• Drag the black solid down the layer stack so that it sits above the two Fractal Noise movies you imported earlier.

• Press Q once to select the Mask tool in the Tools palette; if the Rectangle Mask is active, press Q again to toggle to the Elliptical Mask tool. (You can also click and hold on the Rectangle Mask until the Elliptical Mask tool pops out.) With your new solid layer still selected, double-click the Elliptical Mask tool to add a new full-frame oval mask to this layer.

• The Toggle View Masks button along the bottom of the Comp window controls whether mask outlines are visible in the Comp window. If it is off, enable it now (the button will be darker in color).

22 The **FractalNoise_soft.mov** sits above the **FractalNoise_blocky.mov** in the Timeline window (top) and is set to Overlay mode. Result shown above.

23 Select the Elliptical Mask tool from the Tools palette (above), then double-click the tool icon to create a full-frame oval mask. The Toggle View Masks button at the bottom of the Comp window controls the visibility of mask outlines.

Toggle View Masks

23 *continued:* A vignette effect which darkens the corners of the frame is built by applying an oval mask to a black solid (above), inverting the mask, feathering it, and using Mask Expansion to push it out to the corners (below).

• Type MM (two Ms in quick succession) to twirl down the Mask options in the Timeline window; you should see the Mask Shape, Mask Feather, Mask Opacity, and Mask Expansion properties.

• Check the Inverted switch (to the right of Mask 1 in the Timeline window) so that the black solid is opaque outside the mask, and transparent inside the mask.

• Scrub the Feather parameter, setting it to a nice soft value such as 100. Notice how the feathered edge straddles the mask outline.

We'd like to reveal more of the corners. One approach would be an even larger feather amount, but that may eat away too much from the inside of the mask. We can fix that…

• Scrub the Mask Expansion value. Notice how the feathered edge moves in relation to the mask outline in the Comp window. Set the Expansion value to around +50 or to taste to move the feathered edge outside the mask edge.

• Along the bottom of the Comp window, click on Toggle View Masks to turn it off so you can see the edge of the mask without the yellow border.

And that's it for the background – you can now turn your attention back to the robot arm and the text items it will be pointing to. Go ahead and twirl up any property that may be open in the Timeline window to reduce distractions.

That completes Part 3 so Save your project. You can compare your work against our prebuilt comp [**RoboTV_after Step 23**]*. If you want to pick up this tutorial at this point and focus on animating the robot arm, rename our comp to "My_RoboTV_23" and continue.*

23 *complete:* Your mask should end up with roughly these settings.

Part 4: Rotation Motivation

Remember way back in Part 1, when you set up the Parenting chain for the robot arm? Time to put that groundwork to use in animating the arm. But first, you have to give it some targets to hit in your animation moves.

As we mentioned earlier, the idea behind this spot is a "bumper" (video insert) that will lead into the next section of a sports program. There are four sports highlighted in the next section; the title of each will come on as the arm swings to it to illustrate it.

Adding the Titles

STEP 24: Select the **My_Sources** folder in the Project window and hit Command+I (Control+I) to bring up the Import dialog. Select the layered Illustrator file **SportsTitle.ai** from this project's **Sources** folder. At the bottom of the Import dialog, be sure to select Import As: Composition – Cropped Layers (*not* Footage). Click Open, and two new items will be added to the Project window: a folder and a comp, both named **SportsTitle Comp 1**.

Double-click the comp to open it. This new comp includes four title layers: **Snowboarding**, **Skateboarding**, **Sky Diving**, and **Climbing**. All layers are filled with white, and were aligned along an arc in Illustrator.

STEP 25: In the comp [**SportsTitle.ai**], select the **guides only** layer and hit the Delete key to remove it. (The guides are only visible when inside Illustrator, where they indicate the position of Title Safe areas; we don't need them here.) Select all four title layers and type Command+C (Control+C) to copy them.

STEP 26: Bring your [**My_RoboTV**] comp forward, and Paste.

• Drag these layers down the Timeline window stack until they sit above the **Vignette solid** and the background layers.

• If your [**SportsTitle.ai**] composition had been shorter than 06:00 duration, the pasted layers will appear trimmed shorter than needed in this comp. If that's the case, extend all layers to the full six seconds: with them still selected, go to the end of [**My_RoboTV**], and hit Option+] (Alt+]).

24 The Project window after importing **SportsTitle.ai** as a comp.

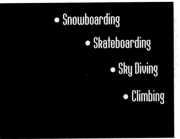

25 The names of the four featured sports have already been typeset in an arc in Illustrator. The font is Conques Demi from T.26 (www.t26.com).

26 Paste the titles into [**My_RoboTV**] and drag them down the layer stack to be just in front of the background layers.

Timeline Markers

The idea is that each title pops on as its respective movie plays. Fortunately, back in Step 17 you placed comp markers at these edit points, which rippled through as layer markers when you nested [**video sequence**] into your main composition. However, numbers aren't very descriptive; you can edit these markers to remind you which sport comes on when.

STEP 27: Drag the Timeline window wider so you've got room for all of your columns plus space to read comments on the layer bars. Then change those comments:

• Hold the Shift key while dragging the time marker until it sticks on **video sequence**'s layer marker 4. Looks like our climbing footage. Double-click the layer marker named 4 to open the Marker dialog. Change the Comment field to say "**Climbing**" and click OK.

• Drag the time marker to layer marker 3, and verify that this is our sky diving footage. Double-click the marker named 3, change its Comment field to "**Sky Diving**" and click OK.

• Drag the time marker to layer marker 2, and verify that this is our skateboarding footage. Double-click the marker named 2, change its Comment field to "**Skateboarding**" and click OK.

27 Edit the comments for the Layer markers attached to **video sequence** to remind you which clips starts where, then add Comp markers at every second through 05:00 to speed up navigation to these video edit points.

• Hit Home, which will take you to the start of the Snowboarding clip. With **video sequence** selected, hold Option (Alt) and hit * on the numeric keypad to open the Marker dialog. Name this one "**Snowboarding**".

• To make this comp easier to navigate quickly, feel free to add comp markers 1 through 5 at times 01:00, 02:00, 03:00, 04:00 and 05:00 (locate, hold Shift, and type their respective numbers). You'll then be able to return to these marked frames by simply typing their respective numbers. Then hit Home to return the time marker to 00:00.

Twisting Your Arms

You may want to take a moment here and play the final **RoboTV.mov** again (you can even import it into the project, so that you can play it from inside After Effects). If you get stuck wondering how the arms could possibly rotate so they align with each sport's bullet point, you can always refer to our finished movie. However, there is no right or wrong way to animate the arms – provided they hit their marks, and seem to be having fun!

If you're not there already, you'll probably want to set the Comp window to display in Full Resolution and 100% Magnification for the following arms rotation steps, so you can see the titles clearly. Feel free to turn off the Video switch for the background layers to speed up previews; we also toggled the Switches/Modes column back to Switches by pressing F4.

Step 28: With the time marker at 00:00, select the **Small Arm, Medium Arm**, and **Big Arm** layers and hit R to twirl down Rotation.

• Turn on Rotation animation stopwatches for all three. You can drag the cursor across all three stopwatches in the Timeline window in one movement, or use the Set Rotation Keyframe shortcut Option+R (Alt+R). This will create the first keyframe for each arm at time 00:00.

• Press F2 to deselect the arms to avoid accidentally editing all three arms at once.

Now here's where the fun starts: You need to change the rotation values for all three arms to create a starting position which has them "tucked in" along the right side of the TV screen.

There are a couple of ways to edit the Rotation values. We personally prefer scrubbing these values in the Timeline window; hold down Command (Control) to scrub Rotation in finer increments. Or, you can use the Rotation tool (W is the shortcut for Wotation) to rotate the arms by dragging them in the Comp window.

We'll give you some clues to get started, then you can complete the animation using your own ideas on what would be fun moves. For example, the arms at 00:00 would tuck in alongside the screen with these settings:

• **Big Arm** rotated –10°

• **Medium Arm** rotated –170° and

• **Small Arm** rotated +160°

Of course, you can always enter in these exact values for the Rotation property for each layer – but where's the fun in that?

Switcheroo!

To switch the Switches and Modes column back and forth, press F4.

Finer Increments

If you're scrubbing the Rotation values to animate the arms, remember that holding the Command (Control) key when you're scrubbing will cause it to rotate in finer increments.

28 The initial, folded-up starting point for the arms at 00:00; the background layers have been turned off to speed up RAM Previews.

STEP 29: Once you're happy with your first set of keyframes, move to time 01:00 by typing 1 to locate its corresponding Comp marker. Change the rotation keyframes for all three arms so that the tip of the small arm hits the bullet at the beginning of the **Snowboarding** title. We suggest you animate the big arm a little clockwise, but make big dramatic moves for the medium and small arms so that they swing out to the right and up (if they swing left as they ascend they will obscure the TV screen). Getting it right will take some tweaking; feel free to nudge the title into position if you can't get the arm to reach the bullet point exactly – just be careful not to disrupt the arrangements between words to the point where it starts to look sloppy.

Our example reaches the bullet with the following settings:

- **Big Arm** rotated −6°
- **Medium Arm** rotated −1 × −41° and
- **Small Arm** rotated 1 × +45°

29 The arms are rotated to hit the first sport's bullet point at 01:00, creating the second set of keyframes.

STEP 30: Once you're happy with the placement of the arms at 01:00, hit N to end the Work Area at 01:00 and do a RAM Preview (shortcut: hit 0 on the keypad) to see how the animation looks.

30 After animating the first move, go to time 01:10 and check another set of keyframes to hold the arms in place for 10 frames. You can drag across all three keyframe checkboxes in one mouse movement.

• Once you're happy with the move, press 1, then Shift+Page Down to advance 10 frames to time 01:10. Add Rotation keyframes to all three arm pieces by checking their keyframe boxes. This should ensure that they have the exact same values as the keyframes at 01:00. This will make the arms "freeze" for 10 frames between 01:00 and 01:10.

In Step 33, we'll convert the keyframes at 01:00 to real "Hold" keyframes, which will ensure that the Rotation value holds steady until the next keyframe is encountered.

STEP 31: As your aerobics instructor would say (if you ever got to the gym), "this is the pattern": The arms reach up to the title at the top of the second, freeze for 10 frames, then move to the next title for 20 frames. So have fun completing the animation as follows, doing a RAM Preview after each title as it is reached:

- At 02:00, animate the arms to reach the **Skateboarding** title. Give the movement some personality – for example, feel free to rotate the **Small Arm** around a full turn. Once you're happy with the placement, hit N to reset the end of the work area, and RAM Preview. (Use this technique to RAM Preview each section as you go – making changes to a section in the middle is difficult once you've completed the progression of keyframes.) If you like the way the arms swing around, Shift+Page Down to advance 10 frames.

- At 02:10, check the Rotation keyframe checkboxes to duplicate the values and introduce a freeze between 02:00 and 02:10.

- Move to 03:00, and rotate the arms to reach the **Sky Diving** title. Press N, RAM Preview this section, and tweak if necessary. Then Shift+Page Down to advance 10 frames.

- At 03:10, check the Rotation keyframe checkboxes to duplicate the values.

- Move to time 04:00, and make the arms reach the **Climbing** title.

- At 04:10, check the Rotation keyframe checkboxes to duplicate the values.

- At 05:00, animate the arms back into a tucked-in position, similar to the beginning.

- RAM preview the entire animation when you're done, and switch back to the Selection tool (V) if the Rotation tool is currently active.

Save! If you're having trouble creating an animation you like, feel free to pick up our prebuilt comp [RoboTV_after Step 31] and call it your own…we won't tell. Just be sure you know how we arrived at this point.

Easy Does It

STEP 32: All the rotation moves so far use Linear keyframes, the default interpolation type when you create temporal keyframes. Although we have a "robotic" design, we don't necessarily want the robotic motion that results from linear interpolation. A quick way to add some elegance (and to make this animation a little more realistic, as a "real" robot arm wouldn't be able to start and stop instantaneously) is to add some ease in and outs to the rotation keyframes.

- Make sure the Rotation properties are still exposed for all of the arm pieces in the Timeline window.

Bullet Hole

When you're animating the arms to hit the bullets, if you temporarily reduce the Opacity of the **Small Arm** layer, you'll be able to see the bullet point underneath. Return Opacity back to 100% when you're done.

At 02:00, the arms reach Skateboarding.

At 03:00, the arms move to SkyDiving.

At 04:00, the arms tuck into Climbing. Footage courtesy Philip and Karen Smith: Getty Images/Mountain Pursuits.

![My_RoboTV • Timeline window showing the timeline with Small Arm, Medium Arm, and Big Arm layers with Rotation keyframes]

32 After all the Rotations keyframes have been selected, press F9 to apply Easy Ease to them.

• Click on the word "Rotation" for the **Small Arm** layer. This will select all the Rotation keyframes for this layer. Now Shift+click on the word Rotation for both the **Medium Arm** and **Big Arm** layers, so that all Rotation keyframes are selected.

• Press F9 to apply Easy Ease to all selected keyframes, or apply it from the menu using Animation>Keyframe Assistant>Easy Ease.

• Deselect All (shortcut: F2).

Looking Square

STEP 33: Since the Rotation keyframes at 01:00, 02:00, 03:00, and 04:00 for all three layers are freezing for 10 frames, it would be helpful if they looked like Hold keyframes in the timeline (Hold keyframes have square icons, or if converted from Linear will have a square shape on the outgoing side). Although it's not necessary for this particular animation, this is an example of "defensive" animation in which you're reducing the chance of accidentally screwing something up later.

Parent Power

To toggle the Parent column on and off, press Shift+F4.

> Hold style keyframes say "do not vary the value of this parameter until the next keyframe." Even if two successive keyframes have the same value, it's still possible for drift to occur between them through mistakes with their velocity curves. It's also a problem with Position keyframes, where errant handles in the motion path can introduce wobbly animation.

• Drag a marquee around the three keyframes at 01:00.

• Hold down the Shift key and drag a marquee around the keyframes at 02:00, 03:00, and 04:00 to select them as well (see figure below).

33 Select the Rotation keyframes at comp markers 1, 2, 3, and 4 by holding down the Shift key and dragging a marquee around them (shown in progress).

• Once these keyframes are selected, Command+Option+click (Control+Alt+click) on any one of the selected keyframes to toggle

![My_RoboTV • Timeline window showing the marquee selection in progress around keyframes at comp markers]

My_RoboTV • Timeline									
My_RoboTV	video sequence	SportsTitles Comp 1							
0:00:05:00 (29.97 fps)									
#	Layer Name	Parent	Mode	T TrkMat					
▽ ☐ 2	Small Arm	⊚ 3. Medium Arm ▾	Normal ▾						
▷ ⓞ	Rotation		2 x +155.0 °						
▽ ☐ 3	Medium Arm	⊚ 4. Big Arm ▾	Normal ▾	None ▾					
▷ ⓞ	Rotation		0 x -155.0 °						
▽ ☐ 4	Big Arm	⊚ 5. Frame ▾	Normal ▾	None ▾					
▷ ⓞ	Rotation		0 x -5.0 °						
			Switches / Modes						

them all to Hold keyframes (or use Animation>Toggle Hold Keyframe menu command). Deselect the keyframes again by pressing F2.

33 *complete:* The selected Rotation keyframes converted to Hold keyframes.

- Rotation is now complete, so twirl up all layers and Save your project.

STEP 34: Since the idea is that the arm reaches up and "turns on" each title, you will need to edit the in point for each title to its "cue in" time. One approach to this is using the In column in the Timeline window.

- Context+click on the column headers in the Timeline window and select Columns>In, or select Columns>In from the Timeline window's wing menu. If you're running short of screen space, close the Parent column (Context+click on Parent heading and select Hide This from the popup, or press Shift+F4).

It helps to drag the In column close to the layer names so you don't inadvertently change the value for the wrong layer. Currently, all layers have an in point of 00:00:00:00 (or at least, they should!).

34 You can customize the Timeline window by opening just the In time column, giving you another tool to set the in point of layers.

- For the **Snowboarding** title layer, click on the value for in point. The Layer In Time dialog will open; type "100" (you don't need to type the colon as in 1:00), and click OK. The in point value will be converted to the 00:00:01:00 display style.

- Using the same technique, set the **Skateboarding** title to start at 02:00.

- Set the **Sky Diving** title to start at 03:00.

- Set the **Climbing** title to start at 04:00.

- Save your project, and RAM Preview again to see the titles "pop on."

34 *complete:* Set the In times for the titles to equal when the robot arm hits their marks. You can either enter values in the In column, or move to the desired in point, select the layer, and press [to move the layer to the current time.

My_RoboTV • Timeline											
My_RoboTV	video sequence	SportsTitles Comp 1									
0:00:04:00 (29.97 fps)											
#	Layer Name	In	Mode	T TrkMat		:00s					
▷ ☐ 4	Big Arm	0:00:00:00	Normal ▾	None ▾							
▷ ☐ 5	Frame	0:00:00:00	Normal ▾	None ▾							
▷ ☐ 6	[video sequence]	0:00:00:00	Normal ▾	None ▾		Snowboarding	2	3	4		
▷ ☐ 7	[Vignette solid]	0:00:00:00	Normal ▾	None ▾							
▷ ☐ 8	Snowboarding	0:00:01:00	Normal ▾	None ▾							
▷ ☐ 9	Skateboarding	0:00:02:00	Normal ▾	None ▾							
▷ ☐ 10	Sky Diving	0:00:03:00	Normal ▾	None ▾							
▷ ☐ 11	Climbing	0:00:04:00	Normal ▾	None ▾							
▷ ☐ 12	[FractalNoise_soft.mov]	0:00:00:00	Overlay ▾	None ▾							
▷ ☐ 13	[FractalNoise_blocky.mov]	0:00:00:00	Normal ▾	None ▾							
			Switches / Modes								

Motion Blur

STEP 35: Make sure the Switches panel is visible (press F4 if it isn't). Turn on Motion Blur (the "M" switch) for all three arm layers, then click on the master Enable Motion Blur switch along the top of the Timeline window so you can see this blur in the Comp window before you render. RAM Preview a couple of seconds to see how the arms look with motion blur applied.

You can set the amount of motion blur in the Composition Settings> Advanced section under Shutter Angle. We set our comp to a relatively high Shutter Angle of 300°.

If the Small Arm is moving more than the other arms, the Small Arm will blur more. Also, the pixels at the tip will be blurrier than those near the joint, since these pixels are moving faster.

Notice how the motion blur fades away right before 01:00 as the arm eases into a stop when it reaches the **Snowboarding** title. The blur amount is based on the speed of each pixel, so the motion blur fades away as the layer slows down.

Motion Blur adds a considerable render hit, so turn off the master Enable Motion Blur switch if you need faster previews. If you decide to render your final version of this tutorial, in the Render Settings

35 By enabling Motion Blur for the robot arm pieces, After Effects will automatically calculate more blur when the pixels in each piece move faster.

Shutter Angle

The Motion Blur Shutter Angle can be set as high as 720°. If you were field rendering the final output, the intensity of the motion blur would appear cut in half (as there are two fields per frame); you can set the Override Shutter Angle as high as 1440° in the Render Settings dialog.

dialog the Motion Blur popup should be set to "On for Checked Layers" to ensure that layers with their M switch checked will render with motion blur in the final render. The Render Settings also includes an Override Shutter Angle field, where you can force the comp (and any nested comp layers) to render using a common shutter angle amount.

STEP 36: Turn on any background layers you might have turned off to speed up your previews. You're done with all of the hard work for this tutorial. Save the project and RAM Preview your final animation.

In the next Part, we're just going to step through some additional enhancements we decided to make to the final animation. Feel free to try out your own variations to customize the result to your own tastes.

If you want to check the results of these final edits, compare your version with our [**RoboTV_after Step 36**].

RoboRender

STEP 37: Hit Command+M (Control+M) if you want to render your comp as a movie. (If not, skip ahead.)

• In the Render Settings dialog, make sure you choose Best Quality, Full Resolution, and set Field Rendering to Off (as our video sources don't have fields, and we want to see all of our motion blur). Set the Motion Blur popup to On for Checked Layers.

• In the Output Module Settings dialog, set Channels to RGB, Depth to Millions of Colors, and Color to Premultiplied (Matted). The Format is up to you, given your hardware; for playback from hard disk, we personally like QuickTime Movie and the Photo-JPEG codec, with the Quality set between 60 and 99 depending on visual quality and disk space requirements (lower numbers equals lower quality and space). Don't forget to enable Audio Output.

If you want to render this project to the NTSC DV format, choose the DV codec in the Format Options, and set the audio to 32kHz or 48kHz. To resize the render to DV spec, enable the Stretch section, disabling Lock Aspect Ratio, setting the Stretch Width to 720, and keeping the Stretch Height at 480. This will create the nonsquare pixels the DV format expects.

37 To render this project to a NTSC DV file, click on Format Options to change the codec to DV NTSC. Then use the Stretch dialog to scale the 640×480 pixel comp up to a 720×480 file.

Part 5: Guided Tour to the Finish

That just about completes the RoboTV animation. There are a few finishing touches we added which we encourage you to explore. Select Window>Close All to reduce window clutter.

Play the **RoboTV.mov** again from the **Final Movie** folder for this tutorial and note the "coming up next" title that types on, and the white-to-yellow color changes in the titles to the right. To study these and other additions, in the **_RoboTV * prebuilt>Final Comps** folder in the Project window, open [**RoboTV_FINAL**], and note the following:

• Select the **Snowboarding** title layer, and hit U to twirl down animated properties if they're not already visible. We felt that the arms "sliding" into position with their ease-in animation called for a softer entry of the titles. So instead of popping on each title, we added a five-frame fade-up that began two frames before the original pop on time. For example: The **Snowboarding** title originally popped on at 01:00, but it now fades up from 00:28 to 01:03. All four titles were treated the same way. RAM Preview a section and see if you like the softer fade ups better. (Often the music will dictate whether layers should pop on or fade up, so try to listen closely for any such musical cues.)

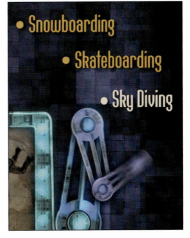

The titles are set to fade up over five frames, and as each new title fades up, the previous title changes from white to yellow thanks to an animated Fill effect.

To start the spot, "coming up next…" types on while the first video is revealed through Effect>Boris BCC3>Boris Mosaic.

Textacy

Animating text is covered in more detail in Chapters 3 (*Hot but Cool*) and 12 (*Flamingo 4*).

We added an Animator for Opacity to this Text layer with the target Opacity set to 0%, and keyframed its Range Selector values to gradually exclude all the characters to reveal them over time for a soft "typing" effect.

• With the **Snowboarding** title still selected, hit F3 to open the Effect Controls window. We added Effect>Render>Fill to each title layer, and animated the Color from white to yellow over 10 frames. Since the yellow has less contrast than white against the predominately blue background, this moves the emphasis to each new white title as it fades up. Select the **Skateboarding** title and hit T to reveal its Opacity keyframes. The timing is such that as each new title fades up to 100%, the previous title turns yellow. So in the case of the **Snowboarding** title, it fades from white at 01:23 to yellow at 02:03, while the second title – **Skateboarding** – fades up from 01:28 to 02:03.

• A small dark drop shadow (Effect>Perspective>Drop Shadow) was added to all titles to give them a little more lift from the background.

• On the left side of the frame just above the video inset, the words "coming up next…" were created using the Type tool in After Effects. We used the font Arial hoping you might have it installed on your computer, and gave it a false ("faux") italic slant. It has the same color as the sports titles, as well as a small drop shadow.

• The soft typing-on effect for the "coming up next" text was created by animating the Opacity of the characters. Twirl open this Text layer's parameters in the Timeline window, they twirl open Text, Animator 1, Range Selector 1, and Advanced in succession. We created an Animator for Opacity, and set the target Opacity value to 0%. With the End of the Range Selector set at 100%, we keyframed the Start value from 0% of all the characters to 100%. This means at the first keyframe, all of the characters (those between 0% and 100%) are selected, and get the 0% Opacity; at the second keyframe, none of the characters are selected (as there is no room between 100% and 100%), and therefore they revert to their normal transform value of Opacity = 100%. We used the default Shape of Square with Smoothness set to 100%, resulting in characters fading from 0% to 100% as they are deselected by the Range Selector.

• From 00:00 to 01:00, the first video in the montage is already showing a snowboarder taking flight, but the **Snowboarding** title has yet to be revealed. To make the first video initially match the pattern in the background, we added the Boris Mosaic effect to the **Montage_precomp_FINAL** layer. Select this layer and hit F3 to see its parameters. By animating the Pixelate X value from 50 at time 00:00 to 0 at 01:00, the mosaic fades out over time. There's no need to also animate the Pixelate Y value because the Lock Pixelation checkbox is on (this locks the Y value to whatever X is set to).

• We also added some more saturation to the snowboarding movie and tweaked the hue and saturation of the rock climbing movie to better match the blue-purple background. If you want to see before and after comparisons, Option+double-click (Alt+double-click) our [**video sequence_FINAL**] nested layer to open our treated precomp. Drag its tab completely out of the Comp window to open a second Comp window where you can see both this comp and our final [**RoboTV_FINAL**] comp side by side. Resize and rearrange the windows as needed.

In the [**video sequence_FINAL**] comp, move to time 01:00 and turn on and off the Effects switch (the "f" switch) for the **AB_Recreation_24.mov** layer – this will toggle the Hue/Saturation effect for the snowboarder. Compare the effect of adding more saturation against the background layers in the final composite. Press F3 to see the effect settings used and edit to taste.

Also in the [**video sequence_FINAL**] comp, move to 05:00 and turn on and off the Effects switch for the **GI_MountainPursuits.mov** layer – this will toggle the Hue/Saturation effect for the climber movie. Compare the original turquoise blue sky against the blue-purple sky, which we feel better matches the blue in the fractal noise background. Press F3 to see the effect controls and edit to taste.

The first video is revealed through Effect>Boris BCC3 Effects>Boris Mosaic; the Pixelate X parameter is animated from 50 to 0; the Pixelate Y parameter follows as it is locked to X.

Going Farther & Bonus Tutorial

You can continue to tweak our final version, if you like. For example, to emphasize each new title appearing, experiment with animating a glow-style effect (perhaps using Effect>Tinderbox-Blurs>T_LensBlur, which comes free on this book's DVD) to each title as the arm turns it on, or spotlight it with a lens flare effect or other visible flash.

We've also included a bonus step-by-step tutorial called **Fractal NoiseBG_Pro.aep** with an accompanying PDF file, which are in the **02_RoboTV>_FractalNoise_Bonus Tutorial** folder. This shows how we created the backgrounds used in this project with the Fractal Noise plug-in included in the Professional edition. It also includes additional tips for creating animated seamless loops with the Fractal Noise effect.

For more information on topics covered in this tutorial, check out the following volumes of *Creating Motion Graphics*:

Volume 1:

Setting anchor points and parenting

Nesting Compositions

Blending Modes

Masking

Comp and Layer markers

Keyframe velocity manipulation

Motion Blur

Animating text

Render settings

Volume 2:

Importing Photoshop files as Comp

Importing Illustrator files as Comp

Field rendering; nonsquare pixels

Some of the footage was further color-corrected to better match the overall spot. For example, the snowboarder had some saturation added (left = before, right = after).

Hot but Cool

A trio of text animation tricks: slamdown, 3D rotation and write on.

This breezy tutorial shares three ideas for animating the words in the title Hot but Cool: jerkily slamming the word "Hot" into place, rotating "but" into position in 3D, and using the Paint tool to write on "Cool" one character at a time. You'll perform these tricks keeping in mind how each animation will work with the soundtrack.

We provide you with a starter composition that already has the marked-up soundtrack in place. You'll create the titles using the Type tool, and then follow the step-by-step instructions for each text trick, with latitude for you to customize the animations to taste. We'll wrap up with a quick guided tour of touches we added to the final project, including layering together a pair of background movies and treating the entire composition with a Lens Blur effect.

OVERVIEW

Main Concepts:

These are the features and concepts we will be focusing on in this project:

- Spotting music
- Creating and animating Text
- "Slam down" text animation
- Continuous Rasterization
- Hold keyframes
- 3D rotation
- Painting in Write On mode
- Paint on Transparent mode
- Set Matte effect
- Adjustment Layers
- Blending Modes
- Tinderbox T_LensBlur effect*

Requirements:

After Effects 6.5 Standard edition.

Getting Started:

** Be sure to install the T_LensBlur effect from The Foundry (www.thefoundry.co.uk), included on the accompanying DVD in the **Free Plug-ins** folder.*

Inside the **Tutorials** master folder on the accompanying DVD, locate and copy the folder **03_HotCool** to your hard drive.

In the folder **Final Movie** inside this main folder, double-click and play **HotCool.mov**.

Inside the **Project** folder you'll find the finished After Effects project file **HotCool.aep**. Open the project file – this is your starting point. We suggest you save under a new name after each major section.

The Tasks

This is what you will be doing in the various parts of this tutorial:

PART 1: Create the *Hot but Cool* title using the Type tool. Animate "Hot" to slam into place using Hold keyframes, then rotate "but" using simple 3D.

PART 2: Use the Paint tools to trace the "Cool" word as if it was handwriting on. Clean up edges with the Set Matte effect.

PART 3: Take a guided tour of our enhanced version of the title, where we add background movies as well as an adjustment layer with Tinderbox's T_LensBlur effect to tie the elements together.

A different text trick is used to introduce each word of the *Hot but Cool* title; the halos around the text shapes are created with the Tinderbox T_LensBlur effect. Backgrounds from 12 Inch Design's ProductionBlox Unit 02 and 03, plus Bestshots.

Part 1: Hot Painting

With the **HotCool.aep** project open, find the composition [**HotCool * starter**] in the Project window's **My_Comps** folder, and open it:

STEP 1: We've added the soundtrack already in this starter comp, and changed the Composition> Background Color to a blue similar to our eventual background layers. A recurring aspect of this tutorial will be timing your animations to music. Open the dialog for Preferences>Previews, and enter "**900**" to set the Audio Duration to 09:00. This will allow you to Audio Preview the entire 08:16 length, plus give you a half-second pause before it starts over again. Click OK to accept.

STEP 2: The audio waveform for layer 4 – **CM_CoolGroove.mov** – should already be visible. If not, select this layer and type LL (two Ls in rapid succession) to reveal it.

Press Home to reset the time marker to 00:00, and press the period key (.) on the extended keypad to preview the audio (hit any key to stop playback).

1 Set the Preferences>Previews>Audio Preview Duration to 09:00 by entering "900" (no colons are needed).

Music Credits

The soundtrack for this project was arranged by Chris Meyer of CyberMotion, using a trio of copyright-clean sampling CDs. The upright bass is played by John Pattitucci, and is from the Spectrasonics *Bass Legends* CD (distributed in the United States by Ilio Entertainment – www.ilio.com). The drums were played by Keith LeBlanc on his *Kickin' Lunatic Beats* CD (distributed by AMG – www.amguk.co.uk), and were edited to fit. The sax riff was transplanted from Zero-G's *Pure Trip Hop* (www.zero-g.co.uk).

2 Some of the major beats in the music are marked with layer markers. To add more markers, select the layer and press * (the asterisk key on the keypad) to add a marker at the current time. Double-click the marker to add a comment. To delete a marker, press Command on Mac (Control on Windows) and click it.

More on Music

To learn more about reading audio waveforms and spotting music, check out the article *Timing Video to Audio* in the **Goodies** folder on this book's DVD.

3 Select the Type tool from the Tools palette. If the Character and Paragraph palettes don't automatically open, click the Palettes button.

The soundtrack has three main sections: a pair of drum rolls at the start, a drum "pickup" with a sax playing on top, then the main groove when the upright bass and drums play together.

Listen carefully as the time marker scrolls through the waveform in the Timeline so you can start to draw a correspondence between the beats and their spikes in the waveform. We've already created layer markers for some of the more important beats; feel free to create more.

> Audio waveforms are slow to redraw in After Effects. After you have a handle on which layer markers correspond to which parts of the music, feel free to twirl the waveform up to save redraw time. Press LL again whenever you need to see the waveform again.

Creating the Text

In this section you'll create the text for the three words "Hot but Cool". We'll use a couple of fonts that came free with the After Effects 6.5 installer CD – Stencil Std and Tekton Pro. (If you're using the Tryout version, substitute these fonts with something similar from your own font library, being careful to pick a font for the "Cool" word that looks easy to trace!)

If you're comfortable creating basic text, you can skip ahead to Step 6 and start instead with comp [**HotCool * starter 2**], where we've typeset the words for you.

On the other hand, if you'd like to use your own font design or need to practice creating text, these steps are for you.

STEP 3: Select the Type tool from the Tools palette (Window>Tools). The Character and Paragraph palettes should open if Auto Open Palettes is checked on. (If you're unfamiliar with these palettes, check out the overview of windows and palettes on pages 2–5.)

• To ensure we're all on the same page, select Reset Character from the Character palette's Options menu (top right corner). This resets all parameters (except the Fill color, for some reason!) to default values.

• Select the Paragraph tab, and then select Reset Paragraph from the Paragraph palette's Options menu to return this palette to its defaults.

• With the [**HotCool * starter**] comp forward, click in the Comp window to start a new text layer, and type "**HOT**" in all caps. Be sure to *press the Enter key to exit editing mode* – the text entry cursor will disappear but the layer will remain selected. Note that the name of the layer is now **HOT**.

When the layer is selected, any changes you make to the Character and Paragraph palettes will apply to the whole word, no matter which tool is active. On the other hand, if you had remained in text editing mode, you would have to select the type in order to make changes. (If you don't select the type, then changes made in the palettes apply only to future text you may type.)

3 After typing "HOT", press the Enter key so that the entire word is selected. Center the text in the Paragraph palette (above). In the Character palette (left), we've set the HOT title to 90pt Stencil Std, and changed the fill color to Red.

• In the Paragraph palette, we clicked on the Center Text button.

• In the Character palette, we selected the font Stencil Std, at a size of 90pt, and changed the fill color to Red.

• We also chose to kern the "HO" character pair to –40 to tighten up the spacing. To kern pairs, place the cursor between the H and O in the Comp window, and press the Option (Alt) plus the left or right arrow keys to tighten or loosen the kerning. Press Enter again when you're done to exit editing mode.

• When the Type tool is active, you can temporarily toggle to the Selection tool by pressing Command (Control) to move the text layer. We moved the HOT title to Position X = 140, Y = 110. You can also press P to reveal Position and enter this value directly.

STEP 4: Create the other two words similarly. With the Type tool selected, click in the center of the Comp window and type **"but"**, then press Enter.

• Change the font to Tekton Pro Bold, size 60pt, fill color pale blue. The type should be aligned center already. Position it around X = 200, Y = 166.

STEP 5: Then create the **"Cool"** title, lower right.

• We used Tekton Pro Bold Oblique, size 110pt. Change the fill color to white by clicking on the white swatch below the eyedropper in the Character palette. Center alignment is fine. Position it around X = 250, Y = 260.

To compare your settings to ours, check out comp **[HotCool * starter 2]**. *Or use it instead from here!*

Hide Selection

Selected type appears in reverse, making it difficult to make color decisions. Press Command+Shift+H (Control+Shift+H) to hide the selection; the text remains selected while you pick colors.

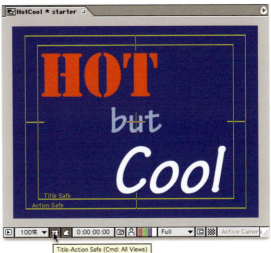

5 After Step 5, all three titles are typeset. You can toggle on the Title-Action Safe overlay to help you position the type.

Hot Slam

To animate the **HOT** layer, we'll employ a "slamming down" technique (play the final movie again to see what this looks like).

STEP 6: Turn off the Video switch (the eyeball) for the **but** and **Cool** layers, leaving just the **HOT** layer visible. You're done with the Character and Paragraph palettes so feel free to close them.

• We've decided to bring the HOT title on in time with the second drumroll at the start of the soundtrack. Move to time 00:21, where we have the hits in this roll marked in the audio layer; select the **HOT** layer and press [to move its in point to the current time.

• Still at 00:21, press B to begin the work area here.

• Move to time 02:28 and press N to end the work area. Press + (on the normal keyboard, not the keypad) to zoom in around this time.

• Press Shift+Home to return to the start of the work area at 00:21.

Center Timeline

When you are zoomed in and viewing only a section of the timeline, press D to center the view around the time marker. Place the time marker in the center of the work area before pressing D to center the work area in the timeline.

STEP 7: You'll animate the type's Position and Scale using a text animator. In the Timeline window, twirl down the **HOT** layer until you see the Text section:

• Click on the Animate button and select Position from the list of text properties. Animator 1 (with Range Selector 1) will be added to the Timeline, with the Position property applied to it.

> The general Path Options and More Options sections will also be revealed. You can ignore Path Options for this tutorial (you will learn how to apply text along a mask shape later in Tutorial 12).

• Click the Add button and select Property>Scale to add the Scale property to Animator 1 (see figure).

In the Comp window, take note of the selector bars encompassing the word HOT. These show the beginning and end of the selection as set by Range Selector's Start and End parameters. Twirl down Range Selector 1 and note that Start is set to 0% and End is at 100%. With all characters selected by Animator 1, any changes you make to the Position and Scale properties belonging to this animator will apply to the entire word. Twirl up Range Selector 1 when you're done.

7 After selecting Animate>Position and then Add>Property>Scale, the timeline should look like this (above). (Don't confuse the Animator's Position and Scale properties with the regular Transform properties!) The Range Selector's left and right selector bars are visible in the Comp window (below).

• Scrub the X value for Animator 1's Position property: the text moves left and right. Edit Position so HOT is roughly centered in the comp.

• Now increase the Scale value: note that each character scales individually. If you were using the regular Transform>Scale property, the entire layer would be affected. Note also that the text defaults to scaling around each character's baseline, not the center of the layer. Both these issues are easily addressed:

• For control over letter spacing, click the Add button again and add Property>Tracking. Increase the Tracking Amount so that the characters don't overlap each other.

• To make the characters scale around their vertical center, twirl down Text>More Options, and set the Group Alignment Y value to –50% (leave X at 0). Scrub the Scale value again and note the difference. You can twirl up the More Options section when you're done to save space.

STEP 8: Now comes the fun part! At time 00:21, turn on the stopwatches for Animator 1's Position, Scale and Tracking Amount properties.

• Adjust Scale to about 400%, then adjust the Position and Tracking values so that the text forms an interesting shape in the Comp window (see figure to the right).

• Advance 3 frames to 00:24 and change all three values again. There is no right and wrong way to edit these properties, but the idea is to gradually reduce the Scale from 400% to 100% over a series of keyframes. So, for instance, we used 300% Scale at this frame. Feel free to decrease the Tracking Amount so that characters overlap, or increase it so that characters go partly off screen.

• Continue to create five more keyframes at 00:27, 00:29, 01:01, 01:03, and 01:06, for a total of seven keyframes. Remember to keep decreasing the size until you reach 100% at the last keyframe at 01:06, but we find it's best not to be predicable about the rate of change. In fact, it's better to decrease the size for a few keyframes, then surprise the viewer by scaling it larger again in the middle!

• At time 01:06, where the text comes to rest, the values should be Scale 100%, Position 0,0, and Tracking Amount 0 – in other words, Animator 1 should no longer be adding any offsets. RAM Preview and tweak values to taste.

8 At 00:21, turn on the stopwatches for Animator 1's Position, Scale and Tracking Amount properties and adjust the values (above) so that the text is filling the frame in an interesting way (below). Note that Text layers automatically "continuously rasterize" so they render cleanly at any size.

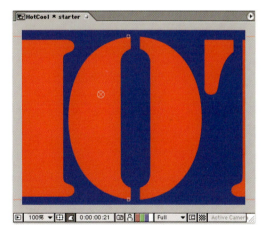

Save your project. Our results are shown below as well as in prebuilt comp [**HotCool_after Step 08**] *which can be found in the Project window's* **_HotCool * prebuilt>_compare comps_after Step ##** *folder.*

8 *complete:* Adjust the Position, Scale and Tracking values for the other five beats; note that we bounced the size smaller then larger again. The last keyframe (at time 01:06) is not shown as it is identical to the starting position shown earlier.

9 Marquee around all the keyframes except the last set to select them, and Toggle Hold Keyframes. This turns off interpolation so that the keyframe value is "held" until the next keyframe.

Return to Linear

To return any keyframe type (including Hold keyframes) back to Linear interpolation (the default "diamond" icon), press Command (Control) and click on the keyframe icon.

STEP 9: You probably noticed when you previewed that **HOT** "slides" between your poses. To change this to a "slamming" action:

• Select all of the keyframes except for the last set at 01:06 (see figure above). Then select Toggle Hold Keyframe from the Animation menu, or use this shortcut: press Command+Option (Control+Alt) and click on any one of your selected keyframes. Hold keyframe interpolation will "hold" each pose until the next keyframe, without interpolating between values. RAM Preview and note the difference.

Save your project. Our prebuilt comp is [**HotCool_after Step 09**].

Simple 3D Rotation

For the **but** layer, we'll use a simple rotation in 3D, demonstrating that you don't need cameras and lights to animate layers in 3D.

STEP 10: Twirl up the **HOT** layer, and turn on the eyeball for the **but** layer. Move the time marker to about where the saxophone comes in – we used 01:12. Select the **but** layer, and press [to slide its in point to this time.

STEP 11: You want to rotate this word around its Y axis which requires that the layer be in 3D space, so turn on the 3D Layer switch for **but** in the Timeline window.

11 Turn on the 3D switch (circled in red), and scrub the Y Rotation value (above). Watch the **but** layer spin around in the Comp window (below).

• With **but** still selected, hit R to reveal its Orientation and Rotation properties. We'll get into the difference between them later in this book in the *Postcards in Space* tutorial; for now, focus on the Y Rotation value, which is in Revolutions and Degrees. Scrub the value for degrees to get a feel for what it does.

• With the time marker still at 01:12, reset Y Rotation to 0° and enable its animation stopwatch.

• To make one revolution during the sax riff, move to around 02:21 and set a second keyframe with a value of 1 Revolution (or 360°).

• With this keyframe selected, press the shortcut F9 – Easy Ease – to smooth out the end of this move. (You can also apply Easy Ease from

HotCool * starter

0:00:02:24 (29.97 fps)

	#	Layer Name			
▷ ☐	1	T Cool			
▽ ☐	2	T but			
		⏱ Orientation	0.0°, 0.0°, 0.0°		
		⏱ X Rotation	0 x +0.0°		
▷		⏱ Y Rotation	1 x +0.0°	◀ ✓	
		⏱ Z Rotation	0 x +0.0°		
▷		⏱ Opacity	100 %	◀ ☐	
▷ ☐	3	T HOT			
▷ ☐	4	[CM_CoolGroove.mov]			

Switches / Modes

the Animation>Keyframe Assistant menu.) RAM Preview, and tweak this keyframe's timing to taste.

STEP 12: The **but** layer pops on abruptly. Fix this by adding a fade up:

• Press Shift+T to also twirl down Opacity, and press I to jump to the layer's in point at 01:12. Turn on the stopwatch for Opacity, and keyframe it from 0% at its in point, to 100% at 02:00, or to taste. RAM Preview and twirl up the **but** layer when you're finished tweaking.

Save your project. Our prebuilt comp is [**HotCool_after Step 12**].

12 The **but** layer is rotated along the Y axis, and a fade up is added.

Part 2: Cool Painting

For our third word, Cool, you'll use the Brush tool to paint animated strokes that trace the underlying Cool title. You'll then remove the underlying text.

STEP 13: Because the Paint tools work only in the Layer window, and you can't open the Layer window for a Text layer, you first need to precompose the **Cool** layer. Precomposing will place the **Cool** text layer into a comp of its own (known as a "precomp"), and the image output by that precomp will become the new source for the current layer. Here's how it's done:

• Turn on the eyeball for the **Cool** layer, select it, and select Layer> Pre-compose. Name your new comp "**Cool_precomp**". Enable the Open New Composition option and click OK. Note that the precomp has now been added as a tab to the Comp and Timeline windows.

> Because you checked the Open New Composition option, the precomp – not the original comp – will be the forward comp. If this option was off, then the **[HotCool * starter]** comp would be forward when you clicked OK and the precomp would not be a tabbed item.

• Before you start tracing the text with the Brush tool, be absolutely sure that you like the font, size and kerning of the Cool title! Although you can change the text in the precomp at any time, doing so may require re-doing the paint job over from scratch. So fix it now!

Pre-compose

New composition name: Cool_precomp

○ Leave all attributes in "HotCool * starter"
Use this option to create a new intermediate composition with only "Cool" in it. The new composition will become the source to the current layer. This option is not available because the layer can not have a source.

● Move all attributes into the new composition
Use this option to place the currently selected layers together into a new intermediate composition.

☑ Open New Composition

Cancel   OK

13 To paint on a text layer, you first need to precompose it (above).

After you precompose, the original text layer will be replaced with the precomp as a nested comp layer (below).

HotCool * starter | Cool_precomp

0:00:02:18 (29.97 fps)

	#	Layer Name	
▷ ☐	1	[Cool_precomp]	
▷ ☐	2	T but	
▷ ☐	3	T HOT	
▷ ☐	4	[CM_CoolGroove.mov]	

15 The palettes button in the Tools palette can be used to toggle the Paint palette open and closed when any of the three paint tools are selected.

15 *continued:* In the Layer window (above), make as many practice strokes as you need to determine what would be the best size brush tip. The stroke needs to be large enough to cover the width of the type, but not so big that it touches adjacent characters. Once you arrive at the right size, delete any practice strokes in the Timeline window (right).

Step 14: Once you're happy with the look of the type in the precomp, click on the tab for the [**HotCool * starter**] comp you were using earlier to bring it forward. Note that what was the **Cool** text layer has now been replaced with a nested comp called **Cool_precomp**.

• Go to time 02:18 and press [to start the **Cool_precomp** layer here.

• Press B to start the work area at 02:18 and then extend the work area to the end of the comp. Zoom out the timeline as needed.

Now that the setup work is done, it's finally time to paint! Double-click the **Cool_precomp** layer to open its Layer window.

Step 15: With the Layer window open, select the Brush tool from the Tools palette. The Paint palette should automatically open, with the Brush Tips palette tabbed with it.

• You can twirl up the Clone Options section of the Paint palette as you won't be using it.

• Set the Paint palette to the settings shown to the right. Set the Foreground color to whatever color your text should be (white in this case).

The brush size needs to be large enough to cover the type easily, but not so large that it starts to cover adjacent characters. So make a few trial strokes in the Layer window to find the right size. Although you can change the width of the strokes after they're drawn because you're painting with vectors instead of pixels, having the right-sized brush radius to start with will be easier in the long run. We chose the Hard Round 19 pixels size from the Brush Tips palette for our example.

• When you have the right size, press PP (two Ps in quick succession) to reveal the Paint effect and delete any practice Brush strokes.

Your practice strokes lasted for the entire duration of the layer, because the Duration popup in the Paint palette was set to Constant. In the next step you'll paint the real strokes in Write On mode.

STEP 16: Still at comp time 02:18 (00:00 in the Layer window), set the Duration popup in the Paint palette to Write On; this option will automatically remember your brush stroke's start and end points in time. Since you can change the playback speed later, *focus on drawing the strokes accurately and at an even pace* rather than perfecting the timing.

• Paint over the "C" as slowly as you like, without touching the adjacent "o". Because it's a write-on stroke, the stroke will disappear when you mouse up. RAM Preview to see it animate. If you didn't like your attempt, Undo (or delete Brush 1), press Home, and try again.

• Press Home and paint the two "o"s and the "l" in a similar way.

• When done, scrub the timeline or RAM Preview to see all four strokes write on. In the Timeline window, you should see four Brush strokes, one for each character. If you want to redo one of the strokes, select its Brush # in the Timeline window (it will be selected also in the Layer window), and paint the stroke again. The original timing will be retained. (The fact that a selected stroke can be easily replaced should serve also as a warning – accidents happen!)

• Press U to reveal the keyframes that were set for the End parameter in Brush 1 though 4. Right now all four strokes start at the beginning of the layer (which should be at 02:18), and end at various times. We'll deal with this "octopus" look next!

If you made a huge mess, delete the Paint effect and redo Step 16, or use our prebuilt comp [**HotCool_after Step 16**].

STEP 17: Each stroke has its own "bar" in the timeline; while you can drag each bar to offset them in time, or drag the ends to change the in and out points for the strokes, in this case it's easier just to move the pairs of End keyframes to control the order the strokes play back.

To make the characters appear to be handwritten, only one character can write on at a time. So Brush 1 should play first; only when Brush 1 is finished should Brush 2 start to paint on, perhaps with a slight delay. And then on to Brush 3 and Brush 4 (see figure on next page).

So take a few moments and move the keyframes in time; your only goal is to have the second End keyframe for Brush 4 (the "l" character)

16 With Duration set to Write On mode, paint over the Cool text one character at a time in the Layer window.

16 *complete:* When done, all four characters will be painting at the same time. Note that the View popup must be set to Paint and the Render checkbox enabled to see the brush strokes.

17 The End keyframes are moved so that the strokes play back in sequence. Two frames were added between each stroke for natural pacing.

18 Turning on Paint on Transparent removes the underlying text.

18 *complete:* The Set Matte effect (above) cleans up the edges by using the original alpha channel of the source layer. The View popup in the Layer window displays the result post-effect.

sync to the music beat at 05:22 and that the animated strokes don't overlap in time. RAM Preview and tweak the timing to taste.

If needed, check out our prebuilt comp [**HotCool_after Step 17**].

Step 18: With the painting done, it's time to tidy up the results:

• With the [**Cool_precomp**] layer selected, press PP (two Ps in quick succession) to twirl down the Paint properties. Set the Paint on Transparent option to On. The paint now draws on a transparent layer.

• Finally, apply Effect>Channel>**Set Matte** at its default settings. This takes the original alpha channel of the layer at its source (before the Paint effect) and reapplies it to the layer after the paint has rendered.

Note 1: Be aware that this technique "traces" the title with flat paint, it doesn't "reveal" the text. To reveal a textured title or logo design, use the paint strokes as a track matte instead.

Note 2: Although you can paint with Channels = Alpha only, the Paint on Transparent option (as of version 6.5) zaps the original alpha resulting in black edges. Hence the Set Matte effect.

• Bring the Comp window forward, zoom out the Timeline, set the work area to equal the length of your comp, and RAM Preview.

That wraps up the steps in this tutorial. If you want to compare your animation with ours, check the prebuilt comp [**HotCool_after Step 18**].

Part 3: All That Jazz

Now that you have animated the Hot but Cool title, feel free to finish the project off as you like – perhaps tint the words, add a background, and otherwise treat the final frame. We've included our own version for you to pick apart: In the Project window, look inside the **_HotCool * prebuilt>Final Comps** folder and open [**HotCool_FINAL**]. Starting at the bottom, here are some highlights:

• The background consists of three movies: a blue background movie (**12_U03_B11.mov** from 12 Inch Design), and rotating musical symbols (**BS_Upbeat.mov** from Bestshots) which uses the layer above (**12_U02_B26.mov**, also from 12 Inch Design) as a luma matte. The **BS_Upbeat** movie is also blended with Hard Light mode.

The final animation was blended further by stacking an adjustment layer with T_LensBlur applied in Hard Light mode. The background movies from 12 Inch Design are available at full NTSC and PAL resolution in the **Free Footage** folder on your DVD.

• The **HOT** and **Cool** layers have their positions animated to slowly drift across the frame after they come on; **Cool** also scales up. We also applied Perspective>Drop Shadow to lift them off the background.

It's worth noting that even though the **but** layer has its 3D Layer switch enabled, because the background layers are 2D we needed to apply a regular Drop Shadow effect to it. While 3D layers can use 3D lights to cast shadows, these shadows will not render on 2D layers.

In addition, to add an effect to a text layer with its 3D switch on, you must use the Advanced 3D Rendering Plug-in. (You set this option in the Advanced tab of Composition Settings, as discussed in Chapter 8.) We've also enabled Motion Blur (the M switch) for the **but** layer and set a Shutter Angle of 500° in Composition Settings>Advanced.

• To enhance the look, we added an adjustment layer (Layer>New> Adjustment Layer) and then applied Tinderbox–Blurs>T_LensBlur (free on your DVD) to it. This effect gives a "blooming" appearance, compared with the normal fuzziness of other blurs. We set this layer to Hard Light mode and lowered its Opacity to 50% so that the bloomed version would interact with the untreated frame underneath.

Experiment with turning layer 1 on and off to get an idea for what T_LensBlur is contributing to the overall look. Pay particular attention to the way the colors bleed between the title and background. Also try some brightening modes such as Add or Screen.

Select layer 1 and press F3 to open the Effect Controls windows, and experiment with T_LensBlur's Radius and Bloom values. In general, applying adjustment layers with effects on top of the final frame is a great technique for blending disparate elements, and pushing your design in a direction you might not have otherwise envisioned.

Connect

For more information on topics covered in this tutorial, check out the following volumes of *Creating Motion Graphics*:

Volume 1:

Animating Text

Continuous Rasterization

Hold keyframes

Working in 3D

Set Matte effect

Track Mattes

Adjustment Layers

Volume 2:

Audio Basics and spotting audio

Paint (3rd edition)

AutoTracker

Using Motion Tracking to composite graphical overlays onto live footage with 3:2 pulldown applied.

This tutorial is derived from a larger project CyberMotion executed for Perception Communications and American Isuzu Motors Inc. for Isuzu's new Axiom crossover vehicle. To illustrate the numerous sensors monitored by Isuzu's Torque on Demand system in the Axiom, we created a fanciful animation in which a number of sensor icons follow points on moving footage of the Axiom, adding numeric readouts down the side to suggest the information being conveyed.

To link these icons to the footage, we used the Motion Tracking feature of the After Effects Professional edition. In this tutorial, we will walk you through tracking specific points on the footage and attaching the icons to them. You will also be encouraged to see how many other points you can track to create a full set of 12. After the hard work is done, we will then walk you through the additional enhancements we made to the final frame.

Another significant subject of this tutorial is handling video footage that originated on film and that uses a luminance range different from what is normally employed by After Effects. You will learn how to remove 3:2 pulldown from footage and to add it back in when you render, as well as how to manage these common luminance range issues.

OVERVIEW

Main Concepts:

These are the features and concepts we will be focusing on in this project:

- Removing 3:2 pulldown
- Managing 16–235 luminance ranges
- Motion Tracking
- Nesting compositions
- Adjustment layers
- Adding pulldown during rendering

Requirements:

After Effects 6.5 or later Professional edition.

Getting Started:

Inside the **Tutorials** master folder on the accompanying DVD, copy the folder **04_AutoTracker** to your hard drive. Inside this is a folder called **Final Movie** – open it, then open **AutoTracker.mov** in the QuickTime Player to preview it.

Inside the **Project** folder you'll find accompanying After Effects project file **AutoTracker.aep**. Open this file, as it is your starting point; we suggest you save under a new name after each major section.

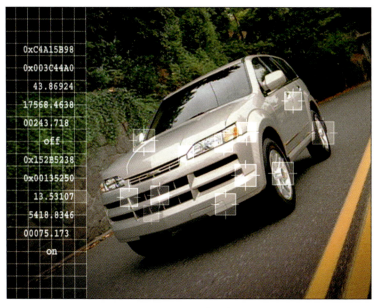

A final frame from this sequence, featuring a number of graphical tracking boxes and faked numeric readouts. Axiom footage courtesy of Perception Communications and American Isuzu Motors Inc.

The Tasks

This is what you will be doing in the various parts of this tutorial:

Part 1: Import the footage, remove 3:2 pulldown, create a new composition at the resulting special frame rate, translate its luminance range, and add the soundtrack. These issues relate to all versions of After Effects.

Part 2: Motion track the footage by trying different techniques, including picking up failed tracks from the middle of a clip.

Part 3: Import and attach the sensor icons, scale and apply blending modes to them to improve their appearance, and exploit nested comps to swap them out quickly.

Part 4: Retranslate the luminance range for video output, and automatically add 3:2 pulldown during the final render.

Part 5: Take a guided tour of additional touches we added to the finished project, including creating a series of randomized numbers using the Numbers effect, making the sensors appear to pulse in time with the music through the use of the wiggle expression and Expression Controls, and treating select areas of the original video using the Mosaic effect applied to an Adjustment Layer.

Standard Edition

If you don't have the Professional edition, you can still benefit from this tutorial. Complete Part 1, skip over Part 2, and pick up again with Part 3 using our prebuilt comp, **[Tracker_after Step 27]** where the tracking data is already complete.

Part 1: Pull Me Down

Not all of the footage items you receive for jobs will be ready to use in a composition as-is. In this case, the main footage was originally shot on 24 frame per second (fps) film, which introduces some interesting frame rate and field interlacing issues. It was also captured on a Media 100 nonlinear editing system, which passes along to the user a luminance range based on its internal digital video format, in which the black and white points are not where you might expect.

Removing 3:2 Pulldown

STEP 1: Select the **My_Sources** folder in the Project window, then select the menu command File>Import by pressing Command+I on Mac (Control+I on Windows). Locate the **04_AutoTracker>Project> Sources** folder on your drive, select **PC_Axiom.mov**, and click on Open.

At the top of the Project window, the movie will report that it has a frame rate of 29.97 fps. After Effects will also detect a tag in the file that says it has separated fields, lower field first. However, this is only part of the story…

1 After you import **PC_Axiom.mov**, the Project window will note it has a frame rate of 29.97 fps, Lower Field First.

STEP 2: Double-click the movie to open it in a QuickTime player window. Single-step through it using the left and right arrow keys, and look for signs of video field interlacing: alternating horizontal lines in the image that seem to be offset from each other, like the teeth of a comb. This is easiest to spot in the ivy hanging over the wall to the left early in the shot, since it has good contrast, and is the object moving most quickly in the image.

These offsets appear because the alternating lines from each field of the image are from different points in time – namely, 1/59.94th of a second apart (half the duration of a single NTSC frame). As you continue to step through the clip, you will notice, however, that only some of the frames exhibit interlacing. Keep stepping, and note the pattern: three "whole" frames with no interlacing, followed by two "split" frames with interlacing. By contrast, normal interlaced video exhibits these lines and split appearance in every frame.

Close the QuickTime window, and Option+double-click (Alt+ double-click) the same item to open it in After Effects' own Footage window. This special window shows you the footage *after* After Effects has separated the frame into two distinct fields. Step through these individual fields using the Page Up and Page Down keys. You should now notice a different pattern, in which an image is repeated for three steps, then the next image appears for two steps. (With normal video, you would observe a different image every field; if a progressive scan camera or mode was used, you would observe a steady pattern of a different image every two fields.)

2 As you step through this movie in a QuickTime player, you will notice some of the frames appear "whole" (left), while others are "split" with field interlacing lines clearly visible (right).

3:2 Pulldown

What is the cause of the strange patterns of repeated images you observed in Step 2? You're seeing the result of a process known as 3:2 pulldown. This footage was originally shot on film, at 24 fps. To transfer this shot to NTSC video with its frame rate of 29.97 fps, the film is first slowed down from 24 fps to 23.976 fps (the same ratio as between 30 fps black-and-white video and 29.97 fps color). The original film frames are then spread across video fields using a method in which the first frame is copied across two video fields, then the next frame is copied across three video fields. This creates a pattern of whole and interlaced (split) frames that matches what you saw in the QuickTime Player, as well as the pattern of two repeated fields followed by three in After Effects' Footage window after the fields have been separated.

In most cases, you can treat this video the same as any other clip. However, when you have to track the detail in every video field – such as rotoscoping, or matching the motion of another layer to an object in

The 3:2 pulldown process spreads four film frames across 10 video fields by repeating the film frames in a 2-3-2-3 pattern. When two different film frames end up in the same video frame, it is said to be "split" (S); when the same film frame is used for both fields of a video frame, it is "whole" (W). This illustration shows a WWSSW pattern.

this video – it is highly desirable to find a way to retrieve the original film frames: It's the difference between having to manage 24 frames or 60 fields of imagery for every second of the shot.

You are witnessing the results of how most film is transferred to NTSC video, commonly known as 3:2 pulldown. This technique spreads every four film frames across 10 video fields (for more details, see the sidebar *3:2 Pulldown* above). Since the main point of this tutorial is to track the motion in this footage, it would require a lot less work to track only the unique source frames, and not the duplicated fields as well.

Step 3: Select **PC_Axiom.mov** in the Project window, and press Command+F (Control+F) to open its Interpret Footage options.

> We often refer to this dialog as "the money box" because making sure its options are set correctly can save you lots of time and/or money. For example, removing pulldown will reduce the number of frames you have to work on. And you can avoid correcting mistakes later in the process because the field separation, frame rate, or alpha channel interpretation were set incorrectly.

The third panel in this dialog is named Field and Pulldown. At this point, the Separate Fields option should be set to Lower Field First (the most common setting for NTSC D1 or DV footage), and the Remove Pulldown option defaults to Off. There are five possible whole/split patterns this footage could have. You could try each one by hand, or you can let After Effects try first.

VideoSyncrasies

Interlacing, 3:2 pulldown, field rendering, non-square pixels, luminance ranges, alpha channel types, and other technical video issues are discussed and demonstrated in a DVD we made: *VideoSyncrasies* from Desktop Images (www.desktopimages.com).

3 If a footage item has 3:2 pulldown, you can either manually remove it by carefully observing the footage and choosing an appropriate whole/split phase setting, or have After Effects guess for you. Note the message that this footage now has effectively the same frame rate as the original film.

3 *complete:* After you've removed the pulldown, the pulldown phase and new effective frame rate will be noted in the Project window.

4 Drag the source footage to the New Composition icon at the bottom of the project window to have its size, length, and frame rate automatically copied into the comp's settings.

Click on the Guess 3:2 Pulldown button. After a brief pause, the Remove Pulldown setting should change automatically to WSSWW, which After Effects thinks is the pulldown pattern or "phase" this footage was created with. Also notice that a line of text has appeared next to this setting, noting that the footage now has an effective frame rate of 23.976 fps after pulldown has been removed – this is the rate the film was running at when it was transferred to video. Click on OK.

Go back to the After Effects Footage window for this item, or re-open it if you already closed it. Now as you step through the source, you should see a new frame of movement for every step you make. Close the Footage window when you're done. (The QuickTime Player window will not show any change, since it presents the footage to you before it has been processed by the Interpret Footage settings.)

Occasionally, After Effects is unable to guess the correct phase – such as when the footage is fading up from black, or has little to no initial motion. You can either hand-count the phase and enter it yourself, or keep trying the different options until you no longer see split frames in the Footage window. If you can't find an option that works, there is always the chance that the phase was disrupted at some previous point in the chain, including placing an edit during the clip, or because the footage was time-stretched. Another possibility is that it uses the alternate 24Pa pulldown phase appearing in some cameras.

If you look at the top of the Project window again, you will note that the information for this clip has been amended to include the 3:2 pulldown phase, and you'll see the new effective frame rate (rounded to 23.98 fps for display purposes only).

Building the Main Composition

Removing 3:2 pulldown has reconstructed the original, whole film frames. The next steps include creating a composition that takes this special frame rate into account, adjusting for differences in luminance space that some video systems impose on their footage, and adding the soundtrack.

STEP 4: You need to create a composition with the same settings – size, duration, and frame rate – as this clip. You could copy down this information from the Project window, create a new comp from the Composition menu, and transcribe these parameters across, or you can let After Effects do the work for you.

• Drag the footage item **PC_Axiom.mov** to the New Composition icon at the bottom of the Project window, and release the mouse. A new comp with these settings will be created automatically for you.

• Drag this comp to the **My_Comps** folder in the Project window.

• With this new comp selected, press Command+K (Control+K) to open its Composition Settings dialog. Verify that the frame rate is 23.976 fps and change its name to "**My_Tracker**". The process of removing pulldown has left some less-than-ideal frames at the end; go ahead and alter the duration to 06:17 to trim these off. Click on OK.

STEP 5: This footage was originally captured on a Media 100 system, which passes its internal 16–235 luminance range directly to other programs. It is much easier to work with clips like these in After Effects if you first convert them to a 0–255 luminance range; that way, you don't have to watch out for accidentally creating colors that are too dark or bright for legal video on output.

• In the composition [**My_Tracker**] select the layer **PC_Axiom.mov**, and apply Effect>Adjust>**Levels**. This will automatically open an Effect Controls window for Levels. Note that the Histogram in this window shows very little visual information at the left and right extremes, giving a further clue that a reduced luminance range is in use.

• Type Shift+F5 to take a snapshot of the Comp window in its current state. You can also click on the camera icon at the bottom of the Comp window to take a snapshot.

• In the Effect Controls window, set the Input Black parameter to 16, and the Input White parameter to 235. This will stretch the luminance for this clip back out to full range.

5 The Histogram in the Levels effect can give a clue as to the luminance range of a captured clip. Here, an arrow points to the gap in the whites, indicating "true white" is probably at 235, not 255 (on a 0–255 scale).

Time Display

You can set the Timecode Base in Preferences>Time to 24 fps if you prefer the time readout to more closely match your frames. We left it at 30 Non-Drop Frame for this tutorial.

A Matter of Black and White

Have you ever received footage that looks more washed out than you would expect? Most digital video systems work with an internal luminance system where, in a range of 0–255, a value of 16 represents true black and 235 represents true white. This allows them to capture hot spots that were accidentally too bright (over 100 IRE), and to output so-called superblack video which is occasionally used to create mattes.

Some systems, such as the Avid and Blackmagic, automatically translate these internal values to the 0=black/255=white ranges most image software –

including Adobe After Effects – expects. However, some systems – such as the Media 100, older DDRs, and some DV codecs – pass along these unscaled internal values directly to other software.

This makes it your responsibility to manually translate to and from these alternate systems, stretching 16–235 out to 0–255 before you use a clip, and squeezing it back down to 16–235 again when you render.

Details on this are covered in detail in *Creating Motion Graphics Volume 2*; in this tutorial, you will be working through an example of this procedure.

5 *complete:* The original 16–235 luminance range movie displayed in a 0–255 colorspace looks washed out (left). After applying Levels and extending its luminance range, the contrast increases (right).

• Press F5 to compare this treated footage with the snapshot you took of the untreated version (or click the "man" icon at the bottom of the Comp window). The treated version should have a nicer contrast to it; you might even notice now that the paint is a subtle shade of gold or beige rather than silver.

• Close the Effect Controls window.

STEP 6: Select the **My_Sources** folder in the Project window, and type Command+I (Control+I) to open the Import dialog. Locate the file **CM_Tracker_music.mov** in the same **Sources** folder where you found the Axiom clip, and click Open. Then type Command+/ (Control+/) to add it to your comp. If the time marker was not at 00:00, type Option+Home (Alt+Home) to start the music track there.

RAM Preview [**My_Tracker**] by pressing 0 on the numeric keypad to get a feel for the overall shot.

Music Credits

Chris Meyer of CyberMotion arranged the soundtrack for this tutorial. It includes rhythm loops from the Spectrasonics sampling CD *Metamorphosis* (distributed by Ilio Entertainment – www.ilio.com), plus an additional snare roll from *Chemical Beats* by Zero-G (www.zero-g.co.uk). The guitar chord was played by Peter Maunu for the Spectrasonics CD *Bizarre Guitar*, and was chosen to match the camera move that slides from a frontal to a partial profile view. The garbled communication voices are from the Sound Ideas *6000 Series* sound effects library (www.sound-ideas.com), and are intended to reinforce the data communications theme.

If you don't have enough RAM or a fast enough computer to preview the entire full-frame shot, reduce the Resolution to Half by pressing Command+Shift+J (Control+Shift+J), and reduce the Magnification to 50% by pressing Command (Control) plus the – symbol along the top of the keyboard. However, in doing so you may notice a quirk in After Effect in which fields reappear in footage with 3:2 pulldown applied when they're viewed at Half Resolution. Ignore it. When you're done, return to Full Resolution and 100% Magnification for the next part.

*To ensure your basic comp is built correctly, compare [**My_Tracker**] with our version [**Tracker_after Step 06**] in the Project's _AutoTracker * prebuilt>_compare comps after Step ## folder. If you prefer, duplicate our comp and rename it "**My_Tracker_06**" to use for the rest of this tutorial. And don't forget to save your project!*

Part 2: Getting On Track

The portion of the video script that this shot was designed to illustrate says: "While driving, the system monitors 12 different inputs, including engine RPM, the brakes, and throttle position. Changes in speed, throttle position, or braking alert the system to possible handling or traction challenges." This was the only guide we had for where to place the sensors.

In this part of the tutorial, we'll walk you through the process of tracking two of these points. The footage was not shot with special markers for us to track; we just chose what we thought would be the best piece of footage from a selects reel – so part of your challenge will be trying to find naturally occurring points in the image to track.

Forward Track

The first motion track we'll do will be fairly simple. We're looking for a section of the car that will be visible for the entire duration of the video, and which doesn't change shape too much during this time. The best shapes to track are ones with high contrast and distinct edges or boundaries. The middle of a line is bad, because it's hard to tell where you are along the line. However, where two lines cross is good, because the X or T formed at the cross is easy to identify and follow. Dots and the ends of lines are also nice, unambiguous shapes to track. For this first track, we'll choose one of the crosses formed by the shape of the car's grill.

Step 7: At this point, we haven't decided what the final tracker shape will be. That's okay; as of After Effects version 6, you can perform your tracks separately from applying the resulting data to another layer. The track data is stored as keyframes in the layer you track, and is therefore saved with the project.

Verify your comp is set to Full Resolution, and select the layer **PC_Axiom.mov**. Then select the menu item Window>Tracker Controls, which will open a new floating palette. Click on the button Track Motion in the upper left of this palette; note that the Layer window for **PC_Axiom.mov** will be opened automatically for you. (All tracking takes place in the Layer window.)

In the Layer window you will see a set of boxes with the name Track Point 1 above – this is your first default track region; we'll be modifying it in just a second. Other clues that you are in "tracking mode" is that the View popup along the bottom of the Layer window will be set to Motion Tracker Points, a faint zigzag line will be drawn through the layer bar, and a dashed line will appear above this bar.

> The set of boxes you see are called Track Point 1 because a motion track may involve up to four individual Track Points. Do not be thrown off when this name is different than the name of the Tracker that appears in the Timeline window.

An Image Problem

The higher the image quality of the footage you are tracking, the better your results. In this tutorial, the footage has been through a composite video dub which reduces it quality, which makes it more difficult to track cleanly.

7 The main controls for the Motion Tracker/Stabilizer exist in the Tracker Controls palette (above). When you click on Track Motion, the clip's Layer Window will open, with a default Track Point created in the middle (below).

STEP 8: The bad news is that setting up the tracker is not entirely intuitive, as many of its parameters are hidden inside an Options window. The good news is, if you've used the tracker in previous versions of After Effects and were frustrated by it, it received a major overhaul in version 6.0, with further significant tweaks in 6.5. The tracker is now faster and more accurate, plus the default options are much better. Still, you should make it standard practice to give them some thought and verify their settings before performing a track.

First, you need to set up the type of track you wish to perform: In our case, the Transform property Position. In the Tracker Controls window, make sure the Track Type popup is set to Transform. Underneath this popup, verify that only the Position option is checked; we don't care about the rotation or scale of the point we will be tracking.

Then click on the Options button below these checkboxes. It will open a separate Motion Tracker Options window. Verify the following settings:

- Under Channel, make sure the Luminance option is selected. As we have a silver car with black details, there isn't a lot of color or saturation to track; we will be selecting track points based on their contrast between silver and black.

- Below Channel, leave Track Fields unchecked; removing the pulldown from the footage means there are no fields in the source footage to worry about.

8 It is essential to verify and properly set the Motion Tracker Options. Probably the trickiest to set are the Adapt Feature options; we find the settings shown here are a good starting point of many tracks.

- Verify that Subpixel Positioning is enabled: This is what allows smooth motion for your track.

- You need to choose a set of "track adaptiveness" options which will take into account how the feature you will be tracking will change over the length of the clip. In our case where the camera angle and zoom is changing a bit, but not drastically from frame to frame, leave "Adapt Feature on Every Frame" disabled, and instead set the "If Confidence Is Below" popup below to Adapt Feature. This tells After Effects to look for changes in the track feature it is following only if After Effects has trouble. Go ahead and leave the Confidence threshold at its default of 80% for now. If you have difficulty performing a track, these settings should be the first you tinker with.

- Leave the Process Before Match section disabled.

In the Crosshairs

When the tracker is active, in the Layer window you will see a set of two boxes, with a + symbol in the middle. We refer to this as a Track Point set. Here's what each part of the set is for, and how to edit them:

• The + symbol is the Attach Point: the place you want to attach the anchor point of another layer that is supposed to track a feature in the current layer. It does not have to be inside the boxes (sometimes there isn't a good feature to track near where you want to pin the new layer), but tracks generally will appear tighter and more accurate if you can keep the feature you're tracking close to the Attach Point.

• The inner square is the Feature Region: the unique pattern or shape that After Effects is supposed to follow around the frame. The smaller you can make this, while still fully enclosing the feature you want to track, the faster and more accurate your tracks will be. You need to take into account that the feature may grow larger during the course of a track if it comes closer to the camera, so don't make the Feature Region too small to start!

• The outer square is the Search Region: how large of an area After Effects is supposed to search from frame to frame to find the pattern inside the Feature Region. After

the feature is found, the Feature and Search Regions are reset, and the process starts over for the next frame. If you know the feature has a particular direction it is more likely to move, you can make the Search Region larger in that direction to better capture its movement.

You can have up to four sets of regions and Track Points, depending on the type of track you are performing. Tracking Rotation or Scale requires two sets of Track Points, as you need a second reference to decide how much the scene has rotated or scaled; a four-corner pin requires four sets of Track Points – one for each corner.

There are several ways to modify the Attach Point plus the Feature and Search Regions:

• Dragging the Attach Point moves it without moving the Feature and Search Regions.

• Clicking and dragging inside the Feature and Search Regions, but not on their outlines or the Attach Point, moves everything as a set. The cursor arrow will be black, followed by a four-pointed arrow icon. The area inside the Feature Region will be magnified as you drag, making it easier to precisely locate the region.

• Option+dragging (Alt+drag-ging) inside the Feature and

A Track Point set consists of an Attach Point (the crosshair in the center), a Feature Region (the smaller box), and a Search Region (the larger box). As you edit these, the cursor icon changes shape to reinforce what you are about to do; this small black icon with the four-headed arrow following means you are about to move the entire Track Point set.

Search Regions, but not on their outlines or the Attach Point, moves just the Regions and leaves the Attach Point where it was. The cursor arrow will be white, followed by a four-pointed arrow icon. The area inside the Feature Region will be magnified as you drag.

• Dragging on a corner of a region box will resize the box symmetrically. You will see a normal cursor as you do this.

• Command+dragging (Control+dragging) on a corner of a region box will move just that corner of the box. You will see a normal cursor as you do this.

• Dragging the side of a region box will move the entire box without resizing it. You will see a white cursor arrow followed by a white box.

9 After Effects will automatically magnify the area inside the Feature Region box as you reposition it. Drag it until the Attach Point (the + icon) is centered over one of the intersections of the grill pieces.

10 Analyze This! Once your Track Point is set up, click on the Analyze Forward button in the Tracker Controls palette to perform the track.

STEP 9: Now let's turn our attention to the Track Point set in the Layer window. The components of this set are described in the sidebar *In the Crosshairs*; now it's time to put them to use. We've decided that the "T" shapes formed by some of the vertical and horizontal elements in the car's grill might make good features to track.

Click and drag in the area between the two region boxes to move them as a set. As you do so, you will notice After Effects automatically magnifies the pixels around the inner box, which is the Feature Region (very handy!). Drag them until the + icon of the Attach Point is centered on a point where the thin central horizontal grill piece just meets the middle horizontal bar of the grill/bumper.

Next, make the Feature Region as small as you think practical. Dragging one of its corners resizes the entire region symmetrically around its center. To adjust an individual corner, hold the Command (Control) key down as you drag one of the corners.

Then resize the Search Region to allow After Effects to capture the roving feature from frame to frame. Taking the philosophy that bigger must be better, we sized this box to make sure we could follow the feature being tracked no matter how much the car or camera moved. Bigger *is* better, right?

STEP 10: Moment of truth: Click on the Analyze Forward button (the "Play" icon) in the Tracker Controls palette, and watch how the Tracking Region boxes move from frame to frame. If you're both lucky and good, they should constantly recenter on that point in the grill you identified until it reaches the end of the clip. But if you see a sudden jump, something went wrong (as it often does in the real world); press any key to stop the track.

In our first attempt, part way into the track the Track Point suddenly jumped to the lower portion of the grill. This is because we made our Search Region too big, and After Effects accidentally thought another point (namely, the near-identical junctions between all the vertical and horizontal grill elements) was a better match. The bigger you made the Search Region, the quicker the track will go awry; in our case, we made it until about 01:20 before things went wrong.

You could go back to Step 9 and start over, defining a better Search Region. Or, you can save the work you've already put in, and redefine the track mid-stream to pick up from the last good point.

10 *complete:* We defined too large of a Search Region; as a result, After Effects jumped from the correct spot (left) to a similar-looking but incorrect spot below it (right).

STEP 11: If your Search Region was close to the right size, there's a chance you don't have to do anything: Just back up the time marker to the last good tracked frame, and click on Analyze again. The tracker will adapt to this new "model" frame as it tracks subsequent frames.

But you may not be that lucky, so back up to this last good frame (around 01:20 in our case; your specific frame will depend on the size of your Search Region box), then carefully resize the Search Region smaller so it no longer encompasses another similar section of the grill either to the left, right or below. Make sure you don't move the crosshairs in the middle of the Tracking Region, or you will confuse the resulting position data. Also, be aware that if you resize the Search region then move to another time, the boxes revert to their old size – so move the time marker first, then resize the box.

11 Reduce the size of the Search Region to miss the similar-looking section of the grill below (where the cursor is pointing).

STEP 12: When you've resized the box, click on Analyze Forward again. You should make it to the end of the clip fine this time. If not, just repeat this step: Back up to an earlier good-looking track, adjust the Search or Feature region, and continue from there. If it seems hopeless, go back to Step 9…

STEP 13: After you have performed a track, you will notice a string of keyframe icons in the Layer window which indicate the tracked path. Scrub the time marker in this window and observe the position of Track Point 1's Attach Point relative to your target on the grill – it should follow it very closely. (If you cannot see this path, make sure the View popup along the bottom of the Layer window is set to Motion Tracker Points, and that the Track Point you are interested in is selected in the Timeline window.)

Press U to reveal this layer's keyframes in the Timeline window. A simple positional motion track such as this one will save keyframes for the Feature Center (the center of the Feature Region), the Attach Point (the small crosshair, which is probably the center of the Feature Region in this case), and the Confidence After Effects has in how accurate the track point is. A drop in the Confidence value means the track point might have drifted; click on the arrow to the left of the word Confidence to twirl down its Value graph for a quick visual check. If the line stays high and fairly even, you're in good shape.

13 Keyframes for your track will appear in the Layer window (above) after you're finished. Type U to reveal these keyframes in the Timeline window; twirl down the Confidence Value graph (below) to make sure it stays high and somewhat even. Dips indicate possible mistracking; scrub the time marker through the Layer window to visually verify the position of the Attach Point.

A Track of One

If you click an Analyze button, and After Effects stops after tracking only one frame, you either clicked on one of the Analyze 1 Frame buttons, or clicked Analyze Forward when you mean Analyze Backward (or vice versa).

Twirl up Tracker 1 in the Timeline window when you're done.

If you were trying to replace a portion of the car, such as a license plate or badge, you would need to be very critical of how precise the track is. For data readouts and other more fanciful graphics, you don't need to be as critical. This application is rather forgiving, so don't be upset if you have trouble creating rock-solid tracking data.

*Save your project. If you are unsure of the results of your first track, compare your work with our prebuilt comp [***Tracker_after Step 13***].*

Backtracking

Not all tracking points are polite enough to stay in the frame for the entire shot. We decided the centerpoints on the wheels would be good points to add sensor icons to, but they aren't visible during the first second of the shot. To work around this, you can try tracking them from the end of the shot backward, then decide how to gracefully cover up the beginning.

STEP 14: In the Timeline window, drag the time marker to the end of the comp. Make sure the Layer window for **PC_Axiom.mov** is still open (if not, double-click this layer in the Timeline window) and forward (select its tab along the top of the Comp/Layer window). Finally, make sure the Tracker Controls palette is still open (if it isn't, re-select it from the Windows menu).

STEP 15: Click on the Track Motion button in the upper left corner of the Tracker Controls palette. A new set of Track Point boxes will appear in the Layer window, and a new Tracker will appear in the Timeline window attached to the **PC_Axiom.mov** layer.

You'll want to use the same set of options as you did back in Step 8:

• Set the Track Type popup in the Tracker Controls to Transform, with only Position checked underneath.

• Click on the Options button in the Tracker Controls.

• Under Channel, make sure the Luminance option is selected.

• Below Channel, leave Track Fields unchecked.

• Verify that Subpixel Positioning is enabled.

• Leave Adapt Feature on Every Frame disabled, and set the "If Confidence Is Below" popup below to Adapt Feature. Leave the Confidence threshold at its default of 80%.

STEP 16: Click in the area between the outer Search Region box and the inner Feature Region box, and drag until the Attach Point crosshair is nicely centered in the black wheel insert for the front wheel. As you drag, After Effects will magnify the area inside the Feature Region to show you what is being selected.

Resize the Feature Region box so it just encompasses that black insert, with about a pixel or two of silver as a border – this will create a nice, high-contrast spot to track. To verify your selection, click and very slightly drag between the Feature and Search Regions to invoke the magnification feature.

STEP 17: Resize the Search Region box, thinking about how much the wheel moves from frame to frame. Remember that just dragging a corner of a Region resizes it symmetrically; Command+dragging (Control+dragging) moves just that corner and leaves the others where they are. We chose an initial size about half the size of the tire, slightly biased to the right as this is the direction the wheel will slide off toward as we track backward through the shot.

17 Set up the Tracking Region box to focus on the black insert in the front wheel, starting at time 06:16 in the shot.

STEP 18: Click on the Analyze Backwards button in the Tracker Controls palette (near the bottom, second from the left). If you've not made your Search Region too large, After Effects should walk backwards through the footage, keeping the Feature Region centered over the wheel's insert.

If the track goes astray, you have the same options here as you did before when you were tracking the grill: either go to your last good point, resize the Search and Feature Regions (without moving the Attach Point), and pick up your track from there, or go back to the first frame of your track and start over fresh.

> If you have a completed track that you *think* might work, but want to take another shot at it without overwriting the track you just performed, then merely start another tracker: Click on the Track Motion button in the Tracker Controls palette to get a fresh Track Point and try again. You don't have to use every track you make. And since each track is saved with the layer, you don't have to worry about losing them. (Indeed, we suggest saving a copy of your project after each track you want to keep!)

19 This track will probably be less solid than your first, especially as you start to view the wheel from the front rather than the side. Locate your earliest good tracked frame and place a Layer marker to remind you where to trim it out in the final animation.

STEP 19: You might have noticed that this track seemed less stable than your first track – especially as it reached the start of the clip, when we view the car from the front instead of the side and don't have a good view of the wheel insert anymore. Twirl open the Confidence Value graph for this new track, and it will probably look more jagged. It follows that it's probably not a good idea to use this entire track.

Scrub the time marker in either the Timeline or Layer windows, watching the Layer window to see how closely your Track Point follows the wheel's center. At the earliest point in the clip where you think the track is still pretty good (probably around

01:05 or so), hold down the Option (Alt) key and press * on the numeric keypad. This will open the Marker window. Type a brief note to yourself to remind you that this is the earliest good point for your second track, then click OK.

> This track probably jitters around more than your first one; the center of the wheel turns out not to be as good of a point to track as a crosshair in the grill. This amount of jitter would be unacceptable if you were trying to replace the wheel on the car, but will work fine for our purposes in this project. Part of motion tracking is knowing when to stop and move on...

Oops – Wrong Layer

Don't forget to select the layer to be tracked, not the layer to be attached, before starting a new track.

STEP 20: You will note in the Timeline that your tracks have generic names like Tracker 1 and Tracker 2. It will become easy to forget which track is which part of the car. To rename a tracker, select its name in the Timeline window, press Return to highlight it, type your new name, and hit Return again. You can also rename a tracker by selecting it, clicking on Options in the Tracker Controls palette, and giving it a new name there.

STEP 21: Remember at the start of this Part, where the script said "the system monitors 12 different inputs"? You guessed it: You have 10 more tracks to perform. Rather than lead you step by step through these remaining tracks, we're going to leave it up to you and your own creative devices to find 10 more suitable points. Here are some tips:

- The sharp angles around the grill, bumper, and lights all present some excellent points to track.

- There are a couple of points along the side worth tracking, such as the back wheel, as well as the door lock or rearview mirror. As with the front wheel, you will probably need to track these in reverse, and trim them to start later in the comp.

- Running out of ideas? Look at points where the windshield meets the body pillars and hood.

- If you find a good track point where it otherwise would not make sense to place one of the sensor

21 Find 10 more features on the car to track. The points we chose are identified by pink squares to make them easier to see. When finished, you should have at least 12 sets of Motion Tracker keyframes in the Timeline.

icons, you can place the Tracking Region around that good point, then move the Track Point crosshair to where you want the sensor to end up.

- Don't forget: Save after each track you want to keep, name your tracks, and there's no lost honor in backing up and resuming a track in the middle.

We encourage you to practice your tracking skills by completing all 12 tracks yourself. If you get too frustrated, look at our comp **[Tracker_after Step 21]** *for ideas on points to track. You can duplicate and rename it "MyTracker_21" if you wish to continue with our version rather than yours.*

Part 3: Iconography

In this part, you will add the sensor icons to your comp and apply your tracking data to them. We will use a "defensive animation" technique that will make it easier for you to swap out different icons later.

STEP 22: Select your **My_Comps** folder, and type Command+N (Control+N) to create a new composition. Set its size to 100×100 (make sure the Lock Aspect Ratio switch is off), pixel aspect ratio to square, frame rate of 23.976, and duration to 06:17 in order to match [**My_Tracker**]. Name it "**My_Sensor**" and click OK. Set its Composition> Background Color to black, to make the sensor easier to see.

STEP 23: Select your **My_Sources** folder, and use Command+I (Control+I) to open the Import Footage dialog. In the same **Project>Sources** folder where you found the video clip and the soundtrack, select **CM_sensor_crl.tif**. Depending on how you have your preferences set, you may get an Interpret Footage dialog asking you to choose an alpha channel type. If so, select Straight Alpha and click OK.

STEP 24: With [**My_Sensor**] open and the forward composition in your Comp and Timeline windows, select **CM_sensor_crl.tif** in the Project window and hit Command+/ (Control+/). This will automatically add the selected footage item to the forward comp.

• Bring [**My_Tracker**] forward, and hit Home to return the time marker to 00:00. In the Project window, select [**My_Sensor**] and type Command+/ (Control+/) to nest this comp inside [**My_Tracker**].

STEP 25: Time to assign your tracking data to sensor icons. If the Tracker Controls palette is not still open, select it from the Window menu. Click on its Motion Source popup menu, and select **PC_Axiom.mov**, as this is the layer that has all the sensor data stored in it. Then select one of your tracks from the Current Track popup below.

• Next, click on the Edit Target button in Tracker Controls. This will open a dialog that lists all of the layers in the current comp. As it makes no sense to apply a track to the source layer or to an audio layer, only one choice will be valid: **My_Sensor**. Select it and click OK.

• Finally, click Apply. This will open the Motion Tracker Apply Options dialog. Its default – X and Y – is what you want in this case. Click OK.

Click on the [**My_Tracker**] tab along the top of the Comp window to bring it forward. You should see our round sensor centered around the track point you selected. Hit 0 on the numeric keypad to RAM Preview the comp, and watch how the sensor tracks the car!

Standard edition

If you don't have the Professional edition, continue with Part 3 using our prebuilt comp, [**Tracker_after Step 21**]. Duplicate it and rename it "**MyTracker_27**" and drag it to the **My_Comps** folder.

23 If you have the interpret alpha choice in Preferences>Import set to Ask User, when you import **CM_sensor_crl.tif** you will be asked to set the alpha type for this file. Choose Straight.

25 In the Tracker Controls, select **PC_Axiom** as the Motion Source, and then select one of your trackers in the Current Track popup.

25 *complete:* After applying tracking data to a sensor layer, it will now follow that point on the car.

Circles and Eggs

The circular icons look egg-shaped in the **[My_Tracker]** Comp window because they are being stretched to match the comp's D1/DV pixel aspect ratio. Toggle the Pixel Aspect Correction switch along the bottom right of the Comp window for a quick confidence check.

You're about to add 11 more copies of this sensor precomp into **[My_Tracker]**; this may get confusing. To avoid this, select the one **My_Sensor** layer currently in your comp, hit Return to highlight its name, type in a new name (perhaps matching the name you gave its corresponding tracker), and hit Return again to accept it.

STEP 26: Creating the rest of the sensors and applying unique tracks to them is easy. Hit Home to return the time marker to 00:00, select **[My_Sensor]** in the Project window, and type Command+/ (Control+/) multiple times to add 11 more copies of it to **[My_Tracker]**. In the Tracker Controls palette, verify that Motion Source is set to **PC_Axiom.mov**. Then follow these steps for each of the 11 sensors you just added to the comp:

- Use the Current Track popup to select a new set of tracker data.

- Verify that Track Type is set to Transform.

- Click on Edit Target, and select your next sensor layer in the Motion Target dialog's Layer popup. Click OK.

- Click Apply in the Tracker Controls, verify the Apply Dimensions popup in Motion Tracker Apply Option is set to X and Y, and click OK.

- Select this sensor in the Timeline window (you may need to deselect **PC_Axiom.mov**), and rename it to match the track data you just used.

When you're finished, click on the **[My_Tracker]** tab along the top of the Comp window to bring it forward. You should now see a dozen round sensors attached to the car. Hit 0 on the numeric keypad to RAM Preview and enjoy!

STEP 27: These sensors are cool, but they look a bit large, and could stand out more against the video. No problem:

- In [My_Tracker], select all of the **My_Sensor** layers, and turn on their Collapse Transformations switch (the one that looks like a sun with rays). Click on one switch, and the switches for all the selected layers will change. This will allow changes in the **[My_Sensor]** precomp such as scalings and blending modes to flow through to **[My_Tracker]** while maintaining maximum quality. Deselect the layers (shortcut: F2).

- Select the **[My_Sensor]** comp. If it occupies the same window as [My_Tracker], click on the [My_Sensor] tab in the Comp window, drag it outside its current window, and release the mouse –

27 Set Collapse Transformations for all the **My_Sensor** layers in **[My_Tracker]**.

it will now have its own Comp window. Resize this new window and position it on your screen so you can see the Comp windows for [**My_Sensor**] and [**My_Tracker**] at the same time.

- In the [**My_Sensor**] comp, select **CM_sensor_crl.tif** and type S to reveal its Scale property. Experiment with different values. After you enter a new value, you will see all of the sensors in [**My_Tracker**] update to reflect the new size. We chose 60%.

- Still in [**My_Sensor**], press F4 to reveal the Modes column in the Timeline window (or click on the Switches/Modes button at the bottom of the Switches column). Change the blending mode for **CM_sensor_crl.tif** to Add mode.

Since Collapse Transformations is turned on for this precomp's layer in [**My_Tracker**], all of the sensors in [**My_Tracker**] will redraw with this mode applied. This new mode will brighten up the appearance of the sensors and make them interact more with the video underneath, resulting in a more "phosphorescent" look.

27 *complete:* The sensor icon has been scaled to 60% and set to Add mode in its precomp (above), which ripples through to all of the sensors in the [**My_Tracker**] comp (below).

Planning for Change

When you have an element that is used multiple times and that may be changed later (either by you or the client), it is a good idea to put it into its own composition, and use this precomp in your final composition. Any changes made to the original element in its precomp will automatically ripple into any comp in which it is nested.

The sensor icon used in this tutorial is a good example. We created two different icons in After Effects, using a combination of solids, mask shapes, and Effect>Render>Stroke. However, you might want to create a different icon in a program such as Adobe Illustrator, use a "dingbat" type font with the Type tool, or even create an animating icon.

If so, place it in [**My_Sensor**], scale it to fit, and see how you like it in [**My_Tracker**]. In our sensor design, we purposely avoided anything that had too clear of a "crosshair" in the very center, as it might imply too specific of a region – as well as tip off the viewer that our tracks were not perfectly accurate.

If you are curious to see how we built our icons, check out the composition [**_sensor icon creation**] inside the Project window's **AutoTracker * prebuilt** folder. Even though we built them in After Effects, we pre-rendered them as stills to save rendering time later.

We built our sensors by drawing a series of mask shapes on a solid, then outlining them with Effect>Render>Stroke.

STEP 28: RAM Preview [**My_Tracker**] to see how your new sensors look. You probably have a few tracks that wobble or jump at the start of the track, such as the wheels. Let's trim the wobble out of those layers, and give them a fade-up:

• Select one of the sensor layers that starts with a wobble.

• Drag the time marker until the earliest point where the sensor seems stable. If you saved Layer markers to note these points on the problem tracks, hold the Shift key while you drag, and the time marker will snap to these Layer markers.

[Timeline window: Tracker_after Step 29 • Timeline]

28 Add fade-ups to any layers where the tracks didn't extend back to 00:00.

• Type Option+[(Alt+[) to trim the in point of this layer to where you want it to start.

• Move 10 or 15 frames past this point – in other words, a nice duration for a quick fade.

• Press T to reveal the Opacity property, and click on the stopwatch icon to set the first keyframe at 100%.

• Press I to return to this layer's in point, and enter an Opacity value of 0%.

• Repeat this process for any other unstable layers that should start after 00:00.

RAM Preview to see if you like this better. When done, twirl up the Opacity properties to clean up your Timeline window again.

What's in a Name

Give your adjustment layers names that make sense, such as "luminance adjust", to help you identify them in the Timeline window. To rename an adjustment layer, select Layer>Solid Settings, or press Command+Shift+Y (Control+Shift+Y) to open the Solid Footage Settings dialog. Adjustment layers are also added to the Solids folder in the Project window, and can be renamed from there as well.

STEP 29: Everything is looking good…until you remember that the client told you the graphical theme in all the print materials is graph paper, and to use boxes whenever you can. Let's import a new square sensor icon and replace the circular icon layers. This is when you understand why you placed the sensor icon in a precomp:

• Bring the comp [**My_Sensor**] forward, and make sure the layer **CM_sensor_crl.tif** is selected.

• Select the **My_Sources** folder in the Project window, and import the icon **CM_sensor_sqr.tif**. If you're asked, set its alpha channel type to Straight.

• With this item still selected in the Project window, type Command+Option+/ (Control+Alt+/) to swap it for the circular icon in [**My_Sensor**]. If you like, scale it down a little smaller to make it less imposing (we left it at 60%).

> In this example, you could have selected **CM_sensor_sqr.tif** in the Project window, and used File>Replace Footage>File to replace this source with the square sensor directly from disk. This would replace the icon throughout the project, even if it was used in multiple compositions. By comparison, importing a new source and using the Replace Layer shortcut lets you be more selective in replacing sources.

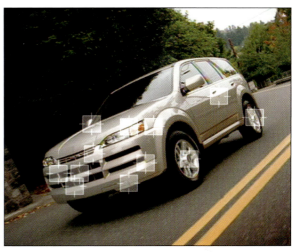

• If it's not already visible, bring the comp [**My_Tracker**] forward, and note that all of the sensors have been updated automatically.

Save your project. That finishes Part 3; the only task left is preparing for the final render. Compare your comp with [**Tracker_after Step 29**].

29 By swapping one sensor image in [**My_Sensor**], all 12 of the sensors update automatically in [**My_Tracker**].

Part 4: Back to Video

The hard work is done. The final steps are getting back to where you started when you were handed this clip to enhance:

STEP 30: If you are rendering back to a system expecting footage with a 16–235 luminance range, then you'll need to reintroduce the original luminance range (if it's expecting 0–255, skip ahead to the next step).

• In [**My_Tracker**], return the time marker to 00:00. Add a Layer>New>Adjustment Layer. Open Layer>Solid Settings and rename it "**luminance adjust**", and click OK.

30 Add an Adjustment Layer to your comp, rename it "**luminance adjust**" and apply the Levels effect to it. (Creating a new Adjustment Layer really just creates a full-frame white solid with the half-moon switch turned on.)

My_Tracker • Timeline

My_Tracker / My_Sensor

0:00:00:00 (23.976 fps)

#	Layer Name		00s	01s	02s	03s	04s	05s	06s
1	[luminance adjust]								
	▷ Levels	Reset	*Adjustment Layer - The effects applied to this layer affect only all layers behind it*						
2	R headlight								
3	UR grill								
4	R fender flare								
5	UL grill								
6	LL/C grill								
7	L bumper insert								
8	LR grill								
9	L windshield								
10	keyhole								
11	rear wheel								
12	front wheel								
13	grill center								
14	[CM_Tracker_mus...]								
15	[PC_Axiom.mov]		keyhole / frnt whl in						

Switches / Modes

30 To reintroduce a 16–235 luminance range before the final render, apply the Levels effect, and set the Output Black and White parameters to 16 and 235 respectively.

D1 to DV

If you want to render to a DV NTSC codec, in the Output module set the Crop parameters to remove two lines from the top and four lines from the bottom. This will resize your rendered frame from 486 lines to 480, while maintaining the same field order.

• With this adjustment layer still selected, add Effect>Adjust>**Levels**. In the Effect Controls window, set the Output Black to 16, and Output White to 235. This squeezes the luminance range back into what some systems expect. Your image will look a bit washed out in the Comp window, but will look normal on final output through your video system. Close the Effect Controls window.

STEP 31: Type Command+M (Control+M) to add [**My_Tracker**] to the Render Queue. Give it a name that makes sense, such as "**TrackerRender.mov**". In the Render Queue window, select Best Settings from the Render Settings templates popup, and click on the text "Best Settings" to open the dialog:

• Set the Field Render popup to Lower Field First, to match what most D1-size NTSC systems use.

• Set the popup for 3:2 Pulldown to any choice other than Off. The exact pulldown phase you choose is irrelevant for video work, and is only an issue if you are creating a video edit that needs to be conformed back to film later.

• The "Use this frame rate" section should now read "29.97". The line above will note that the comp is being sampled at 23.98 fps (really 23.976 rounded to two digits for display purposes). Click OK.

• Choose an appropriate codec for your hardware in the Output Module, turn on the Audio switch, and proceed with the render.

The result of these settings is to instruct After Effects to render your comp at 23.976 fps. After it has rendered these frames, it will then spread them across video frames using the same two field/three field pattern discussed earlier when you removed pulldown from the original clip. After Effects then saves a 29.97 fps interlaced movie with this pattern. If you click on Render, you will observe this stuttering pattern in the timecode under the Current Render progress bar.

There are two advantages to working this way: The render goes much faster, because you are rendering only 24 frames rather than 60 fields per second; and any additional animation you have created – such as the tracking sensors – will be rendered at the same speed as the underlying footage, which will make the final motion appear more coherent.

31 You can reintroduce pulldown at the render stage by selecting a field order and pulldown phase in the Render Settings, and setting the final frame rate back to 29.97.

Part 5: The Scenic Tour

The work you performed in Parts 1 through 4 is enough to hand your client back the original clip with some tracker icons composited on top of the footage. However, we added some design touches to make the clip more than just a technical illustration.

In the Project window folder _Tracker * prebuilt>Final Comps_, double-click on [**Tracker_Final**]. Here are some of the touches we added:

Pulsing to Music

We wanted to tie the graphics more closely to the music, which would add to the impact. We spotted some of the beats in the soundtrack **CM_Tracker_music.mov**, and noted the tempo averaged roughly 12.25 frames per beat (fpb) against a timebase of 30 frames per second. Since we could not track some of the sensor locations back to the start of the clip, we faded up a series of sensors – layers 8 through 11 – in time with the music. You know the saying: If life gives you lemons, make lemonade…

We then decided to make the sensors pulse in time with the music.

Comp Background

When applying an adjustment layer with Levels to reintroduce the 16–235 luminance range, the Composition background color is not effected. Instead, use a background solid layer set to the color you want, and let the Levels effect perform the luminance adjustment.

Our final timeline, with all of our tricks revealed. Open the comp [**Tracker_Final**] to explore some of these tricks in more detail.

Tracker_Final • Timeline

Tracker_Final

0:00:00:00 (23.976 fps)

#	Layer Name	Mode	T TrkMat	
1	[luminance adjust]	Normal		imposes 16–235 luminance range
	Levels — Reset			
2	[numbers_generator]	Add	None	6 alphanumerics in precomp
	Scale — 60.0 , 75.9 %			
3	[numbers_generator]	Add	None	offset –01:00 in time
4	[grid]	Add	None	
	Grid — Reset			
5	[mosaic adjustment]	Hard Light	None	adjustment layer in Hard Light for subtle grid
	Mosaic — Reset			
6	[wiggle controllers]	Normal	None	master controllers for sensor layer expressions
	wig_speed — Reset			
	wig_scale — Reset			
	wig_opacity — Reset			
7	[CM_Tracker_music.mov]			beats spotted for fades
8	front wheel	-	-	SENSOR LAYERS (label = green)
9	rear wheel	-	None	first three faded up in time with music
10	keyhole	-	None	wiggled scale, opacity for all sensor layers
11	R headlight	-	None	Add mode used in precomp; collapsing passes thru
12	UR grill	-	None	
13	R fender flare	-	None	
14	UL grill	-	None	
15	LL/C grill	-	None	
16	L bumper insert	-	None	
17	LR grill	-	None	
18	L windshield	-	None	
19	grill center	-	None	
20	[PC_Axiom.mov]	Soft Light	None	instant sex trick (blur + Soft Light)
	Levels — Reset			
	Fast Blur — Reset			
	Opacity — 50 %			
21	[PC_Axiom.mov]	Normal	None	
	Levels — Reset			

A set of Expression Controls were created to give master adjustments over the speed, scale, and opacity of the wiggle expressions applied to the sensor layers.

We used a "wiggle" expression applied to Scale, and tied it to a set of Expression Controls in layer 7 to give us a master adjustment for speed and amount. For the scale, we chose a value of ±15%, which when multiplied by the 60% scale in the sensor precomp resulted in a final scale range of 51% to 69%. The layers are collapsed, maintaining maximum quality.

We also used a wiggle expression to vary their Opacity ±50% from a starting point of 100%. Since a layer cannot become more opaque than 100%, this means each sensor was full-on roughly half the time, occasionally dipping as low as 50% for the remainder. For the speed parameter, we used 30 fps ÷ 12.25 fpb ≈ 2.44 wiggles per second. Each sensor icon animating also helps reinforce the impression that each is measuring an ever-changing value.

Grid Frame

To lend more structure to the frame, a graph paper-like grid element was added to the left side. This pattern was created using the effect Render>Grid using a spacing of 20 pixels. We nudged its Scale and Position values as needed to get it to line up with our other effects. To keep the same "phosphorescent" look as the sensor icons, its Opacity was reduced to 50%, and the Add blending mode was used.

We wanted to add more of a digital feel to this grid, so we added an adjustment layer that covered just the left portion of the frame, same as the grid layer. Effect>Stylize>Mosaic was employed to break the video into digitized boxes. The effect was made more subtle by using Hard Light blending mode. Set mosaic adjustment's mode back to Normal to get a better idea of what the raw mosaic looks like.

Random Numbers

Next was creating a set of 12 randomized numbers and data readouts to go with the 12 sensors. To save time, and to make it easier to adjust a group of numbers as a block, we set up a row of six of them in the precomp [**numbers_generator**].

Option+double-click (Alt+double-click) on one of these layers in [**Tracker_final**] to open this comp, and feel free to explore how we set it up. For the most part, we used variations on Effect>Text>Numbers, although we also used a Text layer with its Source Text keyframed to create a simple on/off sequence at the bottom. For the sake of this tutorial, we set the font to Courier Bold in hopes you would also have it installed on your system; feel free to try out other fonts if you don't – we used ITC's Conduit on the real job. Comp window guides were used to help align the different numbers.

Once we dragged this comp into our final, we realized the numbers were too big: To get 12 of them onscreen, they would extend outside the frame's safe areas. We scaled them vertically by about 75% so there would be one number for every 1.5 grid cells, and horizontally until we were happy with how they filled the available space. We used two

Grid lines were used in the Comp window to help us align the different types of numbers. The Proportional Spacing option was set in the Number effect to help hold their positions.

The Advanced tab in Composition settings (above) has an option that preserves the frame rate of the comp, even when it is nested in a comp with a different frame rate.

The final frame (right). We had to scale the numbers along the left skinnier than they are tall to get them inside the Action Safe area.

copies of this precomp, and offset one in time so different numbers would appear for each copy of the precomp at the same point in the timeline. Again they were set to 90% Opacity with the Add blending mode so that they would interact better with the image behind.

The Numbers effect defaults to updating every frame, which is often too fast. The trick to force an effect to proceed at a different frame rate is to nest it in a comp with the desired rate. In our case, we placed it in the precomp [**numbers_generator**] and set its frame rate to 12fps. Then in that comp's settings, look under its Advanced tab, and enable its option "Preserve frame rate when nested or in render queue." Now After Effects will obey this precomp's frame rate even when it's nested in another composition or rendered at a different frame rate.

Sex in Advertising

The last touch we added is our "instant sex" trick to make video look more like oversaturated, slightly overexposed film. To do this, we duplicated the footage layer **PC_Axiom.mov**, and set the copy on top to use Soft Light blending mode to increase the apparent saturation. This copy was then blurred by roughly 10 pixels to create the puffy, blown-out look, with its Opacity reduced until we achieved the desired effect.

End of the Track

We normally think of using After Effects' Motion Tracker for tasks in which part of the original scene has to be replaced. This usually requires a lot of preplanning, and the result can take many hours to get right. The shot provided here was not ideal for getting perfect tracks, but it was good enough to coordinate some fun graphical elements. With a few hours' work and a little imagination, we were able to deliver the client a scene with higher production value than the simple text overlays originally requested.

Connect

For more information on topics covered in this tutorial, check out the following volumes of *Creating Motion Graphics*:

Volume 1:

Nesting Compositions

Collapse Transformations

Blending Modes

Adjustment Layers

Levels, Stroke, Mosaic, and Numbers effects, plus "instant sex" trick

Textacy: Animating Source Text

Preserving a comp's frame rate

Volume 2:

Removing and rendering with 3:2 Pulldown

Managing 16–235 luminance range footage

Motion Tracking

Non-square pixels

Expressions

3D Mechanic

Recombining the layers of a multipass 3D render in After Effects to create a more realistic composite.

The best 3D scenes are rarely finished "in camera" in a 3D application; they are massaged further in compositing programs such as After Effects. Performing this layering in After Effects is faster and more powerful than attempting it inside your 3D program.

You may already be familiar with the techniques of rendering separate diffuse, specular, and reflection passes to later mix inside After Effects, or adding some "grunge" to your surfaces to make them more realistic. In this tutorial, master 3D modeler Alex Lindsay of dvGarage takes these concepts to the next level, focusing on details you might not have

OVERVIEW

Main Concepts:

These are the features and concepts we will be focusing on in this project:

- Multipass rendering from a 3D program
- Combining the diffuse, specular, and reflective properties of a surface
- Alpha edge issues
- Blending modes
- Track mattes
- Faking light wrap and edge feather
- Comp snapshots
- Adjustment layers
- Conforming frame rates
- Nesting comps
- Displacement Map & Compound Blur effects (Pro) *(optional)*
- CC Vector Blur *(optional)*

Requirements:

After Effects 6.5 or later Standard edition; Professional edition recommended.

If you do not have the Professional edition, make sure you install the Cycore FX set of plug-ins which comes bundled with After Effects 6.5.

Getting Started:

Inside the **Tutorials** master folder on the accompanying DVD, locate and copy the folder **05_Mechanic** to your hard drive.

In the folder **Final Movie** inside this folder, double-click on and play **Mechanic.mov**.

Inside the **Project** folder you'll find the finished After Effects project file **Mechanic.aep**. This is your starting point; we suggest you save under a new name after each major section.

Credits:

The artwork for this project was created by Alex Lindsay of dvGarage (www.dvgarage.com).

ever considered, but which contribute to making a photorealistic image. Not every 3D job you have will require this much planning and thought, but it's good to at least be aware that these issues exist.

The structure of this tutorial is a bit different from others in this book. Because the final image is essentially a still and involves a lot of layers, we've already imported all the layers for you, and arranged them in their respective compositions. You will perform the mixing of these layers, using a combination of track mattes, blending modes, and simple effects such as blurs. A final version of this work is included in the project file for browsing or comparison when you're done.

A comparison between a simplistic 3D render (left) and one that uses a variety of techniques to create a more realistic scene in After Effects (right). Photograph and model courtesy of Alex Lindsay of dvGarage (www.dvgarage.com).

The Tasks

This is what you will be doing in the various parts of this tutorial:

PART 1: Build up the surface for the spaceship in its own composition, using track mattes, blending modes, and blurring to combine separate diffuse, reflective, specular, grunge, and occlusion render passes.

PART 2: Finish two additional precomps that will serve as luminance mattes for faking edge feather and light wrap effects.

PART 3: Composite the spaceship over its background; create a more realistic shadow and the lighting effects mentioned above.

PART 4: *Optional for Professional edition users:* Use a particle system render to create exhaust heat effects.

Attention To Detail!

Before you get started, play the two **AttentionToDetail** QuickTime movies in the **AttentionToDetail Movies** folder inside your After Effects project; these review important information on the subject of multipass rendering and layering. These movies are part of dvGarage's *Attention to Detail* series, and they provide an excellent overview of the techniques employed in this tutorial – especially from the 3D preparation and rendering side of the equation. Additional tutorials may be found on the web site: www.dvgarage.com.

Part 1: Perfecting Imperfections

The general concept is that the ship was constructed with a metal that has a dull surface, and was then plated with chrome. However, time and use has worn some of the chrome plating away. Therefore, there are two different surface properties you will be balancing against each other:

Mech_diff_hard The diffuse (underlying) surface, lit by an overhead light to simulate the sun.

Mech_diff_dome The diffuse surface lit by a form of global illumination such as a dome light, simulating light from the sky.

Mech_grng_base The model with a "grunge" map placed in the luminance channel, representing the aging of the surface.

Mech_background The image you will composite the ship in front of; also used as a reflection map.

Mech_refl_blur The result of using a blurred version of the background as a reflection map, representing the diffuse surface's reflections.

Mech_refl_shrp A sharp version of the background reflected, representing the chrome surface's reflection of its surroundings.

Mech_occlusion A ray-traced occlusion map for the model. This will be discussed in more detail later.

Mech_spec_soft Softer, broader specular highlights for the underlying surface of the object.

Mech_spec_hard Harder, tighter specular highlights for the chromed surface of the object.

- The diffuse character of the underlying model. Light is scattered or absorbed by this surface.

- The harder specular character of the chrome surface. Light is reflected back to the eye by this surface.

You will be building up the ship from the underlying dull surface to the chrome plating, with reflections and specular highlights on top. As a result, we have rendered eight different passes of this ship (as shown on the opposite page).

STEP 1: In the Project window, twirl open the **Sources** folder. Double-click the files to open them in their Footage windows, if you want to get a better idea of what they look like. You might notice that many are set to have their Alpha channel ignored (see figure), and have rough-looking edges as a result of rendering with a Straight alpha channel but viewing just the RGB channels. You will be using modes to blend multiple copies of these files on top of each other, which can lead to artifacts in antialiased edges. Therefore, one copy with its alpha intact will be used as a stencil over the final stack to clean up the edges. You should still render these layers from your 3D program with a Straight alpha; otherwise, their edges will be premultiplied, and also will not add up correctly. (Straight alpha channels are also covered in *The Planets* tutorial.) When you're done, close any open files.

The Diffuse Surface

STEP 2: In the Project window, double-click on the comp [**1_Ship Composite**]. It should have only the bottom layer (#14) turned on: **Mech_diff_hard.tif**. This represents the sun reflecting off the duller underlying metal surface of the ship.

STEP 3: Turn on the eyeball (the Video switch) for layer 13, **Mech_diff_dome.tif**. This layer represents the broader illumination from the sky hitting the underlying metal surface.

Since this ship has seen some wear, this surface should not look clean. Above it in the layer stack is a copy of our grunge-mapped ship, **Mech_grng_base.tif**. Turn on its eyeball; this is where the aging is going to come from.

1 Many of the layers have had their alpha channels turned off. Their edges will be recut with a Stencil layer later, to make sure they are clean.

Navigation Aids

These are a few general concepts that will aid your navigation of this project:

- We've used the Labels feature in After Effects to color-code all the layers and comps to help you keep track of them.

- The layer property you'll be editing most often is Opacity. The shortcut to reveal it is to select the layer, and press T. We're going to assume you remember this rather than drive you crazy by repeating it throughout.

- You will be toggling the Video switch for many layers to make them visible. We sometimes refer to this switch as the "eyeball" as that's what its icon looks like.

- Finally, many of the layers have both effects and blending modes applied. For this reason, we opened both the Switches and Modes columns at the same time in the Timeline window. If you don't see both, context+click (Control-click on the Mac, right-click on Windows) on any other column in the Timeline window and enable both Switches and Modes. If you don't have a wide enough screen to easily see both, open one and use the shortcut key F4 to toggle back and forth between these two columns.

3 Use the grunge map of the ship as a luma matte for the dome light pass (right). This will reduce the sky's illumination where the ship has been beat up (above).

Grunge

The grunge map used in this tutorial – plus numerous others – is from dvGarage's Surface Toolkit CD-ROM. Grunge maps are essential tools for aging surfaces in 2D or 3D.

Make sure the Modes column is visible, and set the track matte (TrkMat) popup for layer 13, **Mech_diff_dome.tif**, to Luma Matte; the Video switch for layer 12 (the matte) should turn off automatically. This will have the effect of reflecting the sky's illumination only where the ship has not been dinged and nicked. The underlying diffuse image is still visible; toggle layer 14 on and off if you want to check.

STEP 4: Turn on the Video switch for layer 11: **Mech_refl_blur.tif**. This blurred copy of the reflection map represents how the underlying surface is colored by the rest of its environment, not just the sun and sky.

This blurred reflection pass will also be matted by a copy of the grunge pass, already sitting above it in the layer stack. We want these colors to appear in the opposite places that the dome light illumination occurred. Therefore, set layer 11's track matte option to Luma Inverted Matte. Some of the pits created in Step 3 will now have reflected bits of color in them.

Reflections add illumination to a surface. To simulate this effect, set **Mech_refl_blur.tif**'s Mode to Screen. The result is too bright: You just want some subtle highlights at this point, since this is not the main chrome reflection. Reveal this layer's Opacity (select it and hit T), and reduce its value to somewhere around 32%.

4 Use the grunge pass as an inverted matte to reveal blurred reflections in some of the pits (above). Reflections add illumination to a surface, so use Screen mode, and reduce the layer's Opacity to blend it in subtly (right).

The Reflective Surface

STEP 5: Time to turn your attention to the chrome surface of the ship. Turn on layer 9: **Mech_refl_shrp.tif.** Reflections in a hard surface like chrome are much sharper than in a dull surface, so an unblurred map was used for this pass.

5 For the chrome, a sharp version of the reflection map is matted with the grunge layer (upper left), then set to Screen mode and reduced in opacity (upper right).

By now you should be seeing a pattern: A copy of **Mech_grng_base.tif** is sitting above **Mech_refl_shrp.tif** in the layer stack, just waiting to weather it. Set the track matte for layer 9 to Luma. This will add pits to the chrome.

As noted in Step 4, reflections add their coloration to a surface. Set layer 9 to Screen mode. Reveal its Opacity property, and turn it down to blend in these reflections better; somewhere around 63% is good.

STEP 6: A common trick to enhance the richness of 3D images is to duplicate them and apply an "intensifier" blending mode such as Overlay, Hard Light, or Soft Light to the copy on top. This adds saturation and contrast, yielding a warmer version of an object or its environment than mathematically correct renders will.

Turn on layer 7, which is a copy of **Mech_refl_shrp.tif.** Since this copy should occupy only the same areas of the model as the underlying version, yet another copy of **Mech_grng_base.tif** is sitting above it. Set the track matte for layer 7 to Luma, and experiment with these differ-ent intensifier modes. Reveal this layer's Opacity, and reduce it to tone down the effect. We chose Hard Light mode, and an Opacity of 35%.

6 A copy of the mottled hard reflection pass is applied using an intensifier mode such as Hard Light. This helps warm up the image, adding saturation and contrast.

Occlusion

STEP 7: At this point, the ship still looks like a toy dipped in chrome that has been batted around a bit. Phong-rendered reflection maps are a great, quick-and-dirty way to reflect an environment onto a model without enduring the long render times that raytracing often incurs. However, they have a bad habit of appearing in the creases where the model should be dark. Therefore, we're going to use a bit of raytracing to give us a layer that indicates where those creases are, so we can make them dark like they should be.

Turn on layer 5: **Mech_occlusion.tif.** This special pass indicates whether a section of the ship is reflecting the environment or just another portion of itself, such as spaces in the creases.

Traces of the Occult

If your 3D software does not have an occlusion option, here's how you can fake it:

• Set the surface of your model to black, but 100% reflective.

• Apply a white reflection map.

• Render with raytracing, but set the renderer to calculate only one ray bounce – this is all you need to determine if a pixel is reflecting the model or the environment.

The result should be an image that is white for most of the model, and black inside these creases we're trying to obscure.

7 An occlusion pass (upper left) can be thought of as revealing where an object shadows itself inside its various folds. Apply this using Multiply mode with Opacity to taste (above) to darken these folds (upper right).

Set **Mech_occlusion.tif**'s mode to Multiply: This will darken the underlying image where the occlusion pass is dark. The result is a bit extreme; reveal this layer's Opacity, and dial back to taste. We chose 45%.

Specular Highlights

The final touches include adding specular highlights: "hotspots" where the light sources are reflected strongly back to the eye. As has been the case for the other surface properties of the ship, the underlying surface and the chrome surface will get different specular treatments.

STEP 8: Turn on layer 4: **Mech_spec_soft.tif**. This is a render pass of just the specular highlights, with a relatively wide, soft falloff. This corresponds to the highlights from the duller, underlying metal surface of the ship.

As is the case with most of our other surface properties, a copy of the grunge pass – **Mech_grng_base.tif** – has already been positioned above the soft specular layer, ready to be used as a track matte.

Since this softer specular pass is supposed to appear only where the chrome has been pitted or worn away, you will want to use the inverse of this pass. Set the track matte popup for **Mech_spec_soft.tif** to Luma Inverted.

Specular highlights further brighten the surface of an object, just as reflections do. Therefore, set the blending mode for **Mech_spec_soft.tif** to Screen. You can leave its Opacity at 100%; its effect is already pretty subtle.

8 A relatively soft, broad specular highlight pass (upper left) is used for the underlying surface of the ship. The grunge pass is used as an inverted luma matte, so these highlights appear only where the chrome has been worn away (upper right).

Step 9: The chrome surfaces of the ship get a harder, tighter specular highlight. Turn on layer 2, **Mech_spec_hard.tif**, and note how this differs in the intensity of the hotspot from **Mech_spec_soft.tif** (toggle the Solo switches for these layers to compare, turning all Solo switches off when you're done).

Set **Mech_spec_hard.tif**'s blending mode to Screen, as you did above. We chose not to use the grunge pass to matte this layer, because this harder specular highlight is already pretty tight and does not spill over into some of the areas illuminated by the softer specular highlight in Step 8.

Highlights are often perceived as "blooming" – often the result of film or video being overexposed by the bright hotspot of the specular highlight. Select **Mech_spec_hard.tif**, and apply Effect>Blur & Sharpen>**Gaussian Blur**. Experiment with small amounts of blur to soften the bright highlight. We settled on a value of 2.0; you can use a touch more if you want a softer look.

9 A tighter, hotter specular highlight pass (upper left) represents the light hitting the chrome surface. It is also applied in Screen mode, and blurred slightly (upper right) to give the impression of slightly over-exposed film or video.

Step 10: You might have noticed that the edges of the ship look ragged or aliased. All of the render passes you have been layering together so far have had their alpha channels ignored, to avoid potential problems with blending modes incorrectly adding multiple antialiased edges. Time to clean them up.

Double-click layer 1 – a copy of **Mech_diff_hard.tif** – to open it in its Layer window. Click on the Show only Alpha channel switch along the bottom of this window (it's the white tab). Note how the edges look clean; this is a copy of the diffuse pass with its alpha channel turned on and interpreted correctly.

Close this Layer window. Set layer 1's blending mode popup to Stencil Alpha. This tells After Effects you wish to use the alpha of this layer as a cookie cutter, and to trim the alpha channels of all the layers underneath with this layer's alpha. To have the stencil take effect, turn on this layer's eyeball, keeping an eye on what happens in the Comp window – the edges of the ship should clean up nicely.

10 The alpha channel of **Mech_diff_hard.tif** layer will be used as a Stencil Alpha to clean up the edges for the underlying layers in this comp.

*This completes the surface of the spaceship. Save your project under a new name before you continue. If you are concerned you missed a step, compare your composition with our prebuilt [1_Ship Composite-FINAL] in the Project window's 3D Mechanic * prebuilt folder.*

10 *complete:* The rest of the layers in this comp have had their alpha channels ignored, displaying an aliased edge (left); using this top layer in Stencil Alpha mode cleans them up (right).

Building the surface of the ship was over half the work you'll be doing in this tutorial. But before you move on to compositing the ship over its background, you need to prepare some precomps that will be used in this final composite.

Edge Feather Fake

An important technique for compositing an object over a new background is to feather the edges of the foreground object, causing that object to "melt" into the scene. This simulates the way light naturally bends around the edges of real objects. Effect>Blur & Sharpen> Channel Blur has an option to blur just the alpha, but it spreads the alpha to be larger than the layer was originally. You want the edge feather to just cut into the alpha – not enlarge it. Here's a workaround:

11 A copy of the ship render, with alpha channel intact, is filled with white. This is the start of creating a luma matte for the feathered edges.

STEP 11: In the Project window, open the comp [**2_Edge Feather matte**]. It contains two copies of the version of **Mech_diff_hard.tif** where we kept the alpha channel – same as you used in Step 10.

Select the second copy (layer 2), and apply Effect>Render>**Fill**. This replaces the normal color channels with the color of your choice, while keeping the layer's alpha channel. An Effect Controls window should have opened when you added this effect; change the Color parameter from its default red to pure white.

STEP 12: Turn on the Video switch for layer 1. It contains another copy of **Mech_diff_hard.tif** with its alpha channel intact. You will use this copy to cut a hole out of the underlying layer, resulting in just a feathered edge around the outline of the ship.

Make sure the Modes column is open in the Timeline window. Set the blending mode popup for layer 1 to Silhouette Alpha. This inverts the alpha channel for the top layer, making it transparent where the ship would be and opaque beyond it, and uses the result to cut out the alpha for the layer below. At this point, the only piece of the underlying ship layer you can see is a faint line where the antialiased alpha channels of the two layers combine (zoom in if you need to take a closer look).

12 To use the first copy of **Mech_diff_hard.tif** to punch a hole out of the second copy below, set the layer on top to Silhouette Alpha (above). The result is a thin white outline where their antialiased edges are trying to cancel each other out (left).

Step 13: This thin white outline is the beginning of the feathered edge you will need later – but it needs to be wider. Select layer 1, and apply Effect>Blur & Sharpen>**Gaussian Blur**. (You can use Fast Blur if you are working on a slower machine; just make sure the layer is set to Best Quality so Fast Blur will render more cleanly.) In its Effect Controls window, increase the Blurriness parameter until you start to see a small, soft white rim in the Comp window, outlining where the ship should be. While you're scrubbing this value (or any parameter in After Effects), press Command (Control) to scrub in fine increments. We used a value of 6.

> When you're editing the Gaussian Blur effect, if you see jagged edges while you're dragging its Blurriness slider, you have Fast Previews turned on. Click on the Fast Previews button along the bottom right edge of the Comp window and set it to Off. You will see slower but full-resolution previews rather than faster low-resolution previews as you scrub the Blurriness slider.

Note how this rim has a hard edge around the outside, and feathers off only toward the inside. (If you see the opposite, you probably applied the blur to layer 2, not layer 1.) This result will be used later as a luminance matte to fake the feathered edge effect we're after.

Step 14: In the Project window, double-click the [3_Light Wrap matte] comp to open it. The Comp window should look very similar to your result for [2_Edge Feather matte], with just a wider edge. The only difference is that the Gaussian Blur applied to the top layer has been set to a Blurriness of 10. (Since it is otherwise identical, we saw no point in making you go through the same steps again.)

In addition to feathering the edges of the ship, we want to give the impression that light being bounced from the ship's new surroundings is wrapping around or "contaminating" the surface of the ship. You will use this wider feathered edge as a track matte for this effect.

Save your project. If you need to, compare your results for [2_Edge Feather matte] with its corresponding final version in the Project window's **3D Mechanic * prebuilt** *folder.*

13 Blurring the top layer results in a feathered edge that is cropped by the alpha of the layer underneath. This will be used later as a luminance matte.

14 The comp [3_Light Wrap matte] is virtually identical to [2_Edge Feather matte], with just a wider blur to create a larger area to contaminate the edges of the ship with faux reflected light from its new background.

Composite Wizard

If you regularly need to composite 3D objects over new backgrounds, or work frequently with bluescreen or greenscreen images, check out the Composite Wizard effects set distributed by Red Giant Software (www.redgiantsoftware.com). It includes powerful plug-ins for edge blur, edge feather, and light wrap which are easier to use than the workarounds discussed here.

Part 3: Blending In

To blend the spaceship into its new environment, you will need one more special render pass in addition to the precomps you built in the previous two sections. We'll also cover some tricks using blurs and blending modes to further erase the line between models and perceived reality.

Shadow

STEP 15: From the Project window, open the comp [**Main Comp**]. Although it contains nine layers, only one is turned on right now: the new background, which was also used for the ship's reflection map.

Double-click layer 6 – **Mech_shad_base.tif** – to open it in its Layer window. This is a special render pass that shows just where the shadow from the ship would fall on the imaginary ground in 3D. Close this Layer window after you've become familiar with the render.

15 To create a more realistic shadow, render a special pass from your 3D program that shows just where the ship's shadow would fall.

STEP 16: You may be tempted to fill the shadow layer with the color black and use it as is. In reality, shadows are seldom simple pools of darkness – instead, they appear as shadings of the surface they fall on. To simulate this, we've placed **Mech_shad_base.tif** above a copy of the background layer so we can use the shadow pass as a track matte for a treated version of this background.

Turn on the Video switch for layer 7: a duplicate of **Mech_background.jpg**. To help keep all of our copies of the background image straight, click on the name for this layer to select it, hit Return, type in a more descriptive name such as **"BG for shadow"** and hit Return to accept it. Then set its track matte popup to Alpha Matte (Luma Matte would work as well, since our shadow pass was rendered as white against black). Nothing will appear in the Comp window yet, since at this point you just have an exact copy of the background.

16 Use the shadow pass as a track matte for a copy of the background.

With layer 7 selected, choose Effect>Adjust>**Levels**. This is what you will use to change the contrast of the shadow. In the Effect Controls window, drag the gray arrow under the center of the Histogram display to the right to decrease the Gamma value. This will shift more of the image toward levels below 50% gray. Watch the Comp window: You will see the shadow appear.

This may be the only adjustment you need to make to create a realistic shadow. However, if there were any bright white areas inside the shadow's area, adjusting the Gamma may not make them dark enough. If this is the case, lower the Output White value to pull them down.

These are "to taste" parameters; when you're deciding how dark to make your shadow, take into account how strong the light sources would be. Because the scene is evenly lit by an overcast sky, we used a Gamma of 0.8 and Output White to 174 to create a relatively subtle shadow.

Edge Feather

STEP 17: Turn on the Video switch for layer 5, which is the precomp [**1_Ship Composite**] you built in Part 1. Since it uses the same image for its reflection map as is used for the background, it already matches fairly well. But look closely at its edges: They're a bit sharply defined, which is usually a giveaway that an object has been composited over a new background. In reality, the light being reflected by the background should wrap around and soften those edges. Click on the Take a Snapshot icon along the bottom of the Comp window or press Shift+F5 to store a reference copy of the current image.

In Part 2, you built a precomp – [**2_Edge Feather**] – to use as a matte to blend the background into the edges of the ship. Note that we've already nested this precomp as layer 3, and have positioned another copy of the background as layer 4 underneath it.

Select layer 4, hit Return to rename it, type in a more descriptive name such as **"BG for edge feather"** and hit Return to accept it. Turn on the Video switch for this layer, and set this layer's track matte popup to Luma Matte. You should notice a subtle lightening and feathering of the ship's edges, as a portion of the background is matted over them. To compare, press F5 or toggle the Show last Snapshot button along the bottom of the Comp window.

You can decide how strong this effect is by revealing the Opacity property for **BG for edge feather** and reducing it; try 50%. Press Shift+F6 to take a second snapshot of this intermediate result.

16 *complete:* The Levels effect (top) is used to darken a copy of the background copy to create a subtle shadow (above).

17 After turning on the ship, take a snapshot of the Comp window to compare the effect of adding an edge feather treatment.

17 *complete:* Before (below left) and after (below) adding the edge feather effect.

18 A matte with a broader feather is used for the light wrap effect. Blending modes alter the color of the ship based on the background. But study the feet of the ship: We're seeing too literal a copy of the background cutting through them…

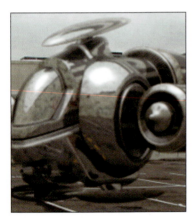

19 Blurring the light wrap effect gives a softer, more diffuse look (above). Your Timeline (below) should now have two sets of edge treatments active on top of the main ship.

Light Wrap

In addition to feathering the edge of the foreground object, another common compositing trick is to give the appearance that reflections from the background are wrapping around or "contaminating" the edge color of an object. This trick is especially useful if the background layer includes a light source that would be naturally illuminating the foreground object, but we can use it in this purely reflective example as well.

STEP 18: Check out layers 1 and 2 in the Timeline window: One is the precomp [3_Light Wrap matte] you inspected in the previous section, and the other is yet another copy of our background plate. Select the name of the latter (layer 2), hit Return, give it a more meaningful title such as **"BG for light wrap"** and hit Return again. Turn on its eyeball, and set its track matte popup to Luma Matte just as you did for the edge feather pair earlier.

The Comp window will show a fuzzier version of your edge feather application in the previous step. But rather than feather the edges, you want to change the color of them – so start experimenting with different blending modes for **BG for light wrap**. If the background had a light source, you might use Add or Screen to further illuminate the ship. In this case, where you want color and contrast instead of light, try out Overlay, Soft Light, and Hard Light to see which coloration you prefer. Press F6 to call up the snapshot of the feather-only version from the last step to compare the effects.

Remember that you can always tweak the Opacity of this light wrap layer, or change the width of the wrap by changing the Blurriness parameter for the first layer back in [3_Light Wrap matte]. In the end, we chose Hard Light, with 100% Opacity. Press Shift+F7 to store a snapshot of this result.

STEP 19: This lighting effect is supposed to be suggestive, rather than a literal reflection of the background. Select **BG for light wrap** and apply Effect>Blur & Sharpen>**Gaussian Blur**. Increase its Blurriness to around 10 or until the effect softens; press F7 to compare your results with your previous preblur snapshot. A good area of the ship to focus on is along the top, where the left wall cuts behind the ship; the white parking stripes that cut through the feet of the ship are another area to watch.

Press Shift+F8 to store a copy of your final light wrap result. If you like, browse through your snapshots saved under F5, F6, F7, and F8 to review your progress at blending the ship into its new scene.

	#	Layer Name	Mode	T	TrkMat		
▷	1	[3_Light Wrap matte]	Normal				
▽	2	BG for light wrap	Hard Light		Luma		
		▷ Gaussian Blur			Reset		
▷	3	[2_Edge Feather matte]	Normal		None		
▽	4	BG for Edge feather	Normal		Luma		
		▷ Opacity			50 %		
▷	5	[1_Ship Composite]	Normal		None		
▷	6	[Mech_shad_base.tif]	Normal		None		
▷	7	BG for shadow	Normal		Alpha		

1_Ship Composite 2_Edge Feather matte 3_Light Wrap matte Main Comp
0:00:00:00 (29.97 fps)

If in a hurry on a particular job, you can combine the edge feather and light wrap treatments in one pass. For example, turn off **BG for light wrap**, set **BG for edge feather** to Screen mode to provide the illumination, and reduce its Opacity to 30%. The result is not as nuanced, but still helps blend the spaceship into its background.

Through the Mist

There's one more trick we'll employ to finish off this composite. If reality is full of imperfections, our attempts to re-create it are even more imperfect. If you were to visit the set of a film production or television show, you might be surprised how rough many of the set pieces and props appear (including some of the human talent). Directors of photography use various tricks to slightly soften the image they shoot in an attempt to smooth over these imperfections. One technique is to apply a spray called ProMist to the camera lens. Here's a way to re-create the digital equivalent of this technique:

STEP 20: The easiest way to add an effect to an entire comp is to add a full-frame Adjustment Layer on top. Any effects applied to this special layer will be applied to a composite of all layers underneath.

With [**Main Comp**] forward and the time marker at 00:00, select Layer>New>**Adjustment Layer**. Notice the half-moon icon in this layer's switches: That's what identifies it as an Adjustment Layer. Select Layer>Solid Settings, rename it **"softening adjustment layer"**, and click OK.

STEP 21: With **softening adjustment layer** still selected, apply Effect>Blur>**Gaussian Blur**. If you have not applied any other effects since Step 19, you can also use the keyboard shortcut Command+Option+Shift+E (Control+Alt+Shift+E) to apply the last effect used. Increase the Blurriness parameter until you see the image go slightly soft; about 2 pixels should do it.

Then set the blending mode for **softening adjustment layer** to Lighten. This means the blur will have an effect only where the blurred pixels are lighter than the pixel underneath, resulting in a slightly puffy look. The result is a subtle softening of the creases in the spaceship, lightening of the graffiti on the rear wall, and brighter white lines on the ground; press F8 to compare it with the snapshot you took at the end of Step 19.

Some compositors use more blur, or a brighter blending mode such as Screen; however, you've done enough work with the edge feather and light wrap layers that you can get by with this light-handed treatment. If you find the result too soft or blurry, reveal the Opacity property for this layer, and scrub it until you have a look you like. We settled on an Opacity value of 40%.

Meet Doris

One nickname for this blur-it-when-you-shoot-it technique is Doris, supposedly named after techniques used to make a popular but aging actress appear perpetually young.

20 Enable the Adjustment Layer switch for the topmost layer.

21 An adjustment layer with a slight blur, applied with Lighten mode, performs the final blending for the scene.

Main Comp • Timeline

	#	Layer Name	Mode	T	TrkMat				

0:00:00:00 (29.97 fps)

▽	1	☐ [softening adjustment layer]	Lighten ▼						
		▷ Gaussian Blur			Reset				(matte for light wrap)
		▸ ⏱ Opacity			40 %				
▷	2	[3_Light Wrap matte]	Normal ▼	None ▼					(matte for light wrap)
▽	3	BG for light wrap	Hard Light ▼	Luma ▼					BG to colorize edges
		▷ Gaussian Blur			Reset				
▷	4	[2_Edge Feather matte]	Normal ▼	None ▼					(matte for edge feather cheat)
▽	5	BG for Edge feather	Normal ▼	Luma ▼					BG wraps around ship
		▸ ⏱ Opacity			50 %				
▷	6	[1_Ship Composite]	Normal ▼	None ▼					ship composite
▷	7	[Mech_shad_base.tif]	Normal ▼	None ▼					(shadow used as matte)
▷	8	BG for shadow	Normal ▼	Alpha ▼					copy of background
▷	9	[Mech_background.jpg]	Normal ▼	None ▼					background

21 *complete:* The Main Comp's Timeline window after all our blending tricks have been applied.

*Save your project. If you're using the Standard edition of After Effects, this completes your work, so compare your result with the prebuilt comp [****Main Comp_FINAL****] to see if you ended up with the same image. Close this comp and twirl up the* **3D Mechanic** * **prebuilt** *folder.*

Third-Party Heat

Several third-party plug-in vendors supply alternate Displacement Map and Compound Blur effects. SmoothKit Gaussian from RE:Vision Effects is the nicest compound blur we've found.

Part 4: Exhausting Measures

Pro This final section is optional, and requires the After Effects Professional edition for the two effects you will be applying: Displacement Map and Compound Blur. However, if you have installed Cycore FX (which comes bundled with After Effects 6.5), you can use its CC Vector Blur plug-in to create a displaced blur which results in a sufficiently similar feel.

This trick covers using a separate particle system render pass to fake the heat wave distortion that would be caused by the engine exhaust from the ship.

Exhaust Particles

STEP 22: In the Project window, open the **Sources** folder, select the **Mech_engine_exhaust.mov** footage, and type Command+F (Control+F) to open its Interpret Footage dialog. This short movie was rendered out of the 3D program at 30 frames per second (fps). However, NTSC video rate is 29.97 fps – so its frame rate was set to conform to 29.97. Close this window when you're done, and twirl the **Sources** folder back closed.

Interpret Footage

Interpretation for "Mech_engine_exhaust.mov" — Δ 0:00:01:00

Alpha
- ○ Ignore   ☐ Invert Alpha
- ● Straight – Unmatted
- ○ Premultiplied – Matted With Color: ▮ ✎
- ⬭ Guess

Frame Rate
- ○ Use frame rate from file: (30.000 fps)
- ● Conform to frame rate: 29.97 Frames per Second

Fields and Pulldown
- Separate Fields: Off
  - ☐ Preserve Edges (Best Quality Only)
- Remove Pulldown: Off
- ⬭ Guess 3:2 Pulldown   ⬭ Guess 24Pa Pulldown

22 Many 3D scenes are rendered at 30 fps, even though the proper frame rate for NTSC video is 29.97 fps. You can enforce the correct frame rate in the Interpret Footage dialog.

Step 23: Still in the Project window, double-click on the comp [**4_Engine Exhaust**] to open it. Hit 0 on the numeric keypad to RAM Preview it.

This series of green and yellow dots was created with a very simple particle system in 3D. The model of the ship was used to create a hole in the alpha of the particles, leaving just dots. You will later use these colors to decide how much to displace the background image for the heat effect. It is important that this pass be rendered with an alpha channel, instead of over a black background; otherwise the Displacement Map effect will interpret the black background to mean it should displace pixels in a negative direction.

Step 24: These dots are too well defined to create a hazy heat effect. Therefore, you will need to blur them. Compound effects, such as Displacement Map and Compound Blur, require that any treatments applied to a layer that will be used as a map must be done in a precomp – otherwise, these attributes will be ignored. That's why we've dedicated a composition to just apply effects to these particles.

In this comp, select **Mech_engine_exhaust.mov**, and apply Effect> Blur & Sharpen>**Gaussian Blur** (or Fast Blur, if you want to save render time – this is the least image-critical blur you've applied in this project, so you can cut some corners). Adjust the Blurriness parameter until the dots become fuzzy and blend together, but not so much that they fade away. A value around 5 works well.

Step 25: You will be using this result as an image map layer for a pair of compound effects in the final composite. In the Project window, drag the icon for [**4_Engine Exhaust**] onto the icon for [**Main Comp**]. This will nest the exhaust comp into your primary comp. Open [**Main Comp**], turn off the eyeball for the new layer **4_Engine Exhaust**, and drag it to the bottom of the layer stack – we like to tuck our maps out of the way, to reduce the chances that we might turn them on by accident. If this layer does not already start at 00:00, select it and type Option+Home (Alt+Home).

Heat Wave

Step 26: Select layer 9 – the original copy of **Mech_background.jpg** that serves as the main backplate for the composite – and change its name to "**Background (with Displace)**". Then choose Effect>Distort>**Displacement Map**. (If you don't have the Professional edition of After Effects, but do have Cycore FX installed, jump to Step 26 Alt below.) In its Effect Controls window, set its Displacement Map Layer popup to layer 10, **4_Engine Exhaust**. You should now see some fairly obvious waves to the right of the ship's engines.

23 A simple particle system with green and yellow dots were rendered blasting from where the engines would be, with a hole cut in their alpha channel by the ship's body.

24 Blur the particle by about 5 pixels to create a blurred map to use in the final composition.

25 In the Project window, drag the icon for [**4_Engine Exhaust**] onto the icon for [**Main Comp**] to nest it.

26 The engine particle system creates some nice, animating heat waves behind the ship (left) when it's first applied with the default values of 5.0 pixels. We reduced the displacement amount to a more subtle 2.0 pixels (right). Note the settings for the popups – especially Displacement Map Layer – if you are having trouble getting this to work.

Displacement Map includes a pair of popups that give you a choice of which properties of the Displacement Map Layer to use when you're deciding how much to displace an image. Since the engine particles were green and yellow, choose Green for Horizontal Displacement, and Luminance for Vertical Displacement as it gives a smoother look.

Then adjust the Max Horizontal Displacement and Max Vertical Displacement parameters until you have obvious, but believable, heat waves behind the ship. RAM Preview to check how they animate: They will be a lot more obvious when they're moving than when you're viewing them as a still frame. We settled on values of 2.0 for both Max Horizontal and Max Vertical Displacement.

26 *Alt:* CC Vector Blur is also capable of creating heat wave distortion effects. The choice of Vector Type is important; the default setting blurs the entire image.

STEP 26 ALT: If you have CycoreFX installed, it has an effect to use in place of Displacement Map. Select layer 9, and apply Effect>Blur & Sharpen>**CC Vector Blur**. For its Vector Map popup, select **4_Engine Exhaust**.

Experiment with its Vector Type options. The first three – Natural, Constant Length, and Perpendicular – will introduce blur just where the engine particles are, and not the rest of the background image. Each gives a different look; we chose Constant Length. Then set its Blur length and Map Softness parameters to taste. We found that a Blur length of 4.0 and Map Softness of 0.0 worked well for us.

Alex Lindsay and dvGarage

Alex Lindsay has worked in computer graphics since the mid 1980s. He spent three years at LucasFilm subsidiaries JAK Films and Industrial Light and Magic working in roles from pre-visualization to creating shots for the movie *Star Wars: Episode I*. His credits also include *Titan AE* and the *ABC Hockey Night* opening title sequence.

Lindsay is co-founder of dvGarage (www.dvgarage.com) and the Pixel Corps (www.pixelcorps.com), which are dedicated to the development of the next generation of visual media artists. dvGarage products, such as its Surface Toolkit and 3D Toolkit, were used in the creation of this tutorial. Two examples of dvGarage's excellent online training are included in this project's folder on the CD.

Main Comp-FINAL • Timeline

	#	Layer Name	Mode		T	TrkMat															00f	00:15f	01:0	
▽ ▷	1	[softening adjustment layer]	Lighten	▾																	△ blur = 2 △ Lighten mode			
		▷ Gaussian Blur					Reset														ƒ			
		Ö Opacity					40 %																	
▷	2	[3_Light Wrap matte-FINAL]	Normal	▾		None	▾														△ (matte for light wrap)			
▽	3	BG for light wrap	Hard Light	▾		Luma	▾														△ blur = 10 pixe △ Hard Light			
		▷ Gaussian Blur					Reset														ƒ			
▷	4	[2_Edge Feather matte-FINAL]	Normal	▾		None	▾														△ (matte for edge feather ch			
▽	5	BG for edge feather	Normal	▾		Luma	▾														△ BG △ blurred by exhaust			
		▷ Compound Blur					Reset														ƒ			
		Ö Opacity					50 %																	
▷	6	[1_Ship Composite-FINAL]	Normal	▾		None	▾														△ ship composite			
▷	7	[Mech_shad_base.tif]	Normal	▾		None	▾														△ (shadow used as matte)			
▷	8	BG for shadow (darkened)	Normal	▾		Alpha	▾														△ copy of background			
▽	9	Background (with Displace)	Normal	▾		None	▾														△ background warped by exha			
		▷ Displacement Map					Reset														ƒ			
▷	10	[4_Engine Exhaust-FINAL]	Normal	▾		None	▾														△ pre-blurred exhaust			

The Final Fake

This final trick is very subtle, but is another example of the kind of attention to detail (to borrow a dvGarage phrase) that will make a viewer's eye less likely to pause and note that "something's not quite right…"

The Displacement Map effect has been applied to the main background plate. However, this is not the only place where we see a portion of the background image – it was also feathered over the edges of the ship back in Step 17. To create the most accurate image, you should displace or blur this edge where the exhaust is just leaving the ship.

Step 27: Select layer 5 – **BG for edge feather** – and apply Effect>Blur & Sharpen>**Compound Blur**. In its Effect Controls window, set the Blur Layer popup to use layer 10, **4_Engine Exhaust** precomp. The default Maximum Blur setting of 20 is a bit extreme; we chose a value of 4.

RAM Preview one more time and compare your result with [**Main Comp-FINAL**] *to verify you made the air move as you should.*

It's All in The Details

As Alex Lindsay of dvGarage notes, it is the subconcious detail that whispers to a viewer's brain whether or not it should believe what it is seeing on the screen. The overall goal is to create 3D composites and effects shots that are so convincing, that the brain can turn its attention back to the storyline and the message being conveyed.

It's true that you may have difficulty seeing the result of some of these tweaks at video resolution with this particular model, but it is good to get into the habit of thinking about such fine points. The day may come when you have to do a job like this at high-definition or at film resolution for a major motion picture.

27 The final Timeline window for [**Main Comp**]. Note the combination of track mattes, blending modes, Opacity settings, and effects.

Connect

For more information on topics covered in this tutorial, check out the following volumes of *Creating Motion Graphics*:

Volume 1:

Track Mattes

Blending Modes

Editing and animating effects

Adjustment Layers

Snapshots

Nesting Compositions

Importing footage and separating fields

Volume 2:

Compound effects, including Displacement Map

Piccadilly Circus

Employing lights, shadows, and blending modes to create a graphical look with 3D.

The client brief for the next two tutorials is to create graphics for a travel series that uses the London Underground (the subway, also known as the "tube") as a central theme. Each segment of the show focuses on the shops, sights, and tourist attractions around a particular tube stop, such as Piccadilly Circus.

There are two parts to the overall design, each of which will be covered in this and the following tutorial: The first is a centerpiece graphic that blurs the lines between flat, print-style art and dimensional 3D through lighting tricks; the second consists of additional graphical dressing based on sequences of words and moving elements. This tutorial is intended to be a gentle introduction to the concepts of using 3D space and lights. Working in 3D doesn't mean you have to

OVERVIEW

Main Concepts:

These are the features and concepts we will be focusing on in this project:

- Creating and animating solids
- Importing Illustrator files as Comps
- Using Null Objects for Expressions and Parents
- Setting up a master color with Expressions
- Parenting
- Creating 3D layers
- 3D Material Options
- Light Options
- Animating a Light
- Saving a Comp as a Proxy

Requirements:

After Effects 6.5 or later Standard edition.

Getting Started:

Inside the **Tutorials** master folder on the accompanying DVD, locate and copy the **06_PiccadillyCircus** folder to your hard drive.

In the folder **Final Movies** inside this main folder, double-click on and play the movies **PiccadillyCircus.mov** and **Underground.mov**. The first movie is what you will be creating in this tutorial; the second shows you how you will use it in the next tutorial.

Open the file **PiccadillyCircus.aep** inside the **Project** folder – this is your starting point; we suggest you save under a new name after each major section.

suddenly start flying around in space; you can use these features to subtly enhance what otherwise would be a flat, 2D design. We will also touch on using null objects, parenting, and expressions. These are all important features added in version 5 that we know many are not yet comfortable with.

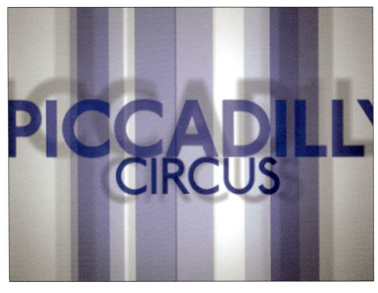

In this tutorial, you will create the comp [**Centerpiece**], which includes all the 3D elements such as the moving solids, the main title, plus the lighting tricks. In the next tutorial, you will add 2D layers such as the text animations along the top and the graphic element at the bottom.

A frame from the final Centerpiece animation. The movie you create in this tutorial will be used as a source in the next tutorial, *Underground Movement*.

While you could complete the entire tutorial in one comp, by splitting it in two you can prerender the 3D comp and use a Post-Render Action to assign it as a Comp Proxy: A very useful time-saving feature. Using a comp proxy will significantly speed up creating and rendering the final comp in the next tutorial.

The Tasks

This is what you will be doing in the various parts of this tutorial (since this tutorial is quite lengthly, feel free to take breaks between sections):

PART 1: Create and animate a set of solids to create the interweaving panels for the background, and assign them a master color through the use of a Null Object and Expressions.

PART 2: Add a light to the scene, adjust shadow properties of the light and solids, add a background to catch the shadows, and adjust the Z depth of each object to increase the shadow interplay.

PART 3: Import the layered Illustrator file with the title elements, parent them to a Null Object, add Expressions to them so that they follow the master color, and edit their Material Options to alter how they react to the light.

PART 4: Animate the title pieces.

PART 5: Animate the master color.

PART 6: Animate the light.

PART 7: Render, and create a composition proxy for the next tutorial, *Underground Movement*.

Sources Diversion

Newly imported sources are automatically placed in whatever folder is currently selected in the Project window, or the folder where a currently selected item resides. To stay organized, select the **My_Sources** folder in the Project window before you import a new source – that way you'll always know where it went!

Part 1: Building a Better Background

The main idea behind the centerpiece you will be creating in this tutorial is animating a series of overlapping, semitransparent solids to create a shifting background for the main title. The trick here will be using 3D space, lighting, and shadows in slightly less than obvious ways to achieve a rich mix of what are otherwise simple elements.

In the process, you will get a good introduction to animating lights and setting the surface attributes for 3D layers in After Effects.

We've created **My_Comps** and **My_Sources** folders for you to put your own work into: They will help keep it separate from the prebuilt versions. When you select the appropriate folder before importing a file or creating a composition, After Effects will automatically add your new elements into that folder for you.

Animating the First Solid

STEP 1: In the Project window, select the **My_Comps** folder. Create a New Composition, 320×240 pixels in size, square pixels, a duration of 03:01, 29.97 frames per second (fps), and name it "**MyCenterpiece**". Notice that the comp will be created inside the **My_Comps** folder, which will help you stay organized.

STEP 2: Your final animation will be over white, so change the Composition>Background Color to white. Setting the background color in this way will allow you to see your initial pieces in context, without having to build a background layer first.

STEP 3: The animated stripes that go behind the title will be created using a total of six solids: three moving left to right, and three moving right to left. Each will be slightly different from the other in width and opacity.

Create the first solid by selecting Layer>New>Solid or use the shortcut: Command+Y on Mac (Control+Y on Windows). Make it 50 pixels wide by 320 pixels high, and name it "**Left to right/50**" (try to give everything a name that will make it easy to remember what it does). You would normally set the color for a solid in this dialog, so for now, go ahead and select a nice blue, and click OK.

You may have noted that we instructed you to make this solid taller than the composition. This is

1 Start by building a new comp, 320×240, 3:01 long, at 29.97 fps (frames per second).

3 Give solids a helpful name: The first solid will move left to right when animated, and is 50 pixels wide – hence the name **Left to right/50**.

a bit of planning ahead: When you start to arrange objects in 3D space, quite often you will move some of them farther away from the virtual camera. This results in objects that previously filled the frame appearing smaller after the move. By starting out with solids taller than you may need, you reduce the chance they may be too small later.

STEP 4: Animate this solid from left to right by setting Position keyframes so that it moves from somewhere around the center of the comp at time 00:00 to the right side of the comp by 03:00. For beginners, here are the steps:

• To reveal Position in the Timeline window, select the layer and hit P: This reveals its animation stopwatch.

• Turn on the stopwatch for Position at time 00:00 to set the first keyframe, and make sure the solid is roughly in the center.

Go Home!

If you drag in a layer, or create a new solid, light, or null object, and it doesn't begin at 00:00 as you'd like, press Option+Home (Alt+Home) to move the selected layer(s) to start at the beginning of the comp.

• Hit the End key to move to time 03:00, and drag the solid to the right side of the comp. Hold down Shift after you start dragging to move the solid in a straight line. Press Home to get back to time 00:00.

If you're curious, we personally chose the positions X = 184, Y = 120 at time 00:00 and X = 285, Y = 120 at time 03:00 – but the result is supposed to look somewhat random, so don't sweat the details quite yet.

*If you'd like to check that you're on track so far, this first solid and its animation are saved in a prebuilt comp, [**Centerpiece_after Step 04**], which can be found inside the **Piccadilly * prebuilt>_compare comps _after Step ## folder**. And remember to save your project as you go…*

4 The first of six solids have been added and animated. The horizontal line in the Comp window (which is the same color as the layer's label and bar in the Timeline window) shows the animation path. Hold down Shift after you start dragging to move the solid in a straight line, or scrub the Position X value in the Timeline.

A Null Swatch; A Master Color

There is an old saying: Measure twice, cut once. The same applies to building animations. Quite often it pays to sit back and think about what you are going to be doing, and if anything repetitive jumps out, to consider if there is a way to save some work before you actually do it.

In the case of this design, you will have six solids with the same color. Since clients are known to change their minds about details such as color, it would be nice if there was a way to change that color only once. Same goes if you decide to animate that color: Wouldn't it be great to animate only one set of color keyframes, instead of six?

Expressions are perfect for just these applications. In its simplest form, an expression is a way to have one parameter follow another. That way, you can change just one parameter, and have others slave along behind it.

Expressions can be applied to any parameter you can keyframe in the Timeline window. Note that the color of a solid is *not* a parameter that fits this description. However, there are several keyframeable effects that give you control over a layer's color; a good one for this job is the Fill effect.

Now that you know how you're going to make a solid's color your slave, the next question is: Who should be the master? You can designate one of the six solids to be the master and the rest slaves; we personally find it easier to keep track of an animation if the master is separate from one of the objects being animated. For this, we like to employ Null Objects.

A *null object* is essentially a small (100×100) solid that has an Opacity of 0%, so it does not render – even though you can still see its outline in the Comp window if its Video switch (the "eyeball") is turned on. Nulls are great tools for parenting chains (and we will exploit this feature later in this tutorial), but they also make great masters for expressions.

Now that you've had a chance to think, instead of creating and animating five more solids first and figuring out how to coordinate their colors later, let's build a master color object and slave the color of our first solid to it. It will then be easy to duplicate this solid – with the color expression already in place – and save time creating the next five.

STEP 5: Select Layer>New>Null Object to create our master null. Make sure it starts at time 00:00 in your timeline – if necessary, select it and press Option+Home (Alt+Home).

Null objects are 100×100 pixel solids set to 0% Opacity (so they don't actually render) with their Anchor Point defaulted to coordinates X = 0, Y = 0. Normally used in parenting chains, they also make great masters for expressions. Although a null doesn't render, it does have a width/height value, which affects how it appears in the Comp window. Open Layer> Solid Settings and you can set the size of the null's display box.

5 Adding a Null Object to a composition is no more difficult than adding a Solid or an Adjustment Layer.

- While it's still selected, press Command+Shift+Y (Control+Shift+Y) and enter a new name, such as "**null/master color**".

- Since we don't need to see the null in the Comp window, go ahead and turn off its Video switch to hide its distracting outline.

STEP 6: Apply Effect>Expression Controls>**Color Control** to your new **null/master color** layer. In the Effect Controls, click on the Color swatch and change its default red to a tasteful blue (we used HSB 220, 73, 87; the corresponding RGB values are 60, 113, 221).

This Color property will be the master color that the six solids will follow. You need to see this parameter to assign an expression to it. Therefore, select **null/master color**, press E to reveal the effect in the Timeline window, then twirl down the effect to reveal its color swatch.

Expressing Color

STEP 7: Apply Effect>Render>**Fill** to the **Left to right/50** solid layer. Ignore its current red color; it will be overridden by the expression you are about to create. Press E for Effects and twirl down the Fill effect in the timeline.

This is saved as prebuilt comp, [**Centerpiece_after Step 07**]. *You can refer to it if you need to compare your progress so far.*

STEP 8: In the Timeline window, Option+click (Alt+click) on the *stopwatch* for the Color parameter in the Fill effect that was applied to the **Left to right/50** solid layer (see the stopwatch circled in the figure above). This adds a = symbol directly after the stopwatch and reveals the expression field. After Effects automatically fills the expression field with a default script, which we'll override by creating a new expression in our next step.

There are a number of ways to add an expression to a property. You can also select the Color parameter in the timeline and choose Animation>Add Expression, or use the shortcut, Command+Option+= (Mac) or Control+Alt+= (Windows).

6 Apply the Angle Control effect to the **null/master color** layer, and change the Color from red to blue.

Sneaky Swatch

To reveal just the Color swatch in the Timeline, turn on its keyframing stopwatch in the Effect Controls window, press U to reveal keyframed properties in the Timeline, and turn keyframing back off by toggling the swatch's stopwatch again.

7–8 The master null has a Color Expression Control applied; the first solid you created has a Fill effect. To add an Expression to the solid Fill's Color property, Option+click (Alt+click) on the stopwatch for Color.

Express Yourself

Expressions are bits of software code, based on the JavaScript language, that create a value for whatever parameter you assign them to. These values are recalculated every keyframe, and are "live" – as you change another parameter the expression is looking at, the expression will automatically update the parameter it controls. If you aren't a programmer, don't worry: After Effects makes creating simple (but exceedingly useful) expressions very easy. If you *are* a programmer, you can really go to town!

9 To create a simple expression, activate Expressions for the target parameter, and in the Timeline window drag its pick whip to the parameter that will be its master (left). After you release the mouse and press Enter, After Effects writes a corresponding Expression for you automatically (below).

STEP 9: Click on the Expression's pick whip (the center button that looks like a spiral symbol) and drag it to the word "Color" on the **null/master color** layer. This is a lot easier to do than to explain, so refer to the figure above. Release the mouse button, and press Enter (not Return) to activate the new expression.

After you press Enter, you will see that After Effects has written an expression for you. Without going into the depths of writing JavaScript, you can still read this expression and make sense of what is going on. A hint is to use the periods to find breaks in the phrasing. For example, what the expression

thisComp.layer("null/master color").effect("Color Control")("Color")

is really saying, is that for the value of the Fill effect's Color, to look in this comp, for a layer named **null/master color**, which has an effect named Color Control, and to use its parameter named Color.

To test that the expression is working, click on the Color swatch for the **null/master color** layer, and change the color to something quite different from blue. The color of the solid should also change, as its Fill Effect follows along. Be sure to Undo to return to that nice blue color…

If you got lost along the way, check out our prebuilt comp, **[Centerpiece_after Step 09]**.

Three-up Solids

At this point you need to build up this centerpiece comp by duplicating the first animated solid layer and creating variations. Being that we're venturing into The Land of Repetitive Work here, if you're short on time you can be forgiven if you just read these steps, then use our prebuilt comp **[Centerpiece_after Step 12]** to continue with Part 2.

On the other hand, if you feel that Practice Is Good, then follow through with Steps 10 through 12 – though we'll leave some of the animation decisions up to you:

STEP 10: Select the layer **Left to right/50** and duplicate it by selecting Edit>Duplicate. Press U to reveal the animated parameters for this duplicate. You'll notice that the expression was duplicated as well. Edit this copy as follows:

• Type Command+Shift+Y (Control+Shift+Y) to rename and resize the solid. We varied the width of each solid to be between 30 and 60 pixels wide. Rename the solid by changing the number at the end of its name to reflect the width you've chosen. For instance, if you change the width to 40 pixels, rename your duplicate solid "**Left to right/40**". Click OK.

• Edit the Position keyframes for the duplicate layer so that the solid starts somewhere left of center at 00:00, and ends up right of center at 03:00. Make sure the solids don't overlap at these keyframes; you're going for variety, and you want to cover a good deal of the comp with your solids rather than leave large white spaces.

• Repeat the Duplicating step again, set a different width and name for the third solid, and animate it so it starts on the far left at 00:00 and ends up left of center at 03:00.

• RAM Preview and check that the solids don't overlap and that they all have slightly different speeds (otherwise they will look like a group of three solids moving in tandem).

STEP 11: Set the Opacity property of each solid so they have a different value, somewhere between 25% and 60% (see figure below). This partial transparency will come in to play later as we overlap solids traveling in the other direction.

Save your project before moving onto the next step.

10–11 By duplicating the first solid, you can easily create two more; just edit their Position keyframes to vary their animation. Don't forget to also vary their widths and give each a different Opacity value. Here you see the third solid selected at time 00:00 (above) and at 03:00 (below).

12 By now you should have six solids of varying widths and opacity, animating to cross over each other. To make the stripes appear a little darker when they overlap, change their blending mode from Normal (top) to Multiply (above).

Six-up Solids

STEP 12: You should now have three solids animating from left to right with different opacities. To create the next three, continue to duplicate one that's already built, but this time edit each so that:

• You have three solids that animate from *right to left*, spacing them apart in more or less a mirror image as you did the first three solids.

• Again, vary the width of the three new solids between 30 and 60 pixels wide, and rename the solids appropriately – i.e., "**Right to left/50**".

• Choose new Opacity values for each solid between 25% and 60%.

• Tweak all six solids so that you have a pleasing animated group, and RAM Preview to check that you end up with a group of solids with differing speeds, widths, and opacities.

• Simple opacity is often the least visually interesting way to blend together multiple objects. Get in the habit of trying different blending modes in search of more interesting looks. In this case, select all six solids and change the blending mode for any one of them from Normal to Multiply; this will change all their modes at once. Multiply will make them appear even darker when they cross over each other.

You can change the blending mode for a layer in a number of ways. The easiest is to reveal the Modes column, then select a mode from the Modes popup. To open the Modes column, click on the bottom of the Switches/Modes column to toggle to Modes, or press F4 to toggle back and forth. To see the Switches and Modes columns side by side, context-click on any column heading and select Modes from the Columns popup. Rearrange the columns by dragging the headers. Hide any column by selecting Hide This from the Columns popup when you context-click a column heading.

12 *complete:* Your Timeline window will now include seven layers: the master null for controlling the color, and six solids with animating Position, as well as expressions applied to their Fill Color. Note that we've opened the Modes column as well.

Save your project and twirl up all layers in the Timeline window.
If that all seemed a bit tedious, then you're probably glad we've
prebuilt those last few steps for you! If you want to use our version,
open the comp [**Centerpiece_after Step 12**] *and rename it*
"MyCenterpiece12" in Composition>Composition Settings.
In the Project window, drag this comp to the **My_Comps** *folder*
and continue with Part 2.

Part 2: Let There Be Light

After the previous step, you will have six solids animating: three from
left to right, and three from right to left, all with different opacities and
widths. They've all been set to Multiply mode, and the colors of
all six solids are controlled by the **null/master color** layer. But
let's be honest…it looks pretty flat, with not enough subtlety to
really create interest. Let's liven things up by adding a light
source so that shadows are falling all around.

Light Setup

STEP 13: In order for lights and shadows to work properly, you
have to set up a number of items:

• Start by adding a Light. The procedure is simple: Click on the
Layer menu or context-click in the Timeline window, and select
New>Light. Use these Light settings (see figure): Light Type of
Spot, Intensity 100, Cone Angle 90, and Cone Feather 50. Make
sure Casts Shadows is checked on and set the Shadow Darkness
to 100% and Shadow Diffusion to 10. The Light Settings dialog
also gives a tip at the bottom that's well worth noting as we'll see
later: "Shadows are only cast from layers with 'Casts Shadows' enabled
to layers with 'Accepts Shadows' enabled." Click OK, and make sure
the layer has been set to start at time 00:00: Otherwise, the light will
not switch on until it reaches its in point.

• Depending on whether you have added a light since you started
up the program, and how you set an option, After Effects may warn
you that some of your layers need to be in 3D for lights to have any
effect. And it's right – so switch the six solids from being 2D layers

13 To add a light to a comp, select
Layer>New>Light. Be sure you enable
Casts Shadows, and heed the warning
at the bottom of the dialog to set up
the shadow options for your 3D layers.
Once you've edited these settings,
they'll be used the next time you
make a new light.

13 *continued:* To interact with
cameras and lights, layers must be
set to 3D mode – a simple switch
in the Timeline window.

13 *complete:* The Material Options for a 3D layer decide how it interacts with Lights. Set Casts Shadows to On for all six solids in your project.

14 Once you've added a comp-sized white solid as a background layer and switched it to 3D mode, you can see the effect of the light on the entire comp.

13 *continued:* After you add a Light and switch the solids to 3D, you will notice their shading changes, as the cone of the spotlight falls off toward the edges of the comp.

(the default) to 3D layers. All this requires is toggling their 3D Layer switch to be On in the Timeline window. You can drag down a row of multiple switches to set them all in one swipe of the mouse.

Immediately, you will notice a difference in the way the layers are shaded in the Comp window. This is the result of how the light is interacting with them. But we still don't have our shadows…

• Select all six solids, and type "AA" (two As in quick succession) to twirl down their Material options. These options are available only for 3D layers. You'll notice that all the solids have Casts Shadows set to Off; this is the default. With all the solids still selected, click on any one of the words "Off" next to Casts Shadows, and all six layers will toggle to Casts Shadows = On. You can also use the shortcut for Toggle Casts Shadows: Option+Shift+C (Alt+Shift+C).

Hmm. Still not looking anything like our finished movie? That's because while the shadows are being cast, there's nothing to catch them. You're going to tackle this issue next, by placing another solid behind them in space. Twirl up all layers before moving on.

Cones and Feathers

If you look closely at the results so far, you might notice that the light has created some shading on the blue stripes, but not on the white background. Lights affect only 3D layers – not 2D layers or a comp's background color. To have the light affect the entire visible area of the comp, you'll need to create another solid to use as a backdrop. Once that's in place, it will be easier to adjust the light's characteristics to get the look you want.

STEP 14: Create another solid as you have above, but this time click on the Make Comp Size option, and change its Color to white. Name it "**white background**" and click OK. Drag this white solid to the bottom of the layers stack, and turn on its 3D Layer switch. Now you should notice the light's falloff shading the background as well. If nothing else, a spotlight is a nice way to add a vignette look to a comp.

If you are new to setting up lights and materials, compare your comp with [**Centerpiece_after Step 14**]. *As always, you can duplicate our comp and just continue from there.*

STEP 15: Nice effect, but the corners are probably quite dark if you used our initial settings. If you want the light to illuminate more of the comp, you can either change the light's position, or in the case of a spotlight, the size of its light cone and the way it falls off. Let's experiment with the latter approach:

• Select the light in the Timeline window and type AA (two As in quick succession) to reveal its Options.

• To see what Cone Feather does, scrub its value in the Timeline. Compare the result of values between 0% and 100%. Lights take a little while to render; be patient and pause on different settings to see their results. Leave this value set to 0% where the light edge is very hard for now – this will make it easier to see the results of Cone Angle adjustments.

• Scrub the Cone Angle value, and compare values from 0° (light contracts to nothing) to 150° (at which point the comp should be covered with light). Since your goal is to have the light cover the entire comp, with a nice falloff around the edges, set the Angle to somewhere around 135°, where the outer reaches of the cone just extend beyond the comp's edge.

• Now go back and tweak the Cone Feather to get a nice falloff that focuses attention back toward the center of the comp. We personally liked 65%.

Save your project before the next step.

15 The Cone Feather parameter adjusts how softly the light falls off from its outer reaches to its center. A Feather value of 0% (left) compared with 100% (right).

15 *complete:* By setting a slightly larger Cone Angle of 135°, (above) the center of the comp is lit more evenly (below). The Feather value is set to 65%. You can also enter these values directly in the Light Settings by double-clicking the light layer.

3D View Shortcuts

The function keys F10–F12 can be used to quickly change the 3D View – for example, F12 defaults to the Active Camera. To choose your own views for these function keys, switch to a different view, and select View> Set 3D View Shortcut>Replace. For this tutorial, try changing the F11 shortcut to the Right view and F10 to the Top. You can then use the function keys to quickly switch your view.

16 The Comp window allows you to view the arrangement of your objects several different ways. In the Right view, the solids default to the center, with the light and virtual camera off to the left.

Shadow Depth and Darkness

Nice light falloff – but still no shadows. For shadows to be visible, you need to create some gaps in depth between the layers. These gaps from front to back create room for a shadow to be cast from one object onto another.

STEP 16: To get a true sense of depth, objects need to be different distances from the virtual camera. This means moving them to different positions along the Z axis, which defines closer/farther compared to X's left/right and Y's up/down.

By the way, where is this camera? When you create a comp, After Effects automatically creates a default camera. You can't see it in the Comp or Timeline windows, but it's there. In the event you're interested, it is based on a 35mm film camera with a 50mm lens and a field of view of 39.6°. It has automatically been positioned back in Z so that a layer the same size as the comp positioned at Z=0 perfectly fits what the camera sees; in the case of a 320×240 comp, this works out to a distance of Z value of −444.4. We hope you got all that, because there's a quiz later on... Although you can create a camera with custom settings, since you're not going to be animating or otherwise editing the camera's settings for this tutorial, you might as well use the comp's default camera and keep things simple.

When you switched these layers from 2D to 3D mode, their Positions automatically added a Z parameter with a default value of zero. Negative values of Z will move the solids closer to you and the virtual camera; positive Z values move them farther away. A slight complication in this plan is that you already set up pairs of position animation keyframes for most of these solids, so you will need to edit the Z value for both keyframes to keep the solids at the same relative distance from the camera as they animate from side to side.

The best way to approach creating these gaps is to change the Comp window's 3D View Popup (it's in the lower right corner of the Comp window – resize the window wider to see it) from Active Camera to Right. Once you're in the Right view, you'll see the side view of the solids in the center of the Comp window, and the icon representing the light on the left side. In this view, positive Z values are toward the right; negative Z values (closer to the light and virtual camera) are to the left.

• Select all the animating solid layers, including the **white background** layer (but not the **null/master color** layer), and press P to view their Position values.

• Deselect all the layers (F2), and in the Timeline window click on the word Position for the first solid (which is probably **Left to right/50**) – this will select *both* of its Position keyframes.

• Press Home to return to 00:00 (if you're not already there), then *use the right arrow key* to nudge the layer's Position value in Z. As the value for Z increases, the layer moves right in the Right view, and thus farther away from the light. Double-check that both Position keyframes remain selected, indicating that both keyframes are being changed.

> When you're editing the value for Position, you can't simply scrub the value or change the value – this will change the value of Position only *at the current time*. If the time marker is parked on a keyframe, this will change just that keyframe, leaving the other keyframe unchanged (and deselected). If the time marker is between keyframes, you'll add a new keyframe at that point in time and deselect the existing keyframes. Using the arrow keys to nudge the layers in the Right or Left view is an easy way to move both keyframes in Z at the same time. Just be sure the time marker is parked on an existing keyframe, as nudging between keyframes will add a new keyframe.

Assume for now that later on your title layers will be placed somewhere around 0 on the Z axis. Therefore, you'll need some separation between the colored stripes and the background so they will cast shadows on each other. You'll also need a little separation between the title and these solid layers if the title is to cast shadows on them as well. So edit the Z values for the first solid to 20. Press End to move to 03:00, and double-check that the Z value for the second Position keyframe is also set to 20.

• Continue with the other five solids down the layer stack, setting their Z values to, oh, say, 55, 35, 80, 95, and 125 respectively. (These values aren't science – the idea is just to have some separation between layers. As long as the Z values range between 20 and 125, the tutorial will work as expected.) Before nudging, be sure to click on Position to select *both* keyframes for each layer and make sure that the time marker is parked at either 00:00 or 03:00.

16 *continued:* 3D layers have an additional Z parameter for Position. Set the first solid to a Z position of 20. Make sure both Position keyframes get this Z value.

16 *continued:* All of the solids have been arrayed varying distances from the light so that shadows will now be visible as they fall from the forward layers to the ones behind.

16 *complete:* Moving an object farther away from the camera makes it appear smaller. This is a problem in the case of your white background, which was supposed to fill the frame.

Nudging Nuances

Remember that nudging increments are based on screen pixels. Set the Comp window to 200% magnification to nudge in half pixels, or 50% to nudge two pixels at a time. Hold down Shift as you nudge with the arrow keys to move layers 10 screen pixels at a time.

18 The background has been made larger, and the Shadow Darkness parameter backed off to a more subtle value of 25%.

- Set the white background solid to a Z distance around 140 so it is the farthest away from the light. This means it will catch the shadows for all of the animating solids in front of it.

Once the Z positions are set, press Home and End a couple of times and compare Position values – the Z values should be the same for the first and last keyframe for each solid. Only the X values, indicating left-to-right movement, should be changing, and the Y values should all remain at 120 (the center of the comp).

Select Active Camera again from the Comp window View popup; you'll notice that the shadows are finally starting to take shape. Move to different points in time to see how the solids and their shadows interact. There's just one small thing (isn't there always)…

Save your project. If you want to compare your progress, check out our prebuilt comp [**Centerpiece_after Step 16**].

STEP 17: Remember way back in Step 3, where we said it was a good idea to create 3D layers larger than you think you'll need them just in case you move them farther away from the camera? And remember we didn't do that in Step 14, when we created the background solid? That came back to bite us here. Now that you've moved the **white background** solid to 140 on the Z axis (away from you), the 320×240 solid is too small. (Look closely, and you'll notice one of the colored solids reaches just short of the top and bottom as well.) If you recall the final design we previewed at the start of this tutorial, this isn't so much of a problem vertically, since in the next tutorial you will mask it down to use just a center stripe for the final frame – but you still need the background solid to reach the left and right edges.

Select the **white background** layer, and open its Solid Settings using the keyboard shortcut Command+Shift+Y (Control+Shift+Y). When you eyeball the comp, you can guess that making this solid half again larger should more than do the trick; change its size to 480×360 pixels.

STEP 18: Shadows, by definition, create dark areas in the image. Twirl down the Light Options (or type AA) and scrub the value for Shadow Darkness. We think you'll agree that 100% darkness is a bit extreme; notice how lower values brighten up the image. Set it to about 25%. RAM Preview your comp, twirl up all layers, and Save your project.

Compare your comp with our prebuilt comp, [**Centerpiece_after Step 18**]*, if your result doesn't seem to match the illustrations. Feel free to use this comp instead if you got lost along the way; just rename it "***MyCenterpiece18***" and drag it to the* **My_Comps** *folder.*

Part 3: Title Treatments

You've used a combination of lights, shadows, and blending modes to create a nice animating background. Now it's time to put the main title on top, taking further advantage of some lighting tricks. If you've been opening the various prebuilt comparison comps as you go, it would be a good idea to clean up your screen at this point and close all of them except for your current [**MyCenterpiece**] comp.

Import and Center

STEP 19: The title for this episode of our travel series is "Piccadilly Circus." Select the **My_Sources** folder in the Project window and File>Import>File the Illustrator file **PC_Title.ai** residing inside the folder **06-PiccadillyCircus> Project>Sources**. Be sure to set the Import As popup near the bottom of this dialog to Composition, and click Import.

You will have both a folder and a comp called **PC_Title Comp 1**. Double-click the comp to open it. The title consists of two layers of black type against a black background color (so they won't be visible), and a guide layer (which you can ignore). Select the two type layers in the Timeline – **Piccadilly** and **Circus** – and Copy them.

• Bring your [**MyCenterpiece**] comp forward, Paste, and the two title layers will be pasted on top. Notice that these layers are a different size than this comp, as they were created at a size of 400×130 pixels in Illustrator. This size difference also caused them to come in off-center.

• You'll want to center the type in your composition as a starting point for performing your animation. With both layers still selected, press P and twirl down Position. Click on one of the values and enter X = 160, Y = 120 (the center of a 320×240 comp). Also make sure they start at 00:00.

To find the center of a non-standard-sized comp, you don't need a calculator. Context+click on the value for Position and select the Edit Value option to open the Position dialog. Set the Units popup to "% of composition," then type 50 in the X-axis field and 50 in the Y-axis field. Click OK, and the layers will appear exactly in the center of the comp.

To change multiple layers at once, click on the word Position in the Timeline window, then Shift+click to select all other Position properties – merely selecting multiple layers isn't enough. Even though all Position keyframes are now selected, only the values at the current time are changed when you context+click and select the Edit Values option.

For single layers, you can open the Position dialog by using the shortcut Command+Shift+P (Control+Shift+P).

19 Open the 400×130 sized [**PC_Title Comp 1**] (above) and Copy the two title layers. Bring the [**MyCenterpiece**] comp forward (below) and Paste. The titles paste in off-center because they retain their original Position values based on the 400×130 comp.

19 *continued:* To center the title, let After Effects do the math for you by using the "% of composition" option in the Position value dialog.

19 *complete:* The font used is Johnston's London Underground, from the foundry P22 (www.p22.com). It is based on Edward Johnston's original typeface design created for London Transport in 1916, which also became the model for the very popular sans-serif typeface Gill Sans.

20 Assign a new parent for the **Piccadilly** and **Circus** type layers. This will make scaling and positioning them easier, without losing the ability to animate them independently.

• Drag the title layers down the layer stack so they are above the six solid layers and below the **null/master color** layer; this is mainly to help us keep organized.

Control through Parenting and Expressions

STEP 20: The title's too big for the frame; you're going to need to scale it down and tweak its position. You'll also be animating both words in the title separately from each other. A convenient yet flexible way to coordinate these actions is to group the two words together using a null object as a parent. Each word can then animate individually, while being scaled and positioned by its parent.

• As you did in Step 5, create a new Layer>New> Null Object. Rename it to "**null/title parent**" – Command+Shift+Y (Control+Shift+Y) will open Solid Settings. Turn off the Video switch for this null, to hide its distracting outline box in the Comp window.

• Again, to help keep things organized, drag this new null object down the layer stack so it sits above the two title layers.

• If the Parent column is not visible in the Timeline, use the shortcut Shift+F4 to reveal it, or context+ click on another column and select Columns> Parent. Select both the **Piccadilly** and **Circus** layers, and set their parent to be **null/title parent**.

• Select the **null/title parent** layer. Press S to reveal its Scale property in the Timeline. Edit its Scale value to 90%, which will scale both title layers from their null's anchor point (its top left hand corner).

If you feel your parenting skills are shaky, compare your work with [**Centerpiece_after Step 20**].

STEP 21: The title is going to get the same color expression treatment you gave the background stripes in Steps 7 through 9:

• Apply Effect>Render>**Fill** effect to both title layers, leaving the settings at their defaults.

• Apply an expression to the Color parameter of these Fill effects so they also follow the Color swatch for the effect applied to the **null/master color** layer; refer back to Step 8 if you need a refresher.

• Select both title layers and change their blending mode to Multiply (again, just as you did with the solids in Step 12). If you don't want to open the Modes column, you can also select Multiply from Layer> Blending Modes, or by context+clicking on the layer bar and selecting Multiply from the Blending Modes in the popup menu.

Reacting to Light

The title appears to be a different color blue from the solids because they are still 2D layers. By switching them to 3D layers, they will then interact with the comp's light, resulting in a more interesting look. But you can go even further than that, manipulating the shadows cast by the title and how the title reacts to the light hitting it.

STEP 22: Turn on the 3D Layer switch for both title layers. They will now react to the light. If you toggled the Switches/Modes column to Modes to set their blending mode above, you'll need to toggle back (shortcut: F4) to see the 3D Layer switch.

With both title layers selected, press Option+Shift+C (Alt+Shift+C) to change Casts Shadows to On. If you want to verify that this worked, type AA to reveal the Material Options and the Casts Shadows setting.

21 Give the title the same treatment you gave the colored stripes: Apply the Fill effect, use the pick whip to create expressions that slave the title's color off of the **null/master color** layer, and set them to use Multiply blending mode so you get varying shades of blue as the title interacts with the background.

22 Toggling the 3D switch on for the title layers makes them interact with the light (left); change their Material Options to Casts Shadows (right).

Shadow Size

Whether the shadow is larger or smaller than the layers that cast it depends on how far away the light is from a layer compared with how far away the camera is. If the light is farther away than the camera, the shadows are smaller than the layer; if the light is closer, the shadows are larger.

STEP 23: The shadows for the title should now be visible. However, our starting point for the light chose a Shadow Diffusion value of 10, which creates very soft shadows in this case. Here's how to adjust it:

• Select the **Light 1** layer, type AA to reveal its Options, and change its Shadow Diffusion parameter to around 5. The shadows should now appear better defined.

The most visible portion of the shadow is being captured by the **white background** layer. Since the six blue stripes are transparent, the shadow is much less apparent on them. If you look closely, you can see broken-up echoes of the title's shadow on these stripes, which adds further visual interest – but the eye is definitely drawn to the main shadow on the background first.

To our eye, the shadow falling from the **Circus** layer is a bit large, to the point of distracting us from the first title layer **Piccadilly**. Closer spacings between layers results in shadows that are closer in size to the object casting them. To tighten the shadow just for the word Circus, you will need to move it closer to the background.

23 To make the shadows more defined, reduce their Shadow Diffusion setting (left). To make a shadow closer to the size of the layer casting it, move that layer closer to the layer catching it, as we did with **Circus** (right).

• Select the **Circus** layer and type P for Position. To achieve a better visual balance in the frame, select a Z value that places it somewhere between behind the **Piccadilly** layer. We happened to choose a value of 30, but please experiment for yourself. Note that as you place it farther back, it will start to move behind some of the blue stripes. Due to a combination of their transparency and the Multiply blending mode, this is not as obvious as you might expect, but don't push your luck. When in doubt, check it at several different points in time as the stripes move about.

STEP 24: To finish up the look of the title, you can experiment a bit with the Material Options for each word (shortcut: AA). The Material Options affect the way a layer reacts to the light hitting it. By choosing different settings, you can get different looks out of layers that otherwise share the same light, without having to apply effects.

- The Diffuse and Specular settings determine how a light glares off a surface. To give the **Piccadilly** layer more punch, try higher values for either one of these parameters. In the end, we cranked Diffuse up to 100 and decreased Specular to 25, but feel free to set these to taste.

> Note that higher Shininess values don't make an object shine more brightly; they tighten up the size of the glare.

- Rather than punch up the **Circus** layer as well, we want to make it recede more into the background. This can be done by reducing its Diffuse value, making it reflect less light back to the eye. We ended up with a value of 25 (see figure below of Timeline). Twirl up all layers and Save your project.

*We left some of those recent steps a little sketchy, since they repeated actions made earlier in this tutorial. If we lost you along the way, compare your result with our prebuilt comp [**Centerpiece_after Step 24**].*

24 The Material Options for a layer define how it is illuminated by lights. By manipulating these, you can increase the glare on the word Piccadilly to make it punch forward more, and reduce the illumination on Circus to make it darker, without changing either layer's color.

To make After Effects more responsive while working with 3D layers, you can turn on Draft 3D in the Timeline window (above). This will temporarily disable lights and shadows (below).

25 Piccadilly moves from right to left and is shown here at time 00:00 (below left) and 03:00 (below right). Title Safe guides (shortcut is ' – the apostrophe key) are turned on to help with placement.

Part 4: Animating the Title

Nice lighting – but the title just sits there. Now it's time for you to make it move. Working in 3D while lights and shadows are turned on can be very slow, so enable the Draft 3D switch for the next step to temporarily disable all lights and shadows. You temporarily won't have as rich a look, but scrubbing parameters and RAM Previewing your animation will be significantly faster in Draft 3D.

Why not select an OpenGL mode in Fast Previews? Although OpenGL acceleration can be a great boon when working in 3D, it currently renders shadows in a way that can be more distracting than helpful. Draft 3D temporarily disables lights altogether, while – like OpenGL – still including them in the final render (just turning the light off is asking for trouble...).

STEP 25: Select the **Piccadilly** layer and animate it from right to left:

• Return the time marker to 00:00 (shortcut: Home), select **Piccadilly**, and type P to reveal its Position property (if it's not already revealed). Remember to scrub just the X values; press Shift while scrubbing to move in larger increments or Command (Control) for finer increments.

• Move it along the X axis so the first character is well right of the left edge of the comp, and the last couple of characters are cut off by the right side of the comp. We liked somewhere around X = 60. Turn on the animation stopwatch to enable keyframing; this also sets the first keyframe to remember the current position.

• Press End to go to time 03:00 and move the **Piccadilly** layer left along the X axis until the last character nicely clears the right edge of the comp (see figures below). We settled on an X value of –36; this meant the Position property in the Timeline window read –36,0,0.

STEP 26: Now animate the **Circus** layer in the opposite direction:

• Reveal the Position property for **Circus**, and at time 00:00 move the layer left until its first character is just a bit to the right of the first character in the word Piccadilly. Its position should read something close to –20,0,30. Enable keyframing for the Position property.

• Move to time 03:00, and adjust the X value until the last character in Circus is just left of the last character in the word Piccadilly – somewhere around 55 should do. Don't just type in our values; scrub the values in the Timeline window to get a feel for the faster screen update in Draft 3D mode.

RAM Preview and check the animation to see if you like the move. If you get lost, compare your version to our prebuilt comp [**Centerpiece_after Step 26**].

STEP 27: You'll eventually be taking just a center horizontal slice of this animation to use in the next tutorial. But after playing around with the positions of the words in the title, you can't be sure they're still centered vertically in the comp. Let's check that, and reposition it as necessary. Stay in Draft 3D mode during this step to speed things up:

• Look closely at the Comp window to see if the title seems vertically centered to you. For confirmation, either press the ' (apostrophe) key to toggle on the Safe Areas overlay to get a center crosshair, or bring the Comp window forward and select View> Show Grid to overlay a virtual graph (its parameters are set in Preferences>Grids & Guides).

26 The Circus layer moves from left to right and is shown here at time 00:00 (left) and 03:00 (right).

27 Turn on the safe area overlays or the grid (pictured here) to verify that the title isn't quite centered horizontally.

27 *complete:* By adjusting the Y Position value for the **null/title parent** layer, both title layers can be easily moved up and down in the comp – without affecting their individual left and right animations.

Since you've already set up animation keyframes for the words in the title, it would be a minor pain to re-edit all of them just to recenter the title. This is where the null parent comes in:

• Select the layer **null/title parent**, twirl down Position, and edit its Y Position value by scrubbing its value. Go for a better vertical position, remembering that the smaller layer **Circus** will take up less "weight" in the overall visual balance. By editing the parent layer in this way, you can move the entire title without messing up the keyframes already assigned to the children. Set the Y Position to about 126 (the Position of the null should now read X = 160, Y = 126).

Note that the parent is a 2D layer, but the children are 3D layers. If you want to move the children as a group in Z, you would need to also turn on the 3D Layer switch for the parent null object. Since you are only moving layers in Y here, you can leave the parent in 2D.

The next steps involve tweaking the colors and animating the light, so turn off the Draft 3D switch so you can see the light's effect. Also turn off any guides or grids (View>Hide Grid) and Save your project.

Adjustment Layers versus Expressions

You may be wondering why we didn't use an Adjustment Layer to set or animate the color of the layers below, rather than drag you down the path of using Expressions. Part of it is we wanted to give you some practice using Expressions. But there are a few advantages to the master color swatch concept described in this tutorial compared with Adjustment Layers, which may not be immediately obvious:

• The obvious one first: Adjustment Layers affect all layers below, which might not be desirable if you want only certain layers to be effected. For instance, if you used an Adjustment Layer to change or animate the color of the bars, any background layers would change color as well.

• The master color swatch can be "expressed" to other layers in any comp, so you could control colors across multiple comps with just one swatch.

• A master color swatch (such as the Color Control effect in this tutorial) could be controlling a color swatch in any other effect, such as the stroke color in the Stroke effect, or one of the replacement colors in a Tint effect.

• Adjustment layers are always 2D layers, and perform as "render breaks" in a 3D animation stack. This means that if you use an adjustment layer to apply an effect to the 3D layers below, these layers are rendered as a "group," and the result is a 2D composite. You cannot then have other 3D layers above the Adjustment Layer casting shadows or otherwise interacting with those layers below.

Part 5: Animating the Master Color

The advantage of setting up a master color as you did earlier is that it's easy to animate all the slaved layers at once. Let's take advantage of that:

Step 28: Select the **null/master color** layer, and press F3 to open the Effect Controls window. With the time marker at 00:00, turn on the animation stopwatch for Color: This sets a keyframe for the original blue color at the start of the animation. Hit End to go to 03:00, and click on the color swatch to change the blue to a nice purple color.

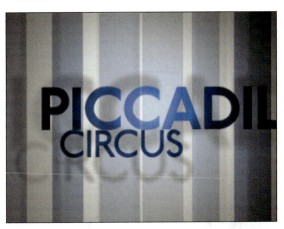

> When you animate colors, After Effects interpolates between those colors by traveling in a straight line between them on the HLS color wheel. If you travel across the wheel in a way that brings you near the center (by using complementary colors), your intermediate colors will be grayish. A workaround is to add additional keyframes in-between to guide it through more saturated colors.

Perform a RAM preview or test render. Note how all the colors change together, even though you had to set up only one pair of keyframes. Thus is the joy of using expressions to create master control layers! This will come in even handier if you have clients who are prone to change their minds about things like color. In our theoretical example of creating a series of graphics for a multipart travel show, you could also use this master to change colors for different segments.

Save your project and RAM Preview and check the animation to see if you like the move. If you got lost, compare your version with our prebuilt comp [**Centerpiece_after Step 28**].

Step 28 Optional: Just because a master color is controlling your layers doesn't mean you can't introduce some variation in those slaves. For instance, you could add Effect>Adjust>**Hue/Saturation** effect to the **Circus** title layer and change the Hue to +25. Now when you change the master color, the **Circus** layer will follow as before, but always with a Hue offset by 25°. You can also write more complex expressions to do these offsets for you, but quite often it might be quicker and easier to just use a familiar effect.

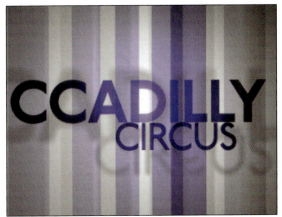

28 By using expressions to create a master swatch, the color of eight layers can be animated together using two keyframes. Here you see the color at the beginning, middle, and end.

Gak Pak Attack

When a design concept becomes popular, it is usually a matter of time until someone develops a plug-in to make it easier. In the case of animating bars, probably the best plug-in is Glider in the Gak Pak from Profound Effects (www.profoundeffects.com/products/gakpak/).

Glider creates a series of animating vertical and/or horizontal bars, with user control over their size, number, opacity, variation, motion, and blending. Glider can also create shapes at the intersections of horizontal and vertical lines for added interest. It does not feature the 3D shadows and lighting you see in this tutorial, but it is still very powerful, and saves you the tedium of keyframing.

The Gak Pak also contains plug-ins which create a series of other animating geometric and organic shapes. It is based on the effects engine in Useful Things (also from Profound Effects), which allows you to create your own plug-ins to create graphical elements. Free demo versions of both are available for download.

Part 6: Animating the Light

We've kept this tutorial fairly straightforward so far, with just a single light and the default camera. But you'll also notice a recurring theme of adding touches that create subtle visual interest. To further this aim we're going to animate the light, which will affect how shadows fall over time. This final effect is also much more "to taste" than some of the animation we led you through above, so we're going to discuss your options as much as tell you what to do.

29 Lights have two steering wheels: the Position of the light in space, and the Point of Interest where the light is aimed. Turn on both stopwatches to animate the light for this tutorial.

STEP 29: Be sure Draft 3D is off so you can see the effect of the light. At time 00:00, select the **Light** layer, press P, and then press Shift+A. This will reveal its Position and Point of Interest properties. Enable the animation stopwatch for both.

Unlike normal layers, lights and cameras have two "position" properties: one for where they are located in space, and a second Point of Interest for where they are aimed. It is true that you could achieve the same results with just one position property, then rotate the object to aim it where you want, but many find it easier to control cameras and lights with this two-position system. (Another technique is to attach a camera or light to a null object, then rotate the null – more on this in the *Postcards from Earth* tutorial.)

Your goal is to set the first keyframe with the light highlighting the left side of the comp. You can do this by re-aiming its Point of Interest or its Position. Note that the relationship between the two decides

29, *at time 00:00:*
By animating the light, the areas that are lit and the resulting shadows will play across the title. Switch between Top View, Right View, and Active Camera to set up the light in 3D space. We start off pointing the light to the left side.

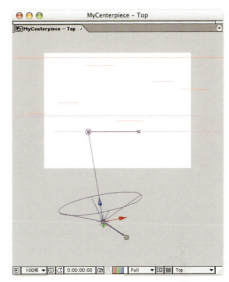

what direction the shadows will be cast. For example, if you moved the Point of Interest left and Position right, the shadows would be cast more to the left as the light raked across the title. If you were to move both the Point of Interest and Position of the light to the left, then the shadows directly under the light will be cast somewhat straight, while shadows farther away appear a bit more rakish.

(If you're new to moving a light, check out the *Moving Lights 101* sidebar on the next page for some tips.)

When you're happy with your look at the start of the comp – and verified that you remembered to enable keyframing – press End to move to 03:00, and move the Position and Point of Interest again so that the spotlight highlights the right side of the comp (in other words, so it scans across the word Piccadilly while it moves in the opposite direction).

The direction the light points as a result of the relationship between its Position and Point of Interest also affects whether the shadows are cast up or down the back wall you created with the layer **white background**. Moving the Position of the light closer to the title will also make the shadows grow in size, while moving it back will make them smaller. Feel free to experiment!

Save the project. To compare your results, open our prebuilt comp, [**Centerpiece**], *from the* **Piccadilly * prebuilt>Final Comp** *folder. If you prefer our version, feel free to use it for rendering in the next step.*

Multiple Views

When positioning elements in 3D, select View>New View to open a second comp window. Now you can set one window to Top or Left view and see the results in the Active Camera view.

29, *at time 03:00:*
The light has moved to point more to the right side of the comp, and also pulls farther away; this tightens the shadows closer to the title. Experiment until you find a move you like.

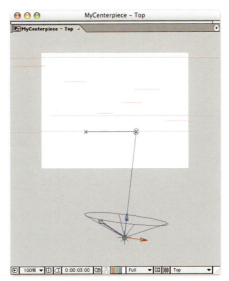

Moving Lights 101

There are a number of ways to move a light around in After Effects, which you should explore if you're new to using lights:

• Scrub the values in the Timeline window or enter values directly. Hold Shift down while scrubbing for larger increments; hold Command (Control) for finer increments.

• Drag the light directly in the Comp window while it's set to Active Camera view. If you avoid the three X/Y/Z axis arrows, you can move the light freely. If you drag one of the X, Y, or Z axis arrows (your mouse cursor will change to show you if you've

Hold down Command (Control) as you move on one axis to move the Position without moving the Point of Interest.

grabbed a particular axis), this will move both the light *and* the point of interest. However, you *can* move the light along a particular axis and *not* move the point of interest by holding down Command (Control) while you drag.

• If you make a mess, click Reset at the top of the Light's Transform section. This only resets the Transform values; it does not affect the light's options you've already set.

• Change the Comp window's view to Left or Top to get a better idea of how the light is pointing, and try moving the light or point of interest in those views. (Same rules apply regarding moving along the axes.) Return to Active Camera view to check your results.

The following tips for moving the light apply to moving any layer, but are particularly useful when you're moving layers in 3D when lights and shadows are slowing things down too much:

• Hold down Option (Alt) as you move the light to temporarily disable realtime updating in the Comp window.

• Set the Fast Previews popup (to the right of the 3D View popup along the bottom of the Comp window) to one of the OpenGL modes. Some of the light's properties (such as soft, subtle shadows) may not render, but you can still see the overall illumination, and the program will be much more responsive.

Part 7: Creating a Comp Proxy

This composition you've created will serve as a centerpiece inside a second composition for the finished design. You will build the rest of the project in the next tutorial. However, there's some final work you can do here that will make your life easier when you move on.

You may have noticed that your comp has been getting more sluggish as you add more layers, turn on shadows, and so on. This is because 3D in general and shadows in particular take longer to render than otherwise similar 2D compositions. You really don't want this render hit to be dragging you down as you try to work on other elements – especially since you've already finished this piece.

Therefore, it's a good idea to prerender this centerpiece comp so that the relatively slow 3D shadows don't try your patience later. In the next tutorial, rather than use your rendered movie directly, you will use this movie as a Comp Proxy, acting as a stand-in for the slower composition. That way, you can still go back and tweak this comp later if you feel the final design requires changes.

Proxies are footage items that act as stand-ins for other footage items or entire compositions. Most users employ them to temporarily link in draft or low-resolution versions of large footage items to speed up their work. However, they're a great tool when you are nesting a finished comp so that it becomes a source layer in another comp. You would render the first comp, link the render as a proxy for the comp, and now you don't have to wait for the first comp to render as you move around the second comp. Proxies are easy to turn off or remove, if you later decide to go back and edit the original comp. Applying and working with comp proxies is covered in the next tutorial, Underground Movement.

Step 30: With your fully tweaked-out **MyCenterpiece** comp open, select Composition>Make Movie. Save the movie to this tutorial's folder on your hard drive, and name it "**MyCenterpiece_proxy.mov**".

• In the Render Queue, use the "Best" Render Settings template or similar (Best Quality, Full Resolution, No Fields).

• In the Output Module, use the "Lossless" template (you don't want to degrade the quality of a Comp Proxy movie by compressing it, since you will be using it in the final render). Click on the word Lossless to open the Output Module settings, and set the Post-Render Action popup to Set Proxy, which will automatically assign the proxy.

30 Render your final **Centerpiece** comp and you can use it as a Comp Proxy in the next tutorial, *Underground Movement.*

• Save your project, and hit the Render button. Now go make a really nice cup of tea (you deserve it). If you like, play back your finished movie when the render is done so you can enjoy all the work you've put in throughout these pages.

To Be Continued…

Once you've given your brain and fingers a rest, move on to the next tutorial: *Underground Movement.* You'll finish off the title animation using tricks such as sequencing words created in Illustrator to create multiple layers of type, and turning a tileable graphic into a seamless "tickertape" that animates across the frame.

Connect

For more information on topics covered in this tutorial, check out the following volumes of *Creating Motion Graphics*:

Volume 1:

Parenting

3D Space, Cameras and Lights

Color effects

Volume 2:

Expressions

Advanced Rendering with Comp proxies

Underground Movement

Looping elements such as lists of text and seamless graphics to create a backdrop for a main title.

The client brief is to create graphics for a travel series that uses the London Underground as a central theme. Each segment of the show focuses on the shops and sights around a particular stop. In the prior tutorial, you created the title for the segment on Piccadilly Circus. In this tutorial, you will create the backplate which is common to all of the segments. This includes multiple appearances of a list of stops to be covered in this series, plus a graphical element based on an Underground route map. The title is then masked to appear in the middle of this backplate.

This project already has one composition in it, [**Centerpiece**]. You will create a new comp named [**MyFinal**] that will incorporate [**Centerpiece**] as a layer. We've also created folders in the Project window named **My_Comps** and **My_Sources** for you to put your own work into, to help keep it separate from the prebuilt versions.

OVERVIEW

Main Concepts:

These are the features and concepts we will be focusing on in this project:

- Using Comp Proxies
- Masking
- Importing Sequences
- Footage Frame Rates
- Looping in Time and Space
- Continuous Rasterization
- Timing to music
- The Offset effect

Requirements:

AE 6.5 or later Standard edition.

Getting Started:

Inside the Tutorials master folder on the accompanying DVD, locate and copy the folder **07_Underground** to your hard drive.

In the folder **Final Movie** inside this folder, double-click on and play **Underground.mov**. This is the overall piece you will be creating in this tutorial.

Inside the **Project** folder you'll find the finished After Effects project file. Open the project **Underground.aep** – this is your starting point; we suggest you save under a new name after each major section.

We suggest you complete the *Piccadilly Circus* tutorial in the prior chapter first – it creates the centerpiece that appears in this project. But don't worry; we have also included instructions for jumping straight into this tutorial.

Select the appropriate folder before importing a file or creating a composition, and After Effects will automatically place your new elements into that folder for you.

The Tasks

This is what you will be doing in the various parts of this tutorial:

PART 1: Apply a comp proxy to save time when RAM Previewing and rendering the final comp.

PART 2: Create a new composition, add and mask the main title animation, and import the soundtrack.

PART 3: Import a sequence of Illustrator files twice, modify their Footage settings to realize different frame rates, edit their appearance, continuously rasterize one layer and blur it, and time the keyframes of a scale animation to match the soundtrack.

PART 4: Use the Distort>Offset effect to tile a graphical element and animate it, render the final movie taking the comp proxy into account, and explore additional tweaks we made, including faking an "inside shadow" on the main title layer.

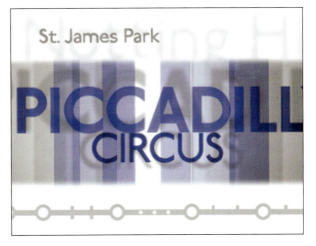

A frame from the final Underground animation. The "Piccadilly Circus" centerpiece was created in the prior tutorial using 3D lighting tricks. This tutorial creates the additional elements at the top and bottom of the frame.

Part 1: Voting by Proxy

The title animation, **Piccadilly Circus**, was executed in 3D, using a light and shadows. These features slow down the responsiveness of the comp considerably. To avoid the wait for it to render every time you jump to a new frame of the backplate animation, you can attach an already rendered movie of the title animation to this composition as a comp proxy. As a result, After Effects will just grab frames from this movie as needed, rather than render the contents of the composition.

STEP 1: If you worked through the *Piccadilly Circus* tutorial, you assigned your final render to automatically become a proxy for the composition you built. Here, we're going to assume you forgot to set the Post-Render Action popup in the Output Module (it happens…).

In the Project window, select the composition [**Centerpiece**]. Then select File>Set Proxy>File. When the Set Proxy File dialog appears, locate and select either the movie you rendered as the last step in the previous tutorial, or the file **PiccadillyCircus.mov** in the **Underground>Project>Proxies** folder inside this tutorial's folder. Click Open to assign the proxy.

1 The Set Proxy option is under the File menu (above); link to the proxy movie in the Proxies folder.

1 *continued:* When a proxy has been assigned to a composition, specifications for both appear at the top of the Project window. The black box to the left is the proxy on/off switch.

Once a comp proxy has been applied, you'll notice along the top of the Project window that the proxy's specifications appear to the right of the comp's own. A square will also appear to the left of the comp's name. When this square is filled, the proxy is in use. Clicking on this box turns off the proxy, but does not remove it.

When a proxy is enabled for a comp, its Comp window will be surrounded with a yellow outline. If you make changes to layers in the Timeline window, you will not see the Comp window update until you turn off the proxy – so be careful!

1 *complete:* When a proxy has been assigned to a composition, its Comp window will be outlined in yellow. Editing its layers will have no obvious effect until you disable the proxy.

Comp Proxy Tips

Comp proxies are great tools to speed up your work or your final render. If you have finished work on a composition that will be nested into another comp, prerender it, and set the Post-Render Action popup in the Output Module to Set Proxy. (This is not unlike how some other graphic workstations "process" layers.) You can always remove the proxy and edit the composition further if needed.

Here are some tips on how to best manage comp proxies:

• Render proxies to the highest quality possible, such as uncompressed. This will preserve maximum image quality, since you will potentially be re-compressing the proxy footage at the final render stage. If the comp you're rendering needs to have an alpha channel, be sure to render to a file format that supports alpha (such as QuickTime Animation, Millions of Colors+).

• Whether it's best to field render a proxy depends on your final output, and how the proxy is being used. If you are not field rendering the final movie, don't bother field rendering the proxy. If you *are* field rendering, and if the proxy will appear full-frame in the final image, then field render the proxy. When

you assign an interlaced comp proxy, separate the fields of the proxy (via File>Interpret Footage>Proxy) just as you would treat any other interlaced source footage. If you're field rendering the final, but the proxy will be animated further, you will achieve the highest quality by rendering the proxy without fields, at twice the frame rate (say, 59.94 fps). Now, one full frame will be rendered in the proxy for each field of output. (Do not separate fields for the proxy.)

• When you archive your finished project, you can throw away these proxies: They tend to be large uncompressed movies, and you still have the under-lying comp to edit or re-render if you need to open the project later. You can either remove the proxies from the After Effects project file before you archive, or after you re-open it and note they are missing.

• If you decide that a comp to which you have a proxy assigned needs additional changes, don't just turn off the proxy; if the prerendered comp proxy is no longer valid – *remove it*! Otherwise, you run the risk of using this now-outdated proxy when you perform your final render (the Proxy Use parameter in Render Settings is covered later in this chapter). To remove a proxy, select the comp in the Project window again, and use File>Set Proxy>None.

This is a good time to Save your project. If you're not sure you applied the comp proxy correctly, compare your version of [**Centerpiece**] *with our prebuilt comp* [**Centerpiece_after Step 01**]. *You'll find it in the* **Underground * prebuilt>_compare comps_after Step ##** *folder.*

Part 2: The Beginning of the End

Time to start building the final composition, which will contain your background elements. First you need to make a new composition, then add in the centerpiece title animation and the music.

Create the Final Comp

STEP 2: Select Window>Close All to close all windows and remove clutter. In the Project window, select the **My_Comps** folder. Create a Composition> New Composition, and set it to be 320×240 pixels, square pixel aspect ratio, 29.97 frames per second (fps), duration 03:01, and call it "**MyFinal**".

> You can save and delete presets from the popup list: To save custom settings, click on the floppy disk icon and name your new preset. To delete any preset, first select it, then click on the Trash icon.

Click OK to create the comp. If it's not already white, change the Composition>Background Color to white.

STEP 3: Select the [**Centerpiece**] comp in the Project window, and type Command+/ on Mac (Control+/ on Windows) to add it to the forward comp. This comp will now be nested as a single layer centered in [**MyFinal**]; because a comp proxy is assigned, it will preview and render very quickly. If it does not begin at the start of the timeline, select it and type Option+Home (Alt+Home) to force it to start at 00:00.

To see the comp proxy in action, turn off the proxy in the Project window (click on the black square next to its name), bring the Comp or Timeline window back forward, and hit 0 on the numeric keypad to initiate a RAM preview. The preview times should be relatively slow, since all the layers in the [**Centerpiece**] comp are rendering. Now turn the proxy back on (click the square icon again) and Preview again. Although the image may look identical, what's playing now is the preren-dered movie from disk which is *significantly* faster. Be sure to leave the proxy turned on!

2 When creating a new comp, you can save your settings as a preset by clicking on the floppy disk icon and entering a name for the new preset.

3 Add [**Centerpiece**] to the [**MyFinal**] comp to nest it as a layer.

4 Create a rectangular mask directly in the Comp window to reveal a center stripe with just the title.

4 *continued:* Make sure Toggle View Masks is enabled (circled above), and double-click the mask shape to bring up the Free Transform Points. Click and drag the points or mask outline to easily rotate or reshape the mask.

Masking the Title

Next comes masking down the main title graphic so that it only resides in the middle of the frame, leaving room above and below for extra graphical details:

STEP 4: Select the **Centerpiece** layer, then select the Rectangular Mask tool from the toolbar (shortcut: Q). In the Comp window, drag a mask shape around the Piccadilly Circus title area to reveal just a center stripe. To do so, start your dragging in the gray canvas area just outside the comp's active image; a good place is the upper left corner, making sure you start above where the shadowed "Piccadilly" appears. When you're done, switch back to the Selection tool (shortcut: V).

The Toggle View Masks switch in the lower left corner of the Comp window must be on to edit the mask in this window. Fortunately, the act of drawing a rectangular mask automatically turns it on for you.

To tweak the mask shape, double-click the mask outline to bring up the Free Transform Points. The cursor icon changes to show if you are about to rotate the mask shape, or drag it taller or wider (move the cursor near one of the square transform points to get this icon). Hold down the Command (Control) key while dragging to resize it symmetrically. Drag the transform outline to move the entire shape. Hit Enter to accept your changes and exit Free Transform mode.

> While it's great to be able to mask directly in the Comp window, sometimes the mask outline gets in the way. Switch Toggle View Masks off when you're done.

If you want to enter exact values for the Mask Shape, with the **Centerpiece** layer still selected press M to twirl down Mask Shape in the Timeline window. Click on the word Shape to open the Mask Shape dialog, and choose Rectangle as the Shape. We used these values for the Bounding Box: Left = 0, Top = 50, Right = 320, and Bottom = 185. Click OK to see the mask shape update.

4 *complete:* The Mask Shape dialog, where you can precisely resize the mask.

5 Press to reveal the Mask Feather parameter, and disable the Constrain Proportions lock (above). Scrub its Y value to add a bit of vertical feather to the mask, giving it a soft top and bottom edge against its background (below).

STEP 5: Next, let's blend the title graphic into the background, instead of having a hard mask edge. With the **Centerpiece** layer still selected, press F to twirl down its Mask Feather parameter in the Timeline window. Turn off the Toggle View Masks switch along the bottom of the Comp window so you can see the edges without distraction.

We want to feather just the horizontal edges of the mask shape. To do this, click on the chainlink icon to the left of its parameters to unlock the Horizontal and Vertical values from each other. Scrub the second value (the Y – or Horizontal – Feather) until you get a softness you like. We chose a value of 5. Deselect the layer (press F2) the layer to see the edge better. Note that the vertical (left and right) edges stayed sharp

If you need to, check your mask against our prebuilt comp [**Final_after Step 05**]. *If you like, you can duplicate our comp, rename it "MyFinal5" and continue on from here.*

Let There Be Music

STEP 6: Time to add the music track. Press Home to make sure the time marker is at 00:00. Then select the **My_Sources** folder in the Project window and choose File>Import>File. Navigate to this tutorial's **Project>Sources** folder on your disc or drive, and import the soundtrack **CM_Underground_music.mov**.

With this footage item selected, type Command+/ (Control+/) to add it to [**MyFinal**]. The Comp and Timeline windows should now be forward. Press the period key (.) on the numeric keypad to preview the music, or do a RAM Preview (press 0 on the keypad) to hear the music with the title graphics.

Twirl up all layers. This is a good time to save your project before you start Part 3.

Music Credits

The music for this tutorial was arranged by co-author Chris Meyer, using samples from Spectrasonics' *Liquid Grooves* (more info at www.spectrasonics.net) and the original BBC Sound Effects library (available from Sound Ideas at www.sound-ideas.com). The sound effects were recorded by the BBC on the Underground's Victoria Line.

Part 3: Sequences in Stereo

The idea of this background is that it is to be used for all the segments in this travel series on the Underground. The top area of the comp is to be filled with a sequence of names of London Underground stations. This sequence is a series of Illustrator files with roughly one station per letter of the alphabet (A is for Arsenal, B is for Baker Street, and so on). This name sequence will be imported twice, with each version at a difference size and opacity, playing back at a different frame rate.

Foreground Sequence

First, let's import the version that will run small and in the foreground:

STEP 7: Select the **My_Sources** folder in the Project window and select File>Import>File. Locate and open the **Stations_Sequence** folder in this tutorial's **Sources** folder. This is a series of Illustrator files, saved in alphabetical order. Select the first file – **Arsenal.ai** – and check the Generic EPS Sequence box at the bottom of the dialog. Click Open. After Effects will ask you to verify how to handle the footage; leave Import Kind set to Footage and Layer Options set to Merged Layers. Click OK.

STEP 8: The Illustrator sequence will appear in the Project window, and will default to one file per frame for a total duration of 00:23. To add the sequence to your comp, make sure [**MyFinal**] is the forward comp with the time marker located at 00:00, and press Command+/(Control+/). It should appear at the top of the layer stack.

RAM Preview the comp. Hmm – goes a bit fast, and 23 frames is woefully short to fill your three-second animation…

7 To import a sequence of Illustrator files, select the first one in the list, enable the Generic EPS Sequence option, and click Open.

STEP 9: You will need to find a way to extend this sequence. Two options include slowing it down so each file's duration is longer than one frame, and looping it so the sequence will repeat once it runs all the way through. Or, you can combine these two techniques:

• In the Project window, select **Stations_Sequence** and choose File>Interpret Footage>Main. Set the "Assume this frame rate" parameter to 8 frames per second, and click OK. (This speed is something you can tweak later to taste, if you wish.) Note that the duration as displayed at the top of the Project window now appears as 02:27: Just a bit shy of the three seconds you require, but all frames will play at least once.

• Open the Interpret Footage dialog again, set the footage to Loop 2 times, and click OK. Now the sequence will start again when it finishes one full sequence, and the total duration reads 05:23.

• Even though you have now changed the effective duration of this footage item, the original duration for the layer is being honored in the Timeline. Drag the layer's out point handle past the end of the timeline so the sequence is visible for the entire duration (you don't have to carefully end at 03:00, as any frames after the end of the timeline will be automatically trimmed).

• RAM Preview the comp again, to check out the new speed and duration.

STEP 10: It's time to find a good position in the frame for this first copy of the sequence, and reduce its Scale and Opacity parameters so it doesn't take attention away from the main title:

• Select the layer **Stations_Sequence** and press S to reveal its Scale. Set this to 75%.

• Set this layer's Opacity to 40%. You can either type T to reveal this parameter in the Timeline window, or use the shortcut Command+Shift+O (Control+Shift+O) to directly open an Opacity dialog.

• Move its position in the Comp window so that it sits above the **Centerpiece** layer in the white area at the top of the frame. Turn on Title Safe guides (shortcut is the apostrophe key) and position the sequence so that it's tucked just inside the Title Safe area in the top left of the comp.

• Select the **Stations_Sequence** layer in the Timeline window and hit Return to activate its name for editing. Rename the layer "**Stations_ Foreground**". Hit Return again to accept the new name. This will help you identify the layer when you import the same sequence again.

9 Set the Interpret Footage parameters for the sequence to play at 8 fps, and to loop twice (top). After lengthening the sequence in the Interpret Footage dialog, drag the out point handle of the layer bar (above) past the end of the timeline so that it lasts for the full duration of the comp.

10 Click on the Title Safe switch to see the guides displayed. Reduce the Scale and Opacity for the first copy of the sequence, and position it just inside the Title Safe area in the upper left corner.

Conforming versus Time-stretching

Are you wondering why we didn't just time-stretch the sequence in Step 9? The advantage to conforming the frame rate in Interpret Footage is that the frame rate is set *before* any keyframes. We can animate our layer and then change the frame rate later without affecting any keyframes that are applied. Time-stretching also stretches keyframes, so if you time an animation to music and then change the stretch value, you also have to adjust any keyframes.

Save your project. If you need to, compare your work so far with our prebuilt comp [Final_after Step 10]; you can use this comp to continue from here if you like. We've also saved a prebuilt comp after Step 9, if you want to back up and start over from there.

Background Sequence

It's time to create a second version of the station names. We want this version to be larger and blurry and set well back in the background. It will also run at a slower frame rate than the first sequence and scale over time. The idea is to use this version to mimic the 3D shadows as a way of echoing the message of the foreground sequence, but in a manner that's quick to set up and fast to render.

STEP 11: Now that you've successfully negotiated importing and positioning one sequence, import it again, setting a different rate:

• Select the **My_Sources** folder and Import the **Stations_Sequence** a second time, checking Generic EPS Sequence checkbox as you did in Step 7 previously.

• Open the Interpret Footage and set the frame rate to 5 frames per second, and click OK. If you want, edit the Comment field in the Project window so you can help tell the two copies of the sequence apart from each other. At this slower speed the sequence will be 04:18 in length, which will more than cover our short animation – no need to loop it.

• Add this second sequence to [**MyFinal**], making sure it starts at 00:00.

• Select this new layer in the Timeline and hit Return to rename the layer "**Stations_Background**". Hit Return again to accept the new name. (Clicking on the column head toggles between the Layer and Source Name.)

• With this new layer still selected, select the Pan Behind tool (shortcut: Y), and move the anchor point in the Comp window so it sits at the left-hand corner of the text. For instance, if you're viewing the first Station name – Arsenal – move the anchor point to the bottom left-hand corner of the capital A. This will ensure that when you scale the text, the scaling will occur around this point. The Anchor Point value should read approximately X = 32, Y = 24; you can verify this by revealing the Anchor Point parameter in the Timeline (shortcut: A). Switch back to the Selection tool when you're done (shortcut: V).

11 Import the sequence of station names a second time, setting this copy of the sequence to 5 fps. You can enter comments for the two copies in the Project window to help tell them apart.

• Press S to twirl down Scale, and set the value to 200%. Yes, we know we're the same ones who told you elsewhere that scaling past 100% is a Bad Thing, and you'll notice that the text now looks a bit fuzzy in the Comp window. We'll get to that…

• Position the layer so it's tucked inside the Action Safe area at the top of the comp (Position about X = 18, Y = 48). Since this second text layer is intended to be more of a background wash than a main element, you can get away with placing it outside the Title Safe area.

• Time to tackle that fuzzy text. It originated as an Illustrator file, and was built out of vectors rather than pixels. After Effects has the ability to re-rasterize vector artwork to a size larger than it was originally created in, while keeping it sharp. This toggle is the one that looks like a sunburst icon in the Switches column of the Timeline window. Click on it for this layer to enable Continuous Rasterization. Notice how the text becomes much sharper now.

> You do not need to turn on Continuous Rasterization unless you're scaling an Illustrator layer past 100%. Doing so won't make the artwork look any better, and may render more slowly.

11 *continued:* The second copy of the text has been scaled 200%, and moved up to the left corner of the comp. Note that the Anchor Point (where the cursor is pointing) has been moved with the Pan Behind tool to the lower left corner of the text.

11 *continued:* The layer has been set to Continuously Rasterize (the switch with the red circle in the Timeline, top), so the vector-based text will now be sharp (above). The comp is shown here with Action/Title Safe guides on.

STEP 12: This may seem trivial to you, but it's the kind of thing we sweat on a real job: A problem with the animation is that both sequences start in sync at time 00:00, resulting in both layers showing the word "Arsenal" at this time. We like to make coincidences like that less obvious. Therefore, the goal is to offset the **Stations_Background** layer in time to knock it out of sync with the **Stations_Foreground** layer – at least at the very beginning and end. Experiment with sliding the **Stations_Background** layer bar earlier in time; be careful not to move it so early in time that the layer ends prematurely.

Another simple solution is to select the **Stations_Background** layer, press End to move to 03:00, and hit] (right square bracket) to move this layer so its out point equals the current time. At 03:00, you should now see the Waterloo text, which is the last station in the sequence. Press Home to return to 00:00; the background sequence should now start with Holborn.

- If Scale is twirled up, press S to twirl it down. Turn on the animation stopwatch for Scale to create a keyframe at 00:00 with a value of 200%.

- Hit End and change the Scale value to 300% at time 03:00.

- Press Shift+T to twirl down Opacity, and set the opacity for the layer to 10% so it's now a *very* light gray.

- Drag the layer to the bottom of the layer stack so it's behind all other layers – the bottom of the descenders on the text should disappear behind the top of the **Centerpiece** layer. Reposition the layer to taste.

12 A second copy of the station sequence has been scaled up and made transparent, acting as a form of echo for the foreground copy. The layer has been slid in time to start before the beginning of the comp to disrupt a too-obvious sync issue, and dragged to the bottom of the stack.

- RAM Preview to check your final text animation. You should have a lot of motion going on now, which will help keep the viewers' interest from episode to episode as they see other versions of this title.

Here comes another example of where we like to take an animation one step further: Notice in the soundtrack that the whine of the subway car taking off starts somewhere between 20 to 30 frames in. Instead of having the **Stations_Background** layer scaling over the entire length of the comp, change its animation so its scale matches this feature of the music:

- Select **CM_Underground_music.mov**, and type LL to reveal its audio waveform in the Timeline window. Press Home to return to 00:00. Preview the audio (shortcut: the decimal key on the extended keypad) while looking at the waveform around 00:20 to 01:00 and try to identify a good trigger for when the whine sound effect starts to rise.

- Drag the time marker to your chosen frame (we personally selected 00:20 to synchronize with a drum hit around this time), then drag the first Scale keyframe for **Stations_Background** to this time. Add the Shift key after you start moving the keyframe, and it will "stick" to the time marker. RAM Preview and tweak to taste.

- Consider applying the Animation>Keyframe Assistant>Easy Ease Out to this first keyframe, so the scale builds slowly like the whine. Twirl up all layers in the Timeline window.

*That was a long couple of steps – feel free to compare your comp with our prebuilt version [**Final_after Step 12**]. Don't forget to Save!*

Blurring the Background

Call us picky, but that second copy of **Stations_Sequence** looks too sharp. After all, it's supposed to be the farthest-back element we've created so far, acting as a stylized variation of a shadow for the foreground copy. A great way to fake the impression of distance is to use blurs.

For the longest while, you could not apply effects to Continuously Rasterized layers – instead, you had to resort to precomposing, Adjustment Layers, or other trickery. That changed in After Effects version 6:

Step 13: Select **Stations_Sequence** and apply Effect>Blur & Sharpen> **Fast Blur** (or any preferred blur effect). Its Effect Controls window will open; adjust the Blurriness value to taste (we used 4.0 pixels). If you like, increase this layer's Opacity to make it more visible.

> The "gotcha" with applying effects to Continuously Rasterized layers is that Effects are now calculated *after* Transforms. As the layer scales larger, you may notice the blur amount remains the same in absolute terms – in other words, it does not scale to match the layer's size. It's too subtle here to worry about, but something to keep in mind.

*Save your project and compare your comp so far with our prebuilt version [**Final_after Step 13**]. You're almost done...*

12 *complete:* To make the animation of the second stations sequence tie in better with the soundtrack, spot when the sound effect of the whine of the car speeding up begins, and have the sequence's Scale keyframe Easy Ease away from this point in time.

13 A recently-added feature is the ability to add effects directly to Continuously Rasterized layers.

Part 4: Last Stop

You're on the home stretch: The only things left to do are finish off the bottom of the frame. For this you'll be employing a different take on the concept of "looping" a layer.

Offset Tracks

Our final element is a graphic that was created using the P22 Johnston Underground Extras font, stringing along symbols into a representation of a map of an Underground track. By using similar symbols at the start and end, we've created a tileable graphic that is seamless on the left and right sides.

14 The track dropped into place. The next trick is to make it animate as if it were a never-ending ribbon.

STEP 14: Select the **My_Sources** folder in the Project window and use File>Import to add the **TubeTrack.psd** footage item (located in the same **Sources** folder as you found the music back in Step 6). After Effects will ask whether you want a specific layer or to merge the layers; use the Merged Layers default; leave Import Kind to Footage. Click OK.

• Add it to your [**MyFinal**] comp. Make sure that it begins at 00:00.

• Position the **TubeTrack.psd** layer so it is more or less centered in the white area along the bottom of the comp (about 214 on the Y axis). It will roughly straddle the Title Safe line, but should stay inside the Action Safe area. If you want, you can toggle these guides on and off by using the ' (apostrophe) key. Turn off Title Safe guides after you've placed the graphic, as they obscure it somewhat.

STEP 15: You have just one copy of the track, barely wider than the comp. This doesn't give you a lot of room to animate it across the frame using Position keyframes. But when we created it, we made sure it would tile end to end – so you're going to do the animation inside a plug-in instead.

• Apply Effect>Distort>**Offset** to the **TubeTrack.psd** layer. The Offset effect allows you to pan an image within a layer, so that as one side moves off frame, it will wrap around to the opposite side. Because the TubeTrack graphic is identical on the left and right edges, you will not notice any seam as it wraps around.

• In Offset's Effect Controls window, turn on the animation stopwatch for the Shift Center To parameter in order to create the first keyframe at 00:00.

• Change this keyframe's value to X = 0, Y = 15 (since you'll be moving only horizontally, be sure the Y value stays at 15). By resetting the X value to 0, you'll be easily able to gauge the correct value for the second keyframe. If you were keeping one eye on the Comp window, you'll notice you still see a complete track extending across the width of the frame.

• Hit End to move to 03:00. Scrub the X value to the right to increase its offset, watching the Comp window to see how much of the track graphic is being shifted.

15 Apply the Offset effect to the track, and enable keyframing for the Shift Center To value.

With experience, you'll get a feel for how many pixels a second is a good speed to move an object. Since this animation is only three seconds long, and the first keyframe is set at X = 0, it's pretty easy to do the math in your head to calculate this speed: Divide the X value you choose for your second keyframe by 3 to arrive at its speed in pixels per second.

For instance, we had an idea that we wanted the graphic to move at about 50 pixels a second, so we used a value of X = 150, Y = 15 for the second keyframe. If you're not ready to do this kind of math in your head, of course you can feel free to experiment with different values, RAM Previewing as you go, until you get a speed you like.

• Finally, set the Opacity for this layer to 50% to knock it back a bit, and RAM Preview one last time.

Don't forget to Save your final project, which we'll render in the next step. If you suspect you got a little lost along the way, open our prebuilt [**Final_Comp**] *to compare your results.*

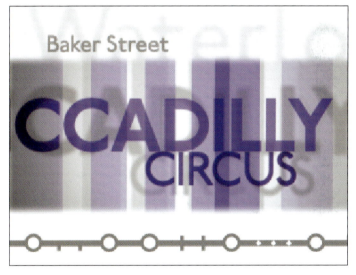

15 *complete:* The final frame at time 03:00 (top), with the track offset over time and reduced in opacity (below).

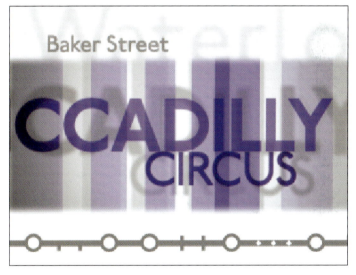

Final Render

Yes, we know you know how to render a movie…but don't run away without finding out how to render your comp proxy correctly!

STEP 16: Select Composition>Make Movie to render your composition [**MyFinal**]. Name it and select a location on disk to save it to.

• In the Render Settings dialog, pick a template that renders at Best Quality/Full Resolution, with Field Rendering Off (320×240 movies are never field rendered). To be absolutely sure the **Centerpiece_proxy.mov** is used in place of the much slower [**Centerpiece**] composition, make sure to set the Proxy Use popup to Use Comp Proxies Only.

If the Proxy Use popup is set to Current Settings, this means proxies are used only if they are switched on in the Project window. That leaves your final render open to a bit of chance, as you might have accidentally switched it off. We personally change all our Render Settings templates intended for final rendering to Use Comp Proxies Only. That way, whenever we take the time to prerender a comp proxy, the final render will use them. Just be sure to remove any obsolete comp proxies – don't just turn them off. The Use Comp Proxies Only setting also ensures that any proxies assigned to footage items (which are usually low-resolution temporary files not intended for the final render) will be ignored – Current Settings doesn't assure you of that. (You could also select the Use All Proxies option, which would also use Footage proxies if assigned.)

• For the Output Module, be sure to pick a template that is capable of outputting audio, such as a QuickTime movie (sequences don't support audio). Also check that the Output Audio checkbox is turned On. If you use the default Lossless template, edit the template by turning on the Output Audio checkbox. (You can save this modified template by selecting Make Template from the bottom of the Output Modules template popup; give it a useful name like "**Lossless+Audio**".)

16 It is important to make sure the Proxy Use popup in the Render Settings dialog is set to Use Comp Proxies to ensure the right files will be used.

Wrapping Up

If you made it all the way through the previous tutorial to build the centerpiece as well as this tutorial, congratulations! It took a bit of time, but hopefully you found this a nice little workout that created a pleasing graphic out of relatively few source materials: a little text; a few solids; and judicious use of lights, blending modes, and opacity to blend them all together.

Going Further

There are several ways you could enhance this final animation. Here are a few ideas to try out:

• To enhance the sense of depth, add a drop shadow to the **Centerpiece** layer.

To see a shadow cast above and below the center section in order to simulate a light placed closer to the layer than the virtual camera (a concept mentioned in the previous tutorial), you can apply two copies of Effect>Perspective>**Drop Shadow** and set them to cast their shadows above and below, respectively. Another trick you could employ is to mask, blur, and reduce the opacity of a black solid slightly larger than the **Centerpiece** layer, placed behind it.

One possible enhancement is to add a shadow to the centerpiece, giving more dimension. How would you create an inner shadow such as this?

Challenge: How would you create an inner shadow that casts on the **Centerpiece** layer instead of the white background? We already gave you a hint above about trying masked solids instead of effects. If you can't figure it out, look at our prebuilt comp [**Final_Inner Shadow**].

• Since we were trying to create a nicely balanced 320×240 pixel frame (and didn't want to make you execute dozens of repetitive steps), we included only two copies of the Stations sequence. If you were composing a full video frame and wanted a busier look, you would probably use more copies, scaled at various sizes. Take a shot at creating a busier frame by creating more variations of this element.

• Find a map of London, or images that reflect some landmarks one might find around the stops highlighted in our fake program, and use those as a background for this project. Try reducing their opacity to make them recede into the white background, or tint them to match the color of the title.

• To make the **TubeTrack.psd** element more interesting, consider creating alternate versions with colored dots that fill in the circles. Animate these dots to make it appear as if these various stops are blinking on an animated map of the Underground. One approach to doing this enhancement is to Layer>Pre-compose the **TubeTrack.psd** graphic, using the Leave All Attributes option. This will move just the original source into its own precomp. Make a small circle by creating a new small solid and applying a circular mask. Position the circle behind the tube graphic and animate the color (in a Fill effect perhaps) or Opacity. Duplicate this circle layer as often as is needed. This precomp will now be used in place of the original still image graphic in the final comp, where the Offset effect is still being applied.

You could also open the **TubeTrack.psd** in Photoshop, and create circles on separate layers. Save as a new name, and import the new file as a Composition, where you can animate the circles to taste. Then replace the original layer in the final comp with this new comp.

Connect

For more information on topics covered in this tutorial, check out the following volumes of *Creating Motion Graphics*:

Volume 1:

Masking

Importing sequences, footage frame rates, looping footage

Keyframe animation

Continuous Rasterization

The Offset effect

Volume 2:

Prerendering and Comp Proxies

Working with Illustrator

Audio Basics and Effects

Postcards in Space

Using cameras and 3D space to create dimensional graphics.

This tutorial will serve as an introduction to using the 3D space features in After Effects, focusing on camera animation, 3D transformations, nesting 3D compositions, and combining 2D and 3D layers.

It covers two separate projects: **Camera.aep**, where you will build a simple multilayer animation that will teach you the basics of manipulating layers and cameras in 3D (including nesting 3D precomps and collapsing their transformations), and a guided tour of the more complex **Postcards.aep**, which employs 3D space to build a

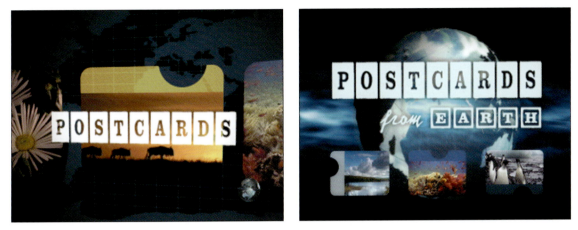

more involved opening sequence for a fictional program. This second project includes additional tricks of interest, such as using expressions to integrate pseudo-3D effects into this new 3D space, and the intelligent use of nested compositions.

The next tutorial – *The Planets* – will extend these concepts by discussing the Auto-Orientation and Depth of Field options for the camera. Lights and shadows were covered in a previous tutorial, *Piccadilly Circus*. We will briefly cover lights in this tutorial as well.

The Tasks

This is what you will be doing in the various parts of this tutorial:

PART 1: Learn how to place layers in 3D space, including using different Comp views. We'll also cover render order concerns.

PART 2: Create a new camera and experiment with different presets, understand Angle of View and Zoom; learn tips on moving the camera and using the Track Camera tools to customize the Comp views.

PART 3: Add a background, employ different techniques to animate the camera, add a second camera, and switch between them.

PART 4: Understand the differences between Rotation and Orientation, including a side trip on the subject of layer intersections.

PART 5: Add more layers to your composition, precompose and collapse transformations for 3D layers, composite a 2D layer on top, and take a brief refresher course on adding a light.

PART 6: Read an overview of the more complex project **Postcards.aep**. A detailed walk-through of this project is included in a PDF file on the DVD named **08B_Postcards_Bonus.pdf**.

In this tutorial, you will create a simple animation that involves a combination of 2D and 3D layers (left). We will then walk through a more complex project that uses the same principles (right).

The footage inside the "postcards" are from the Artbeats stock footage libraries Penguins, Under The Sea, Animal Safari, and Timelapse Landscapes 3; the texture map in the earth is from Digital Vision's Inner Gaze; the background in the complex project is a composite of movies from Artbeats' Digital Edge and from Digital Vision's Atmospherics.

Part 1: A Space Odyssey

1 Your initial comp contains a pair of 2D layers: **Title.ai** (the font is Childs Play Block from P22), and the background **Postcards_animals.tif**.

The plan for this and the next several sections is to use some of the elements from the *Postcards from Earth* project to create a simplified version of this opening title. Along the way, you will learn about 3D space and manipulating the camera. You do not have to exactly re-create the images shown here or the animation **Camera.mov**; feel free to experiment and pursue your own ideas of how you might use these tools.

In this first section, we will focus on placing layers in 3D, and becoming comfortable viewing and navigating around this space.

STEP 1: Make sure you have opened the project **Camera.aep**, not **Postcards.aep**. Then open the composition [**Camera*starter**]. It contains two layers – **Title.ai** and **Postcards_Animals.tif** – which are currently in their default 2D space.

2 Layers default to 2D space, unless their 3D Layer switch (where the cursor is pointing) is enabled. Once set to 3D, their Position property gains a third value: Z Position.

2 *complete:* When 3D layers are selected, they are drawn in the Comp window with a set of three axis arrows to tell you which way they are oriented. The blue arrow is hard to see in this view, because it is pointed straight at you along the Z axis.

STEP 2: Select both layers, and type P to reveal their Position properties in the Timeline window. Make sure the Switches column is visible in the Timeline window; if not, hit F4 to reveal it.

Turn on the 3D Layer switch for both layers (its icon looks like a wireframe cube). In the Timeline window, you will notice that the Position properties have gained a third parameter: their Z Position. Where X is left and right, and Y is up and down, Z can be thought of as closer or farther away.

You should also notice that in the Comp window, 3D layers that are selected are drawn with three arrows extending from their Anchor Points. The colors of these arrows – red, green, and blue – correspond to which way their own X, Y, and Z axes are pointing. The blue Z arrow is hard to see right now, because it is pointed straight at you.

You might also have noticed what *didn't* change: the position and size of the layers in the Comp window. Every composition has a default camera that ensures layers placed at Z = 0 that have not otherwise been rotated in 3D space (more on that later) appear the same way in 2D or 3D. In the next section, you will create a new camera, where you can change how it views these layers.

3 The 3D View Popup along the bottom of the Comp window allows you to see the layers from different angles, including Top view (left). Beneath the camera views are six *orthographic* views, with no perspective distortion – we use Top and Left a lot to help us see what is happening in Z space. The three Custom Views (right) allow you to examine a scene with perspective without having to move a camera there yourself.

The View from Here

When you're working in a comp with 3D elements, the default view is the Active Camera, which is what will be rendered on final output. However, you will often want to look at your virtual set from different perspectives, such as from the side or from above.

STEP 3: Explore the different Comp window views either by using the menu item View>Switch 3D View, or the 3D View Popup along the bottom right of the Comp window (resize the window wider to see it). The first six views – Front, Left, Top, Back, Right, and Bottom – look at the scene from specific sides. For example, Top View is akin to floating above all of your layers. These six views, referred to as *orthographic* views, are also special in that they have no perspective distortion. They are useful for checking how your layers are truly arranged in 3D space, without having to take camera or perspective distortions into account.

The other three views – Custom View 1, 2, and 3 – give you different perspectives on the scene without having to create a camera and move it to that position. They include perspective distortion, which is more representative of how a camera will render on final output.

STEP 4: After Effects reserves the function keys F10, F11, and F12 to quickly jump between different views. You can decide what view each key jumps to: Set the view you want in the Comp window, then hold Shift while you press F10, F11, or F12 to assign that key.

For example, we like to use the Left view to see the Z Positions of layers: Positive Z values extend to the right; negative Z values to the left. Choose Left view from the popup at the bottom of the Comp window, and press Shift+F11. Verify that F10 is set to Top and F12 is set to the Active Camera; if they aren't, reassign them using the same procedure. Verify your key assignments by checking the View>Switch 3D View menu.

Exposé Issue

With OS X, some vital function keys may be taken over by Exposé. Reassign them in System Preferences>Personal>Exposé.

5 Scrub the Z Position value for **Postcard_Animals.tif** (above right) and notice how the layers separate in space (above).

6 Set the Z Position for **Postcard_Animals.tif** to 100. Since it is farther away than before, it is drawn smaller in the Active Camera view.

Letter of the Law

Dragging an axis arrow automatically constrains movement to the letter of the axis that pops up next to the cursor – there is no need to hold down the Shift key while you're dragging.

STEP 5: Select Custom View 3 for the Comp window. In the Timeline window, scrub the Z Position for **Postcard_Animals.tif** while you're watching the Comp window. Notice how **Postcard_Animals.tif** separates from **Title.ai** in space.

If you set Z Position for **Postcard_Animals.tif** to a negative value, it will render in front of the **Title.ai** layer, even though it is below **Title.ai** in the Timeline window. Since their distance from the camera must be taken into account, 3D layers rewrite the old rules on which layers get rendered in front of other layers – see the sidebar *New World Order* for more details.

If layers do not move in the Comp window while you scrub their values in the Timeline window, check the status of the Live Update switch along the top of the Timeline window: It should be on (highlighted). We also suggest for now that you set the Fast Previews switch along the bottom right of the Comp window (drag it open wider to see it) to Off, as you do not need OpenGL acceleration for these simples moves.

STEP 6: Press F12 to return the Comp window to Active Camera view. Continue to experiment with scrubbing the Z Position for **Postcard_Animals.tif**. Notice that the higher the Z Position value, the farther away it appears, not unlike the effect of scaling a layer. This is part of normal 3D perspective. When you are done experimenting, set this layer's Z Position to 100; you will be using this arrangement later.

If you are still not clear on the implications of the orthographic views, change the view to Front. Notice that the layers look the same as they did before you changed the Position for **Postcard_Animal.tif**. This is because orthographic views such as Front, Left, and Top do not take distance perspective into account. Change back to Active Camera view when done.

STEP 7: Select the **Title.ai** layer and in the Comp window, click on the left or right side of the layer (away from the X, Y, and Z arrows), and drag it around in the Comp window while you're keeping an eye on its Position values in the Timeline window. Because you are looking straight on at the layer, moving it changes only the X and Y values, not the Z value. You can also press the Shift key after you start dragging to constrain movement to the X or Y axes. Also, if you move the cursor to either the red arrow (X axis) or green arrow (Y axis), you can drag the layer along a single axis. When you're done exploring, Undo until you return the layer's Position to 160, 120, 0, or enter these values directly.

New World Order

When you build a composition with just 2D layers, it is easy to look at the Timeline window and know which layers would be rendered on top or in front of other layers: The layer at the bottom of this window renders first, and each layer farther up renders on top of the layers underneath. Track Mattes cause minor but easily understood exceptions to these rules (see *Creating Motion Graphics* Volume 1 for details).

3D layers use different criteria: After Effects studies the 3D layers, calculates their relative distance from the active camera, and renders the layers that are farther away before the layers that are closer.

When you combine 2D and 3D layers in the same comp, the 2D layers break the 3D layers into groups that are rendered together. For example, say you had a composition with six 3D layers, and one 2D layer stacked in the middle of them in the Timeline window. All the 3D layers below the 2D layer would be calculated and rendered as a group. The 2D layer above them would then be rendered on top of this composite. Finally, the 3D layers above the 2D layer would be rendered as their own group, and composited on top of the layers underneath.

One important implication of these groups is when you have a light casting a shadow, and the 3D layers are also set to cast shadows: *shadows can fall only on other 3D layers in the same group.* (Shadows can never fall on 2D layers, and 2D layers don't cast shadows.) For purposes of rendering, Adjustment Layers are considered to be 2D layers; if they're placed between a number of 3D layers, they'll break those layers into groups above and below the adjustment layer.

So, even though the 3D rendering order is dependent on the distance of the layers to the cameras, you still need to be aware of the layer ordering in the Timeline when you're mixing 2D and 3D layers.

Move the cursor to the Anchor Point area of this layer until the cursor shows a Z beside it, and drag the mouse. Dragging up or to the right moves the layer closer (negative Z values); dragging it down or to the left moves it farther away (positive Z values) until it moves behind the **Postcard_Animals.tif** layer.

Although this works, it's quite difficult to control the movement along the Z axis in this view because it's straight on to the current view. If you want to move a layer on one axis, it's a good idea to pick the most appropriate view. For instance, press F10 or F11 to change the Comp's view to Top or Left views respectively. Now the blue Z axis is much easier to grab and move.

Return to Active Camera view (F12), and Undo until you return the layer to a Position of 160, 120, 0 – you will be relying on these values later.

Save your project. We have saved the composition at this point as [**Camera_after Step 07**]; *you will find it in the project folder* **Camera * prebuilt>_compare comps_after Step##.** *If you need to, you can compare your work with this one, or duplicate our comp and use it for the following sections.*

7 Although you can grab the Z axis arrow in a straight-on view (such as Active Camera view), it can be hard to see exactly what is going on. Get in the habit of switching views to see the axis you are interested in more clearly – such as the Left view to edit Z.

Part 2: Creating a New Camera

Now that you have some familiarity with objects in 3D space, in this section you will create a new camera and learn how to manipulate it around these objects. We will discuss some of the camera's settings, and several ways to manipulate it in the different Comp window views.

STEP 8: Make sure that the Comp window is set to Active Camera view and that the time marker is at 00:00. Then create a new camera by selecting Layer>New>Camera.

This will open a large dialog box with a lot of parameters. If you are trying to match a scene in After Effects to one created in 3D or captured in real life, these parameters give you a lot of control. If you are a graphic artist who is just interested in cool imagery, they can be a bit daunting. If you fall into the latter category, you can ignore most of these parameters and just use different presets, or vary the Angle of View or Zoom properties (they are related) to create different looks.

You are not committed to these settings; you can open this dialog again later, or access these parameters in the Timeline window. Pick the 50mm preset for now, and note the Zoom property directly below the preset popup; if the Units popup in the lower left of this dialog is set to Pixels, the Zoom value should equal 444.4. This property does not exist in a real camera, but it's handy inside the After Effects world: A layer this distance from the camera will appear to be the same size whether it is in 2D or 3D.

Click OK. With your new **Camera 1** layer selected, type P to reveal its Position property. Note that its Z Position equals –444.4: New cameras default to a Z Position equal to their initial Zoom setting (changing the zoom or selecting another preset later does not change the Z position to match).

The 50mm preset is the same as the comp's default camera. Save a snapshot of what this looks like by pressing Shift+F5 so you can easily compare what different camera presets look like.

8 Create a new camera, and select the 50mm preset.

8 *complete:* The 50mm preset is the same as the comp's default camera.

STEP 9: Everything else being equal – including the camera's position relative to the layers it is looking at – shorter lens presets equal a wider Angle of View. Wider Angles of View result in the layers appearing smaller in the frame, since the virtual lens would be taking in a wider overall image. A result of this is that the more layers are spaced apart, the greater the exaggeration in distance between the layers.

Double-click on **Camera 1** to re-open the Camera Settings dialog. Note the current Angle of View and Zoom settings, then pick the 28mm preset: The Angle of View will increase, and Zoom will decrease. Click OK; the two layers will appear much farther away. Press Shift+F6 to save a snapshot of this. Note the Z Position parameter for **Camera 1**: It is still –444.4. Change it to –248.9, which corresponds to the Zoom parameter for the 28mm preset (and would have been the Z Position you would have gotten had you created a new camera with the 28mm preset in the first place). Notice that the **Title.ai** layer – which is at Z = 0 in the comp – now appears about the same size as it did with the 50mm camera preset. You can press F5 to recall the 50mm snapshot to compare. However, the **Postcard_Animals.tif** layer appears farther away when you're using the 28mm preset: This is a result of the exaggerated perspective of using a shorter lens that has a larger Angle of View.

STEP 10: Set **Camera 1**'s Z Position back to –444.4 so you have a common camera position to compare other lens presets with. Double-click **Camera 1** again, choose the 135mm preset, and click OK. This preset is more akin to a telephoto lens, resulting in the layers appearing much closer. Press F5 and F6 to compare it with the 50mm and 28mm presets, respectively.

STEP 11: The 135mm preset zooms so close to the layers that they are blown up past their original size, resulting in some fuzziness. However, **Title.ai** was created in Adobe Illustrator, and contains vector outlines instead of pixels. This means you can take advantage of the Continuous Rasterization feature to render it sharply at its new size. Click on the sunburst icon for **Title.ai** in the Timeline window, and notice how much sharper the title now appears.

9 The 28mm preset has a wider Angle of View, resulting in the layers appearing farther away if the camera is kept at the same position (above). When the camera is moved closer (below), you can see how perspective is exaggerated by the wider view angle.

10–11: If the camera is left at the same position, the 135mm lens preset works as a telephoto, magnifying the layers (far left). Unfortunately, this scales the images past their original size, resulting in a fuzzier image. Fortunately, **Title.ai** contains vector artwork; turn on its Continuous Rasterization button (above) and note how much sharper it appears (left).

11 *complete:* The 135mm preset with the Camera's Z Position set to –1200.

The "longer" 135mm preset has a much narrower Angle of View. To reinforce how this affects perspective, set the Z Position of **Camera 1** to –1200, which equals this preset's Zoom value. Notice the relative lack of perspective: The relative sizes of the two layers are almost the same as when they were both in 2D, even though **Postcard_Animals.tif** is placed farther back in Z. Set **Camera 1**'s Z Position back to –444.4 when you're done.

STEP 12: Open the Camera Settings one last time, choose the 35mm preset, and click OK. Be sure its Z position is set to –444.4. This is the preset you will use for the remainder of this tutorial.

Save your project. If you suspect you may have crossed up your camera settings, compare your comp with [**Camera_after Step 12**].

Moving the Camera 101

Next you will be animating this camera around your layers, taking advantage of the resulting perspective to create more interest. If you already have experience moving the camera, you can skip ahead to Step 17. If you are not yet comfortable with the camera, here are a few techniques that are good to practice:

13 The shortcut key A reveals a camera's Point of Interest property – the point in space the camera is aimed at.

STEP 13: Select **Camera 1**. Its Position property should already be visible; press P if it isn't. Then press Shift+A: Instead of a normal layer's Anchor Point, this action reveals a second control point called the Point of Interest.

The Position of a camera can be thought of as where it is looking *from*, and the Point of Interest as where it's looking *to*. Some 3D programs, such as Electric Image, use this "two point" or "two node" camera approach. In many cases, this makes the camera easier to control, as you can explicitly set where it is looking – such as the center of a certain layer. You can also use a simple pick whip expression to tie the camera's Point of Interest to another layer's Position.

On the downside, this often means you have to keyframe both Position and Point of Interest when you animate the camera, which makes coordinating some moves more difficult. Later we'll discuss ways to turn off the Point of Interest if you find it is getting in your way.

Scroll Zoom

If you are using a mouse with a scroll wheel, place your cursor over the Comp window and use the wheel to quicky change its Magnification setting.

STEP 14: With **Camera 1** still selected, press F10 to switch to the Top view. Hit the comma key (,) to set the Magnification to 50%, and/or enlarge the window until you can see the camera in its entirety.

If the Info window is not open, press Command+2 on Mac (Control+2 on Windows) to open it – this will give you numeric feed-back as you move the camera. Practice moving the camera using these different techniques:

- In the Timeline window, scrub the values for the camera's Position or Point of Interest.

- In the Comp window, grab and move the Point of Interest as you would a layer's anchor point.

- Still in the Comp window, you can drag the camera around freely provided you grab the camera icon where X, Y, or Z do *not* appear next to the cursor.

- Place the cursor near the camera's axis arrows until you see X, Y, or Z appear, then drag. *Both the camera and its Point of Interest will move together*, constrained to the axis indicated next to your cursor.

- To move the camera along a selected axis *without* moving the Point of Interest, place the cursor near the camera until you see either X, Y, or Z appear, then hold down the Command (Control) key as you drag.

Press F12 to toggle back to the Active Camera view to see the result of your new camera positions as you work, then F10 to go back to the Top view.

Track Camera Tools

The Comp window can be a bit cumbersome to handle in these alternate views: As you change its size or Magnification, it insists on recentering the rendered area inside the middle of the window. This rendered area provides only a limited preview of the frame in anything other than an actual Camera view, and there is a set of tools you can use to reposition your objects inside this area:

STEP 15: Change the Magnification back to 100%. Hitting the period key (.) is a shortcut to zoom up to the next level. Rearrange your screen so you can still read Camera 1's Position property in the Timeline window while the Comp window is forward.

- Make sure the Tools window is visible; if not, press Command+1 (Control+1) to open it.

- Click and hold on the third tool down on the left. An additional window will pop open – these are the Track Camera tools. Select the bottom one: Track Z Camera.

- As you move your cursor over the Comp window, it will change to an icon of this tool. Once it's over the Comp window, click and drag downward or to the left; the drawing of the camera and layers will get smaller. Drag until the camera and layers are about half the size they were when you started. If the camera is selected, you will see its wireframe outline; if it's deselected, you will see just a small box icon.

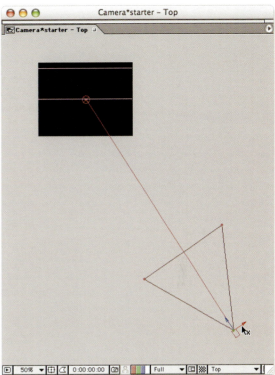

14 Alter the size and zoom level of the Comp window and use the hand tool (hold down the spacebar) to pan around the pasteboard until you can see the camera and layers from the Top view, and practice moving the camera. The letters X, Y, or Z next to the cursor mean dragging is constrained to this one axis.

15 There are three Track Camera tools (from left to right): Orbit Camera, Track XY Camera, and Track Z Camera. Press C to select the Track Camera tool, and press C repeatedly to cycle through the three choices.

15 *complete:* The Track Camera tools allow you to zoom and reposition the objects in the orthographic or Custom views without changing the Position properties of any objects. Note that *the size of the camera icon does not change* (compare this to using Magnification).

Keep an eye on the Timeline window while you're doing this; you will note that **Camera 1**'s Position property does not change. If you are not in a Camera view, the Track tools change only your view – not the positions of any object.

• Watch the Tool window, and press C twice. This will scroll through the track icons, landing on the Track XY Camera tool. Then drag upward in the Comp window until your objects are centered in this view.

Feel free to practice using these tools in the other orthographic and Custom views. You will quickly find that these are much better suited than Magnification for altering the view in the Comp window.

STEP 16: Press F12 to return to the Active Camera view. While you're keeping an eye on **Camera 1**'s Position property in the Timeline window, use the Track Camera tools to change the Comp window. Notice that in this case, the Position of the camera *does* change. (The same will be true in the Camera 1 view.) Tap C to toggle between the different tools, and practice using each one – the Orbit Camera tool is particularly fun and very useful for manipulating the Custom Views as well.

16 If you use the Track Camera tools in a Camera view (left), the camera's Position values will change (right).

The Track Camera tools have different functions in different views – it's important to remember which view you are in and what you are trying to do before using them.

Another option for manipulating views is the Zoom tool: Press Z to select it, and click in the Comp window in the middle of the area you wish to zoom closer to. Press the spacebar and drag to pan around with the Hand tool. Option+click (Alt+click) to zoom out.

STEP 17: When you're done experimenting, position the camera at an angle to the existing layers, so you can see a little perspective (something like our first camera position, as seen here). Set the Comp window to Active Camera view, and 100% Magnification. In the next section you will add more layers and animate the camera around them.

Save your project. If you are already familiar with manipulating the camera and views and therefore skipped this Part, duplicate our comp [Camera_after Step 17] to use from here forward.

Part 3: A Moving Experience

You should now feel more comfortable manipulating the camera and the different views. With that under your belt, it's time to have some fun continuing to build this project. You will add additional layers and cameras, plus animate the cameras.

STEP 18: In the Project window, open the **MySources** folder. Select **MapBackground.tif** and add it to the comp, placing it at the bottom of the layer stack and starting at time 00:00. The shortcuts are Command+/ (Control+/) to add it to the comp, Option+Home (Alt+Home) to start at 00:00, and Command+Shift+[(Control+shift+[) to move it to the bottom.

Notice that the layer is rendered behind the other layers; a 2D layer at the bottom of the Timeline is rendered first. Press F10 and F11 to check the Left and Top views: 2D layers keep the same placement in the Comp window regardless of what view you are using. Press F12 to switch back to the Active Camera view.

STEP 19: With **MapBackground.tif** still selected, hit P to reveal its Position property. Note that there are only two values – X and Y – because new layers default to 2D.

Turn on the 3D Layer switch for **MapBackground.tif**. You will notice in the Comp window that it jumps to the same perspective as the other 3D layers.

It also renders in front of the **Postcard_Animals.tif** layer: This is because its Z Position defaults to 0 – the same as the **Title.ai** layer – so it is technically in front of the **Postcard_Animals.tif** layer placed at Z = 100, regardless of where they are in the layer stack.

18 Add the source **MapBackground.tif** to the bottom of the layer stack (above). Note that 2D layers look the same in every view (below).

19 Turn on the background's 3D Layer switch (above), and it will be shown in the same perspective as the other layers (right). Since it is located at Z = 0, it renders in front of the **Postcard_Animals.tif** layer.

19 *complete:* **MapBackground.tif** is placed at Z = 200. Here, we are dragging its Z axis arrow; it's alright if black shows around the map's edges.

As you remember from Part 1, there are several ways you can edit the Z Position of **MapBackground.tif**:

- If the Selection tool is not already active, press V. You can select the layer and move your cursor into the Comp window, positioning it over the blue Z axis arrow until the cursor shows a small Z next to it. Drag your mouse right and left to see how the layer can easily be positioned in front of the title (negative Z) or behind the other two layers (positive Z values larger than 100).

- Scrub its Z Position value in the Timeline.

- Enter an exact value in the Z Position field.

We settled on a value of Z = 200, which leaves us some room to later position more postcard layers in-between the title and background.

20 Set comp marker 0 at 00:00, and enable keyframing for both Position and Point of Interest.

Animating Cameras

STEP 20: With the time marker at 00:00, press Shift+0 to set a Comp marker. This will give you another way to jump back to the start of the comp. Then enable the keyframe animation stopwatch for **Camera 1**'s Position *and* Point of Interest properties. You can tweak the camera's pose if you like.

STEP 21: Press Command+G (Control+G) to open the Go To Time dialog, type "**300**" and click OK. The time marker will jump to 03:00. Verify that the work area ends at this time (hit N if it doesn't), then press Shift+3 to set a comp marker at this point in time.

Move **Camera 1** to a new position by selecting the Orbit Camera tool (shortcut: press C until it cycles to it), and dragging in the Comp window; note how only the Position of the camera has changed, not the Point of Interest. (The Track Z and Track XY Camera tools change both values.) Feel free to use alternate views to move the camera and Point of Interest; our animation move is shown below in Top view. Hit F12 to jump back to the Active Camera to see what the camera sees. Press 0 and 3 to jump between 00:00 and 03:00 to check your beginning and ending poses, then RAM Preview to see the animation you created.

21 The default motion path is linear (right). This often causes the camera to pass closer to the layers than you intended in the middle of its move. Use the motion path's Bezier handles to create a smoother arc for its path (far right).

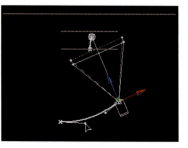

The camera's Position and Point of Interest have Bezier motion paths, just like Position or the Anchor Point for any other keyframed layer. The default motion path is linear, which often does not work well for camera motion – especially if you are trying to get it to swing in an arc. (This is true even if you used the Orbit Camera tool to swivel around your pose.) The result can be that the camera passes closer to the layers than you intended in the middle of the move, then pulls back as it reaches its second Position keyframe. Press V to return to the Selection tool, and practice using the Bezier handles on at least the Camera's Position path to create a more artistic swoop for your animation. RAM Preview until you're happy with the move.

Make sure the handles are not tugged in the opposite direction you want to move; this will result in some strange "loops" to your animation near the keyframes – especially if your Bezier handles are very short. Use the trick of pressing Z to select the Zoom tool and clicking on the keyframe points in the Comp window to get a close look at your handles and path. Option+click (Alt+click) to zoom back out, then press V to return to the Selection tool.

Twirl up the Camera layer when you're done.

Hidden Handles

If you can't see the ends of the motion path handle to grab, Command+drag (Control+drag) out away from the "X" keyframe icon to pull out a new handle. It's best to move to a point in time where the camera back is clear of the keyframe icon.

Viewing a Second Opinion

Switching between the Active Camera and the various orthographic views can be cumbersome. Fortunately, After Effects allows you to have more than one view open simultaneously for the same composition.

With **[Camera*starter]** selected, choose the menu item View>New View. A second Comp window will open, which will also display the contents of your composition. You can then set its 3D View Popup to an alternate view. We usually leave one view on Active Camera, and then use the other to choose alternate views when moving 3D layers or cameras.

When you RAM Preview, by default After Effects will play the window that has the Active Camera chosen for its view. You can turn off this behavior by disabling Previews Favor Active Camera in the Time Controls wing menu (click on the arrow in its upper right corner). Another way of deciding which view will preview is to click on the arrow in the lower left corner of the Comp window: Always Preview This View. You can enable this button for any Comp, Layer, or Footage window, and that window will be the one that caches and plays back when you initiate a RAM Preview.

Use View>New View to open a second window into your composition. Set one to Active Camera, and use the other to try out alternate views. By default, the one with the Active Camera selected will RAM Preview; one way to override this is to enable the Always Preview This View button (circled) for the desired window.

Zoom ≠ Move

There are two ways to zoom or push in on a layer: move the camera closer (which will give a new visual relationship between layers), or change its Zoom property (which scales the image as viewed by the camera as it changes the Angle of View).

Handheld Camera

Next you will create a second camera, and animate it using a different technique. Compositions in After Effects can have multiple cameras. If the Comp window is set to Active Camera, the camera that is nearest the top in the layer stack at the current time, with its Video switch turned on, is the one that renders. You can also select specific cameras from the Comp window's View popup.

STEP 22: Press 3 to locate to comp marker 3 at 03:00. Then select Layer>New>Camera. You can try out a different preset if you like; we chose 50mm. Keep the default name – **Camera 2** – and click OK.

• Press F10 or F11 to switch to the Top or Left view. You will see two camera icons. The currently selected camera will also display its Point of Interest, Angle of View, and axes arrows. If you need to, use the Camera Track tools to see both in the Comp window at the same time.

22 Move to 03:00 and add a Layer>New>Camera. It will automatically be placed at the top of the Timeline (above). In Top or Left view, you should see both cameras at the same time (right).

Workspaces

You can also use Window>Workspace>Two Comp Views and >Four Comp Views to open additional Comp windows, but we prefer the View>New View option as it doesn't resize or reposition the other windows.

• Press F12 to return to the Active Camera view. If the time marker is at 03:00, you will see the view from your new camera, **Camera 2**. Press Page Up to back up in time to 02:29. The Comp window will jump to **Camera 1**'s view: Since **Camera 2** has not started yet at this time, **Camera 1** is the Active Camera.

• Press Page Down to step back to 03:00, where **Camera 2** is active again. Turn off **Camera 2**'s Video switch in the Timeline window. Since this makes **Camera 2** inactive, **Camera 1** underneath takes over.

• Switch **Camera 2** back on, then experiment with the View popup in the Comp window, switching between **Camera 1** and **Camera 2**. This allows you to directly pick which camera to use, regardless of which one is on top in the Timeline, or whether or not their Video switches are on. *This is for previewing only – when you render, the Active Camera is used, **regardless** of which view you have chosen with this popup.*

• Press F12 to return to the Active Camera view.

> You cannot set Opacity keyframes to crossfade between different cameras; they simply switch at their in and out points. If you want to crossfade between cameras, they will need to be in their own compositions; you can then fade between these comps as if they were normal layers. You could also render a single comp in sections, with different cameras active for each render, then crossfade the overlapping frames in your video editing application (or do a final edit in After Effects in a master comp).

STEP 23: With **Camera 2** selected, press P to reveal its Position, then Shift+A to reveal its Point of Interest.

Type Command+Option+O (Control+Alt+O) to open the camera's Auto-Orientation dialog. The default is for the camera to point (orient) to its Point of Interest. Select Off, and click on OK. (We'll discuss the middle option – Orient Along Path – in the next tutorial, *The Planets*.)

Notice in the Timeline window that the Point of Interest property disappears. With **Camera 2** still selected, press F10 or F11 to view the Top or Left views. You will still see the camera as well as the cone that indicates its Angle of View, but you will no longer see the anchor point-style icon for its Point of Interest, or a line connecting the camera to this point.

STEP 24: Press F10 to switch to Top view, then Shift+R to reveal **Camera 2**'s Orientation and Rotation properties. 3D objects have two different ways to rotate them; we'll use just Orientation for now.

Scrub Orientation's X, Y, and Z values (which default to 0, 0, 0), and note how the camera reacts in the Comp window. If you are having trouble corresponding the two, remember that the RGB arrows relate to the XYZ axes: For example, scrubbing the X Orientation value has the same effect as twirling the Red arrow around its axis. (If you make a mess, return the Orientation property to 0, 0, 0, and start over.)

22 *complete:* You can choose which camera to view, regardless of which one is active in the timeline. However, rendering always takes the Active Camera view.

23 Switch the Auto-Orientation option for **Camera 2** to Off. This will make the camera react more like a handheld camera, in which you point it just by moving the camera's body.

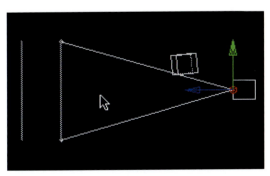

23 *complete:* When the camera's Auto-Orientation is turned Off, the Point of Interest as well as the line connecting it to the camera disappear (shown here in Left view).

24 Scrubbing Orientation's values (left) twirls the camera around its corresponding axes (right).

Several 3D programs use this "one-point" camera model, and you may be more comfortable with it. Without the Point of Interest, however, it can be harder to visualize what a camera is looking at in the alternate views; read the sidebar *Viewing a Second Opinion* for a tip to see the Active Camera's result while you're in one of these other views.

STEP 25: Press 3 to make sure the time marker is at 03:00, and B to start the work area at this point. Then enable keyframing for **Camera 2**'s Position and Orientation. Play around and choose a placement you like that is different from **Camera 1**'s final keyframes, employing the tools you've learned.

Press End to locate to the end of the comp (05:29). Press Shift+6 to set a comp marker here, and N to extend the work area to this point.

Edit **Camera 2** again for a different framing of your scene. RAM Preview to see your new move. Remember that the Position path is a Bezier curve; if your animation wobbles a bit around the keyframes, your path handles are probably pointing at angles that don't describe a smooth path.

25 Set up an animation for your second camera. Don't forget to smooth its motion by tweaking its path between keyframes (below).

When you have a second camera animation that you like, double-click the ribbed area of the work area bar along the top of the timeline. This resets the work area to the entire length of the comp. Press F12 to switch back to the Active Camera view and RAM Preview, noting the switch when **Camera 2** starts in the timeline. If you don't see a switch, make sure the Video switches for both cameras are turned on.

Twirl up **Camera 2**'s properties when you're done.

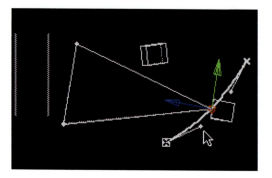

We encourage you to practice and create your own camera animations. If you become frustrated, check our prebuilt comp [Camera_after Step 25] *for ideas, but remember that your animation doesn't have to be the same as ours. And don't forget to save your project.*

Orbiting Camera

It can be difficult to craft a Bezier motion path for the camera that creates a perfectly smooth "orbit" animation. You can use Parenting (covered in *RoboTV*, *Piccadilly Circus*, and *Flamingo 4*) and a null object (also covered in *Piccadilly Circus*) to help execute this move:

- Create a new camera, and set its Auto-Orientation to Off. Position it so that it is pointing along the Z axis at the point you want it to orbit around, with no Rotation or Orientation offset.

- Create a Layer>New>Null Object, enable its 3D Layer switch, and place it at the point in Z space you want to orbit around. It should have the same X and Y coordinates as your camera.

- Parent the camera to the null object.

- To orbit the camera, rotate the null object – the camera will be swung around by the null.

- To zoom the camera in and out, change just the camera's Z Position in the Timeline window.

- For a more advanced setup, add a second Null as the master parent, and animate only its Y Position to move the camera rig up and down.

This animation technique is used for **Camera 2** in **[Camera_after Step 25_alt]**.

Part 4: Rotation Re-orientation

In this section, you will experiment with rotating layers in 3D space, adding more 2D and 3D layers, and precompose a few into their own comp. Precomposing is as useful for grouping together 3D layers as it is 2D layers – especially since you can still Collapse Transformations and have their 3D positions ripple into your final composition.

Throughout this book we've encouraged you on occasion to vary from our choices when you're building your comp. This is even more true for the next two sections: Have fun, compose an elegant frame, make a mess, whatever; the main point is to learn the tools. In the last section and corresponding PDF on the DVD, we will walk through a more carefully thought-out project in detail.

Work Area = Comp

Double-click the ribbed area of the work area bar to reset it to the length of the comp.

26 Reveal **Title.ai**'s Transform properties in the Timeline window, and click on the word "Reset" (circled in red) to return all properties to their default values.

27 3D layers have two sets of rotation properties: Orientation, which sets an XYZ rotational pose, and individual Rotation values for the X, Y, and Z axes.

27 *complete:* Practice animating the three Rotation properties; feel free to have a bit of fun. **Title.ai**'s axes' arrows in the Comp window help show which way it is pointing.

Rotation versus Orientation

STEP 26: To start fresh, make sure all the properties of **Title.ai** are twirled up in the Timeline window, and twirl it down again. The subsection Transform should also be twirled down at this point. Click on the word "Reset" next to the word "Transform": All the values for Anchor Point, Position, Scale, Orientation, Rotation, and Opacity will return to their defaults. (This is probably where the values already are, but we're just being safe.)

STEP 27: Make sure the Comp window is set to Active Camera view. Select the **Title.ai** layer again, and press R. When a layer is 2D, R will twirl down a single property: Rotation. When a layer is 3D, as in this case, Rotation consists of four properties that you can edit: Orientation, plus individual X, Y, and Z Rotations.

The Orientation values consists of X, Y, and Z values, so a keyframe set for Orientation will remember a "pose" (more on this in the next Step). The Rotation values are used for animating the rotation of, rather than merely posing, a layer. Unlike Orientation, you can set Rotation values for multiple full rotations – not just an angle from 0 to 360.

• Turn on the stopwatches for X, Y, and Z rotation and set up some keyframing over a second or so, so you can see how this works. Have fun rotating around all three axes, and don't worry about making a creative mess – we will reset these values in a moment. Make sure you animate at least one axis through a full rotation.

• When you've set some keyframes, RAM Preview and see how it looks. (You can also turn on Motion Blur for this layer by checking both the layer's M switch and the Enable Motion Blur button.) Rotation and Scale occur around the Anchor Point, which is currently in the center of the **Title.ai** layer; leave it here, as it works fine in this case.

STEP 28: After you've had some fun with Rotation, reset **Title.ai**'s Transform properties again: In the Timeline window, twirl up the **Title.ai** layer, twirl it down again, and click on the word "Reset" – all the Rotation values will return to their defaults. If you have set any keyframes, turn off keyframing for these values. Then press R to show just the Orientation and Rotation properties.

At the risk of repeating ourselves, Orientation should be thought of more as a "pose" than a way to rotate a layer. If you try to keyframe a rotation animation using Orientation, you will be disappointed:

• Change the Comp window to Front view to remove any perspective distortion and ignore the camera's animation.

• At time 00:00, turn on the stopwatch for Orientation to set a first keyframe with a value of 0,0,0. Press B to start the work area here.

• Move to 01:00, and press N to end the work area here.

• Scrub Orientation's X value – the first of the three numbers – around almost a full rotation to about 350° (be sure to scrub, don't just type in numbers). You will see **Title.ai** flip around in the Comp window.

• Do the same for Orientation's Y and Z values, scrubbing their values to about 350°. The title should end up facing the front again, albeit at a slight angle.

• Press 0 on the numeric keypad to RAM Preview your animation. You might expect, after rotating in all three axes and seeing these exciting flips and tumbles happen as you scrubbed their values, that you had created a wildly flipping animation. Instead, you're greeted with a very sedate move of 10° in the opposite direction.

What happened? Orientation takes the shortest path to move from one keyframe to the next; it feels no obligation to carry every twist and turn that the Rotation properties do. Keep this in mind when you're deciding which property to use when you're animating a layer.

If your Orientation animation did not turn out as we described, compare your version against [**Camera_after Step 28**]. *Feel free to continue with this prebuilt comp if you prefer. Save your project; you'll be adding more layers in the following Part.*

28 Even though you keyframed a 350° move for each axis of Orientation (above), the resulting animation (below) moves only 10° in the opposite direction. Unlike Rotation, Orientation takes the shortest path between keyframes.

Intersection Dissection

Let's take a moment to talk about intersections between layers – or the lack of them, as is sometimes the case. The **Title.ai** layer is 320 pixels wide, which means that if you rotate this layer's Y value to +90° or −90°, it should intersect the **Postcard_Animals.tif** layer positioned only 100 pixels behind it in Z space.

Open **[Camera_for intersections]** in this project's **MyComps** folder, and try the following steps:

- First off, change the Fast Previews popup in the Comp window to Off to avoid confusion. (The OpenGL renderer supports intersections, but your final render will use the Comp's rendering plug-in.)

- Press F12 to use the Active Camera view. If the Rotation properties for **Title.ai** are not already exposed, select this layer and press R.

- Scrub the degrees portion of **Title.ai**'s Y Rotation value from 0 to 300, and watch it swivel around in the Comp window. It does not appear to collide with the **Postcard_Animals.tif** layer.

- Set the Y Rotation value to 90°, and press F11 to change to Left view. In this view, you can see that the P on the left side of the title is crossing over the line where the layer **Postcard_Animals.tif** sits.

- Return to Active Camera view (F12). Because this comp is using the Standard 3D Rendering Plug-in, which doesn't allow for layers to intersect, the Active Camera view ignores this incursion and doesn't render the intersection. This speeds up rendering, and allows you to be less precise with your arrangement and animation of layers in 3D space.

For layers to intersect (above), use the Advanced 3D plug-in from the Composition Settings>Advanced tab (below).

- That said, there are certainly times when you *do* want to see these intersections. Fortunately, After Effects ships with two alternate Rendering Plug-ins: Advanced 3D and OpenGL Hardware.

- Select Composition Settings and click on the Advanced tab. In the Rendering Plug-in popup, select Advanced 3D, and click OK.

- In the Comp window, you will now see the P in **Title.ai** cut off by the layer it is intersecting with.

Why not use the Advanced 3D plug-in all the time? It does tend to render slightly slower than Standard 3D (particularly when it comes to shadows), and – at least as of version 6.5 – there are still a couple of features such as Stencil Alpha that the Advanced plug-in does not render. The OpenGL Hardware plug-in (which is the same rendering engine as used by the OpenGL Fast Previews) has even more restrictions, and should only be used when you need to crank out a really fast preview render.

Aside from the intersection issue, these plug-ins can have very different looks, especially when it comes to shadows – so experiment!

Using the Standard 3D rendering plug-in, layers never seem to intersect (left), even though alternate views (such as Left view) show they do in certain poses (right).

Part 5: Adding and Collapsing

We'll wrap up this portion of the tutorial by adding more 2D and 3D layers, plus a light.

To make the final composite easier to manage, you will group some of your layers into a precomp. It is possible to have 3D layers in a precomp and still manipulate them in 3D space in the comp they are then nested in; you can also collapse transformations for nested 3D comps with interesting results.

Again, the point of this section is to have fun while you're mastering a few additional concepts, so we're going to give you looser instructions than normal. However, you will also find we've saved prebuilt comps of most of these steps showing our own ideas, if you want to just poke around or compare your results with ours.

Step 29: Press Home to return the time marker to 00:00, and F12 to return the Comp window to Active Camera view.

Reset the **Title.ai** layer to its original placement. This includes turning off any animation keyframes for its Rotation or Orientation properties and zeroing out these values. Twirl up its properties to create more room in the Timeline window.

Step 30: In the Project window's **MySources** folder, we've already imported some additional "postcards" for you to play with. Drag one or more into [**Camera * starter**].

OpenGL Acceleration

Manipulating 3D layers and lights can be slow. OpenGL hardware acceleration is available under the Fast Previews popup in the lower right corner of the Comp window (resize it open wider to see it). OpenGL makes working with multiple 3D layers much more responsive, at the cost of some quality tradeoffs.

Turn their 3D Layer switches on, and array them as you please in 3D space. The only suggestions we'll make are to keep them in front of **MapBackground.tif**, and to not obscure **Title.ai**. If you are having trouble fitting them in, you don't need to rely on their Z Position to make them smaller; go ahead and reduce their Scale as well.

For our own version, we brought in two more layers, placed them to the left and right of the **Postcard_Animals.tif**, and scaled all three postcards to 80%.

30 We've provided three more postcards for you to play with. The images inside are from the Artbeats volumes Penguins, Timelapse Plants, and Under The Sea.

> Rather than pose multiple layers in 3D space, you could set up one layer, duplicate it, and replace the duplicate layer's source by Option+dragging (Alt+dragging) a new layer from the Project window to the comp. The new layer will have identical attributes (3D Layer switch, scale amount, and so on) – you need only to reposition the duplicate in 3D space.

31 Practice using the Orientation and Rotation properties to add interest to the arrangement of your layers (left). Remember that alternate views, such as Top view (right), can help you better visualize what is happening.

32 Select your postcard layers in their current arrangement (above), and Layer> Pre-compose them. Unfortunately, the result is the postcards jumping to new positions (below). Don't panic…

STEP 31: Experiment with the Orientation and Rotation properties of the postcard layers – make them seem more like elements of a mobile hanging in space, or pose them to give the appearance they are facing the main title. This may require some tweaking of their Position properties as well.

We chose to orient the two cards on the sides in toward the title. Remember that alternate views such as Top come in very handy for arranging layers in 3D space; this is a case where it is useful to have a second View>New View open set to Active Camera.

Precomposing 3D Layers

Layers in 3D have more properties to keep track of. It is not unusual to reach a point where you think "This idea looks good – but now I need to scale them all down and rotate them a bit. What a pain." Fortunately, there are a couple of tools in After Effects that make it possible to act on a group of layers as if they were one object: the Parenting feature discussed in the *RoboTV, Piccadilly Circus*, and *Flamingo 4* tutorials, and good ol' fashioned Layer>Pre-compose, which we will use here.

STEP 32: Set your Comp window to Active Camera view. Select all the postcard layers, and select Layer>Pre-compose, or use the shortcut Command+Shift+C (Control+Shift+C). The Pre-compose dialog will open; disable Open New Composition, give this new comp a useful name such as "**Postcards_precomp**" and click OK.

When you precompose 2D layers, you are used to the Comp window not changing; the only action happens in the Timeline window, where the previously selected layers are replaced with a precomp. However, in this case the Comp window may have changed considerably: The postcards act like they are being seen in Front view, while the rest of the layers appear in their normal Active Camera view poses.

The problem is related to After Effects not knowing whether or not you also wanted to precompose the cameras as well, and how to treat this precomp in the main composition. The precomposed layers are now using the default camera in [**Postcards_precomp**], with the result appearing as a 2D layer in [**Camera * starter**].

This can be remedied with a single click of the mouse: In the Timeline window for [**Camera * starter**], turn on the Collapse Transformations switch for the layer **Postcards_precomp**. This will instruct the 3D layers in the comp [**Postcards_precomp**] to ignore their own camera (and any lights), and to use the active camera in [**Camera * starter**]. The Comp window should return to displaying the same poses as before you precomposed.

Note that merely turning on the 3D switch for the precomp layer is not the solution – this just sets the precomp's 2D composite output as a 3D layer in the main comp, where it reacts to the camera in a different way. You need to also Collapse Transformations.

STEP 33: As with any precomp, you can further transform this layer in the current comp:

• Turn on the 3D Layer switch for **Postcards_precomp**. You need to do this to manipulate this precomp in 3D space. Since you've collapsed this precomp's transformations, all 3D transforms performed here will be factored into the 3D transforms for each individual layer in the precomp.

32 *complete:* Turn on Collapse Transformations for your nested precomp. This will instruct the 3D layers in the precomp to use the cameras in this higher-level comp.

33 Scrub the Y Orientation parameter for **Postcards_precomp**. Although it may seem you should just be twirling this layer around its center (below left), since it has been collapsed you are also swinging all of the nested layers, with their 3D offsets taken into account (below right). The Advanced 3D Rendering Plug-in was used here, allowing intersections between the layers.

Camera*starter • Timeline

33 *complete:* Scrubbing the Z value of the precomp's Anchor Point (above) moves the entire group in relation to their center (left). This also changes the arc they will rotate in.

- With **Postcards_precomp** still selected, press R to reveal its Orientation and Rotation properties. Experiment with scrubbing their different parameters – especially Y. Your entire set of postcards will rotate around **Title.ai**, *in 3D space.*

Okay, that was kind of freaky; what's going on? 3D layers – including precomps – have 3D Anchor Points, as well. If a layer's Anchor Point is set to be forward of the surface of the layer, rotating or orienting it will swing it around as if it was on a stick attached to that anchor in 3D space. A precomp defaults to having its Position and Anchor Point at Z = 0, which is the same location as **Title.ai**. However, since some of your postcards are probably set back at a different Z value, rotating their collapsed precomp swings the nested postcards around the precomp's anchor.

If you want to get a better handle on this, press Shift+A to also reveal **Postcards_precomp**'s Anchor Point, and scrub its Z value. You will see the entire group of postcards move closer to and farther away from the center of the comp where **Title.ai** is. Then continue to scrub the Orientation and Rotation properties, noting how the postcards swing in different arcs depending on the anchor's position.

STEP 34: Feel free to experiment with the other Transform properties of **Postcards_precomp**, such as Position, Scale, and Opacity. These should all work as you would expect. Finish by placing this precomp in a pose you like. We personally settled on our arrangement at the time we precomposed. When you're done, twirl up all layer outlines to tidy up your Timeline window.

Effecting 3D

A new feature in After Effects 6.x is the ability to add effects to precomps that have their Collapse Transformations switch enabled. Note this changes the render order a bit, performing effects after transformations (resulting in the "size" of effects not changing as the Scale changes).

Stationary Bugs

As mentioned earlier, After Effects allows 2D and 3D layers to be mixed in the same comp. This comes in handy if you have an object that needs to stay in the same place in a frame, regardless of what the camera is doing.

Step 35: With the time at 00:00, press the apostrophe key (') to toggle on the Title-Action Safe grid in the Comp window.

Then locate the **EarthBug.tif** in the **MySources** folder, and drag it to the lower right corner of the Comp window, near the Title Safe lines. You are going to be using this as a "bug" to overlay on top of your composition. Scale it down (shortcut: S) to an appropriate size – around 15% to 25% is good – and tweak its Position. Toggle the title safe guides back off.

Jump around to different points in time in the comp. Note that the bug stays in the same position regardless of the camera move. This is because new layers default to being 2D, which aren't affected by the camera. If you place this layer on top of the stack in the Timeline window, it will also render on top of all the other layers, regardless of their Z Positions.

35 The earth "bug" in the lower right corner (top) is not affected by the camera's animation, because it is a 2D layer (above).

A Light Touch

The final optional element you might add is a spotlight to further enhance the feeling of depth, and to add a vignette effect to the edges of the frame. Lights were covered in more detail in the tutorial *Piccadilly Circus*; if you are not familiar with them, you might want to come back to these final steps after you have worked through that tutorial. Here we will remind you of a few general tips.

Step 36: Return the time marker to 00:00, and twirl up all layers. Select Layer>New>Light. The Light Settings default to the last light you created; use a Light Type of Spot and enable Casts Shadows. We used the values shown in the figure to the right, but you can always tweak all of these parameters later.

New lights also tend to be positioned too close to layers that are near Z = 0; move the light's Z Position to at least –300 to illuminate more of the scene.

Layers default to *receiving* shadows, but not *casting* shadows. You want the main title to cast shadows on the postcards behind. Select the layer **Title.ai**, and type AA to reveal its Material Options. Toggle the Casts Shadows option from Off to On.

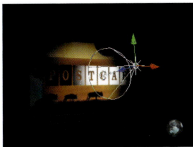

36 At 00:00, add a spotlight (above). For shadows to work, they need to be enabled both for the light, and for a forward layer to cast them (below). New lights may not fully illuminate layers that are near 0 on the Z axis (left).

37 Aim the Light's Point of Interest at the title layer, move it back to illuminate the entire scene, and animate a sweep.

Instant Shadows

The shortcut to toggle a layer's Casts Shadows property on and off is to select it and type Option+Shift+C (Alt+Shift+C).

Draft 3D

Lights and shadows require a lot of extra rendering time. To speed up previews, turn on the Draft 3D switch in the Timeline to temporarily disable the effect of lights and the camera's optional Depth of Field.

38 Frames from the final animation. Note the shadow cast by the title, and how the 2D earth bug in the lower right corner is not affected by animating the light and cameras.

Step 37: Since you want the light to focus on the main title, check the Position of **Title.ai** (it should be 160,120,0) and check that these values are also being used for the Point of Interest of your light. The same shortcut – A – reveals the Point of Interest for both cameras and lights.

With the light selected, type Shift+P to reveal its Position property, and enable it for animation. Since we have not animated the layers, animate the light to perform a mild sweep during the length of the comp so the result does not appear static. Everything you've learned about moving the camera applies to lights, including taking advantage of the different views, and making sure your motion path is smooth.

Step 38: RAM Preview and see if you are happy with your light and animation. If not, feel free to tweak away. Here are a few tips to keep in mind when you're working with lights and shadows:

• A light's falloff darkens an image, as it is no longer fully illuminated. Increase the light's Intensity past 100% if needed – there is no penalty.

• If the light is closer to the layer casting shadows than the camera is, the resulting shadow will be larger than the layer casting it. The farther away the light, the tighter the shadow.

• In order to see a shadow, there needs to be some separation in space between layers casting shadows and those receiving them. You might need to move **Postcards_precomp** farther away from the title to better see the shadows they are receiving.

• For Shadow Diffusion, an amount of 5 to 15 pixels should work well for a 320×240 pixel comp. As you reduce the Shadow Diffusion amount, your shadow may appear darker; if needed, reduce the Shadow Darkness amount to get a less heavy-handed shadow effect. If you are using the Advanced 3D Rendering Plug-in, the sharpness of shadows are also influenced by the Shadow Map Resolution parameter found in Composition Settings>Advanced>Options; larger maps render sharper (and more slowly).

When you're finished, RAM Preview and optionally render your final composition. Our favorite features in After Effects are those that give us new "looks" to use in our designs and animations; 3D space – including lights – certainly qualifies for this award.

Part 6: Postcards from Earth

The techniques you've learned in this tutorial are easily extended to more complex projects. Go back and play the file **Postcards.mov** in this tutorial's **Final Movies** folder. The project that created this movie – **Postcards.aep** – is broken down in great detail in the document **08B_Postcards_Bonus.pdf** on your disk. To give you a taste, here are the highlights:

• 2D and 3D layers are interwoven throughout the spot. The opening space flythrough is 2D footage, which dissolves away with a gradient wipe to reveal a 3D world behind. A pair of 2D layers provide a steady backdrop throughout. The main title is also in 2D, composited over the 3D world. The postcard precomps are used both in 3D space in the middle of the spot and as 2D elements in the main title at the end.

• Four different 3D cameras are used to view the same world from different angles. The cameras are trimmed to cut on musical beats.

• The "hero" of the 3D scenes – a stylized earth floating in the middle of the frame – is created using the Cycore FX plug-in CC Sphere (Cycore FX come bundled with After Effects 6.5; don't forget to install them!). We will detail how we created the texture map for this translucent globe, and a series of relatively simple expressions which keep CC Sphere's 2D layer always oriented towards the currently active camera, creating the illusion that it has true 3D depth.

• The postcards were built using a series of template precomps for their shapes and the circular cutout animation. Different footage was then used inside these templates. This means changes made in one composition – such as altering the basic postcard shape – automatically ripple through to all of the postcard precomps. Expressions also allow us to control the Opacity of the solid-colored frames for all the postcards from one slider in the final composition.

• Notice how the background flashes in time with the soundtrack? We'll walk you through how to use Time Remapping to force the pace of one clip to follow another.

The 3D space features in After Effects have indeed opened up new worlds for graphical design. Have fun exploring them!

The project **Postcards.aep** extends the techniques learned in this tutorial. The earth is created with the CC Sphere effect, and expressions make it follow the camera, creating the illusion of real 3D. The opening movie (left) is from the Artbeats CD Space and Planets; the gradient wipe is from Pixelan's Video SpiceRack.

Connect

For more information on topics covered in this tutorial, check out the following volumes of *Creating Motion Graphics*:

Volume 1:

Continuous Rasterization

Precomposing

Collapsing Transformations

Rotating around the Anchor Point

3D Space, Cameras, and Lights

The Planets

Swooping through a universe of 2D layers that auto-orient toward the camera.

This tutorial serves two purposes: to teach a series of useful tricks that help manage layers in 3D space, and to prepare elements that will be used in the next tutorial. You will animate a 3D camera through a number of objects – flat art of fanciful planets – arranged at varying distances in Z space. The camera and light will both auto-orient along the path they're traveling, and the flat objects will auto-orient toward the camera as it flies past to help maintain the illusion that they have depth. You will then prerender this action as separate color and matte layers to use as part of an opening title sequence (the next tutorial).

OVERVIEW

Main Concepts:

These are the features and concepts we will be focusing on in this project:

- Auto-Orient Camera along Path
- Expressing the Light's Position
- Auto-Orient Light along Path
- Multiple view windows
- Pixel Aspect Ratio correction
- Auto-Orient layers toward Camera
- Creating a 3D layer
- Adding camera roll
- Depth of Field & Focus Distance
- Field rendering
- Adding Output Modules
- Rendering a separate fill and matte
- Rendering with straight alpha

Requirements:

After Effects 6.5 or later Standard edition.

Getting Started:

Inside the **Tutorials** master folder on the accompanying DVD, locate and copy the folder **09_Planets** to your hard drive.

In the folder **Final Movie** inside this main folder, double-click on and play **Planets.mov**.

Inside the **Project** folder you'll find the finished After Effects project file **Planets.aep**. Open the project file – this is your starting point; we suggest you save under a new name after each major section.

Much of the tedious work of arranging the camera and the faux planets in Z space has already been done. This will allow you to focus on the core of this tutorial: using tools in After Effects to orient the camera, light, and objects for you. Afterward, you will position one remaining planet, tweak the position of another, and swap out other planets to taste. On the technical side, you will also be working in a DV NTSC composition with non-square pixels which you will need to field render for the next tutorial.

We're going to assume you already have some experience working in 3D comps, or have already completed the previous tutorial *Postcards in Space*. If not, work through at least enough of that tutorial to familiarize yourself with navigating After Effects' 3D toolset.

A frame from the final *Planets* fly-through. Depth of Field is turned on which renders the planets in the foreground and background out of focus.

The Tasks

This is what you will be doing in the various parts of this tutorial:

PART 1: Use Auto-Orientation to automatically point the camera and light along their paths and the planets at the camera, express the light to follow the camera, and create a second viewer window.

PART 2: Add another planet and place it in 3D space, tweak the positions of some of the planets, and swap out planet layers with alternate planets.

PART 3: Improve the camera's motion by adding an ease out and banking rotation, plus use Depth of Field for selective focusing.

PART 4: Learn how to render a composition as separate RGB and alpha channel movies.

Draft vs. Best

After Effects defaults to creating layers in Best Quality. If you find the RAM Previews too slow on your computer, switch the planet layers to Draft Quality. They will shimmer a bit, but the time savings may be worth it.

Part 1: The Orient Express

After Effects has long had the ability to automatically orient layers so they would point along a 2D animation path. With the addition of 3D space in version 5.0, Auto-Orientation has been expanded to include auto-orienting cameras and lights as well as layers along a 3D path. Layers can also be set to automatically orient themselves toward the camera so you can always catch their good side.

#	Source Name		
▽ ■ 1	ৠ Camera		
	▷ ◉ Position	27.6 , 171.0 , -557.5	✓ ▶
▷ □ 2	♀ Light		
▷ ■ 3	■ TO DO!		
▷ □ 4	aF_PS_CreamRockXtra.tif		
▷ □ 5	aF_PS_Moonish.tif		
▷ □ 6	aF_PS_PittedRock.tif		
▷ □ 7	aF_CB_ChrisStone.tif		
▷ □ 8	aF_PS_RedGreen.tif		
▷ □ 9	aF_PS_Patina.tif		
▷ □ 10	aF_PS_Reflection.tif		
▷ □ 11	aF_CB_Basalt.tif		
▷ □ 12	aF_CB_LayeredTerrain.tif		

1–2 In the starter comp, only the camera's Position property is animating. The layer comments applied to **Camera** and **Light** spell out what else you will be doing to these layers; we also added a solid with its Video switch turned off to give more room for comments.

Scroll Zoom

If you have a mouse with a scroll wheel, place the cursor over the Comp window and use the wheel to quickly zoom in and out while keeping the window size the same.

4 To zoom the 3D views to fit inside the Comp window, first select the Track Z Camera tool.

STEP 1: In the project **Planets.aep**, double-click the [**Planets*starter**] comp to open it. The default view should be the Active Camera; press Shift+F12 to make sure the F12 key is assigned to this view, making it easier to jump back to this view later.

STEP 2: Use Command+A on Mac (Control+A on Windows) to select all the layers, press U to reveal any animation keyframes that have already been applied, then press F2 to deselect the layers. You will notice that only the Camera is animating, with two Position keyframes.

STEP 3: Select the **Camera** layer, then select the Left view from the View popup at the bottom-right of the Comp window. Press Shift+F11 to ensure that F11 has been assigned to this view. This will make switching views easier as you proceed.

From this angle, you should see the camera and a portion of its motion path, but you might be zoomed in too close to see its full path and all the layers. You can either enlarge the Comp window and/or reduce the comp's magnification until you see the entire path, or – better yet – use the Track Camera tools:

STEP 4: To quickly resize the Left view, follow these steps:

- Make sure the Tools palette is open; if not, press Command+1 (Control+1) to open it.

- Press C until the Track Z Camera tool is selected.

- Click in the Comp window and drag either left or down to zoom out until you can see all of the layers and the entire length of the camera's motion path.

> When you're in any of the orthogonal views (Top, Left, Right, and so on), the Track Camera tools can be used to zoom in and recenter your view of the world – without affecting the X, Y, and Z values of your camera layers. These tools only affect values in Active Camera view.

To get another perspective on the camera's path, select the Top view, and press Shift+F10 to make sure this shortcut key has been assigned. With the Track Z Camera tool still selected, click and drag in the Comp window to zoom back as necessary to see the entire path. If the layers

4 *continued:* In the Left view, zoom the 3D views in to fit inside the Comp window (left) by clicking and dragging in the Comp window with the Track Z Camera tool until the camera path and all of the layers fit.

are a bit off-center in the Comp window, press C twice to toggle around to the Track X/Y Camera tool, then drag them inside the Comp window until they are centered to your taste. When you're satisfied with your views, press V to return to the Selection tool.

STEP 5: Drag the time marker in the Timeline window and watch the camera move along its path. Note that only the "back" of the camera is moving, with its Point of Interest remaining behind the farthest layer.

Orienting the Camera along its Path

The current camera animation just pushes forward past the planets, rather than swooping between the planets as you might hope. You could try animating the camera's Point of Interest to change the direction the camera is looking as it sweeps along its curved path, but the effort will soon feel like you're trying to steer both the front and back wheels of a car independently from each other. In other words, it's tricky. Using the Auto-Orient option tells After Effects to do the steering for you.

STEP 6: Select the **Camera** layer, twirl up its properties to hide the Position keyframes, and twirl the layer down again to reveal all of its Transform properties.

STEP 7: With the **Camera** layer selected, press Command+Option+O (Control+Alt+O), or use the menu command Layer>Transform>Auto-Orient. A dialog will appear with a set of choices of how you want the object to orient. Choose Orient Along Path and click OK.

Out of the corner of your eye, you may have caught that the Timeline display changed. Look closely, and you will notice that the Point of Interest parameter has disappeared, since it is no longer being used.

4 *complete:* The Top view gives a different perspective on the camera's path. Use the Track Camera tools to alter this view to taste.

5 As the camera moves along its path, the Point of Interest (where arrow is pointing) remains stationery.

7 Select Layer>Transform>Auto-Orient for the **Camera**. Select the option Orient Along Path.

8 The camera defaults to orienting toward its Point of Interest (left). When Auto-Orientation is set to Path, it points along a tangent to its Position path (right).

STEP 8: Still using the Top view (shortcut: F10), scrub the time marker and observe the camera's path now. Notice it now points at a tangent to its current position on its Position path, rather than at its Point of Interest (which is now gone). Press F11 to switch to Left view, and scrub the timeline here also. If you want to compare the difference, just bring up the Auto-Orientation dialog and set the option back to Orient Towards Point of Interest and notice the difference. Be sure to set it back to Orient Along Path when you're done.

> The third Auto-Orientation choice – Off – also disables the Point of Interest, but it does not force the camera to look along its path either. In this mode, you use Rotation and Orientation to point the camera, which mimics the way some 3D programs work.

If you need to compare your work so far, we've saved a comp in your project with the camera already oriented correctly, under the name **[Planets_after Step 08]**. *You can find it in the* **Planets * prebuilt> compare comps_after Step ## folder.** *Don't forget to save your project.*

The Collapse of Auto-Orient

If you precompose a group of 3D layers that are set to Orient Towards Camera, and then Collapse Transformations, you might expect the layers from the precomp to continue to auto-orient toward the camera. But they won't.

Expressive Lighting

To illuminate your way as you travel among the planets, it would be handy if the light always pointed the same way as the camera. This is very easy to set up with expressions (refer to figures on the next page).

STEP 9: With the **Camera** layer selected, Shift+select the **Light** layer. Type P to reveal both of their Position properties. Note that they are currently different from each other.

Expressionless?

If you are new to Expressions, they are the focus of Tutorial 11. Don't worry; we use only a very simple one here.

STEP 10: Option+click (Alt+click) on the **Light** layer's Position animation stopwatch. This will enable expressions for this property and write a default expression that means "Position = position."

Drag the pick whip tool for the **Light** layer to point at the word Position for the **Camera** layer (see figures on next page). Release the mouse, and hit Enter to accept the new expression. Look at their Position properties, and note that they are now the same.

10 Option+click (Alt+click) on the stopwatch to enable Expressions for the **Light** layer's Position property.

Once the Expression is enabled, click on the pick whip (the spiral icon) and drag it to the Position property for the **Camera** layer.

Release the mouse, and hit Enter to accept the new Expression.

STEP 11: With both the **Light** and **Camera** layers still selected, press F11 to recall the Left view, and scrub the time marker along the length of the timeline. The **Light** layer does indeed stay attached to the **Camera** layer…but it doesn't point in the same direction; it's still pointing at its own Point of Interest. Use the same cure as you did for **Camera**:

- Make sure **Light** is the only layer selected.

- Press Command+Option+O (Control+Alt+O) to bring up its Auto-Orientation dialog.

- Select Orient Along Path, and click OK.

11 The light has been expressed to have the same position as the camera, but it's still aimed at its own Point of Interest (below left). It needs its Auto-Orientation also set to Orient Along Path (below right).

Bright Lights/ Big Universe

You can set a light's Intensity to greater than 100. If you find the planets too dark, select the light, press T, and scrub its Intensity higher until you're satisfied. If later you find the plants to be too bright, reduce the Intensity.

12 Use View>New View to open a second Comp window. You can look at alternate views in the first window (below left) and see the result of the Active Camera in the second window (below right).

The **Light** layer will lose its Point of Interest, and instead snap to point in the same direction as the **Camera** layer. You'll notice that the light has no visible motion path, since it's following the camera's path via the expression. You can scrub the time marker and check out the different views to verify this, if you wish. Twirl up their Position properties when you're done.

You could have achieved a similar result by Parenting the light to the camera, but both would need to have been set to the exact same position and orientation at the moment you parented. On the other hand, if you wanted the light to be offset from the camera's positioning, it would be easier to set up this offset and then parent, rather than use an expression.

We've saved a version with the light already expressed and oriented under the name [**Planets_after Step 11**], *if you need to compare your version with ours.*

Second Sight

Use F12 to switch [**Planets*starter**] to the Active Camera view, and RAM Preview the comp. The **Camera** and **Light** layers now are flying nicely along their paths, but the overall scene just doesn't look that good – the planets are darkly lit, and something funny is going on with their aspect ratios (they should all be perfect spheres). To get further insight to what's going on, we'll create a second Comp window for [**Planets*starter**] in which you can view your edits.

STEP 12: Select the menu item View>New View. A second Comp window will open, set to view the Active Camera, which also displays the contents of [**Planets*starter**]. Arrange the two comp windows so it's easy to see them both. On a 1024×768 or similar monitor size, setting both to 50% Zoom and Half Resolution and placing them side by side works well.

Choose one Comp window – say, the one on the right – to always be your Active Camera view. Click on the other one to bring it forward, and use the F10 and F11 keyboard shortcuts to switch between the Top and Left views, respectively. Set it to Top view for now.

STEP 13: When you start a RAM Preview and you have more than one view open for a comp, by default After Effects previews the Active Camera Comp window. To ensure this always happens, click on the Options arrow in the upper right corner of the Time Controls palette, and verify that Previews Favor Active Camera is toggled on.

13 When you have more than one view open for the same comp, make sure the one with the Active Camera renders when you start a RAM Preview.

STEP 14: As we noted in the introduction, this comp is set to use DV NTSC non-square pixels. When your final render is played back on a real video monitor through a DV signal chain, the final image will be scaled horizontally by about 90%. In the meantime, the comp you are viewing on your computer monitor looks about 111% as wide as it will on playback.

If this distortion bothers you, drag your Active Camera Comp window wider until you can see the Toggle Pixel Aspect Correction button along its lower right edge (it's to the right of the 3D View Popup). Click on it to enable it. The display in the Comp window will now shrink horizontally about 10%, to give you a more accurate view of their true aspect. It may look a little rough; this scaling is done using the equivalent of Draft Quality (no antialiasing), and is only for preview – the comp would not be rendered this way. After Effects will warn you of these consequences – but this mode is still good for a quick check.

> For more details on managing D1/DV NTSC non-square sources, check out the tutorial *AutoTracker* earlier in this book, and the chapter *Working with D1/DV NTSC* in *Creating Motion Graphics Volume 2*.

14 Enable Pixel Aspect Correction for your Active Camera Comp window to view your spheres using a square pixel aspect ratio.

Angling for Attention

Set the time marker to around 01:10, and study your comp. The spheres roughly in the center of the window look taller than they should; the sphere in the lower left corner looks wider than it should. These distortions are not caused by their pixel aspect ratio, but by the fact that they do not face the camera head-on. Viewing them at an angle causes this perspective distortion. Fortunately, just as you can orient cameras and lights along a path, you can orient other layers to face the camera.

15 If the planets do not face the camera, the resulting perspective distortion makes them look like out-of-round spheres.

Auto-Orientation

Auto-Orientation
- ○ Off
- ○ Orient Along Path
- ● Orient Towards Camera

Cancel   OK

15 *continued:* Set all the planets to Orient Towards Camera.

STEP 15: Select all the planet layers (select layer 4, then Shift+click layer 12 to select it and all of the layers in-between), and press Command+Option+O (Control+Alt+O) to open the Auto-Orientation dialog. Pick the option Orient Towards Camera, and click OK. You will notice three things happen:

- In the Top view Comp window, you should notice all of the planet layers will snap to new orientations, pointing at the camera. While they are still selected, note their axis orientation arrows: Their blue Z arrows are all pointed straight at the camera.

- All of the planets in the Active Camera view should look more like true spheres.

- The spheres should also look brighter. Not only are they facing the camera, they're facing the light you expressed to the camera back in Step 10. This light is now getting bounced straight back at the camera, resulting in better illumination.

15 *complete:* After you set the planets to orient toward the camera, notice how their blue Z axis arrows now all point at the camera (left). The result the camera sees (right) is less perspective distortion, and better illumination. Compare this with the otherwise identical figure for Step 15 on the previous page.

With one of your views still set to Top, scrub the time marker and watch how the planets continue to rotate to face the camera as it travels along its path. As you scrub, both Comp windows will update, with the other view (Active Camera) showing you what the camera sees. RAM Preview, and observe that you don't really notice these planets rotating around as the camera flies by them – the result looks surprisingly natural, and helps sell the illusion that they are 3D spheres, rather than cardboard cutouts of spheres.

- Deselect All (F2) when you're through exploring.

*Now would be a good time to Save your project. If you want to make sure the light, camera, and planets in your comp are behaving correctly, compare it with our version [**Planets_after Step 15**].*

Virtual Planets

All of the "planets" in this project are simple spheres created in and rendered from the 3D program Electric Image (www.electricimage.com). The camera and light were aimed straight toward their centers, to remove any sense of directional lighting that would have caused perspective problems later in After Effects. Their surfaces were created using a procedural shader called aFraktal, distributed by Triple D Tools (www.tripledtools.com). Virtually all of the planets use presets provided with aFraktal; the second pair of letters in their names denote who created the preset:

CB = *Chris Bernardi*

ML = *Mark Lewno*

PS = *Paul Sherstobitoff*

Part 2: Building a Better Universe

The basic flythrough is working well now. In this part, you will enhance it further by adding one more planet and tweaking the positions of others or swapping them out.

The Final Frontier

We purposely left out a planet so you could get a little practice adding and positioning a 3D layer.

Step 16: Press Home to return its time marker to 00:00. Make sure your alternate view Comp window is set to Top view (select it and press F10). If you can't see all the planets in this view, press C until the Track Z Camera tool is selected, and zoom the display back a little.

If you find After Effects to be a little sluggish, open the Comp windows wider until you can see the Fast Previews button to the right of the 3D View Popup. Set it to OpenGL with Static Textures. If you have an older OpenGL card in your computer, lights might be disabled while moving layers; don't worry – your final render will be okay.

Step 17: In the Project window, open the **_Planets * prebuilt> Sources** folder. Select the footage item **aF_PS_CreamRock.tif** and press Command+/ (Control+/) to add it to [**Planets*starter**].

Step 18: From the Top view, all of the other planets are being viewed from above, meaning they appear as thin slivers. However, as soon as you add **aF_PS_CreamRock.tif** to the comp, you'll notice that it's quite large and that it's facing directly at you. If you were to switch to the Left view (press F11), it would still be facing you. This is because it

16 To speed up interactions during the next few steps, enable OpenGL acceleration using the Comp window's Fast Previews popup.

17 When you add the still image **aF_PS_CreamRock.tif** to your comp, it will dominate the frame because it is still a 2D layer.

18 Set the new planet's 3D Layer switch (A), scale it to roughly 40% (B), and set it to auto-orient toward the camera (C). The Timeline window reflects the changes so far (right).

OpenGL

To manipulate 3D layers more quickly (including cameras and lights), set Fast Previews (lower right of Comp window – open the window wider if needed to see it) to one of the OpenGL modes. The tradeoff is less accurate rendering – especially with lights and shadows.

defaults to being a 2D layer, ignoring these 3D perspective changes. To put it in its place, from the Top view:

• Enable **aF_PS_CreamRock.tif**'s 3D Layer switch in the Timeline. It will now shift in perspective to match the other planets, but it's still larger than they are.

• With the layer selected in the Timeline, press S to reveal its Scale property, and enter 40% to start with – roughly the same value as used by the other spheres. It will now match the other planets in size. But if you look at the Active Camera view, you will note it looks oblong instead of round – because it isn't oriented toward the camera like all the other planets are.

• With this layer still selected, use the shortcut Command+Option+O (Control+Alt+O) to bring up its Auto-Orientation dialog. Select Orient Towards Camera, and click OK. It will now face the camera just as all the planets do.

Step 19: We felt this new planet should go just forward, to the left, and slightly above the nice blue-gold planet (**aF_PS_Patina.tif**) that's roughly in the center of the arrangement. Practice using some of After Effects' different tools while you're placing it to your taste:

• With **aF_PS_CreamRock.tif** still selected, press Shift+P to also reveal its Position property. Scrub the X, Y, and Z parameters in the Timeline to position it.

• Press V to make sure the Selection tool is active. Directly click on **aF_PS_CreamRock.tif** in the Comp window and move it. You may want to zoom into the comp 200% in order to see the object clearly (press the period key on the keyboard, or use the scroll wheel on your mouse when your cursor is over the Comp window). If the characters X, Y, or Z appear near your cursor as you are about to click, your movements will be constrained to just this axis. A cursor with no characters means you can move it freely, though clicking outside the object will deselect it. Try clicking on the left side where there is no axis arrow if you want to move the layer freely.

• Scrub the time marker in the Timeline window to see how the planet interacts as the camera gets closer: It will swivel away slightly as it tries to stay oriented toward the camera. This might change your opinion on where to place the planet, and how large you want to scale it.

We decided on a Scale of 33% and Position of X = 330, Y = 300, Z = 360. If you would like to place it somewhere else, feel free to do so – just make sure the camera doesn't crash into it during its flythrough! When you're done, drag **aF_PS_CreamRock.tif** down the layer stack in the Timeline so that it sits between other planets near it in the Top view, to help keep things organized.

> 3D layers do not need to be sorted in the Timeline, as the render order is based on their position in space (layers farthest away from the camera are rendered first). We did it here just to help us better keep track of which planet is which.

19 Place your new planet along the camera's flight path. Here, we are parked at 00:24; we're using the Top view in one Comp window (left) to position it and the Active Camera view in the other window (right) to check the result. The X by the cursor means that if we were to click and drag now, movement would be restricted to the X axis.

19 *complete:* After you've set the Position and Scale of the final planet, drag it down the layer stack until it rests between adjacent planets in the comp.

209

20 Toggle between "RAM Preview Options" and "Shift+RAM Preview Options" by clicking on their names.

Planet Tweaks

All of the planets are now in place, so this is a good time to Save. The next steps will fine-tune their positions and replace some of the planets:

STEP 20: Press 0 on the keypad to perform a RAM Preview. If it is taking too long to render, stop the preview, and hold down Shift when you press 0: This calls up an alternate set of preview parameters. The default is to preview every other frame, but you can adjust these settings in the Time Controls window. If you can't see the Time Controls, press Command+3 (Control+3) to open its window. (Note that OpenGL is not used during RAM Previews.)

STEP 21: As we mentioned earlier, one of the side effects of using Auto-Orientation is that the planets tend to swivel aside as the camera gets close to them. This reduces the excitement of some of the closer encounters you might have noticed back before Step 12 – especially as you pass by the second-to-last planet **aF_CB_Basalt.tif** at around time 04:00. Feel free to alter the Position or Scale of some of the planets to increase the fear factor. We nudged **aF_CB_Basalt.tif** over to X = 540, for example.

21 Move **aF_CB_Basalt.tif** closer to the camera as it flies by to create more excitement.

STEP 22: We supplied you with more planets than we used in the final comp. Feel free to swap out some of the planets for ones you prefer.

In the Timeline, twirl up all layers. In the Project window, look at the **_Planets * prebuilt>Sources** folder. Resize the window, or reduce the size of the Name panel along the top, until you can see the Comments panel; note that we have entered "unused" in the Comment field for some (see figure on left). You can also select one of these footage items, and look at the top of the Project window to see if they are already used in compositions. Press the up and down arrows to scroll through them.

To see what a planet looks like, double-click it to open its Footage window. To swap it in for another planet:

- In the comp, select the planet layer you wish to replace.

- In the Project window, select the planet you wish to use instead.

- Press Command+Option+/ (Control+Alt+/) to swap in the new planet for the old, keeping the old planet's Scale and Position values as well as its Auto-Orientation options. You can also Option+drag (Alt+drag) the replacement to either the Comp or Timeline windows.

Don't forget to Save! Feel free to customize your universe to your own tastes, and delete our layer marker reminders if you like. To compare your results, check out our prebuilt comp, [**Planets_after Step 22**].

Part 3: A Classier Camera

In this section of the tutorial, you will refine the camera move in three ways: making it pick up speed at the start of the composition, adding a bit of banking as it swerves between the planets, and enabling its Depth of Field to automatically vary the focus depending on how close the camera is to each planet at any point in time.

You can close your second view now. Set the remaining Comp window to show the Active Camera (and if you have the room, set it to 100% Magnification and Full Resolution). If your screen updates are a bit slow, set the Fast Previews popup to OpenGL with Static Textures.

Easing Out

As useful as it is, the Easy Ease keyframe assistant is not the answer for every situation in which you want an animation to speed up or slow down. In this case, we just want a small speed-up at the start of the camera's animation, rather than the full ease-out from a standstill that Easy Ease would create.

STEP 23: Press Home, and select the layer **Camera**. Press P to reveal its Position property in the Timeline, then twirl down the arrow next to the word Position to reveal its velocity graph. Press Home to return the time marker to 00:00, and select the Position keyframe at this time.

STEP 24: When you select this keyframe, a handle will appear on the velocity graph line right underneath it. Drag this handle down about two-thirds of the way, until the pixels/sec readout to its left is just above 100 pixels per second. Also extend the handle's length until it's about two-thirds of the way to the first comp marker, at 01:00.

24 Pull the velocity handle for the camera's first Position keyframe down about two-thirds, to give a slight ease-out from its initial position.

STEP 25: If you look at the right end of the velocity graph, you will notice that it dips slightly before the last keyframe. Since you slowed down the initial velocity, After Effects had to make up time by speeding up the animation later in the timeline – but it was bound by the second keyframe, which forced this slight slowdown at the end. Drag this second handle up slightly until you have a flat line entering the second keyframe.

25 Correct the slowdown at the second keyframe by raising its handle until the velocity curve is flat at this point.

Rotation versus Orientation

3D layers have two different ways to rotate them: normal Rotation and Orientation. As a general rule, use Rotation when you want to animate the rotation of an object and ensure that just that axis will rotate. Use Orientation when you are trying to pose an object, rather than animate it. You can animate the Orientation property, but After Effects will take shortcuts to get from one orientation to the next, which might not be what you want. A good analogy is to think of a spinning top: Animate the Y Rotation parameter for the spin, and animate Orientation to make it wobble about as it spins.

28 Add some Z Rotation keyframes to simulate banking. Instead of just flying on a flat path between the planets, you will swoop between them. Select all the Rotation keyframes and apply Ease Ease (shortcut: F9) to smooth them out.

RAM Preview this new animation: The difference should be subtle compared with a full Easy Ease, but it still adds interest as it builds up speed toward the end. If you like, tweak these velocity handles further to get the speed change you want.

Since you attached the light to the camera with an expression, there is no need to redo its Position velocity as well; this is an advantage over simply copying and pasting keyframes.

Bank 'n' Roll

The partial ease-out was a nice addition, but we want to add more drama to the animation and make it appear as if the viewer is really swooping around these planets:

STEP 26: With the **Camera** layer still selected, press R. This will twirl up the Position property and velocity graph, and twirl down its Rotation and Orientation values. Press Home to go to time 00:00, and enable the animation stopwatch for Z Rotation.

STEP 27: The goal is to make the camera bank into and out of its turns, as you would expect a plane to. We looked at the Top view and scrubbed through the timeline, looking at how much the camera's path was curving at different points in time as an indication of how much banking to include. Go to the following times, and enter the corresponding Z Rotation values:

00:00	**Z Rotation 0°**
01:15	**Z Rotation +5°**
04:00	**Z Rotation −10°**
04:29	**Z Rotation −5°**

STEP 28: Click on the words "Z Rotation" in the Timeline to select all of these Z Rotation keyframes, and use the menu command Animation>Keyframe Assistant>Easy Ease, or use the shortcut: F9. (Okay, we just told you Easy Ease wasn't the answer to every animation problem. That doesn't mean it isn't the perfect solution to some problems…)

RAM Preview again to check the results. If you start to feel a little seasick, reduce the Z Rotation amounts slightly, or if you'd like a wilder ride, double the values. When you are satisfied, select the **Camera** layer, and press R again to twirl up the Rotation and Orientation properties.

Save your project. You can compare your modified camera animation with our prebuilt comp [**Planets_after Step 28**].

Camera Depth of Field

After adding drama, now you're going to add some depth of character to your final piece. To do this, you will be using an option where only objects a certain distance from the camera are in sharp focus, while others closer or farther away are progressively out of focus.

Step 29: If you enabled OpenGL previews earlier, set Fast Previews to Off now. (As of version 6.5, OpenGL does not render Depth of Field.) Press 2 to jump to 02:00 in the timeline, where you have planets both near and far to better see the effects of the following adjustments.

Step 30: Hit Command+A (Control+A) to Select All, and press P to reveal the Position properties for all the layers. Scan down the list of layers, paying attention to the third Position parameter: their Z position. The planets are arrayed from about –100 to +900. The Depth of Field parameter uses distance from the camera to decide who is in focus and who isn't; looking at these numbers will give us a clue as to a good starting value. Press P to twirl up Position, and press F2 to Deselect All.

Step 31: Select the **Camera** layer, and press AA (two As in quick succession) to reveal its Options. Click on the word Off to the right of the Depth of Field property; this will toggle it On. Increase the Blur Level to 300% so you can better see what effect changing the Focus Distance has. Experiment with the Focus Distance until you get a look you like; lower values bring the foreground objects into focus, while larger values bring background objects into focus. We used a Focus Distance of 500 (roughly the middle of our planet array, from front to back), and left the Blur Level at 300%.

If you have a little time to wait for the render, RAM Preview again to see how the objects that are in focus change throughout the flythrough. If you're impatient, initiate a Shift+RAM Preview, or simply check out the Comp window at a few different times along the Timeline.

Save your project. If you are completely lost, open our prebuilt **[Planets_FINAL]** *comp to compare your results.*

Aperture

The Aperture parameter in After Effects determines how many pixels in Z depth stay in focus, centered around Depth of Field. Objects outside this zone get progressively blurrier.

Delay of Field

Depth of Field adds a significant render hit. Enabling the Draft 3D switch along the top of the Timeline window temporarily disables Depth of Field as well as lighting effects, providing an alternative to OpenGL to make the program more interactive.

31 The difference between Depth of Field switched Off (above left) and On (above). Feel free to experiment with the Focus Distance and Blur Level parameters (left).

When Depth of Field is enabled, you will see two boxes drawn for the camera. One indicates the Focus Distance, where objects are their sharpest (in this case, the rightmost box); the other indicates the Zoom setting, where objects appear the same size in 3D as in 2D.

Alpha Panic

Most editing systems require a straight alpha. The edges around objects in the RGB movie will be expanded – often in ugly ways – to provide additional information for the alpha channel to fade away. This occasionally causes panic in editors who receive your footage; tell them to apply the alpha matte before they freak out…

Adding Modules

An additional Output Module was added by selecting the original render queue item and selecting Composition> Add Output Module. You can add as many Output Modules as you need.

In the Render Queue, you will find one composition to render, with two Output Modules: one for RGB, one for alpha.

Part 4: The Render Queue Tour

The planets flythrough animation is finished. We've already rendered the [**Planets_FINAL**] version to use in the next tutorial: an opening title for a mythical show called *Cosmopolis*. The render was created in two pieces – one movie with the RGB color information, and one with an alpha matte – which requires two Output Modules. If you want to learn how we set this up, read the following section.

Many editing systems can import movies rendered from After Effects with the alpha already embedded in the movie, in which case you would need only one Output Module. In it, set the Channels to RGB+Alpha, and Depth to Millions of Colors+ (the plus symbol indicates an alpha channel will be included). It's still safest to set the Color to Straight (Unmatted) for best results.

If your editing system has a codec that supports an embedded alpha, choose it under the Format Options button in the Output Module. We prefer the QuickTime Animation codec, set to Millions of Colors+, with the Quality slider set to 100%: This makes it lossless. This is our codec of choice when we're prerendering elements to be reused in After Effects. (Do not use the None codec: Contrary to a popular myth, its quality is no better, and it creates unnecessarily large files.)

Two Paths, One Goal

The title designer has been looking over your shoulder while you've been working on this animation, and says that she has an idea for making the title appear from behind the planets. This means you will need to deliver this render with an alpha channel, to ease compositing later. Some editing systems (such as the Avid) are also happier if you deliver separate color and alpha/matte movies; that's what we're going to do in this case just to give you the practice.

Open the Render Queue window (under the menu item Window> Render Queue). We have already queued up [**Planets_FINAL**] (our version of this project), with two Output Modules: one for the RGB information, and one for the alpha channel matte.

Click on "Best/Full/LowerFF/ALL" to the right of Render Settings to open the dialog. This is a template we have created for typical NTSC output: After Effects will render each frame of the animation at the comp's rate of 29.97 frames per second (fps), at Best Quality, with Full Resolution, Lower Field First, and the entire length of the composition. Click OK or Cancel when you're done reviewing its settings.

As After Effects renders each frame to these specs, it holds in memory an RGB image and its associated alpha channel. This frame is then passed to the Output Modules, which perform further processing on it before saving it to disk. In this case, we need two Output Modules: one to save the RGB information, and one to save the alpha.

Click on the text "FILL[QT-Anim]_RGBstraight" for the first Output Module (shown at right). In the Video Output section, note that the Channels popup is set to RGB, with a Depth of Millions of Colors. What is slightly unusual is the Color setting: Straight (Unmatted). If you glance at the bottom of the dialog (see figure to the right), you will also see the message "Warning: you should also output an alpha channel to use straight color."

Most editing systems require a Straight, rather than Premultiplied, alpha. Ironically, the alpha channel is identical between these two settings – it's the color channels that differ. For Premultiplied, the color channels look exactly like the final result. For Straight, the color channels have additional pixels spreading past the edges of

Premultiplied color channels (left) look exactly like the final result. Straight color channels (middle) have extra pixels that are faded later by the alpha channel (right): Look closely at the curvature along the top left of the blue planet.

The second Output Module saves the alpha as a grayscale movie.

the alpha channel, which will be faded later by the alpha. This looks strange in isolation, but it gives a slightly better result.

The second Output Module – ALPHA [QT-Anim_256gray] – makes use of just the alpha channel from the 32-bit image created during the render, and saves it as a 256-gray-level movie (some editing systems may require Millions of Colors even for the alpha). This is later used as a luma matte for the color channels saved by the first output module.

If you want to use your own version of the Planets flythrough in the next tutorial, add **[Planets*starter]** *to the Render Queue and duplicate the settings above. Set the Output To destinations and name the fill and matte movies appropriately. Save, and click the Render button.*

Connect

For more information on topics covered in this tutorial, check out the following volumes of *Creating Motion Graphics*:

Volume 1:

Auto-Orientation

Nesting Compositions

Replace layer source

Keyframe velocity

Easy Ease Keyframe Assistant

Output Modules

Volume 2:

D1/DV NTSC pixel aspect ratios

Straight versus Premultiplied alphas

Cosmopolis

An effects and transition workout to create a spacey show title at DV NTSC resolution.

In this project, you will create a DV-resolution opening title sequence for a show called *Cosmopolis: Planet of the Cosanauts*. To do so, you will use the planet flythrough you created in the previous tutorial, combining separate color and matte movies to reconstruct the main footage element with an alpha channel. You will then employ a combination of Illustrator files and clever effects to create the text treatments.

To save time (or if you haven't had a chance to do the previous tutorial), we've prerendered the planet flythrough; you can swap in your own version if you like. We've also saved most of the effects settings

OVERVIEW

Main Concepts:

These are the features and concepts we will be focusing on in this project:

- Separating interlaced footage
- Combining fill and matte movies
- Nesting compositions
- Choosing a title font
- Importing Illustrator files as Comps
- Applying effects and presets
- Gradient Wipe effect
- Displacement Map effect [Pro]
- Block Dissolve effect
- Adjustment Layers
- Knoll Light Factory LE effect*
- Velocity controls for effects
- Using modes to enhance footage
- Snapshots for comparing effects
- Field rendering for D1 and DV

Requirements:

After Effects 6.5 or later; Professional edition recommended for Displacement Map effect, but this effect is optional.

Third-party effects: Knoll Light Factory LE and Tinderbox T_LensBlur (both included on this book's DVD in the **Free Plug-ins** folder).

Getting Started:

* Be sure to install the Knoll Light Factory LE effect from Red Giant Software (www.redgiantsoftware.com) and the Tinderbox T_LensBlur effect from The Foundry (www.thefoundry.co.uk) included in the accompanying DVD's **Free Plug-ins** folder.

Inside the **Tutorials** master folder on the accompanying DVD, locate and copy the folder **10_Cosmopolis** to your hard drive.

In the folder **Final Movie** inside this folder, double-click on and play **Cosmopolis.mov**.

Inside the **Project** folder you'll find the finished After Effects project file **Cosmopolis.aep**. If you have the Professional edition, open the file ending in **_Pro**. This is your starting point; we suggest you save after each major section.

used here as Animation Presets if you want to skip the keyframing and parameter entry we'll be leading you through. One step calls for the Displacement Map effect, which is available only in the Professional edition; you can skip it without compromising the final result.

The Tasks

This is what you will be doing in the various parts of this tutorial:

PART 1: Import your sources, check field separation of the prerenders, use track mattes to recombine matte and fill movies in a nested comp, and start building the main composition including background and soundtrack.

A frame from the final *Cosmopolis* title sequence.

PART 2: Bring in the Illustrator artwork for the main title, apply a variety of transition and displacement effects to build them on in an interesting manner, and tweak their timing.

PART 3: Nest the title into the main composition, scale it over time, and use an Adjustment Layer to tint the title and background.

PART 4: Animate a lens flare along a Bezier path, with additional tweaks to its parameters and velocity. This part includes the concepts of applying an effect to a solid, and using blending modes to mix it on top of other layers.

PART 5: Use snapshots and the "Instant Sex" technique to further enhance the planets.

PART 6: Take a guided tour through the opening and closing transitions, and field render your final movie.

Matching Pair

Command+− (the minus key) on Mac (or Control+− on Windows) will zoom down and resize the Comp window; use the shortcut Command+= (Control+=) to zoom up and resize. Match resolution to magnification: Full Resolution at 100%, Half Resolution at 50%.

Part 1: Music of the Spheres

In this section, you will import your source material, recombine the separate RGB and alpha layers of the planets flythrough sequence, and add a soundtrack.

Open the **Cosmopolis.aep** project. The **Cosmopolis * prebuilt** folder in the Project window contains both the final version and partial comps saved after various crucial steps; feel free to explore them before you start, but close all extraneous windows before diving in.

1 You can import an entire folder in one click, including any folders of media nested inside the selected folder.

STEP 1: Type Command+I on Mac (Control+I on Windows) to open the Import dialog. Inside this tutorial's folder, open the **Project** folder, then select – but do not open – the **Sources** folder. To import all the sources at once, click the Import Folder button at the bottom of this dialog.

One of the items you are importing is an Illustrator file. After Effects will present you with a dialog asking how you want to handle the layers inside it. Use the default Merged Layers option and click OK.

Select this **Sources** folder in your Project window, and hit Return to highlight its name. Type "**My_Sources**" and hit Return again. Click on the arrow next to it to twirl it open, then twirl open the **Planets_render** folder inside of it to see all the items you just imported.

If you rendered your own version of the planets flythrough in the previous tutorial, you can easily replace the sources: Select **Planets_fill.mov** *in the Project window, type Command+H (Control+H), navigate to and select your own RGB render, and click Open. Do the same for* **Planets_matte.mov***.*

1 *complete:* You now have all the sources you will need for this project, including the two layers that make up the planet flythrough.

Interlacing and Edges

Individually select **Planets_fill.mov** and **Planets_matte.mov** in the Project window, and note the information displayed at the top. After Effects automatically detects movies with a size of 720×480 pixels as having a D1/DV NTSC pixel aspect ratio. It also detects these movies as being lower field first, because After Effects placed a tag in their files when they were rendered. Verify that this separation is taking place:

STEP 2: Double-click on **Planets_fill.mov**. It will open in a QuickTime player. Move the time marker to about one-third of the way into the movie, then use the left and right arrow keys to step through individual frames. The "comb teeth" effect you see on some of the faster moving planets is the result of two interlaced fields, from different points in time, being drawn in the same frame. Close the player window.

2-3 The QuickTime window (left) will show both interlaced fields in the same frame. After Effects' Footage window (right) shows each field after it has been separated.

Step 3: Option+double-click (Alt+double-click) the same movie in the Project window to open it in After Effects' Footage window. Make sure Magnification is set to 100%, and move the time marker to about the same point in the file. Use the Page Up and Page Down keys to step through the movie; you shouldn't see any interlacing teeth as you did in the QuickTime viewer. This is because the Footage window displays files after they have been processed by the Interpret Footage settings, so you're stepping through the already separated fields.

If you want to check that the field separation has been set correctly, select the footage, press Command+F (Control+F) to open the Interpret Footage window, and verify that Separate Fields has been set to Lower Field First.

Check the field separation for both **Planets_fill.mov** and **Planets_matte.mov**. Close their Footage and QuickTime windows when you're done.

> More information on interlaced fields is contained in Part 1 of the *AutoTracker* tutorial earlier in this book, as well as in the chapter *Playing the Field* in *Creating Motion Graphics Volume 2*.

3 *complete:* If the fields are not separated correctly for **Planets_fill.mov** or **Planets_matte.mov**, use the Interpret Footage dialog to choose Lower Field First.

Planets Track Matte

The planets flythrough was rendered as separate RGB (fill) and alpha channel (matte) movies. Some stock footage CDs deliver their content as separate color and matte files; it allows them to compress the fill movie to take up less space on the CD. (This is also a popular way to import footage with an alpha channel into some editing systems). You will build a precomp that recombines these two pieces.

Step 4: To reduce clutter and potential confusion, make sure any other compositions are closed right now (select Windows>Close All). Select **Planets_fill.mov** and drag it to the New Composition icon at the bottom of the Project window. This will create a composition that is the same size, duration, and frame rate as the source footage. Press Command+J (Control+J) to verify it is set to Full Resolution. This comp will be named **Planets_fill.mov Comp 1** and will appear in the **Planets_render** folder in the Project window. Rename it "**My_Planets_precomp**" (either by selecting it in the Project window and hitting Return, or by editing it in Composition>Composition Settings). In the Project window, drag the renamed comp to the **My_Comps** folder.

Step 5: Select the footage item **Planets_matte.mov** in the Project window, and type Command+/ (Control+/) to add it to [My_Planets_precomp]. It will appear above **Planets_fill.mov** in the Timeline window, which is exactly what you want.

New Comp from Multiple Sources

You can drag multiple sources to the New Composition icon to have them all added at the same time.

4–5 Drag the **Planets_fill.mov** to the New Composition icon (above), and rename the resulting new comp "**My_Planets_precomp**". Then add the **Planets_matte.mov** to the comp.

6 Press F4 to reveal the Modes column, and set **Planets_matte.mov** to be a luminance matte for **Planets_fill.mov**.

STEP 6: Bring [**My_Planets_precomp**]'s Timeline window forward, and press F4 to reveal the Modes column (if it's not already visible). Under the TrkMat (Track Matte) heading, click on the popup menu for **Planets_fill.mov** and select Luma Matte "Planets_matte.mov". This will use the luminance of the matte movie as an alpha channel for the fill movie. The Video switch (the "eyeball") for **Planets_matte.mov** will automatically turn off (otherwise you would still see the matte movie).

STEP 7: To verify that the matte is doing its job, click on the Show only Alpha channel button (the white swatch) along the bottom of the Comp window – the result should look a lot like the **Planets_matte.mov** did. Turn this button off, and the comp's background color will now show between the planets. This color isn't important here, but setting it to black will more closely match the night sky it will be composited against later. (If you need to change the background color to black, go to Composition>Background Color.)

7 After the matte has been applied, the edges of the planets will be clean.

STEP 8: If you want to save screen real estate, or if your computer is short on memory or CPU power, feel free to reduce the Magnification to 50% and Resolution to Half. Press 0 on the keypad to RAM Preview the matted movie.

> For those who have not worked through the *Planets* tutorial, the camera flies in 3D space between flat 2D layers of planets that auto-orient toward the camera, so you never see them on edge (which would otherwise give the illusion away).

Planets in the Cosmos

The last steps in this section include creating what will be your main comp, and adding the background, planets, and soundtrack to it.

STEP 9: Select the **My_Comps** folder in the Project window. Either click on the New Composition button at the bottom of the Project window, or type Command+N (Control+N) to make a new composition. Pick the NTSC DV 720×480 preset (not the Widescreen one), verify that the frame rate is 29.97 frames per second (fps), and set its duration to 08:01. Give it the name "**My_Cosmopolis**" and click OK.

9 Create a new comp using these settings. This will be your main composition.

Step 10: In the **My_Sources** folder in the Project window, select **CM_CosmoMusic.mov**, then Command+click (Control+click) on **xTB_Nightsky.mov**: Both will now be selected. Press Command+/ (Control+/) to add them to the [**My_Cosmopolis**] comp. They should both start at 00:00, with **xTB_Nightsky.mov** centered in the Comp window.

Step 11: Drag the [**My_Planets_precomp**] into the [**My_Cosmopolis**] Timeline window, positioning it in-between the **CM_CosmoMusic.mov** and **xTB_Nightsky.mov** layers. Make sure it starts at 00:00; if not, select it and press Option+Home (Alt+Home) to make it start at that time.

Because you composited the fill with the matte in a precomp, you can easily transform or add effects to this composite in [**My_Cosmopolis**] as it is now a single layer. In the precomp, you can also apply effects to either the fill or matte individually, while still dealing with just one layer in your final comp. Prudent use of precomps often yields a nice combination of flexibility and convenience.

Step 12: Hit 0 on the keypad to RAM Preview this composite with the soundtrack. Between 04:00 and 05:00, pay attention to the way the last two planets part, revealing the starfield background. You will use this in the next section to help reveal the show's title.

Save your project before diving into the next part. If you want to make sure you got this far intact, compare your comp with our [**Cosmo_after Step 12**] *in the* **Cosmopolis * prebuilt>_compare comps_after Step ##** *folder.*

11 Drag [**My_Planets_precomp**] into [**My_Cosmopolis**]'s Timeline window, carefully positioning it until you see a bar between the two other layers. When you release the mouse, it will be placed here in the layer stack.

Digital Night

The movie **xTB_Nightsky.mov** was created using the Tinderbox T_NightSky effect from The Foundry's Tinderbox 2 set (www.thefoundry.co.uk).

12 At the end of this section, you have the planets composited in front of a night sky, with the soundtrack in place (right and below).

Part 2: Title Effects

This is the main section of this tutorial, where you will be treating the show title with a variety of transition effects.

STEP 13: When we told you in the first step to go ahead and import the Illustrator file with the title as Merged Layers, we got a bit ahead of ourselves.

Under Preferences>Import>Default Drag Import As you can set Photoshop and Illustrator files to automatically import as Compositions when you drag them from the Finder to the Project window, or when they are included in a folder of sources imported at once. We're assuming this preference has been set to its default of Footage.

In the Project window, look in the **My_Sources** folder for the file **CosmopolisTitles.ai**, and double-click it to open it in its Footage window. You will see a main title and a subtitle, created with white type and saved as outlines from Illustrator (so that we can use any font we want without assuming you'll also have it installed). You need to re-import this file so that the two titles are on separate layers. Close this window, and delete this file (make sure it is still selected in the Project window, and hit Delete).

While there is a handy new option in version 6.5 to convert a Merged file into a layered file (File>Replace Footage>With Layered Comp), it defaults to using the Composition – Cropped Layers option, so we can't use it here.

- Select the folder **My_Sources** in the Project window, and press Command+I (Control+I) or select File>Import>File. Locate the layered Illustrator file **CosmopolisTitles.ai** from the **Project>Sources** folder on your disk. In the lower left portion of this dialog, select the option Import As: Composition. Click Open. After Effects will create a folder and a composition, both named **CosmopolisTitles Comp 1**.

13 The merged Illustrator file contains both the main and subtitles in the same footage item, but later you will be treating them separately. The fonts used are Mason Alternate and Mason Sans Regular from Emigre (www.emigre.com).

13 *continued:* When you re-import **CosmopolisTitles.ai**, be sure to use the Import As: Composition option in the Import dialog so that the layers are the same size as the comp.

Music Credits

The soundtrack **CM_CosmoMusic.mov** was arranged by Chris Meyer of CyberMotion. The rhythm track is from the sampling library *Metamorphosis*, and the echoed guitar stabs (played by Peter Maunu) are from the library *Bizarre Guitar*. Both libraries are from Spectrasonics (www.spectrasonics.net), and are distributed in the United States by Ilio Entertainment (www.ilio.com).

• Drag the comp [**CosmopolisTitles Comp 1**] into the **My_Comps** folder.

STEP 14: Double-click the comp [**CosmopolisTitles Comp 1**] to open it. Press Command+K (Control+K) to open Composition Settings, verify that its duration is at least 05:00, and rename it "**My_Titles_precomp**".

This comp's size and pixel aspect ratio are copied from the original Illustrator file. We created this file at a size of 720×534 square pixels so we could work in square pixels and not lose any resolution when we later fit it into a 720×480 nonsquare pixel NTSC DV composition. Click OK to close the dialog.

STEP 15: Turn off the **POTC_Subtitle** layer's Video switch: We'll work on applying effects to the **Cosmopolis** title first.

This would be a good time to Save your project.

Don't forget the File>Increment and Save feature, which automatically adds a number onto your project name and increments it each time you use this feature. The keyboard shortcut is Command+Option+Shift+S (Control+Alt+Shift+S).

14 The title was built in Illustrator at 720×534 pixels.

15 For now turn off the **POTC_Subtitle** layer.

Choices, Choices...

How do we decide what font to use for a title? First we consider a few different stylistic directions: for this job, computerish, Egyptian, or '60s kitsch. We then hunt through our font libraries, looking for fonts that match our themes or otherwise catch our eye. We'll then build a page in Illustrator, repeating the words we will be typesetting with our different font choices applied. It's important to use the actual words instead of gibberish or a series of letters so you can see how the specific characters work – sometimes a font will have some characters you really like or dislike. Finally, we eliminate the fonts we don't like until a winner emerges, bouncing our "short list" off each other or the client to help break ties.

Some of the fonts we auditioned in Illustrator for the Cosmopolis opening title. The winner, Mason from Emigre, is shown in the center.

16 Gradient maps don't need to have any color, but they should have good black-to-white contrast with lots of intermediate gray values.

Gradient Wipe

For your first effect, you will use the Gradient Wipe effect to bring on the title "Cosmopolis" in an interesting way:

STEP 16: In the **My_Sources** folder in the Project window, select **FractalNoiseMap.tif** and press Command+/ (Control+/) to add it to [**My_Titles_Precomp**]. Press Option+Home (Alt+Home) to make sure it starts at 00:00, and after checking it out, drag it to the bottom of the layer stack.

• Turn off its Video switch: You will not see this layer in the final composite; it will only be used by the Gradient Wipe effect to modify the main title layer.

> **FractalNoiseMap.tif** was created using the Fractal Noise effect that comes with the Professional edition. If you have this version, the project used to create it is included in the **FractalNoiseMap_Pro** folder inside the **10-Cosmopolis** folder. The Fractal Noise effect was also covered in Chapter 2's Bonus Tutorial.

STEP 17: In [**My_Titles_Precomp**], select **Cosmopolis_Title** and apply Effect>Transition>**Gradient Wipe**. This will automatically open the Effect Controls window for Gradient Wipe.

• The Gradient Wipe effect looks to a second layer to determine the pattern used to reveal the layer it is applied to. In this window, click on the popup menu for Gradient Layer, and select **FractalNoiseMap.tif**.

17 Add the Gradient Wipe effect to **Cosmopolis_Title**, and pick **FractalNoiseMap.tif** to be the Gradient Layer.

STEP 18: Transition effects can be used to transition a layer on or off; here you will be using it to transition the main title on. Scrub the Transition Completion slider to preview the way you want it to animate. In this case, it will become obvious that you need to animate from 100% to 0% to wipe your layer on. Set the slider to 100%, where the title has completely disappeared.

• In the Effect Controls window, enable the animation stopwatch for Transition Completion. This sets the first keyframe to 100% at time 00:00.

• Press U to reveal this now-animated property in the Timeline window.

• Move to 01:10 in the timeline. Set the Transition Completion value to 0%; a new keyframe will automatically be created at this time and the title should be fully revealed.

• Set the work area to end at this frame by pressing N (for eNd work area), and RAM Preview.

18 The result is an interesting, fractured effect as the title transitions on (above). Soften the "popping" of the chunks by setting the Transition Softness to around 15% (below).

• Remembering what the **FractalNoiseMap.tif** looked like, note how the title appears in fractured chunks. However, the way entire chunks of the title pop is a little abrupt. Go to some time in the middle of the transition (such as 00:20) and scrub the Transition Softness parameter: This will make the chunks fade instead of pop. Set it to 15% or so, and RAM Preview again.

• The nature of this gradient wipe map is that the title initially seems to be reluctant to transition on, but it speeds up near the end. Smooth this out by context-clicking on the second Transition Completion keyframe in the Timeline window and selecting Layer>Keyframe Assistant>Easy Ease (or select the keyframe and press F9). RAM Preview again; the transition should have a more interesting pace.

Save! If you had trouble setting up this compound effect, compare your [**My_Titles_Precomp**] *with* [**Titles_Precomp_after Step 18**].

18 *complete:* The Gradient Wipe effect transitions over 01:10, easing into the second keyframe, with a Transition Softness of 15%.

Pro Displacing Cosmopolis

The next step calls for using the Professional edition's Displacement Map effect to further fracture the word Cosmopolis. If you don't have this effect, ignore this step and skip ahead to **Step 21**.

STEP 19: In [**My_Titles_Precomp**], move the time marker to around 00:20, so you can see it partway through its transition. Select the **Cosmopolis_Title** layer, and apply Effect>Distort>**Displacement Map**. This should bring the Effect Controls window back to the foreground. Change the following settings:

• Set the Displacement Map Layer popup to the **FractalNoiseMap.tif** layer.

• Set Max Horizontal Displacement to 0.

• Set Use for Vertical Displacement to Luminance (the Red, Green, or Blue channels will also work; with grayscale maps, the luminance information is the same for each of the RGB channels).

• Scrub the Max Vertical Displacement parameter and notice how the title takes on a broken mirror effect. Set it to 75.

19 Set the Displacement Map effect (above) to displace in just the vertical direction by 75 pixels, using **FractalNoiseMap.tif** as the Displacement Map Layer. Set the Max Horizontal Displacement to 0 as we will not be displacing the title to the left and right. The result (below) is an unusual, broken mirror echo.

Spicy Gradients

For the ultimate in gradient fun, check out SpiceRack Pro and OrganicFX from Pixélan Software (www.pixelan.com). (Free samples are included in the **Goodies** folder on the DVD that comes with *Creating Motion Graphics Volume 1*.)

Step 20: Hit Home to return to 00:00. You won't see anything, because the Gradient Wipe is completely faded out at this point – but you're going to start the Displacement Map animation at the same time as the transition.

The order you apply effects is important. Here, you are displacing the wiped pieces, so they stay aligned. If Displacement Map was placed before Gradient Wipe, the wipe would not be aligned with the displaced pieces.

• Enable the animation stopwatch for Max Vertical Displacement in the Effect Controls window. This sets the first keyframe to 75.0 pixels at time 00:00.

• Press U twice to reveal the animated parameters for **Cosmopolis_Title** in the Timeline window (the first U twirls up the previously revealed parameter; the second U reveals all the keyframes). You should see keyframes for Transition Completion and Max Vertical Displacement.

20 Keyframe the displacement animation to occur over the same time as the gradient transition, also easing into the last keyframe. (Use the keyframe navigation arrows to make sure new keyframes you create line up with ones you've already set.)

• In the Timeline window, click on the arrow to the right of the keyframe checkbox for Transition Completion. This will forward the time marker to 01:10, the time the transition finishes.

• Enter a value of 0.0 for Max Vertical Displacement to create a new keyframe, which will also be selected. Press F9 to apply Keyframe Assistant>Easy Ease to it.

Your work area should still be set to extend from 00:00 to 01:10. RAM Preview the composition to see how the Gradient Wipe and Displacement Map effects work in tandem.

Save your project and twirl up all layers. If you need to, compare your result to our prebuilt comp [**Titles_Precomp_after Step 20**].

20 *complete:* The Gradient Wipe and Displacement Map transitions combine to enhance the fractured effect.

Preset Pleasure

We also saved the stack of effects for the **Cosmopolis_Title** layer as an Animation Preset. If you'd rather use the preset, select the layer and choose Effect>Remove All. At time 00:00, select Animation>Apply Animation Preset. Navigate to the **_Presets** folder inside the **Cosmopolis** main folder on your disk. If you're using the Standard version, apply the preset **CosmopolisTitle_Std.ffx**; if you

have the Professional edition, apply the preset **CosmopolisTitle_Pro.ffx** which will also apply Displacement Map. Note that presets also apply all the keyframes added including the Easy Ease!

One problem with Presets is that they don't apply the map layer in a compound effect, but default to None. For both the Gradient Wipe and Displacement Map effects, you'll need to reset the map layer popups to the **FractalNoiseMap.tif** layer.

Effecting the Subtitle

That finishes the main title; next is using a different type of transition plus a track matte to reveal the subtitle.

STEP 21: Make sure [**My_Titles_Precomp**] is set to Full Resolution and 100% Magnification. Turn off the Video switch (the "eyeball") for the **Cosmopolis_Title** layer for now, and turn on the Video switch for **POTC_Subtitle**. With **POTC_Subtitle** selected, move to time 01:00, and hit [(the left square bracket key) to start the layer at this time.

STEP 22: Type Command+Y (Control+Y) to create a new Solid layer. Name it "**Block Dissolve solid**", make it 720×200 pixels in size, and set its color to white. Click OK, and drag this new layer down the Timeline window stack so that it sits directly above the **POTC_Subtitle** layer: Mattes need to sit above the layer they reveal.

22 Create a 720×200 pixel solid, and place it just above **POTC_Subtitle** – you will be using it as a track matte for the subtitle layer.

STEP 23: With **Block Dissolve solid** still selected, apply Effect> Transition>**Block Dissolve**. Scrub the Transition Completion slider from 0 to 100% and see how the white solid dissolves. The default for this transition is to use one-pixel blocks. Change this to use very wide blocks, and animate the block height as the transition plays out:

• Leave the Transition Completion slider at around 50% so you can see how changes to the other parameters will affect the block style.

• Set the Block Width to 120, resulting in six horizontal divisions (720 ÷ 6 = 120).

• At time 01:00, set the Block Height to 10, and enable keyframe animation for this parameter (see figure to the right).

23 At 01:00, the Block Width is set to 120 and the Block Height to 10; enable keyframing for Block Height.

23 *complete:* By default, Block Dissolve has a softer, blobbier look (above left). If you prefer a harder-edged look (above right), disable Block Dissolve's Soft Edges option in the Effect Controls window (below).

Comp Markers to Layer Markers

When you nest a composition, its comp markers become layer markers in the master comp.

• Press Shift+1 (on the keyboard, not the keypad) to create comp marker #1 at this frame. You can hit 1 whenever you need to return to this point. Press B to set the work area to also start here.

• Move to 02:00, and change the Block Height value to 1.

• Press Shift+2 (on the keyboard) to create comp marker #2 at this frame. Press N to extend the work area to end at this time.

• Toggle the Soft Edges (Best Quality) checkbox in the Effect Controls window on and off; it defaults to on. We'll use the harder version in our examples, but if you prefer soft edges, leave this option on.

STEP 24: Now let's animate the transition so that the solid changes from completely black to completely white, which will serve as a matte to transition on the subtitle.

• Hit 1 (on the keyboard, not the numeric keypad) to jump back to 01:00. Enable keyframe animation for the Transition Completion parameter, and set its value to 100%. The solid should be invisible.

• Hit 2 to move to 02:00, and set the Transition Completion slider to 0%: The solid will now be all white.

• Hit U to see your Block Dissolve keyframes in the Timeline window. Drag a marquee selection around the two keyframes at 02:00, and hit F9 to apply Easy Ease to them. If you like, RAM Preview to get a feel for the matte's animation.

24 After keyframing the Block Dissolve, select the last two keyframes, and hit F9 to apply Easy Ease.

STEP 25: If the Modes column is not currently revealed in the Timeline window, press F4 to toggle it on. In the Modes column, set the Track Matte (TrkMat) popup for **POTC_Subtitle** to Alpha Matte "[**Block Dissolve solid**]". This will take the transparency of the layer above (the **Block Dissolve solid**) and use it as a matte, creating transparency for the subtitle. Since you made the solid white, you could also apply it as a Luma Matte.

You may be wondering why we didn't just apply the Block Dissolve effect directly to the text layer. While this will work, it's difficult to tell exactly what is going on since the blocks are seen only inside the shape of the text. If the layer was a full-frame video layer, we would have elected to apply it directly; in this case, we felt for illustrative purposes that it was better to use it as a matte layer. Of course, you could also just "rehearse" the effect on a solid and then copy and paste it to your text layer.

25 Set the Track Matte popup for **POTC_Subtitle** to use the alpha of the **Block Dissolve solid** layer as a matte.

Save your project. Twirl up the **Block Dissolve solid** layer, and turn the Video switch for **CosmopolisTitle** back on. Begin the work area at 00:00, and RAM Preview your title transitions.

If you got lost, we saved an Animation Preset with these parameters and keyframes in this tutorial's **Projects>_Presets** *folder on your disk. Delete the Block Dissolve effect you added in Step 23 but keep the solid selected, press 1 to go to 01:00, and select Animation>Apply Animation Preset>***Block Dissolve_subtitle.ffx.*** We also saved the entire comp at this point in the* **_compare comps…** *folder as* **[Titles_Precomp_after Step 25].**

25 *complete:* The subtitle is now revealed through a flickering series of progressively thinner bars.

Part 3: Reveal, Scale, and Tint

You now have your precomps in order; the following sections will focus on combining them and adding some overall effects. First up is adding a scale animation to the title, followed by using an adjustment layer to tint the titles and stars to work better with the planets.

STEP 26: To reduce clutter, close the comps [**My_Planets_precomp**] and [**My_Titles_precomp**], leaving just the comp [**My_Cosmopolis**] open. Locate to 04:00 in this comp. Hit Shift+4 to create a comp marker at this time.

STEP 27: In the **My_Comps** folder in the Project window, locate [**My_Titles_precomp**] and drag it to [**My_Cosmopolis**] icon in the Project window. This will add the first comp to the second, centered and at the current time. In the Timeline window for [**My_Cosmopolis**], drag **My_Titles_precomp** down the layer stack until it is between **My_Planets_precomp** and **xTB_Nightsky.mov**.

Scrub the time marker from 04:00 onward. Note that as the planets part, the titles are revealed. This is because the titles are underneath the planets in the layer stack.

27 Nest [**My_Titles_precomp**] in [**My_Cosmopolis**], and place it above **xTB_Nightsky.mov** in the layer stack. Note the comp markers in the titles precomp came in as layer markers: We'll use those to aid navigation.

28 Zoom down the Comp window and note that the **My_Titles_precomp** layer is larger than the composition (above). Scale it to 90% to fit the comp window (below).

Scroll Wheel Zoom

If you have a mouse with a scroll wheel, position your cursor over the Comp window, and slowly move the scroll wheel to quickly change the Comp window's magnification.

STEP 28: Shift+drag the time marker along the timeline to 06:00 – it should snap to layer marker 2 in **My_Titles_precomp** (this is comp marker #2 in the precomp, where both titles are fully on). Press Shift+6 to set a new comp marker for this time.

• Press , (the comma key) to zoom the Comp window down and see more of the gray pasteboard around it. The layer outline you see is the outer edges of the **My_Titles_precomp** layer: It's larger than the comp. This title was created at a size of 720×534 with square pixels, and has been nested in a 720×480 comp with NTSC-spec nonsquare pixels. The pixel aspect ratio correction automatically scales up the width of the title layer to adjust for this, resulting in a "fatter" image (720 × 10 ÷ 9 = 800 pixels wide). However, we want these 720 square pixels to map across the width of the comp on a 1:1 basis, and for the 534 pixels in the height to be scaled down to 480.

• With **My_Titles_precomp** selected, press S to reveal Scale in the Timeline window. Note that its current value is 100%. Change the Scale value to read 90%, and the layer will fit the comp window.

• Reset the Comp window's Magnification back to where it was by pressing the period key (on the keyboard, not the keypad).

STEP 29: To add interest to the title as it becomes the center of attention, increase its size over time:

• Move to 07:00, and turn on the animation stopwatch for **My_Titles_precomp**'s Scale property to create a keyframe of 90%.

• Press F9 to add an Easy Ease interpolation to this keyframe.

• Press N to set the end of the work area here.

• Hit 4 to jump to the comp marker you set at 04:00, and change the scale value to 70%, which will create a second keyframe. (If it didn't, you forgot to enable the animation stopwatch above.)

• Press B to set the beginning of the work area here and RAM Preview.

STEP 30: After Effects helpfully created this new keyframe with the same interpolation method as your first keyframe. Twirl down the arrow next to the word Scale in the Timeline window to see Scale's velocity graphs. Unfortunately, we don't want an Easy Ease on this first keyframe; we feel the animation works better if the title is scaling steadily as it is revealed behind the planets. That's easy enough to fix by holding down the Command (Control) key and clicking on the first Scale keyframe until it reverts to the Linear keyframe's diamond icon. Note the change in the velocity graph, and twirl it up when you're done. Press S to twirl up the Scale property.

STEP 31: Last in this section is using an Adjustment Layer to tint the white title and stars to a beige color that better matches the warm brown colors in the planets.

• Hit Home to return to 00:00. The Adjustment Layer will need to start from the beginning to tint the entire duration of the **xTB_Nightsky.mov** layer.

• Select Layer>New>Adjustment Layer. Press F4 to reveal the Modes panel, and note its icon.

> Adjustment Layers apply effects to the composite of all layers below the Adjustment Layer in the Timeline window's layer stack.

• You want to tint only the background layers; not the planets. Therefore, drag this new layer in the Timeline window below the **My_Planets_precomp** layer; it should now sit above the **My_Titles_precomp** and **xTB_Nightsky.mov** layers.

• With the Adjustment Layer still selected, apply Effect>Image Control>**Tint**. This will open its Effect Controls window; set the Amount to Tint parameter to 100% so you can see the results of your color choices.

• Go to somewhere between 04:15 and 04:20 in the timeline where you can see both the title and the planets. Set Tint's Map White To color to a pale, warm beige or straw. Either pick a color by eye, or eyedrop the planets to get a good starting point. We used HLS colorspace settings of Hue 45, Saturation 30, Lightness 100 (RGB 255/236/179). Then hit 6 to jump to comp marker 6, and see how the title looks on its own in this color. (This Tint color is saved as a preset as **Tint_beige.ffx** in the **10_Cosmopolis>_Presets** folder on disk.)

• With the Adjustment Layer still selected, type Command+Shift+Y (Control+Shift+Y), rename it to "**AL/Tint**," and click OK.

30 The **My_Titles_precomp** layer scales from 70% to 90%, starting linear and easing into the last keyframe.

31 Create a new Adjustment Layer, and drag it down the layer stack to be just above the title and nightsky layers.

31 *complete:* Use the Tint effect (above) to more closely match the title and stars to the planets (bottom).

*This completes Part 3, so it's a good time to Save your project.
If you think you might have missed a step, compare your comp
with* [**Cosmo_after Step 31**]. *And don't forget to save your project!*

View Options

You can enable or disable a
number of optional displays in
the Comp window, such as the
outlines of 3D cameras and
lights, or the effect point. Click
on the arrow in the upper right
corner of the Comp window to
open its Options menu, and
select View Options.

Part 4: Lens Flare Arc

Lens flares can be an overused cliché, but they're a great way to add
light sources to the frame – just avoid the temptation to get too carried
away (you know who you are). In this project, we were inspired by
the star shapes in the center of the O characters in the main title,
and decided to animate a flare between them to better tie the word
together. (If you want to refresh your memory, play the final movie
Cosmopolis.mov.)

In this section, you will animate the effect point for the flare along
a Bezier path. Make sure you have installed the free copy of Light
Factory LE provided by Red Giant (www.redgiantsoftware.com)
before proceeding.

STEP 32: Go to 05:20, and press Command+Y
(Control+Y) to create a New Solid. Click on the
Make Comp Size button to make it full frame, and
select black as its color. Name it "**Lens Flare Solid**"
and click OK.

STEP 33: With this solid still selected, apply
Effect>Knoll Light Factory>**Light Factory LE**.
We'll use the default Flare Type of Warm Sun Flare,
since it already has yellow and orange tones that
match the rest of our layers.

STEP 34: In the Timeline window, press F4 to
toggle the Switches column back to Modes, and set the mode for **Lens
Flare Solid** to Add. Since the solid is black, it doesn't "add" any color to
the layers behind, so the black areas will disappear, revealing just the
flare while adding its brightness to the image underneath.

For the next step, we suggest you view the comp at 100% Magnification,
and set it to Full Resolution by pressing Command+J (Control+J). If
you're short on monitor space, resize the window vertically to crop
the top and bottom; you need to see only the Cosmopolis title.

34 The black solid initially shows
just the flare, and nothing behind
(top). Set its Mode to Add to drop
out the black areas and mix the
flare with the background (above).

STEP 35: Now you will animate the flare's center. From the Comp
window's Options menu, select View Options, and make sure Effect
Controls is enabled. This will allow you to position the flare's center
while you're seeing the title, rather than working in the Layer window.

• In the Effect Controls window, click on the stopwatch next to the
parameter named Light Source Location to enable keyframing for it.

Hit U to twirl down animated properties in the Timeline window, and check that all is well.

• Make sure the name of the effect is highlighted in the Effect Controls window. In the Comp window, you should see a circle with a cross in its middle located where the flare's light source seems to be. Drag this point so it's on top of the dot in the first O (in the "Cos" of Cosmopolis).

• Move to 06:20, and drag the center of the flare so that it's on top of the dot in the last O (in the "pol" of Cosmopolis). This should add a second keyframe for Light Source Location.

• With the **Lens Flare Solid** still selected, press Option+] (Alt+]) to trim out the layer at 06:20, for a one-second duration.

• Set the work area to the exact length of **Lens Flare Solid** by pressing Command+Option+B (Control+Alt+B). RAM Preview (0 on the keypad) to see what you have so far.

35 Enable keyframing for the Light Source Location, and make sure the effect's name is selected in the Effect Controls window (left). Then in the Comp window, move the effect control point for the Light Source Location until it sits in the center of the first O (right).

35 *complete:* Set the second keyframe for the Light Source Location to be the center of the last O (above). Trim the layer to end after this second keyframe, then set the work area to equal the length of this layer (below).

36 Open **Lens Flare solid**'s Layer window, and enable viewing of Light Factory LE's motion path.

36 *complete:* In the Layer window, pull the effect path's handles upward to form an arc.

STEP 36: There are a few problems with our initial lens flare animation. The first one to solve is its motion: Currently, it moves in a straight line from the first O to the last. We want a nice arc that rises above the title in the middle. Fortunately, you can create Bezier paths for effect control points; you just need to do it in the Layer window (this is because the X, Y coordinate values are in relation to the layer, not the comp).

• Double-click **Lens Flare Solid** to open its Layer window. Verify that the window's View popup is set to Light Factory LE, and that the Render box is checked: This allows you to see the rendered effects and its motion path in the Layer window.

• The motion path should default to using Auto Bezier spatial keyframes, in which case you should see a dot indicating the position of the handle at each keyframe. Right now, this dot is in line with the motion path, making it harder to see (look for the slightly larger dot). Selecting the Light Source Location parameter in the Timeline window will also make it easier to see.

If you can't find the handles, press the Command (Control) key and drag a new handle out of the keyframe icon.

• Select one dot and drag the handle upward, then repeat for the other dot. Tweak their positions until you have a gentle arc (see figure). Be sure not to reposition the keyframe icons by accident – just move their handles. If you like, you can bring the Comp window back forward and RAM Preview to check out the path. When you're happy with the shape, close the Layer window.

STEP 37: Now let's animate the lens flare so it grows from nothing at the start, to a larger size in the middle, then dies away at the end.

• Move the time marker to 06:05 – the center of the lens flare section – and enable keyframing for the Brightness parameter. This sets a keyframe in the middle of the layer's animation at its default value of 100. Press U to reveal this newly animated parameter in the Timeline.

• With the flare layer still selected, hit I to return to the layer's in point at 05:20. Enter a Brightness value of 0. This will create a second keyframe at the beginning of the layer, which will also be selected in the Timeline window.

• Select the Timeline window to bring it forward. With the first keyframe above still selected, choose Edit>Copy or press Command+C (Control+C) to copy its current value.

• Hit O to jump to the layer's out point at 06:20, and choose Edit> Paste or Command+V (Control+V) to paste a new Brightness keyframe with a value of 0. RAM Preview and observe how the lens flare now acts more like a signal flare shot across the sky.

Step 38: The lens flare animation is getting there, but it's moving a bit fast. Let's try extending it to last 40 frames, instead of 30. Fortunately, After Effects makes it easy to redistribute keyframes across time:

• Make sure the **Lens Flare Solid** layer is still selected, with the Brightness and Light Source Location parameters revealed in the Timeline window.

37 Make the flare animation more interesting by having it grow and recede in brightness as it flies across the sky.

• Move the Time Marker to 07:00: The new target for when the animation is supposed to end. Press Option+] (Alt+]) to trim **Lens Flare Solid** to this new duration.

• Click on the word Brightness in the Timeline window to select this parameter's keyframes. Then Shift+click on the parameter name Light Source Location to add this second row of keyframes to the selection.

• To expand the keyframes, hold down the Option (Alt) key, and drag one of the keyframes currently at 06:20 to the right. After you start dragging the keyframes, also hold down the Shift key. When you get close to the time marker at 07:00, holding down Shift will make the cursor snap to this time. Notice that the keyframe in the middle is also moving, maintaining the relationship it has as the "middle" keyframe.

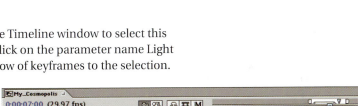

38 Select all of **Lens Flare Solid**'s keyframes, and hold down the Option (Alt) key while you're dragging the last one. The timing for all the keyframes will expand or contract to match. Add the Shift key after you start dragging and the keyframes will snap to the current time marker.

> Summary: Whenever you need to expand and contract a set of keyframes, select them first, hold down the Option (Alt) key, and drag either the first or last keyframe(s) in the set. Add the Shift key to snap to the time marker. This feature works across multiple layers as well!

• Press N to trim the work area to end at this new time (07:00), and RAM Preview to see if you like the slower animation. We think this pace matches the music better as well: The flare dies away with the last guitar sting. When you're done, press F2 to deselect the keyframes to make sure you don't accidentally edit them.

Refinements

Some animators would stop here and move on to the next effect. However, we believe that spending the extra time to refine an animation is worth the resulting polish. When you're animating effects, it's often the subtle timing differences that make the effect really work.

When you want to tweak the speed of a parameter or movement, it's tempting to add additional keyframes. However, with some judicious velocity curve editing, you can add subtle interpolation while still using a minimum number of keyframes.

Selective Deselection

Press Shift+F2 to deselect all keyframes, without losing any layer selections. Pressing F2 by itself deselects all layers and all keyframes.

STEP 39: One concern we have after RAM Previewing is that the flare still moves so fast that the viewer might not pick up its exact start and stop points. With **Lens Flare Solid** selected, press I to jump to its in point (05:20), and press Page Down and Up to play the frames at the beginning of the layer. Notice that the Light Source moves away from the dot in the first O before the viewer has a chance to notice it in the frame. Let's make it linger a bit longer before taking off:

- Twirl down the velocity graph for the Light Source Location. It is currently a flat line, indicating constant speed.

39 With linear velocity, by 05:24 the flare has moved well beyond the O (above left), making it hard to spots its origin. By applying Easy Ease to the movement, the flare lingers closer to the center of the O before it takes off (above right). These speed changes are visible in the Timeline's velocity graph (right).

- Click on the parameter name Light Source Location in the Timeline window to select both of its keyframes, and hit F9 to apply Keyframe Assistant>Easy Ease. Now the velocity graph is an arc, indicating it moves more slowly at the start and end points.

- Page Down again from 05:20 to 05:25 and notice how much slower the light leaves the dot location. This gives the viewer enough time to register that the dot in the O was the origin of the light.

- Move to 06:25 and Page Down frame by frame into the last keyframe. Notice that the ease into the last O is also slower.

• RAM Preview again and see if you agree that the origin of the light source is better defined, and that its exit into the second dot is better illustrated.

• Twirl up the velocity graph for the Light Source Location.

STEP 40: We have the opposite concern with the Brightness animation: We wish it built up to maximum brightness more quickly, and lingered at this value in the center of the animation. Fortunately, there's a keyframe in the middle of the animation, which will make controlling its speed easier:

• Twirl down the velocity graph for the Brightness control. Notice how the Linear keyframes ramp the value from 0 at the in point to 100 at 06:10, then sharply down to 0 again at the layer's out point.

• Press 6 to move to 06:00 (between the first and second Brightness keyframes) and see how small the lens flare appears in the Comp window. The numbers in the Timeline window tell you it has a Brightness value of 50 at this point in its interpolation.

• Select the middle keyframe, and hit F9 to apply Easy Ease keyframe assistant. Notice how the curves change in the velocity graph, and that the value of Brightness at 06:00 has changed to almost 64%.

RAM Preview and see if you like this animation better. To tweak how long this brightness peak lasts, Option+ double-click (Alt+double-click) the middle keyframe to open its Keyframe Velocity dialog, and change its influ-ence numbers: Larger influence percentages mean a longer time spent near the maximum value at this keyframe. If you don't like the extended brightness, Command+click (Control+click) on the middle keyframe to return its interpolation method to linear. When you're done, twirl up the Brightness velocity graph and the layer.

Save your project. If you had trouble with the interpolation amounts, compare your lens flare effect with our [**Cosmo_after Step 40**] *comp. The Light Factory LE effect is also saved as a preset. To use it, remove your copy of the effect from the* **Lens Flare Solid** *layer, hit I to jump to the in point, mouse to Animation>Apply Animation Preset, and select* **LightFactoryLE_cosmo.ffx** *from the* **10_Cosmopolis>_Presets** *folder.*

40 The initial Brightness animation has a linear rise and fall, resulting in a value of 50 at 06:00 (top). Applying Easy Ease to the middle keyframe adds some roundness to this curve, resulting in a value near 64 at 06:00 (above).

40 *complete:* You can increase the influence this keyframe has in its Keyframe Velocity dialog. (As a guide, the Easy Ease keyframe assistant uses a 33.33% influence value.)

CC Composite Trick

If you have Cycore FX installed (free with After Effects 6.5), you can perform the Instant Sex trick with one layer: Apply your blur, followed by Channel>CC Composite. Then select your blending mode and mix amount in CC Composite.

41 The planets before (left) and after (right) adding a copy in Overlay mode on top.

42 Adding another copy of the planets layer, blurred and in Screen mode, brightens the image and blows out the highlights slightly.

Part 5: Sex in Space

In our experience, many 3D renders tend to have a flatter look (no pun intended) than often desired for hot, sexy motion graphic design. A good technique to enhance them is to duplicate a render, and mix in the one on top using blending modes. You can extend this trick by applying a blur to the version on top, which adds a filmic, blown-out look. Multiple duplicates can be used with different modes to fine-tune the effect. We dubbed this technique "Instant Sex", and it's what you will use to improve the planet render we provided.

STEP 41: Move the time marker to a place where you can see a lot of planets onscreen at once, such as around 02:00. Make sure the Modes column is still visible in the Timeline window (press F4 if it isn't).

Select the **My_Planets_precomp** layer, and type Command+D (Control+D) to duplicate it. Rename this duplicate layer so you can keep track of it: Hit Return, name it "**Planets+Overlay**" and hit Return again to accept the new name.

Set the Mode for **Planets+ Overlay** to Overlay. This really pumps up the saturation and contrast on the planets – perhaps too much. Hit T to twirl down the Opacity property for **Planets+Overlay**, and scrub its value until you see a blend you like. We set our layer to 40%.

STEP 42: With **Planets+Overlay** still selected, type Command+D (Control+D) to duplicate it again; this second duplicate will be above the other two planet layers. Hit Return to enable editing, rename it "**Planets+Blur/Screen**", and hit Return again. Press T to reveal its Opacity property.

Change the Mode for this layer to Screen: Notice how the image now brightens and even blows out slightly. With this topmost copy still selected, apply Effect>Blur & Sharpen>**Gaussian Blur** (if you have a slower computer, Fast Blur will do). Set its Blurriness slider to a small value, such as 5. Then scrub its Opacity value until you get a blend you like; we used 60%.

Experiment with turning the duplicated layers on and off to get a feel for what they are adding to the original image: In general, the Overlay layer is adding contrast and saturation, and the Screen layer is enhancing the highlights.

Snap Comparisons

There are numerous third-party blurs to choose from. If you have already installed the Tinderbox T_LensBlur effect (included free on this book's DVD), let's use After Effects' snapshot feature to compare some different looks.

To best see what's going on, hit Home to return the time marker to 00:00, and verify that the Comp window is set to Full Resolution and (space permitting) 100% Magnification.

Step 43: Select just the **Planets+Blur/Screen** layer. If its Effect Controls window is not already open, press F3 to reveal it. You might want to close the effect tabs for other layers, to reduce clutter and potential confusion.

• Click the Take Snapshot icon at the bottom of the Comp window (the camera icon), or use the shortcut: Shift+F5. This saves a copy of the image currently in the Comp window to memory for later recall. This will be your reference of what the Gaussian Blur effect looks like.

• In the Effect Controls window, turn off the Gaussian Blur effect by clicking on the stylized "*f*" to the left of its name.

• Apply Effects>Tinderbox – Blurs>**T_LensBlur** to **Planets+Blur/Screen**. Its default settings are a bit enthusiastic. In the Effect Controls window, twirl down its Controls, and set the Radius to about 8. Verify that the Process Alpha popup is set to Yes.

• To compare these two effects, recall the snapshot by pressing F5, or click on the Show last Snapshot icon (the one that looks like a little man) along the bottom of the Comp window. As long as you are holding down this button (or F5), After Effects will display the previous snapshot you stored to memory – in this case, of the Gaussian Blur effect. Note that the T_LensBlur effect yields a brighter center to the planets, and gives a softer look overall.

• Press and release this switch to decide which you prefer. Make sure the effect you choose is turned on, and the other turned off, in the Effect Controls window. (For a cleaner project, it's best to delete unused effects once you're sure you won't be needing them again. We left both of them in our comparison versions of this comp, in case you wanted to compare them later.)

Snapshots times 4

There are four snapshots available: Press Shift+F5, F6, F7, and F8 to take a snapshot in the Comp, Layer, or Footage windows. Press F5, F6, F7, and F8 to display a snapshot in the active window (which means you can take a snapshot in one window and display it in another).

43 The Take Snapshot button is along the bottom of the Comp window. It will store a copy of the image in the Comp window for later recall.

43 *continued:* Tone down T_LensBlur's defaults by reducing Radius to about 8. Be sure to set Process Alpha to Yes so that the blur is applied to RGB+Alpha.

Snapshots are useful for comparing different values in effects. For instance, you could set the T_LensBlur to different Radius and Bloom Gain values and toggle back and forth to see which one you liked best. However, there is no way to "return to the snapshot values" – you need to be aware of what values were used to create a snapshot, and use Edit>Undo or Edit>History to revert back to that state.

*Save your project before going to the next section and twirl up all layers. You can compare your version of the planets with ours in [**Cosmo_after Step 43**]. We chose the Gaussian Blur for a harder look; feel free to use T_LensBlur in your version.*

43 *complete:* The Comp window normally shows the current state of the composition – in this case, with the T_LensBlur effect applied. Click on the Show last Snapshot icon (where the cursor is pointing) to compare it with the last snapshot you created.

Ten Step

Holding the Shift key while scrubbing most parameters cause them to increment by multiples of 10. In the case of small decimal values such as Gaussian Blur's Blurriness, the Shift key scrubs the value by whole numbers.

Part 6: Transitions Tour

This final part consists of combinations of effects and techniques covered earlier, so we'll just give you a guided tour of how we finished off the tutorial. To check out these effects, in the Project window open the comp **Cosmopolis * prebuilt>Final Comps>Cosmopolis_FINAL** and poke around the upper layers as noted below. If you want to finish off your [**My_Cosmopolis**] comp, there should be enough information in the steps below to do so now that you have the basics down (or you could cheat and apply the Animation Presets to Adjustment Layers as noted below).

STEP 44: In our final comp, select the **AL/Wipe Off** layer, and type Command+Option+B (Control+Alt+B) to set the work area to equal it. If its animated properties are not already revealed, hit U to twirl them down, and then F3 to reveal its Effect Controls window. RAM Preview to see this transition in action.

• At time 07:00, we created a new Adjustment Layer and renamed it **AL/Wipe Off**. Of course, naming it "Wipe Off" doesn't mean it will do anything – so don't forget to apply the effect!

• We applied the Gradient Wipe effect to this Adjustment Layer. We then added the **FractalNoiseMap.tif** to the comp and turned off its Video switch. (This layer is 720×534, but there's no need to prescale it, as the Gradient Wipe effect will automatically stretch the gradient to fit the 720×480 layer size.)

• In the Gradient Wipe effect, we set the Gradient Layer to the **FractalNoiseMap.tif** layer.

• We animated the Transition Completion from 0% at 07:00 to 100% at 08:00. This will wipe off all layers below, revealing the Background color (which should be black).

![Timeline window showing Cosmopolis_FINAL composition with layers]

Timeline window for Cosmopolis_FINAL:

```
Cosmopolis_FINAL • Timeline
0:00:07:00 (29.97 fps)
```

#	Layer Name	
1	[CM_CosmoMusic.mov]	Select All and hit U to twirl down keyframes
2	[AL/Wipe On]	wipes all on
	Gradient Wipe — Reset	
3	[AL/Wipe Off]	wipes off
	Gradient Wipe — Reset	
	Transition Completion — 0%	
	Radial Blur — Reset	
	Amount — 0.0	
4	[FractalNoiseMap.tif]	fx map
5	Planets+Blur/Screen	Screen/60% Opacity
	Effects	
	Gaussian Blur — Reset	
	T_LensBlur — Reset	
6	Planets+Overlay	Overlay/40% Opacity
7	[Planets_precomp]	Original layer/Normal/100%
8	[Lens Flare Solid]	Add Mode
	Light Factory LE — Reset	
9	[AL/Tint]	purple layers are adjustment layers
	Tint — Reset	
10	[Titles_precomp]	1 2 (title in precomp)
11	[xTB_Nightsky.mov]	

Switches / Modes

• We set the Transition Softness to 25% to soften the transition of the individual pixels so that they fade as they transition off.

STEP 45: We also added the Radial Blur effect, using the default Spin blur setting. The Radial Blur Amount ramps up in intensity as the gradient wipe is transitioning off.

When you first apply Radial Blur it will look quite grainy. Radial Blur is a slow effect to render, so its antialiasing is set to Low while the layer is in Draft Quality, and gives you options of how to antialias the effect when the layer is set to Best Quality. This popup defaults to Low. To get better render quality, you must change its Antialiasing (Best Quality) popup in the Effect Controls window from Low to High. This will ensure that when you render using Best Quality for all layers (which they default to), Radial Blur will appear smooth. If you have a fast computer, set the layer to Best Quality while you work. You can always revert the layer back to Draft Quality if the render hit is killing you – but don't change the Antialiasing popup to Low, or your final render will also look grainy.

The final Timeline window. Note the Adjustment Layers added near the top: These create transitions for all of the layers underneath.

44–45 The ending transition is a combination of Gradient Wipe using the now-familiar **FractalNoiseMap.tif** map, and a Radial Blur effect.

AL/Wipe Off • Effect Controls

AL/Wipe Off

Cosmopolis_FINAL * AL/Wipe Off

▽ *f* **Gradient Wipe**	Reset	About...
Animation Presets	None	
▷ Ō Transition Completion	100 %	
▷ Ō Transition Softness	25 %	
Gradient Layer	4. FractalNoiseMap.tif	
Ō Gradient Placement	Stretch Gradient to Fit	
Ō	Invert Gradient	
▽ *f* **Radial Blur**	Reset	About...
Animation Presets	None	

▷ Ō Amount	8.0	
Ō Center	360.0 , 240.0	
Ō Type	Spin	
Ō Antialiasing (Best Quality)	High	

45 *complete:* The Effect Controls window for the transition effects. The cursor is pointing at the Anti-aliasing popup for Radial Blur, which is important for managing quality versus render times.

Layer, Go Home

Need a layer to start at 00:00? Select it, and type Option+ Home (Alt+Home) to quickly snap it back to zero.

46 The opening also includes a Gradient Wipe effect, this time using the planets as the gradient layer.

• The Radial Blur defaults to applying a blur Amount of 10. We originally animated the Amount from 0 at time 07:00 to 8 at 08:00.

• We also added an Easy Ease to the first Amount keyframe, so the blur ramps up slower, and then moved this keyframe to 07:05 by dragging it along the timeline, biasing the Radial Blur effect to come on even more toward the end.

This stack of effects is also saved as a preset. To use it, go to 07:00, add the **FractalNoiseMap.tif** *layer to your comp, and turn off its Video switch. Make a new Adjustment Layer, and apply Animation>Apply Animation Preset>* **GradWipeOff.ffx***. Reset the Gradient Layer popup in the Effect Controls window to* **FractalNoiseMap.tif***.*

STEP 46: The transition at the beginning is a variation of the transition used to wipe everything off at the end. Select **AL/Wipe On**, hit F3 to reveal its Effect Controls window, set the work area to equal this layer's duration, and RAM Preview to see this effect.

• At time 00:00, we created a new Adjustment Layer and renamed it **AL/Wipe On**.

• We applied the Gradient Wipe again, but this time we set the Gradient Layer to the **Planets_precomp** layer. This will wipe on the animation based on the luminance values of the planets.

• We animated the Transition Completion from 100% at 00:00 to 0% at 01:10. This will wipe on all layers below over 40 frames, using the luminance of the planets as a guide. Notice how the **xTB_Nightsky.mov** layer appears only toward the end of the transition, after 01:00; we set the second keyframe to Easy Ease In to lengthen this final fade.

• We set the Transition Softness to 25% to soften the transition of the individual pixels; this is especially important when the gradient layer was not designed to be a map for the Gradient Wipe effect and the values don't smoothly step between the 0–255 gray levels.

- We trimmed the adjustment layer's out point to 01:10, so it will not be sampled after this point (although it won't have any effect, it will add a little rendering time each frame as After Effects looks at it).

*This effect is also saved as a preset. To use it, make a new Adjustment Layer at 00:00. Load the effects by applying Animation>Apply Animation Preset>**GradWipeOn.ffx.** Be sure to reset the Gradient Layer popup to the **Planets_precomp** layer (any one of the three **Planets_precomp** layers will do; compound effects refer to the source of the layer only, before effects and modes are applied).*

Rendering with Interlaced Sources

If you'd like to render your finished Cosmopolis comp, remember that it included field-rendered, interlaced sources (**Planets_fill.mov** and **Planets_matte.mov** are separated as Lower Field First). In order to output both fields, you must turn on Field Rendering in your Render Settings. Then select your DV codec in the Output Module dialog.

If you are using a D1 system, then render to the D1 codec of your choice, still remembering to (in most cases) Field Render with Lower Field First. NTSC D1 has a frame size of 720×486, not 720×480, so you will need to compensate for this by adding pixels to the final rendered frame. In the Output Module, use the Crop section (not Stretch!) to add two pixels to the Top (by cropping –2 pixels), and four to the Bottom (by cropping –4 pixels), which will convert the 720×480 DV Lower Field First output to a 720×486 D1 movie and maintain the field order.

If you just want to save a small test movie to playback on a computer monitor, then render with Best Quality and Full Resolution, but turn Field Rendering *off* – there is no interlacing on computers. In the Output Module, pick a codec of your choice, and Stretch the final output to any small size (240×180, 320×240, and so on). Be sure to use a 4:3 aspect ratio so that you end up with a square pixel movie for playback on a computer – don't simply divide the 720×480 size – and keep in mind that some codecs are optimized for multiples of 8- or 16-pixel blocks in each dimension. We rendered the version in the **Final Movie** folder at a size of 384×288 (which we hope will play well from most hard drives).

Saving Presets

You can save your own favorite stack of effects, including key-frames, by selecting the effects in the Effect Controls window and choosing Save Animation Preset from its Animation Presets popup. If you save them in the Presets folder inside the main After Effects folder, they will appear in the Effects & Presets palette.

Connect

For more information on topics covered in this tutorial, check out the following volumes of *Creating Motion Graphics*:

Volume 1:

Importing footage, folders, and separating fields

Track Mattes

Comp window Magnification, Zoom, and Resolution, plus Snapshots

Nesting Compositions

Editing and animating effects

Animation Presets

Easy Ease Keyframe Assistant

Transition effects, including Gradient Wipe and Block Dissolve

Adjustment Layers

Applying effects to solids

Blending Modes

Rendering Queue

Volume 2:

Compound effects, including Displacement Map

Working with D1/DV NTSC

Just an Expression

A gentle introduction to creating and modifying several common, useful types of expressions, including synchronizing them to music.

Expressions certainly have been one of the most powerful additions to After Effects. They let you automate a great number of tedious animation tasks, causing layers and their properties to react to other layers in ways that would otherwise be difficult to keyframe. To use this tool at an advanced level, however, you must not have too strong a fear of math or of reading JavaScript code. Because of this, learning how to manage expressions is a daunting task for many artists. However, learning just a little lets you do a *lot*.

Other tutorials in this book, such as *Piccadilly Circus* and *The Planets*, have already introduced simple forms of expressions that require a single "pick whip" move to tie one layer's properties to another. In this tutorial, we will introduce a series of slightly more advanced – but still easy to master – expressions that are useful for a number of common

OVERVIEW

Main Concepts:

These are the features and concepts we will be focusing on in this project:

- Expressions
- Animation Presets
- Effect Controllers
- 3D animation
- Orientation
- Bevel Alpha effect
- Texturize effect
- Tint and Fill effects
- Blending modes
- Animating Type
- Set Matte effect

Requirements:

After Effects 6.5 or later Standard edition

Getting Started:

Inside the master **Tutorials** folder on the accompanying DVD, locate and copy the folder **11_Expressions** to your hard drive.

In the folder **Final Movie** inside the project's folder, double-click on and play **Expressions.mov**. (This movie was built with the **MusicalExpression.aep** project which is described in the file **11B_Expressions_bonus.pdf**; you will learn the concepts behind it here and then explore the more complex bonus project later.)

Inside the **Project** folder you'll find the finished After Effects project file **Expressions.aep**. Open this project; this is your starting point.

animation tasks. While we're building those expressions, we will also try to expose the most common trip-ups, and how to solve them. In the process, you will gain a fundamental understanding of how expressions work and how to manage them in your own projects.

The final movie demonstrates what might look like a rather complex project. However, the underlying concepts are easy to master. In the following pages, rather than construct this complex project, we will discuss these concepts using simple shapes. This tutorial then continues on the DVD with a bonus PDF tutorial, **11B_Expressions_Bonus.pdf**. That document covers in detail how we constructed the project that created the final animation you see in **Expressions.mov**.

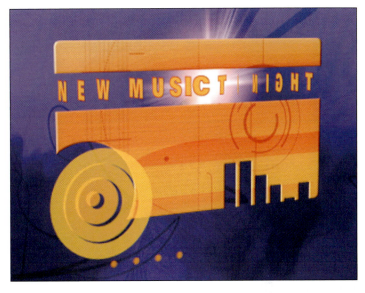

A frame from the *Musical Expression* bonus project in which a series of rings, text-based dots, and volume bargraphs jump in time to the music while the text and edges of the frame react to the camera and another 3D layer.

Surface elements include footage from 12 Inch Design's Unit 03 and the Getty Images/Pop Psychedelia CD; background from the 12 Inch Design's Unit 06 library.

The Tasks

This is what you will be doing in the various parts of this tutorial:

PART 1: Learn how to create, modify, and disable simple expressions, including how to match parameters with different value ranges or number of dimensions.

PART 2: Scale a layer to create a bargraph animation by borrowing keyframed values from another layer or effect.

PART 3: Employ an alternate method to animate the volume bargraph by having one layer's position follow another.

PART 4: Learn an expression modifier that allows one layer to borrow another layer's animation, offset in time.

PART 5: Make one layer point at another in 3D space.

PART 6: Coax 2D effect parameters to react to the 3D position of a camera or light.

PART 7: Take a quick tour of the **MusicalExpression.aep** project where a variety of objects and effects react to the soundtrack or each other, employing expressions that build on the above concepts.

DVD BONUS TUTORIAL: An indepth PDF guided tour of the more complex *Musical Expression* project which employs techniques covered here, plus others. See the file **11B_Expressions_Bonus.pdf**.

Hold That Thought

The best way to save an expression for re-use later is to save it as an Animation Preset. Apply the expression to an Effect Controller or a layer's normal Transform properties, and use Animation>Save Animation Preset. This is discussed in more detail in *Creating Motion Graphics Volume 1 (3rd Edition)*.

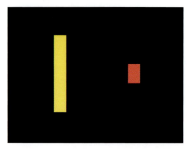

Part 1: A Gentle Introduction

If you're new to expressions, this section will lead you through the easiest way to create expressions: using the pick whip tool to tie one property to another. A large number of useful expressions can be created using this simple tool. If you've already mastered this much, jump ahead to Step 5 to learn how to link dissimilar parameters together, or skip to Part 2 to start exploring more advanced techniques.

1 The comp [**1_simple * starter**] contains two bars, one of which already has its Scale property animating.

STEP 1: In the Project window, locate and double-click the comp [**1_simple * starter**] to open it. It contains two bars made from solids. Note the Scale keyframes applied to the **bar 2** layer (if the Scale property is not already visible, select the **bar 2** layer and type S). We've already created some simple Scale keyframes for it; press 0 on the numeric keypad to RAM Preview this animation.

STEP 2: The easiest expression to create is one in which a property of one layer exactly mimics what a similar property of another layer is doing. Follow these steps to make the Scale property of the **bar 1** layer animate exactly the same as the Scale of the **bar 2** layer:

• Select the **bar 1** layer and type S to reveal its Scale property.

• Click on the word Scale to select it, and use the menu option Animation>Add Expression to enable expressions for this property.
  Scale will twirl itself open in the Timeline window, and reveal a line that says Expression: Scale. To the right will be the word **scale**, currently highlighted. This preliminary expression says "Scale equals scale." Simple, but boring…

2 Use the pick whip tool to tie the Scale of the **bar 1** layer to the Scale of the **bar 2** layer.

• Click on the pick whip tool: The one that looks like a small spiral. With the mouse held down, drag this tool to the word Scale under the layer **bar 2**.

• After you release the mouse, After Effects will write a more useful expression for you:

thisComp.layer("bar 2").scale

The language this expression is written in is called JavaScript. The secret to reading JavaScript is that the periods give you clues on how to break up the expression. This expression says that for the property you've applied it to (**bar 1**'s Scale), After Effects is going to:

look inside this comp:	**thisComp**
for a layer called "bar 2":	**.layer("bar 2")**
and use its Scale property:	**.scale**

- To finish off the expression, either hit the Enter key on the numeric keypad (not the Return key – this will just start another line of text) or click somewhere else in the Timeline window. After

Effects will check to see if you wrote a valid expression – if not, you'll get an error message, and the expression will be disabled. Since After Effects wrote this expression, there shouldn't be any problems.

- RAM Preview and observe that **bar 1** and **bar 2** both scale together.

2 *complete:* After hitting Enter to accept the expression, the Scale value for the **bar 1** layer equals **bar 2**'s Scale. Note that "expressed" values (where the cursor is pointing) appear in red in the Timeline window.

STEP 3: An important feature of expressions is that they are always "live": If you edit a parameter that is being looked at for an expression, the "expressed" layer will automatically update and follow along. You can test this by editing one of the Scale keyframes for the **bar 2** layer. Or select all of the Scale keyframes for **bar 2**, and change their interpolation method: Either Command+click on Mac (Control+click on Windows) on one of the keyframes to change them all to the Auto Bezier interpolation method, or press F9 to set them all to Easy Ease. RAM Preview, and note that the two bars still animate exactly the same without having to rewrite the Expression.

STEP 4: Expressions are easy to turn off. In the Timeline window, click on the = sign to the left of the word Scale for **bar 1**. This will change it to a ≠ symbol. You'll notice that its value jumps back to its original 100%, and the bar will return to its full height in the Comp window. Leave the expression disabled for now.

4 To disable an expression, click on its = symbol to the left of the parameter's name. It will change to a ≠ symbol as confirmation. (To re-enable the expression, click on it again.)

STEP 5: Expressions can be created to link dissimilar properties – it just takes a little extra care. For example, Rotation can be linked to Scale. The potential problem is that for 2D layers, Rotation has one parameter, whereas Scale has two parameters: X and Y. The pick whip tool often allows you to make this distinction:

- If not already disabled, disable **bar 1**'s Scale expression by clicking on the = sign to the left of the word Scale.

- Select **bar 1**, and press R to reveal its Rotation property.

- Enable expressions for Rotation using a shortcut: Hold down the Option (Alt) key, and click on the stopwatch to the left of the property's name. This will twirl down the Expression line; you'll see the word **rotation** which is a basic expression that means **Rotation = rotation**.

- If you were to drag Rotation's pick whip tool directly to **bar 2**'s Scale property, After Effects wouldn't know which dimension of Scale you wanted – so it would assume the first dimension, which is X. But you want Y because it is the value that's animating (X's value is 100%

Deleting Expressions

To remove an expression, select the parameter in the Timeline window and use the menu command Animation>Remove Expression. You can also Option+click (Alt+click) on the animation stopwatch.

throughout). So click on Rotation's pick whip tool, and carefully drag it just to **bar 2**'s Y Scale parameter (the rightmost one of the pair).

• When you release the mouse, the following expression will be written for you:

thisComp.layer("bar 2").scale[1]

This is very similar to the expression you created in Step 2, except the word "**scale**" is now followed with the designation **[1]**. This is JavaScript's way of noting which dimension of a property to use. The designation **[0]** means use the first dimension – X, in this case – and the designation **[1]** says use the second dimension, Y.

• Hit Enter to accept this expression, and note how **bar 1**'s Rotation value now matches **bar 2**'s Y Scale value. RAM Preview to see the result.

5 Rotation has one dimension, while Scale has two dimensions: X and Y. To express Rotation to Scale, drag the pick whip to the specific Scale dimension you want.

STEP 6: Not only do Scale and Rotation have a different number of dimensions, they have different value ranges as well: Whereas Scale goes from 0% to 100%, Rotation goes from 0° to 360° to define one full rotation. If you want 100% of scale to equal 360° of rotation, you will need to make a simple modification to the expression:

• Calculate how much you need to modify the Scale parameter to get the desired Rotation result. In this case, you want 100% to equal 360°, so you need to modify it by a factor of 360 ÷ 100 = 3.6. You can add this modification to the beginning or end of the value you want to modify – if you're at the front, you would say **3.6 *** ; at the end you would say *** 3.6**. (You could also enter *** 360 / 100** for the same result. The asterisk says multiply; the slash says divide.)

5 *complete:* The result is that **bar 1**'s Rotation follows **bar 2**'s Y Scale. When you want to access just one dimension of an overall value, JavaScript requires an additional designation inside brackets to know which one to use.

• In the Timeline window, click somewhere in the expression's text field to select it. Move your cursor to the front of the expression; pressing the left cursor arrow should do the trick.

• Type **3.6 *** at the beginning of this expression.

• Hit Enter, and either scrub the time marker or RAM Preview to see your new result. Feel free to try different values to get different relationships between Scale and Rotation – for example, if you want 100% to equal 180°, change **3.6** to **1.8**.

6 You can use simple math to modify how an expression responds. Here, the Y Scale for the **bar 2** layer is being multiplied by 3.6 to produce **bar 1**'s Rotation amount.

Save your project. To check whether you created these two expressions properly, compare your comps with [**1_simple_after Step 02**] *and* [**1_simple_after Step 06**]. *They are saved in the Project window's* **_Expressions * prebuilt>_compare comps_after Step ##** *folder.*

Part 2: Scaling New Heights

These next two Parts will explore using expressions linked to other parameters to alter the scale or position of a layer. The task you will be working on is animating bargraph-style volume indicators in sync to music, similar to what you saw in **Expressions.mov**. Of course, these techniques are easily applied to other animations.

STEP 7: Close any extraneous comps that may be open, then open comp [**2_bargraph * starter**] and hit Home. It also contains two bars filled with audio icons using the Image Club font Mini Pics Digidings.

STEP 8: In the Project window, twirl open the **Sources** folder. Locate the file **CM_Express_music.mov**, and type Command+/ (Control+/). This will add it to the top of the [**2_bargraph * starter**] timeline, starting at 00:00. With the Comp or Timeline window forward again, RAM Preview to get a feel for the music.

STEP 9: We have already created a set of keyframes that follow the volume of a few of the musical parts in the soundtrack and that have value ranges of roughly 0 to 100. You can do this using Animation> Keyframe Assistant>Convert Audio to Keyframes; we prefer the extra power and flexibility provided by the Trapcode plug-in SoundKeys (see the sidebar *Sound Keys* later in this chapter for more information). These keyframes have been applied to an Expression Controller and saved as an Animation Preset.

• Select the layer **bar 1**.

• Select the menu item Animation>Apply Animation Preset. Navigate to the **_Presets** folder inside this tutorial's folder on your disk, open it, and select the file **2_SoundKeys.ffx**. Click Open.

• The Effect Controls window will open, showing an effect called Slider Control, with one parameter: Slider.

• In the Effect Controls window, select the effect's name, and hit Return to enable it for editing. Type in **"audio level"** and hit Return again. It can be useful to rename effects to keep better track of what they do.

• This Slider parameter holds keyframes representing the loudness of a combination of the bass drum and the guitar line. With **bar 1** still selected, press U to reveal these keyframes in the Timeline window. Twirl open the arrow next to the Slider to see the value graph for these keyframes. Twirl up the value graphs when you're done, but keep the Slider parameter exposed.

Music Credits

The soundtrack for this tutorial was arranged by Chris Meyer of CyberMotion. The ethnic drums and bells came from the sample library *Ethno Techno* by Bashiri Johnson (distributed by Ilio Entertainment – www.ilio.com). The guitar and fast pop drums are from Zero-G's library *Total Drums and Bass* (www.zero-g.co.uk). The whoosh sound came from an "Acidized" version of Bill Laswell's *Sample Material* (mediasoftware.sonypictures.com).

9 We saved an Animation Preset with keyframe data for three different musical lines, applied to dummy effects. Their value graphs give you an idea of how they fluctuate over time.

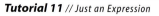

STEP 10: You want to adjust the height of **bar 1** to follow these keyframes. Since we already adjusted the keyframe value ranges to be 0 to 100, this would seem like a simple task:

- With the layer **bar 1** still selected and the sound keyframes revealed, type Shift+S to also reveal its Scale property.

- In the Timeline, Option+click (Alt+click) on the animation stopwatch for Scale to enable expressions.

- Drag the Scale's pick whip to Slider. Release the mouse, and hit Enter to accept it. The result is a two line expression. You may need to click just under the first line of it in the Timeline window and drag down until you can see both lines. It says:

> temp = effect("audio level")("Slider");
> [temp, temp]

This means temporarily store the value of the slider, and apply it to both the X and Y dimensions of Scale. But is that what we wanted?

- RAM Preview. Oops; the bar is scaled both horizontally and vertically. The pick whip was an overachiever, in that it assigned the value of the slider to both dimensions.

STEP 11: You want to affect only the Y dimension of Scale. However, the expression language requires you to provide an answer for both the X and Y dimensions. *These two values must be stored inside a pair of brackets separated by a comma* – for example [**X, Y**].

You want to use Slider for Y; you also need to tell After Effects to use the previous X scale value for X. This latter parameter goes by the name **scale[0]** (the **[0]** says use the first dimension – X – of Scale).

- Click on the expression's text field to select it, then hit Delete to erase it.

- To fill in the answer for X, carefully type:

> [scale[0],

- Now use the pick whip to drag to the parameter name Slider in the Timeline window (see figure on next page). After Effects will automatically type in the correct effect and parameter name.

- In an expression, every open bracket or parenthesis needs a matching close bracket or parenthesis. Finish off the expression by typing] and hit Enter. RAM Preview; now only the height should be animated.

> [scale[0], effect("audio level")("Slider")]

10 Dragging the pick whip from Scale to Slider results in its values being used twice, for the X and Y dimensions of Scale.

Arrays and Dimensions

When a property has more than one dimension, its overall value is referred to in JavaScript as an *array*. For 2D scale, its value is an array with the dimensional parameters X and Y.

Step 12: The height of **bar 1** now scales in time with the music, but it's scaling from its center. A bar graph should scale up from its bottom. Fortunately, this does not require an expression to solve:

• Press Home to return to 00:00, where the value of Slider (and therefore, Scale Y) is 0. Type in a value of **"100"** for Slider 1.

• Select the Pan Behind tool from the Tools palette (shortcut = Y)

• Make sure **bar 1** is selected. Position the cursor over its Anchor Point icon – the circle with the X in the middle – in the Comp window. Click on the Anchor Point, and then press the Shift key, which will constrain your movements to just the X or Y axis. With Shift depressed, drag the Anchor Point icon down until its crosshairs center on the bottom of the layer. If you have the Info window open, it will tell you how far you've dragged; 50 pixels is correct. Press Shift+A to twirl down Anchor Point in the Timeline; its value should now read X = 10, Y = 100.

• Set the first keyframe for Slider 1 back to its original value of 0. RAM Preview: **bar 1**'s height should scale correctly now.

• Drag **bar 1** to line up with the bottom of the Comp window (Y Position = 240), and it will behave just like a bargraph meter.

If you had trouble creating this expression, study the prebuilt comp [2_bargraph_after Step 12] *to make sure you entered it correctly. Save your project before moving onto the next section.*

11 To alter just the Y dimension, tell After Effects to use its previous X scale value for X and then use the pick whip to assign Slider to Y (top), and finish off the expression with a close bracket. Notice how the Scale property now uses Slider's value for just the Y dimension (above), which makes the bar's height jump in response to the loudness of some of the musical parts.

12 Shift+drag **bar 1**'s Anchor Point down to the bottom of the bar so that it will scale from the bottom.

Part 3: Raising the Bar

Although scaling is a versatile way to animate a layer, there are times when it's a bad solution – such as when the layer contains an image you don't want to squish and stretch. An alternative approach is to use expressions to animate the Position of a layer. This is not much more difficult than animating its Scale.

For this part, you can continue using the comp you created in Steps 7 through 12. If you are jumping straight into this Part and have skipped the previous one, open the comp [**3_bargraph_2** * **starter**].

13 The expression to make **bar 2**'s Y position follow **bar 1**'s Slider is not much different from the Scale expression you created in Step 11 (above). However, the animation is in the wrong place (below)…

STEP 13: You want to animate the position for **bar 2** to make it jump up from the bottom of the comp like **bar 1** does, just without the stretching effect that scaling creates. Like Scale, 2D Position has two dimensions: X and Y. Again, *these two values must be stored inside a pair of brackets separated by a comma* – for example [**X,Y**]. You want to animate only the Y dimension, and leave the X dimension alone. Fortunately, this is a problem you already know how to solve:

- Make sure **bar 1**'s effect parameters are exposed in the Timeline window (if not, press E to twirl them down).

- Select **bar 2**, and type P to reveal its Position property.

- Option+click (Alt+click) on Position's animation stopwatch in the Timeline window to enable expressions.

- To tell After Effects to leave the X position alone, type:

  [**position[0]**,

- Drag Position's pick whip up to **bar 1**'s effect parameter Slider. Note that the expression fragment After Effects writes for you is a little longer than before, because it's pointing to a property in another layer.

- Type] to close off the brackets, and hit Enter to enter the expression.

   RAM Preview and notice that **bar 2** hops in a similar manner as **bar 1**. However, there are some problems: **bar 2**'s location in the Comp window is all wrong, and it moves in the opposite direction. These take a little thought to fix, but the concepts are easy.

STEP 14: The sound keyframes we saved in Slider increase in value as the sound gets louder. However, to make an object move "up" in After Effects, you need to *decrease* its Y position value. This contradiction is easy to solve with a minus symbol:

- In the Timeline, click on **bar 2**'s expression field to highlight it.

- Click again just after **[position[0]**, to place the cursor in front of the statement for the Y position.

- Type – (a minus symbol on the keypad, or hyphen on your keyboard). This says use the negative of the value for **bar 1**'s Slider. Press Enter to accept your edit.

```
[position[0],-thisComp.layer("bar 1").effect("audio level")("Slider")]
```

14 To make the bar rise in the frame as the sound gets louder, you need the negative of Slider's value.

   If you RAM Preview now, you will notice that the two bars now move in the same direction – but **bar 2** is hanging off the top of the Comp window, not the bottom like **bar 1** is.

STEP 15: The layer **bar 2** is now correctly bouncing up in time with the music. But where should it be bouncing up from? The bottom of the composition. This comp is 240 pixels high, so fixing this is a simple matter starting with 240, then subtract Slider's value from it. If you were to type **240** in front of the minus sign you added in Step 14, you would have this result. But there is a more clever trick you can use, which makes After Effects do some of the work for you:

- Select the expression, and place your cursor just before the minus symbol you entered above. Carefully type:

   thisComp.height

   This expression fragment is what it says: After Effects will automatically figure out this comp's height in pixels, so you don't have to remember its size. If you were to resize this comp later, After Effects would automatically take this new size into account, keeping the bar at the bottom.

- Hit Enter and RAM Preview again: The motion is correct; **bar 2** just starts higher than it should. We'll fix that problem shortly.

Sound Keys

We created the keyframe data used in this project with a plug-in from Trapcode (www.trapcode.com) called **Sound Keys**. Sound Keys is able to analyze individual frequency bands and loudness ranges of audio, and to create streams of keyframes from this data (the graphical portion of the user interface is shown above).

   As it allows you to focus in on these individual bands of frequencey, Sound Keys has a lot more control than the keyframe assistant Convert Audio to Keyframes or the old Motion Math audio scripts. It also has the bonus of being able to create keyframe data with more fluid motion.

16 You can increase or decrease the height of the area where you read an expression by click+dragging on the line just below it.

STEP 16: If you can't read the entire expression at this point, make the Timeline window wider. This already-long expression is also about to get longer, so open up more height for it in the Timeline window. Place your cursor just underneath the expression field, until a double-arrow icon appears. Click and drag downward to open up a larger expression window.

• Clean up the expression to make it more readable: add spaces on either side of the minus sign. Place the cursor just before the long fragment created by the pick whip tool in Step 13 (just after the minus symbol), and hit Return to move it down to another line. Expressions ignore space and most returns, so these edits won't alter what the expression does.

• Hit Enter to accept the modified expression. It should now read:

**[position[0], thisComp.height -
thisComp.layer("bar 1").effect("audio level")("Slider")]**

16 *complete:* Your modified expression now takes the height of this comp and subtracts from it the value of **bar 1**'s Slider. This will give you the jump-up motion you want.

17 Set **bar 2**'s Anchor Point to its top. That way, the layer will extend off the bottom of the comp.

STEP 17: The motion is correct but **bar 2** starts higher than it should. As in Step 12, we can fix this easily by moving the Anchor Point (since the value of Position used by the expression is the value of the Anchor Point in the Comp window):

• Double-click **bar 2** to open its Layer window.

• Set the View popup (bottom right) to Anchor Point Path.

• Drag the Anchor Point to the top, not the bottom, of the layer – when at rest, you want it to extend off the bottom of the comp. Remember that you can hold the Shift key while you're dragging to constrain your movement. When you're done, close the Layer window.

• RAM Preview for the final time. The two bars are now jumping in unison – but since we used Position rather than Scale to accomplish this with **bar 2**, you don't have to worry about the image inside this bar getting squished.

Save your project. We've saved prebuilt comps for most of the steps in this section for you to compare your results with.

Part 4: Shifting Time

The next trick is using a simple expression to make one layer's animation follow another, but shifted in time. The example we'll use here is creating a "wave" type animation, but this technique has many uses – such as setting up a transition animation for one layer, and having all other similar layers use the same animation at different points in time.

STEP 18: Close any extraneous compositions, and open the comp [**4_time delay * starter**]. It contains three bars made from simple solids. The first one (which appears left-most in the Comp window) already has an expression assigned to it similar to the ones you created earlier: its Y Scale follows the values stored for an Expression Control's Slider that has already been applied.

STEP 19: Make sure the Scale property for **bar 1** is visible in the Timeline window. Then select **bar 2**, and type S to reveal its Scale property. Create an expression for its Scale to follow **bar 1**'s Scale using the pick whip:

• In the Timeline window, Option+click (Alt+click) on the animation stopwatch next to **bar 2**'s Scale property to enable expressions.

• Drag the pick whip for **bar 2**'s Scale to point at the word Scale for **bar 1**. Make sure you drag the pick whip to the word Scale next to the animation stopwatch, and not the next line down that says Expression: Scale.

• Hit Enter, and RAM Preview – the two bars animate together.

STEP 20: The expression for **bar 2** should say:

thisComp.layer("bar 1").scale

To make it look at a different point in time to borrow **bar 1**'s Scale property, do the following:

• Select the expression field for **bar 2**, and move your cursor to the end of the line.

• Type the following immediately after the word **scale** at the end of the expression:

.valueAtTime(time - 0.05)

The *method* (a command to calculate something) **valueAtTime** says "When looking at that other layer's Scale property, check out what its value would be at the time detailed in the following set of parentheses." In this case, that value is the current time minus 0.05 seconds. Press Enter.

Methods of Madness

A parameter value of a property such as Scale or Position is referred to as an *attribute*. A command to calculate something – such as **valueAtTime** – is called a *method*.

19 Use the pick whip to make **bar 2**'s Scale follow **bar 1**'s Scale.

20 The highlighted area shows the attribute that tells an expression to look at a different point in time when it's borrowing another parameter's value.

One Frame Offset

To calculate one frame of delay, you can divide one second by the comp's frame rate, or have After Effects calculate it for you by using the attribute **thisComp.frameDuration** in place of a specific number. For two frames, add *** 2**, and so on.

22 Copy **bar 2**'s expression and paste it into the expression field for **bar 3**. Modify it so that it looks at **"bar 2"** instead of **"bar 1"** so it will follow one more frame behind.

• RAM Preview and note how **bar 2**'s movement now lags slightly behind **bar 1**.

• You can enter any amount of delay you want in place of the 0.05 we had you type in. For example, replace **0.05** with **0.033**, which works out to one frame of delay at 30 frames per second (fps). RAM Preview, and notice how **bar 2**'s movement seems to follow **bar 1** more closely.

STEP 21: Now make **bar 3** follow behind **bar 2**. You can do this by copying and pasting the expression from **bar 2** to **bar 3**, changing just one number:

• Select the Scale expression for **bar 2**, and Edit>Copy it.

• Select the layer **bar 3** and type S to reveal its Scale property.

• Option+click (Alt+click) on its animation stopwatch, and Edit>Paste the expression you copied.

• Hit Enter, and RAM Preview. The layers **bar 2** and **bar 3** move together. This is because **bar 3** is also looking at **bar 1**'s animation, not **bar 2**.

STEP 22: Highlight the expression text for **bar 3**. Modify the phrase "**bar 1**" to say "**bar 2**" so it will look at the next layer in line.

• Hit Enter, and RAM Preview. The three bars will now follow each other, delayed by one frame each.

Remember that the entire chain of expressions remains live: Any changes to **bar 1**'s animation will ripple through to the other bars.

Save your project. As with the previous example, prebuilt comps have been saved for most of the steps in this section. Compare your final result with [**3_time delay_after Step 22**].

Part 5: Here's Looking at You

These next two parts will extend expressions into the realm of 3D space. Part 6 will show a trick to make certain 2D effects appear to be tracking a 3D object, such as a camera or light. Here we will demonstrate a simple expression that makes a layer track another object: the **lookAt** method.

STEP 23: Close any extraneous comps, and open [**5_lookat * starter**]. It contains two layers: a stylized profile of an eye (**CM_eye.tif**), and a sphere from Tutorial 9: *The Planets* (**aF_CB_Venusian.tif**).

> **CM_eye.tif** was created using masks paths and the Stroke effect. The comp it was made in is stored in the **Expressions * prebuilt** folder in the Project window.

STEP 24: This expression requires the objects to be in 3D space. In the Timeline window, make sure the Switches column is visible – press F4 if it isn't – and enable the 3D Layer switch (the checkboxes under the wireframe cube) for both of the layers.

STEP 25: The **lookAt** expression method compares the position of two layers, and re-orients the layer it is applied to so that it faces the second layer. To use the pick whip tool to create this expression, you need to reveal the Position property of both layers – so select them both and press P.

You will apply this expression to the Orientation property of the **CM_eye.tif** layer, so select it by itself, and type Shift+R to reveal this property.

STEP 26: You're going to build this expression using a combination of typing, popup menus, and the pick whip tool. The format to keep in mind when you're working with expression methods – commands to calculate new values – is *the name of the method, followed by a set of parentheses that contains the parameters it is operating on*. If there is more than one parameter, these parameters are separated by commas. For example:

> methodName(parameter1, parameter2)

• Option+click (Alt+click) on the animation stop-watch next to Orientation to enable the expression.

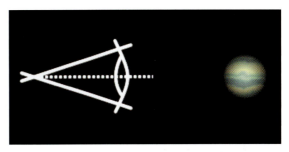

23 The initial comp contains a small planet, and an eye that will look at it using an expression.

24 This expression requires that both layers be in 3D space. Enable their 3D Layer switches (the cube icons).

25 Reveal the Position property for both layers, and the Orientation/Rotation properties for **CM_eye.tif**.

Revealing Expressions

To reveal all expressions used for a layer, select that layer and type EE (two Es in quick succession). Typing U reveals all properties that have keyframes or expressions attached, but it does not reveal the expressions themselves; twirl these properties open to read their expressions.

26 If you can't remember the exact wording for an attribute or method, After Effects has an extensive popup menu that will type the correct letters for you.

Turn Your Back

The After Effects manual says the order of the parameters for **lookAt** are the "from point" followed by the "to point." This is incorrect, and should read "to point" followed by the "from point."

• Click on the arrow to the right of the pick whip tool. A large menu will appear; it contains a library of pretyped expression attributes and methods. Mouse over to the one called Vector Math (the second from the top), then mouse over and down to the one that says **lookAt(fromPoint, atPoint)** and release the mouse. After Effects will automatically type this method for you (with no typos), as well as dummy names for the parameters you need inside the parentheses.

• The first parameter you need is the position of the point you will be looking at, which After Effects mysteriously calls **fromPoint** (yes, it's a mistake). Select the words **fromPoint** (you can double-click them to select them), click on the pick whip tool, and drag it up to the Position property for **aF_CB_Venusian**. Release the mouse, and After Effects will replace the words **fromPoint** with the phrase **thisComp.layer("aF_CB_Venusian.tif").position**.

26 *continued:* The first parameter is the position of the layer you are looking at. Select it using the pick whip tool.

• The second parameter you need is the position of the layer you will be looking from – namely, the eye itself. Select the words **atPoint**, (yes – counter-intuitive), click on the pick whip tool, and drag it up to the Position property for **CM_eye.tif**. Release the mouse, and After Effects will replace the words **atPoint** with the word **position**.

26 *continued:* Next, use the pick whip to select the Position property of the layer you are looking from – namely, the eye layer itself.

	#	Source Name													:00s		05s		10s		15s	

▽ ☐ 1 ■ **aF_CB_Venusian.tif**
   › ⟳ Position   310.0 , 150.0 , 0.0
▽ ☐ 2 ■ **CM_eye.tif**
   › ⟳ Position   100.0 , 150.0 , 0.0
   ▽ ⟳ ≣ Orientation   0.0 ° , 270.0 ° , 0.0 °
      › Expression : Orientation   ⊚ ▶   lookAt(thisComp.layer("aF_CB_Venusian.tif").position, position)
   › ⟳ X Rotation   0 x +0.0 °
   › ⟳ Y Rotation   0 x +0.0 °
   › ⟳ Z Rotation   0 x +0.0 °

Switches / Modes

- Hit Enter. Your final expression should read:

lookAt(thisComp.layer("aF_CB_Venusian.tif").position, position)

STEP 27: Now turn your attention to the Composition window. The **CM_eye.tif** layer has turned sideways in relation to the **aF_CB_Venusian.tif** layer so that its Z axis points at the planet. This is easier to see if you use a different camera position; to get a better perspective, try selecting Custom View 1 from the View popup at the bottom of the Comp window.

Select the **CM_eye.tif** layer and note how the eye's blue Z axis coordinate arrow points directly at the planet (to be exact, the planet's anchor point).

Experiment with moving the **aF_CB_Venusian.tif** layer, either directly in the Comp window or by scrubbing its Position coordinates in the Timeline window. The eye will continue to face the planet. Now change the **CM_eye.tif** layer's Position, and notice that it continues to re-orient itself toward the planet. This will also be true if you keyframed an animation path for either layer.

STEP 28: A design issue with the current arrangement is that **CM_eye.tif** was drawn to *point* at another layer, not face it. This is where having two different sets of Rotation properties for a layer comes in handy.

The eye needs to be rotated on its vertical – or Y – axis to change where it points. Watching the Comp window, scrub the Y Rotation property in the Timeline until the **CM_eye.tif** (and its red Y axis arrow) points toward the planet. This might be easier to see from the Top view; the correct value is 90°. To verify that this works, move either layer around and observe that the eye continues to point at the planet.

If your pointer layer was originally drawn pointing up or down, modify its Z Rotation to aim it in the direction you want. If you need to also animate the layer's rotation, you could apply this expression to a null object, and parent your animating layer to the null. (Parenting a layer to a null object is covered in Tutorial 6, *Piccadilly Circus*.)

Save your project. This finished expression, with Y Rotation offset, is saved as prebuilt comp [**5_lookat_after Step 28**].

26 *complete:* Hit Enter, and your **lookAt** expression is done.

27 After this expression has been applied, the eye layer faces toward the planet along its Z axis (the blue arrow) as viewed in Custom View 1.

28 Entering a Y Rotation value of 90° redirects the eye to point at the planet along the correct axis.

Part 6: 2D Meets 3D

Even though After Effects has a concept of 3D space, all of the individual objects in this space are still flat 2D layers with no depth. Several effects, such as Bevel Alpha and Texturize, fake 3D depth by changing the apparent light levels across a layer's surface. Expressions can be employed to make this fakery appear to track a 3D camera or light (or other layer). This expression can be applied to any effect that has a rotational parameter, such as Directional Blur, Twirl, Wave Warp, or even the normal 2D Drop Shadow effect (if you want to avoid the render hit 3D lights and shadows incur). It does contain some more complex math than what we've dealt with so far, but fortunately, it's a standard formula that you can use as-is and just paste in as needed.

Step 29: Close any extraneous comps, and open [**6_faux 3D** * **starter**]. It contains a solid called **Gold Slab** enabled for 3D, and an animating camera. RAM Preview and note how the camera's perspective changes.

Step 30: Select **Gold Slab**, and apply Effect>Perspective>**Bevel Alpha**. Its edges will now appear to be affected by a light that's where the camera starts. (In the next step we'll build on this idea by using a Light layer.) In its Effect Controls window, increase the Edge Thickness parameter to 4.00 so you can see this more clearly.

   RAM Preview again, and the illusion breaks down: Even though the camera moves, the lighting on the beveled edge does not. You could try to hand animate Light Angle's value to keep the illusion alive, but there's a better way…

Step 31: Delete the Bevel Alpha effect (select it in the Effect Controls and hit the Delete key). Make sure **Gold Slab** is still selected, then go to Animation>Apply Animation Preset. Navigate to the _**Presets** folder inside this tutorial's folder on your drive, select **CameraBevel.ffx**, and click Open. This preset applies the Bevel Alpha effect, with an expression already written.

   With **Gold Slab** still selected, type EE to reveal the expression applied to the Light Angle parameter. You will probably need to drag

30 The Bevel Alpha effect creates the illusion that a layer is being lit from a certain angle (above). However, this angle does not automatically track objects such as a 3D camera (below).

31 Applying this expression to Bevel Alpha's Light Angle parameter causes it to track the camera's relative position (sequence below).

the thin white line below the expression text field downward to see the entire expression; it is four lines long:

```
angle_offset = 90 + rotation;
target_layer = thisComp.activeCamera;
rel_pos = sub(position, target_layer.position);
(Math.atan2(rel_pos[1], rel_pos[0])*180/Math.PI) - angle_offset;
```

This could have been written in one long line, but we broke it up into more easily digestible pieces. This required naming some "variables" to equal intermediate values along the way.

The first line helps compensate for the way different effect parameters behave. You need to determine by observation what value works for each effect. An offset of 90° works for the Light Angle parameter; Drop Shadow's Direction parameter would require you to replace the **90** with **270**.

We also considered that the layer might be rotating as well by adding its Rotation property to **angle_offset** in the first line. To try this out, type Shift+R to also reveal this layer's Rotation property, and scrub the Z Rotation parameter: Note how the light still appears to come from the camera's position.

The second line indicates which object you want to track; in our case, it's the active camera. If you wanted to track a different layer instead, select the phrase **thisComp.activeCamera** and pick whip to the name of the layer you wish to track.

The third line finds the difference in positions between the layer the expression is being used on and the object you're tracking. The fourth line uses the math function arc tangent (**atan2**) to calculate the rotational angle between these two layers, including an offset you can adjust in the first line.

A finished version of this comp is saved in the **_Expressions * prebuilt>_compare comps_after Step ##** *folder as* [**6_faux 3D_after Step 31**].

Step 32: Open comp [**6_faux 3D_light**]. This is a prebuilt variation of [**6_faux 3D * starter**], with a stationary camera and an animating light. The expression has been modified to track the light instead of the camera (drag the expression field larger so you can read the entire four lines of code).

Select the **Light 1** layer and scrub the Timeline to see how the bevel edges appear to follow the light's direction. (To see the motion path for the light, with the light still selected, set View>Set 3D View to Top view or Custom View 2.)

There are several ways to trick this expression into not working, such as placing the camera or light at the same position or on the same plane as the object – after all, 2D effects don't understand "in front" or "behind"; just left, right, up, or down. But overall, this expression has many applications in making the layer it is applied to appear to react to other 3D objects.

Further Reading

If you don't have any prior experience with expressions, you may want to first read a column we wrote for *DV* magazine (www.dv.com) called **DV_Expressions.pdf**. It is located inside the **Goodies>Further Reading** folder on your disk.

There are numerous books on the JavaScript language; our personal favorite is *JavaScript: A Beginner's Guide* by John Pollock (Osbourne/McGraw Hill). You can ignore the chapters on web programming – the bulk of most books – and focus on the language itself.

There is also information available on several web sites; our picks are AE Enhancers (www.aehancers.com) and Dan Ebberts' MotionScript.com.

Finally, there's always (gasp!) the manual and online Help. They contain good, condensed information on expressions.

32 A simple variation of this expression can track an animating light. This is saved as **LightBevel.ffx** in this chapter's **_Presets** folder on the DVD.

33 The overall shape was created by masking a solid.

33 *complete:* The three bars on the left are animated with an expression attached to their Y Scale; the three on the right have their Y Position animated.

34 The dots and outmost ring have their Z Position animated in the same way as the bargraph's Y Position in the previous comp. The other rings follow the first one, delayed in time by one frame each. The dots are created with the Type tool, their locations are expressed to follow along with the music as they flow around a Mask shape. The Hue of the rings is also offset using a simple expression.

Part 7: Musical Expression Project

Go back and play **Expressions.mov** from the **11_Expressions>Final Movie** folder on disk. All of the expressions used to create this movie are derived from those you learned in the previous sections. The individual pieces have been broken down into their own precomps; we'll give a brief overview of those here. For more detail, read the file **11B_Expressions_Bonus.pdf** in the **11_Expressions** folder on your disk.

STEP 33: Open the **MusicalExpression.aep** project; you'll find it in the **11_Expressions>Project** folder. Then open the composition [**ME_1 shape build**]. RAM Preview it and watch how the black bars along the lower right side jump in time with the music.

The overall shape was built by masking a white solid. The six bars are black solids that knock holes out of the overall shape. The three on the left are animated using the Scale trick demonstrated in Part 2; the three on the right are animated using the Position trick demonstrated in Part 3.

STEP 34: Open the comp [**ME_2 ring/dot bounce**]. It has a lot of keyframes; if your screen is redrawing too slowly, twirl up the **SoundKeys** layer. It is easier to see what is going on if you view these 3D layers at an angle, such as with Custom View 1. Locate to 03:00 to see the animation at its peak, then RAM Preview.

The outermost ring has its Z Position animated with an expression similar to that used to move the bar graphs up and down. The other rings have their Z Position tied to the first ring, but are delayed in time one frame each using the same method discussed in Part 4.

Each of these rings has the Fill effect applied. The first ring is having its hue value shifted by scaling down the values of one of the **SoundKeys** keyframe sets. The other rings again just follow the first, delayed in time.

The characters (bullets on Mac; unfortunately Yen symbols on Windows) are created using the Type tool,

with the Path Options set to follow an open mask shape which curls around the rings. The First Margin parameter is offset in much the same way that you learned to offset Position in Part 4; the Tracking Amount is adjusted similar to the way you manipulated Scale in Part 3. This layer also has its Z Position animated in the same way as the outermost ring.

STEP 35: Open the comp [ME_3 title look-at] and RAM Preview it. Each of the individual characters of the title use the **lookAt** expression you learned in Part 5 to follow the flare layer (prerendered using Knoll Light Factory) as it flies through the scene in 3D.

All of the characters were created in white with black outlines. The Tint effect was applied to each of them. These in turn were expressed to the layer **master tint**: Change the colors in its Tint effect, and watch all of the characters follow. Additional simple expressions were used to blink the Opacity of each character in time with the music, including a trick in which all of the layers are faded to full opacity using a separate dummy slider. This trick is explained in detail in the companion PDF file, **11B_Expressions_Bonus.pdf**.

STEP 36: Open the comp [**ME Final Build**]: This is where it all comes together. Select layer 4 – **ME_1.1 surface precomp** – and type EE to reveal its expressions. Both the Bevel Alpha and Texturize effects use the same angle expression discussed in Part 6.

35 Each of the characters are individually expressed to look at the flare layer as it flies by (above).

36 The main surface (left) has the Texturize and Bevel Alpha effects applied, expressed to follow the camera's position.

Although this is not expression related, you might also note that the precomps [**ME_2 ring/dot bounce**] and [**ME_3 title look-at**] have their Collapse Transformations switches turned on. You can collapse 3D compositions; they will then use the camera and lights of the comp they are nested into. This is how we could build 3D elements in precomps and have them integrate with the camera animation in our final scene.

36 *complete:* The final comp. Note that some of the precomps have their Collapse Transformations switch enabled; even 3D layers and comps may be collapsed.

Thanks to Michael Natkin – Adobe's expression wizard – for his support and advice, and to fellow user JJ Gifford whose use of expressions inspired some of the ideas in this tutorial.

Connect

For more information on topics covered in this tutorial and its accompanying PDF file, check out the following volumes of *Creating Motion Graphics*:

Volume 1:

Animation Presets

Anchor Point, Pan Behind tool

Mask Shapes

Bevel Alpha, Set Matte, Tint, Fill effects

Type tool

Nesting Compositions

Blending Modes

Collapse Transformations

Volume 2:

Compound Effects

Expressions

Importing layered Photoshop files

Flamingo 4

Using Illustrator artwork and other vector-based elements to create an animation for the Macromedia Flash file format (SWF).

The artistic brief behind this tutorial is creating web animations to teach kids about numbers. Today's number is 4, and you've enlisted a flamingo to help illustrate this. You'll import a flamingo and a background already created in Illustrator. To animate the flamingo, you will need to set up anchor points and a Parenting relationship for its layers. You'll also add a water element to the background, then create text on a curve using the new Type tool and a Wiggly Selector. Since you want to export the final animation as a Macromedia Flash format file (SWF), you will need to take care to keep all the elements as vector art throughout. After the hard work is done, you can have fun making the flamingo dance to the accompanying music.

OVERVIEW

Main Concepts:

These are the features and concepts we will be focusing on in this project:

- Importing Illustrator files as Comps
- Pan Behind Tool
- Anchor Point
- Parenting
- Keyframe interpolation
- Spotting music
- Masking a solid shape
- RotoBezier mask shape
- Text on a curve
- Wiggly Selector
- Exporting as SWF

Requirements:

After Effects 6.5 or later Standard edition. Adobe Brush Script font (free on your After Effects 6.5 installer CD). If using the Tryout version, use any similar font from your own font library.

Getting Started:

Inside the **Tutorials** master folder on the accompanying DVD, locate and copy the folder **12_Flamingo** to your hard drive. In the folder **Final Movies** inside this project, double-click on and play **Flamingo.mov**. Alternatively, you can open and play the file **FlamingoR.htm** or **Flamingo.swf** in your web browser.

Open the file **Flamingo.aep** inside the **Project** folder – this is your starting point; we suggest you save under a new name after each major section.

Credits:

The concept and artwork for this project were created by Kristin Harris Design (www.kristinharrisdesign.com). Music by Carolyn West.

The Tasks

This is what you will be doing in the various parts of this tutorial:

PART 1: Import the layered Illustrator file that contains the flamingo, set anchor points, and build a parent/child hierarchy for its body parts.

PART 2: Resize the flamingo, add a layered Illustrator file which contains most of the background elements, and animate its clouds.

PART 3: Add the soundtrack and spot the beats in it for animation cues, and animate the legs of the flamingo to form the number "4".

PART 4: Create a water element by masking a solid, animate a bouncing title using the Type tool and a Wiggly selector, and add your own dance moves for the flamingo.

PART 5: Rendering for SWF (pronounced "swiff") output.

The flamingo in its final pose. Artwork © 2001 Kristin Harris Design, Inc. Music © 2001 Carolyn West.

Part 1: First Steps

The folder **Flamingo * prebuilt comps** in the accompanying project contains a number of compositions saved after various pivotal steps below, so you can check your own work if you go astray. Feel free to explore these comps before you get started, but be sure to Close All (Windows>Close All) when you're done. Also in the Project window, we've created two folders called **My_Comps** and **My_Sources** for you to put your own work into and keep it separate from the prebuilt versions. Select the appropriate folder before creating a new composition or importing a file; After Effects will automatically sort it into that folder for you!

Import the Flamingo

STEP 1: First, you need to get a flamingo into your project. Guest artist Kristin Harris has already created one in Illustrator, so select the **My_Sources** folder in the Project window, and use File>Import File>File to locate the layered Illustrator file **Flamingo4.ai** from the **12_Flamingo>Project>Sources** folder on your drive. In the Import File dialog, select the Composition – Cropped Layers option, and click Open. The result is a folder with the individual layers, and a comp with a size of 370×530 pixels.

The Import As popup offers two choices for establishing the layer size when importing a layered Illustrator file. The Cropped Layers option will create layers that are only as big as necessary to hold the layer's imagery.

2 Open [**Flamingo4 Comp 1**] to view the individual layers. (Note that we changed the layer color from Pink to Violet to see the layer handles more easily against the pink flamingo.)

The alternate option – Import As Composition – considers each layer to be the same size as the composition, which means the anchor point is less likely to be in a useful spot.

No matter which option you use when you import an Illustrator file as a Composition, the comp will be created at a size just large enough to include all the elements. If you'd rather predetermine the comp size, draw a rectangle in Illustrator CS around the elements and convert it to crop marks (Object>Crop Area>Make). If you want the Artboard size to be used as the comp size in After Effects, select Object>Crop Area>Make when nothing is selected. (You can adjust the size of the Artboard in File>Document Setup.)

STEP 2: In the Project window, double-click [**Flamingo4 Comp 1**] to open it, and make sure it's set to Full Resolution.

STEP 3: The flamingo has an alpha channel, which means the comp's black background color will be visible around it. This background color is often irrelevant to the final render, but it may appear when you render to SWF. In any case, change Composition>Background Color to white for this tutorial.

Setting the Anchor Points

STEP 4: When you import a layered Illustrator file with the Cropped Layers option, each layer's anchor point will be placed in the center of the layer. However, when the flamingo animates, each part needs to rotate around an anchor point that makes sense for that part: for example, the upper legs should rotate from the hip, and the lower legs should rotate from the knee.

To change the anchor point for the layers, select the Pan Behind tool from the Tools palette (shortcut: Y) and start by selecting the top layer, **Wings**. Its anchor point is visible in the center of the comp. Click directly on it and drag it to the left side of the **Wings** layer, about where the wings would naturally rise if they were flapping.

4 Move the anchor point for the **Wing** layer from its center to a more natural position. The Pan Behind tool edits both the Position and Anchor Point values together, so the layer remains stationary in the comp.

The Pan Behind tool is also referred to as the "Anchor Point" tool. With it you can move the anchor point directly in the Comp window. If you were to change the Anchor Point in the Layer window with the Selection tool, it would offset its position in the Comp window to reflect this new center – you would then have to reposition the layer in the Comp window to get back to where you started. Moving the Anchor Point with the Pan Behind tool automatically changes the Anchor Point and Position values in concert with one another so the layer keeps its same relative position in the comp. Very handy!

STEP 5: Continue selecting layers one by one and moving their anchor points to positions that make sense for each body part. Keep in mind that some of the layers are partially hidden by other layers: for example, **Leg 2** (the leftmost one) is tucked partially behind the body. Feel free to turn layers off or solo layers to see the layer you're working on more clearly.

As this illustration has a loose, fun style, you don't have to place your new anchors exactly at the right pixel, but here are some guides:

- **Foot 1 & Foot 2:** Move these anchors near the top of the feet, where the ankle would hinge, but still inside the foot.

- **Legs Upper:** Move their anchors to the top of the upper leg (the hip).

- **Legs Lower:** Move their anchors to the top of the lower leg (the knee).

- **Body:** Move the anchor to the center of body.

- **Neck:** Move the anchor point to the bottom end of the neck – you will probably want to solo this layer to see it more clearly.

To test that parts such as the **Wings** or **Neck** will rotate correctly, select a layer, hit R for Rotation, and scrub its value. Or, select the Rotation tool (shortcut: W for "wotate") and drag around the layer's anchor. Tweak the anchor points using the Pan Behind tool until you're happy. Be sure to use Undo (or otherwise return all rotations to 0°) and revert to the Selection tool (shortcut: V) before the next step.

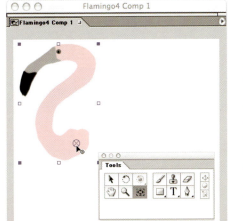

5 When you're setting the anchor points for the remaining layers – in particular the **Neck** layer – the Solo switch (circled below) is useful for isolating a layer that may be obscured by another layer.

5 *complete:* To make sure your new anchor points work as expected, scrub a layer's Rotation property while checking how the corresponding body part moves, or use the Rotation tool and drag the layer clockwise in the Comp window.

Color Coding

When animating a character with many parts, color code the different layer groups. To do this, select the layers you want to be part of a particular group and context+click on the color swatch in the Timeline window to pick another color.

Solo Selecting

You can view each layer separately by clicking the layer's Solo switch. You can solo more than one layer at once; Option+clicking (Alt+clicking) on a Solo switch will turn off any other solo layers. Remember to turn off (not on!) all solo switches to view all the layers again.

We interrupt this tutorial to note that if you are completely lost, open our [Flamingo_after Step 05] *comp to compare your results; you will find it in the* **Flamingo * prebuilt>_compare comps_after Step ##** *folder. You can also use this comp to continue with the tutorial.*

Parenting

You've probably heard the children's song "the thigh bone's connected to the hip bone…" These connections are a good thing, because you wouldn't want to move your hip, and not have your leg follow along with it – like the flamingo's foot in the illustration on the previous page.

This concept is supported by a feature called Parenting where you connect layers to each other. As you move, rotate, or scale the parent, all the connected children will follow. This is an exceptionally handy way to group together layers, and in many cases replaces the need for nesting layers together in subcomps. But Parenting goes beyond grouping, allowing you to set up "kinematic" chains of layers which are useful for character animation and other similar techniques.

Step 6: The **BODY** layer is the centerpiece of the flamingo, and therefore will be the center of our parenting. Now consider how the body parts connect to this: the wings, neck, and both upper legs would be direct children of the body; the lower legs would be children of the upper legs; the feet would be children of the lower legs. Now let's hook up the body parts of your flamingo in the same way.

• Be sure the Selection tool is active and make sure the Parent column is visible in the Timeline window. If it isn't, press Shift+F4, or context-click on one of the other column headers to reveal the Columns popup menu, and select Parent. You can slide most columns left and right to re-arrange them; we prefer it near the layer's name.

• Start with the **Wings** layer. You can either click on the popup for this layer under the Parent column and select the **BODY** layer, or use the pick whip tool: Click on the pick whip (the symbol that looks like a tiny spiral), and drag it to the layer you wish to be the parent.

6 The pick whip tool makes it easy to set up child/parent relationships.

• When you know that more than one layer will have the same parent, you can assign them all at the same time. Select the layers **Leg 1 Upper**, **Leg 2 Upper**, and **Neck**. Remember that you need to Command+click on Mac (Control+click on Windows) to select multiple layers that are not right next to each other in the Timeline window. Now use the popup menu or pick whip for any one of the selected layers to choose the **BODY** layer, and the rest of the selected layers will get the same parent.

A child can have only one parent. However, a child can act as a parent for another layer, which is exactly what we need to finish hooking up the rest of our body parts. You're probably already ahead of us:

- Connect **Leg 1 Lower** to **Leg 1 Upper**

- Connect **Foot 1** to **Leg 1 Lower**

- Connect **Leg 2 Lower** to **Leg 2 Upper**

- Connect **Foot 2** to **Leg 2 Lower**

Save your project. If you're lost, open our [**Flamingo_after Step 6**] *comp to compare your results.*

6 *complete:* Our final parenting hierarchy for the flamingo. Note the **BODY** layer's parent is set to None; it's the master of the entire chain.

Part 2: Composing the Frame

In this part, you will scale down the flamingo to its final size, and add a multilayered background behind it. You will make the background elements semitransparent, to get a more interesting visual mix.

Comp Size and Scaling

The flamingo is larger than you will need in the final composition. To reduce it and the comp down to their final sizes, you'll take advantage of the Parenting feature:

STEP 7: When you imported the flamingo's layered Illustrator file as a composition, the resulting comp received the same name as the Illustrator file. Type Command+K (Control+K) to open Composition Settings, and make the following changes:

- Change the Composition Name to "**MyFlamingo**" (all together now: "My, my, mmyyyyy flamingo!").

- Set the comp Width to 400 and Height to 300. If one number changes when you type in the other, verify that the Lock Aspect Ratio checkbox is turned off. Make sure the Pixel Aspect Ratio is still set to Square Pixels.

- Change the Frame Rate to 12 frames per second (fps) – this is the same as most cartoon animation.

- Set the Duration to 15:00, and click OK.

The following step will scale and position the flamingo character in the resized composition.

Counting Off Base

Since After Effects can't count in the timeline at 12 fps, the File>Project Settings have been saved at 24 fps (the best choice as it's a simple duplicate).

7 Edit the comp's settings from their imported defaults to something that will fit the final animation better. Note that you can type "1500" for 15:00.

7–8 After you resize the comp, the flamingo will appear cropped top and bottom (above).

If your comp's duration was originally less than 15 seconds, you might notice that your layers appear trimmed in the Timeline window to prematurely stop at the old duration's time. There's a sequence of keyboard shortcuts that can quickly fix this:

• Press the – (minus) key on the keyboard to zoom the timeline out to its full duration.

• Hit the End key to locate to the end of the comp.

• Use Command+A (Control+A) to select all of the layers.

• Press Option+] (Alt+]) to trim the out point of all selected layers to the current time.

• Hit F2 or Command+Shift+A (Control+Shift+A) to Deselect All layers.

• Hit the Home key to locate back to the beginning of the comp.

STEP 8: The flamingo now appears larger than the comp. To scale the entire character, all you need to do is scale the master parent – and the children will follow along. Select the **BODY** layer, hit S for Scale, click on the Scale value and enter a value of 50%.

If you've executed all the steps to this point correctly, the entire flamingo will now be 50% of its original size – and floating a bit too high in the frame. Make sure the Selection tool (shortcut: V) is active. With the **BODY** layer still selected, drag it down until it is roughly centered in the frame. Again, the body pieces followed because of the parenting chain you set up in Step 6.

Twirl up all layers and Save your project. If you think you missed something, open our comp [Flamingo_after Step 08] to compare your results, or use this comp to continue with the tutorial.

8 *complete:* To bring the flamingo into view again, Scale the **BODY** layer to 50%, and reposition it towards the center of the frame. Since the **BODY** layer is the master parent, these changes will scale and position the entire character.

Adding the Background

STEP 9: The background was also created in Illustrator, at the intended final size of 400×300. Import it as a composition, as you did with the flamingo in Step 1, but this time select the alternate Import As option:

• Select the **My_Sources** folder in the Project window, then File>Import>File the **Background.ai** from the **Project>Sources** folder. In the Import File dialog, select Composition from the Import As popup, and click Open.

STEP 10: You'll now have a composition and a folder of sources, both called [**Background Comp 1**]. Double-click the comp to open it, and explore the three layers inside: **BG_Palm Trees**, **BG_Clouds**, and **BG_Beach**. Note that all three layers are the same size as the composition itself.

STEP 11: Deselect All (F2), then select layers 1, 2, and 3. Command+C (Control+C) to copy these layers and press Command+W (Control+W) to close the comp windows.

> If you've been exploring different layers and properties, it's best to Deselect All (F2) or Deselect All Keyframes (Shift+F2) before Copying and Pasting layers. If you don't, After Effects defaults to copying any selected keyframe or property value rather than copying the layer itself. For instance: If you select the **BG_Clouds** layer and move it to see what it might look like when it's animated, the Position property is selected along with the layer. If you now Copy, you're actually copying the Position value, not the layer. When you then try to Paste this layer into another comp, either nothing will happen, or you'll paste a new Position value to another (unsuspecting) selected layer. So if you've ever pasted a layer and nothing happened, you're not going crazy...
>
> Just to make life more confusing: In this example, if you used Cut instead of Copy, the layer will disappear, but only the Position keyframes – not the cut layer – can be pasted. Although you can Undo when you realize that Paste isn't working, play it safe and always Copy – don't Cut – layers when pasting from one comp to another.

STEP 12: The [**MyFlamingo**] comp should now be forward. Paste the three background layers. While they are still selected, drag them to the bottom of the layer stack and check that they appear in the same order as before (top to bottom): **BG_Palm Trees**, **BG_Clouds,** and **BG_Beach**.

9 The **Background.ai** file Kristin Harris created consists of three layers: the palm trees, the clouds, and the beach. Verify that Best Quality is turned on for all layers so that they appear antialiased. (Whether new layers are created in Best or Draft Quality is a choice you can set in Preferences> General; the default is to set layers to Best Quality.)

10 Open [**Background Comp 1**], select all three layers and Copy. You can then close this composition.

11 Paste the layers into [**MyFlamingo**] and drag them to the bottom of the stack.

Since your final output will be SWF, you must place all the vector artwork in one composition. This is why you can't simply nest the [**Background Comp 1**] into the [**MyFlamingo**] comp. If you did, the background layers would render out as pixels, not vectors, making your SWF unnecessarily large.

STEP 13: Finish off the background layers by setting all three layers to 35% Opacity (shortcut: T to twirl down Opacity). This will appear to lighten the background layers, since earlier the comp's background color was set to white. The less saturated background should also make the flamingo stand out more.

Note how the semitransparent background layers appear: Even the tree trunks in the **BG_Palm Trees** layer are see-through. When you later export this comp as a SWF, you can also choose to have each vector shape in a layer be individually semitransparent rather than the entire layer looking like one semitransparent image. This creates yet a different look, as even the individual leaves on the trees will be semitransparent, overlapping in interesting ways.

We're using transparency here because we want to show off these features of the SWF file export; if your only goal was to make the background lighter, you could just change the colors in Illustrator. Note that, when you're planning on using SWF export, you shouldn't use a plug-in effect to adjust their color in After Effects: Most plug-ins convert vector art layers to pixels, which will greatly reduce the efficiency of a SWF file.

13 At this point, the background layers are behind the flamingo, and made partially transparent to create more contrast and interest.

STEP 14: To create additional interest, animate the clouds from right to left. At time 00:00, select just the **BG_Clouds** layer, hit Shift+P to also reveal Position in the Timeline window, and turn on its keyframing stopwatch. Set the first keyframe by dragging the layer in the Comp window to the right, or scrubbing the value for X position in the Timeline window. A Position of roughly X = 250, Y = 150 should

14 As you drag the **BG_Clouds** layer in the Comp window at 14:22, the pink line in the middle of the Comp window shows the motion path.

If you don't see both keyframes of the motion path, set Preferences>Display>Motion Path to "All Keyframes". The default is to show only 15 seconds worth, which means that long animations will have truncated motion paths.

The timeline window shows "MyFlamingo • Timeline" with time 0:00:14:22 (12.00 fps).

	#	Layer Name	Parent		:00s	05s	10s	15s
▷ ■	1	Wings	@ 5. BODY ▼					
▷ ■	2	Foot 1	@ 4. Leg 1 Lower ▼					
▷ ■	3	Leg 1 Upper	@ 5. BODY ▼					
▷ ■	4	Leg 1 Lower	@ 3. Leg 1 Upper ▼					
▷ ■	5	BODY	@ None ▼					
▷ ■	6	Foot 2	@ 8. Leg 2 Lower ▼					
▷ ■	7	Leg 2 Upper	@ 5. BODY ▼					
▷ ■	8	Leg 2 Lower	@ 7. Leg 2 Upper ▼					
▷ ■	9	Neck	@ 5. BODY ▼					
▽ □	10	BG_Palm Trees	@ None ▼					
		◦ Opacity	35 %					
▽ □	11	BG_Clouds	@ None ▼					
▷		◦ Position	150.0 , 150.0	◀ ✓	◆			◆
		◦ Opacity	35 %					
▽ □	12	BG_Beach	@ None ▼					
		◦ Opacity	35 %					

Switches / Modes

be good. Hit the End key to go to the last frame (14:22), and move the clouds to the left to roughly X = 150. You can RAM Preview this if you like by hitting 0 on the keypad.

Twirl up all layers and Save your project. If you had trouble following along, open our [**Flamingo_after Step 14**] *comp to compare your results. You can also use this comp to continue with the tutorial.*

Part 3: Let's Dance

We like to coordinate our animation to audio whenever we can, as this often increases the combined impact. Since you're ready to start making the flamingo move, now would be a good time to import the music track that goes along with this piece, and "spot" some beats or other key moments to suggest good points in time to place the keyframes.

Motivating Music

STEP 15: If you want to get some practice spotting the music yourself, select the **My_Sources** folder in the Project window (to help keep your own files sorted), and import the music track **Come_to_the_Island.aif** by Carolyn West – it's in the same **Sources** folder on the disk where you found the Illustrator files. Drag it into the [**MyFlamingo**] comp, making sure it starts at time 00:00. Reveal its audio waveform by twirling down the corresponding property in the Timeline window, or use the short-cut LL (two Ls in quick succession).

You can either RAM Preview the work area of the comp by hitting 0 on the keypad, or audition just the audio from the current time forward by hitting the . (period) key on the keypad. The duration of the audio-only preview is determined by Preferences>Previews>Audio Preview. We suggest you set it to 15:00, since that's the length of this project.

14 *complete:* Animate the **BG_Clouds** layer to drift from right to left by setting keyframes for Position.

Parent Column Toggle

You can toggle the Parent column open and closed by pressing Shift+F4. Close it anytime after Part 2 to save screen real estate.

Audio Shortcuts

Hit L to twirl down audio Levels, and LL (two Ls in quick succession) to twirl down the audio waveform.

Marking Time

You can add layer markers to any layer by selecting it and hitting the * (asterisk) key on the keypad. This creates a layer marker at the current time.

Option+* (Alt+*) will let you name layer markers as you add them; you can also double-click them later to add or edit a name.

Note that you can add layer markers while pre-viewing audio; this allows you to tap along to the music. When the preview is done, the layer markers will appear along the selected layer.

You also have 10 Composition markers, which you can set by pressing Shift+# (number from 0–9 from the keyboard, not the keypad). Press the number alone to jump to that point in time.

You can also create Web Links and add URLs to any Layer Marker (which can tell your web browser to switch pages as the file plays), and export these with the SWF file. These options are covered in the Help> After Effects Help menu under *Creating Web links from markers* and *Including Web links in a SWF file*.

Music Spotting

Spotting the music in a separate project file is a great way for a team to share the music on a large job. The artist with the best sense of time can annotate the music with layer markers, and everyone else can import this project into his or her own animations. Plus, everyone will agree where the beats fall!

Make a note of where the major beats seem to fall – we counted four measures and an ending. Now add layer markers to the music track at these points (see *Marking Time*) to mark the major beats so that you can close the waveform display, which slows down timeline redraws and takes up a lot of screen space.

If that sounds like more work than you're up for right this moment, we've prepared an After Effects project file which you can merge with your current project. To do this, select the **My Sources** folder in the Project window, go File>Import>File, select the **_music_spotted.aep** project file which is loose in the **Project** folder, and click Import. A folder will be created, holding the audio layer and a comp named [**Music Spotted**]. Open this comp and check out the audio: On average, we've marked only every other beat; we know from listening to the music that there is an additional beat in-between most of our markers – and we'll actually spot to some of those in the animation later on.

Select the audio layer, and Copy. Now Paste this layer into your [**MyFlamingo**] comp. (Don't delete the **_music_spotted.aep** project folder, as it holds the source for this audio layer.)

If that still seems like too much work, you can always cheat by opening our finished composition [**Flamingo_Final**]. Select the audio layer (Layer 1), Copy, and Paste it into your own composition. Our layer is already annotated with layer markers. But where's your sense of adventure and accomplishment?!

Animating the Legs

It's time to make your flamingo dance. We'll start by animating the grand finale: where the Leg 2 chain rotates to form the number 4. You can return later and add more animation to the wings, neck, and legs.

STEP 16: Go to time 08:00 – where music measure 4 begins – and select three layers: **Foot 2**, **Leg 2 Upper**, and **Leg 2 Lower**. Hit R to twirl down their Rotation properties, and click+drag across these stopwatches to turn on keyframing for all three layers. This will create the first set of Rotation keyframes at the current time.

• Press F2 to Deselect All. Go to time 08:16, which is about one beat after the start of this musical measure, and rotate **Leg 2 Upper** to +45°. Notice how the lower leg and foot follow, as they are children of the upper leg. (If they don't, double-check your work from Step 6.)

• Go to time 10:00 – about three beats into this measure – and rotate **Leg 2 Upper** to +35°. Why back up from the previous keyframe's value? Because a regular component of character animation includes overshooting the mark, especially if you then need to fold other limbs into position.

• Also at 10:00, rotate **Leg 2 Lower** to –125°. This should form the number 4 and leave the foot visible behind the other leg.

• Still at 10:00, rotate the **Foot 2** layer to –100°, so that its lowermost toe is pointing horizontally.

• Move to time 11:16, right before the music's final statement, and rotate **Foot 2** to –65°. This will move the foot slowly as the music dies down. Like overshooting, relaxing is another technique you can use to add interest to character animation.

15 Spot the beats in the music as a guide to help time your animation. We like to use layer markers for individual beats and events in the music, and comp markers for overall sections.

16 Through the use of Parenting, the flamingo's leg can be folded up into the number 4 using just Rotation keyframes, without having to animate the position of the limbs as well.

	MyFlamingo • Timeline	

MyFlamingo

0:00:10:00 (12.00 fps)

	#	Layer Name	Parent			
▷ □	1	[Come_to_the...]	@ None ▾			△4a △4b △5 △6 △7 △8
▷ □	2	Wings	@ 6. BODY ▾			
▷ □	3	Foot 1	@ 5. Leg 1 Lower ▾			
▷ □	4	Leg 1 Upper	@ 6. BODY ▾			
▷ □	5	Leg 1 Lower	@ 4. Leg 1 Upper ▾			
▷ □	6	BODY	@ None ▾			
▽ □	7	Foot 2	@ 9. Leg 2 Lower ▾			
		▷ ⊚ Rotation	0 x -100.0 °	◀ ✓ ▶		◆ ◆ ◆
▽ □	8	Leg 2 Upper	@ 6. BODY ▾			
		▷ ⊚ Rotation	0 x +35.0 °	◀ ✓		◆ ◆ ◆
▽ □	9	Leg 2 Lower	@ 8. Leg 2 Upper ▾			
		▷ ⊚ Rotation	0 x -125.0 °	◀ ✓		◆ ◆
▷ □	10	Neck	@ 6. BODY ▾			
▷ □	11	BG_Palm Trees	@ None ▾			
▷ □	12	BG_Clouds	@ None ▾			
▷ □	13	BG_Beach	@ None ▾			

Switches / Modes

17 The linear rotation keyframes are set with the work area encompassing them for RAM Preview purposes. Zoom into the timeline to see the keyframes more clearly by using the + and – keys on the keyboard. (You can also center the view around the time marker by pressing D.)

18 To alter a bunch of keyframes at the same time, drag a marquee around them and pick a new interpolation method. Easy Ease is a good start for a less robotic animation, but is not always the right fix…

STEP 17: Set the work area to encompass this section of your animation (08:00 to 12:00), and render a RAM Preview (0 on the keypad). Notice how jerky the animation is: This is because all the Rotation keyframes are Linear, with no ease in and outs added.

STEP 18: Select all the Rotation keyframes by dragging a marquee around them in the Timeline window. (You can also select them by clicking on the word Rotation in the Timeline window for **Foot 2**, which selects all Rotation keyframes for this layer, and then Shift+clicking on Rotation for **Leg 2 Upper** and **Leg 2 Lower**.)

Once all the Rotation keyframes are selected, context-click on any keyframe and select Keyframe Assistant>Easy Ease (shortcut: F9). RAM Preview again and see if you like the smoother animation.

For the most part Easy Ease works well – especially when the music softens toward the end. However, the first move for the upper leg hits on quite a sharp musical beat, which asks for a sharper animation move. Therefore, try changing **Leg 2 Upper**'s middle keyframe (at time 08:16) to an Auto Bezier (or "smooth") keyframe. To do this, be sure to Deselect All (F2) and then Command+click (Control+click) on the middle keyframe for **Leg 2 Upper**. This will revert it to Linear interpolation (denoted by a diamond icon). Now Command+click (Control+click) a *second* time to change its interpolation method to Auto Bezier (circle icon). RAM Preview again, and see if you like the result better.

If the flamingo kicked you in the head instead of posing for the number 4, compare your result with our comp [**Flamingo_after Step 18**]. *Then twirl up all layer outlines and Save your project.*

Graphical Speed

To get a better idea how the keyframe interpolation types are affecting the Rotation, twirl down the Rotation velocity graph for **Leg 2 Upper** and zoom into the timeline. Repeat Step 18, changing the middle keyframe from Easy Ease to Linear and back to Auto Bezier, and observe how the velocity graph changes. Notice how the Auto Bezier method even includes a little "overshooting" for a few frames after the middle keyframe: Although the middle keyframe has a value of 45° and is interpolating to 35° at the third keyframe, it rotates a little more than 45° as it moves through the middle keyframe. Auto Bezier is a good option for middle keyframes where you don't want a full ease in/out feel, but where a linear move is too bumpy.

The Value graph (upper line) shows how the value changes over time; the Velocity graph (lower line) shows changes in speed over time. The small gray bar (where the arrow is pointing) indicates an overshoot in the velocity. (Overshooting means that the velocity is interpolating in the opposite direction than the keyframe values would lead you to believe.)

Part 4: Final Touches

Time to add the final strokes. This will include adding a water layer to the background and animating the title text across the screen using additional tools in After Effects that will render as vectors. You will then finish off the flamingo's animation by improvising your own moves.

Just Add Water

After Effects can also export shapes created using masks and solids as SWF vector shapes. We're going to add some water to the background using this technique.

STEP 19: With the [**MyFlamingo**] comp forward and the current time marker at 00:00, make a new solid (Layer>New>Solid), name it "**Water Solid**", pick a nice blue color using the color swatch in the Solid Settings dialog, and click on Make Comp Size to make sure it's big enough to fill the frame. Click OK, then move the new solid down the layer stack in the Timeline window so that it's below the flamingo but above the three background layers.

19 Use the Pen tool to mask a solid, adding SWF-friendly water to the background. The Toggle View Masks button at the bottom of the Comp window determines whether mask outlines are visible or hidden in the Comp window.

• Select the Bezier pen tool (shortcut: G) and make sure the RotoBezier option is turned off (you'll use it later). Draw a funky shape at the bottom right corner of the beach to make it look like the water is about to wash up on the flamingo's toes. Don't forget to click on the first mask point again to close your mask shape – open mask shapes won't mask out any of the layer.

Masking Mischief

If you animate this mask shape, a new object will be added to the SWF file on each frame the layer appears!

Note that Masks applied to solids are exported to SWF as vectors provided you don't use a feather or mask expansion value other than zero. Other issues are covered in the *Export Exceptions* sidebar later in this chapter.

Comp [**Flamingo_after Step 19**] *shows how we masked the water layer. (Feel free to copy and paste the Mask Shape to your solid!)*

Creating the Title

In addition to Illustrator artwork and masked solids, you can add text with the new Type tool that will render as SWF-friendly vectors. In the next few steps, you'll create the "Flamingo" title, animate it along a curve, then add a Wiggly Selector to jiggle the individual characters.

If Auto Open Palettes is checked, the Character and Paragraph palettes will open automatically when you select the Type tool.

STEP 20: To create the title, move the time marker to 10:00 and select the Type tool. The Character and Paragraph palettes should open automatically provided the Auto Open Palettes option is checked in the toolbar. (If all else fails, you can click the Palette button in the toolbar.)

• In the Character palette, to clear out any lingering settings, select Reset Character from the palette's Options menu.

• Bring the Paragraph palette forward, and select Reset Paragraph from this palette's Options menu.

• With the Type tool, click in the lower half of the Comp window (right around the shin of the flamingo's standing leg). This creates the initial text layer. Type "**flamingo**" then press Enter when done to exit *editing mode*; the layer name will change automatically to **flamingo**. The text layer should now be selected, which means that any changes you make in the Character or Paragraph palettes will be applied to the entire layer.

• With the Paragraph palette forward, click on the Center text button. The text should now be centered around where you initially clicked (if not, be sure you pressed Enter to exit editing mode; if the text entry cursor is still visible, any changes you make will only apply to characters you enter in the future).

• Bring the Character palette forward, and with the layer still selected, pick a fun font from your library (we used Brush Script which is bundled on the Adobe After Effects 6.5 installer CD).

• To change the foreground color, click on the Fill Color swatch and select a color using the Adobe Picker. We chose purple; and who can argue with purple?

• Change the Font Size to 60pt by either scrubbing the T icon to the left of the Font Size field, or entering the value directly.

Depending on your chosen font, you may need to track or kern your title. Tracking will affect the entire title, while kerning will fix problems between specific character pairs.

• To track the title, adjust the Tracking value in the Character palette while the entire layer, or a range of characters, is selected.

• To kern characters, place the Type tool *between the problem pair* and press the Option (Alt) plus left/right arrow keys to tighten or loosen the kerning, respectively. Don't track or kern letters too tightly as they may crash into each other when they wiggle! Press Enter again when done to exit editing mode.

You have two choices to reposition the title:

• With the Type tool still selected, press the Command (Control) key and move the cursor over the title. The cursor will temporarily change to the Selection tool (see figure at right). Drag the layer to reposition it.

• Press V to revert to the Selection tool, and move the layer in the Comp window normally.

20 *complete:* The title is set to 60pt Brush Script, changed to purple, and repositioned over the lower leg.

20 With the layer selected, click the Center text button in the Paragraph palette (above), then set the font, color and size in the Character palette (below). Note that you can scrub the T icon to edit the size.

RotoBezier

Create new masks with automatic curves

Text Along a Curve

The next step is to have the text slide in from the right side in front of the flamingo, and stop in the middle of the frame. Instead of using Position keyframes, though, you'll create a mask shape and set the text to slide along this curve:

STEP 21: Select the Pen tool from the toolbar, and this time check on the RotoBezier option. This allows you to draw a "zigzag" line and have After Effects create the curve automatically, rather than you having to manipulate each set of Bezier handles.

21 An open mask shape was created directly in the Comp window with the Pen tool set to RotoBezier mode. In the Timeline window (below), set the Text>Path Options>Path popup to Mask 1 and the text will snap to the mask shape.

21 *complete:* First Margin is animated to move the text along the curve; Easy Ease is applied to the second keyframe (below).

- In the Comp window, click to create the first mask point on the left side, just off the frame on the pasteboard. Click a few more times to create mask points across the frame until you reach the other side (see figure at left). You don't need to click-and-drag to pull Bezier handles to create curves, as you would if RotoBezier was turned off. Revert to the Selection tool, and edit the position of the mask points as needed; you can also drag the line segments to adjust the curve.

- In the Timeline window, twirl down the **flamingo** text layer, and then twirl down the Text>Path Options sections. Set the Path popup to Mask 1, and additional options will appear (these should be familiar if you've used the Path Text effect). You'll animate the First Margin parameter to move the type along the mask shape.

Sometimes it's easier to work backward. So first create a keyframe at the point in time the animation is supposed to stop, then back up and build the start of the animation:

- Go to time 12:16 – a nice beat before the ending flourish in the music – and turn on the animation stopwatch for First Margin. Scrub the value for First Margin until the word "flamingo" is centered in the frame; depending on your mask shape, it may be a value other than 0.

- Press I to return to the in point at 10:00, and increase the value for First Margin until the text slides off the right side of the frame.

- Set the beginning of the work area to 10:00 and the end to 12:16 or later, and hit 0 on the keypad to RAM Preview this section. The text should slide in from the right side, then stop abruptly.

- For a smoother stop, select the keyframe at 12:16 and press F9 to apply Ease Ease (or select Animation>Keyframe Assistant>Easy Ease).

STEP 22: To finish up, you'll add a Text Animator with a Wiggly Selector to automatically jiggle the type, without having to add lots of keyframes:

- Twirl up Path Options to save space, and return to time 12:16, where the title is centered.

- In the Timeline window, click on the Animate button for the text layer, and select the Position property. Animator 1 will be added to the timeline. If you scrub the value of Animator 1>Position, the entire title will be offset left/right (X axis) or up/down (Y axis). Undo to return the values to 0,0.

- To jiggle each character individually, click on the Add button (to the right of Animator 1) and select Range Selector>Wiggly from the popup menu.

- Scrub the Position X and Y values and notice that each individual character is now being offset in space in a random fashion. RAM Preview and then edit the Position value to taste; we chose X = 0, Y = 25, so that characters wiggled only up and down.

22: Click on the Animate button and select Position; this adds Animator 1 with the Position property applied.

22 *complete:* Click on the Add button (red arrow) and select Range Selector>Wiggly. This adds Wiggly Selector 1 to Animator 1. The Position property value will now apply randomly to individual characters. We faded out the wiggly effect by animating Position from Y = 25 down to 0,0.

Vector Synthesis

The Audio Waveform and Audio Spectrum effects also export as vectors when exporting to SWF. Open the prebuilt comp [**Flamingo_waveform**], preview it, and poke around to check this out.

To create this effect, Effect>Render>Audio Waveform was applied to a New Solid layer set to Best Quality (results can be different in Draft Quality). The Audio Layer popup was set to the music layer, **Come to the Island.aif**. We also created a mask in the Comp window with the Pen tool and made the waveform follow this curve by setting the effect's Path popup to Mask 1. The Maximum Height and Thickness settings were set to taste. Try the Display Options popup set to Analog Dots for another fun effect!

For more details, refer to Help>AE Help> "Exporting Audio Spectrum and Audio Waveform to SWF". It includes tips on using these plug-ins with SWF export and describes a few unsupported features (Outside Color, Softness, and Composite on Original for starters).

• Expand Wiggly Selector 1 to reveal its options. We set the Wiggles/Second rate to 1 to slow down the wiggling.

• The Correlation parameter determines whether characters wiggle differently from each other (values near 0%), or more similar to each other (values closer to 100%). Experiment with this value and set to taste.

• Feel free to fade out the wiggle once you hit the big music beat at 12:16. You can do this by animating the Position value back down to 0,0.

Save your project. Open comp [**Flamingo_after Step 22**] *if you'd like to compare your results.*

Flamingo Antics

STEP 23: Okay, now it's your turn to have some fun without having us telling you everything to do. We left 00:00 through 08:00 for you to add your own animation to the flamingo character. Have fun rotating the wings up and down, as well as rotating the legs and neck – all in time to the music, if you can. You could even add a simple walk cycle if you're feeling empowered! Check out the prebuilt comp [**Flamingo_Final**] to compare approaches.

23 Help the flamingo strut its stuff by animating the neck, wing, and legs according to your own tastes for the first eight seconds of the comp.

Export Exceptions

When you're creating compositions for output to the SWF format, it's best to avoid features and effects that cannot be represented as vectors. Maintaining vectors throughout means working with a limited feature set, and avoiding such After Effects standards as multiple effects per layer, nested comps, blending modes, motion blur, and track mattes. Of course, you can use all these features if you must – but any such layers will be JPEG'd on export to SWF. And that sort of defeats the whole purpose of creating SWF (small files, fast downloads, scalable art).

To see a full list of supported features, we encourage you to pull up Help>After Effects Help and search for "SWF". This should turn up a few pages worth reading carefully, including *Exporting to Macromedia Flash (SWF) format*, and *Supported features for SWF export*.

Symbols and Meaning

There are two main approaches to helping After Effects create an efficient SWF file. One is using only layers or effects that generate vectors; otherwise, those pieces of artwork will be rasterized into far less efficient JPEG images. That has been the focus of this tutorial. The other is minimizing the number of "symbols" After Effects creates.

A symbol is one instance of an object in a SWF. The SWF format is smart enough to reuse symbols where possible – such as realizing one symbol is animating in different places in the frame, or that 10 identical objects are actually just copies of the same symbol. However, the SWF file has to be told this.

After Effects manages Illustrator artwork best: If you duplicate the same Illustrator layer in an animation, After Effects will save the symbol for that layer only once. See also the section in the online help called *Using references in the SWF file* for more info.

If you want to better understand how After Effects converts your layers into SWF, it is worth investing in a copy of the Macromedia Flash authoring tool to peer inside the result. Some have also reported that re-saving an After Effects-generated SWF through Flash further decreases its size.

Special thanks to Jim Tierney of Digital Anarchy (www.digitalanarchy.com) for the information on symbols.

Part 5: A SWF Resolution

STEP 24: Once you're happy with your animation, you can export it to SWF by selecting File>Export>Macromedia Flash (SWF). Be aware that exporting defaults to outputting the *work area only*, so set the work area to the full comp if you want to export the entire animation.

The Save File As dialog will prompt you to name your file – call it "**MyFlamingo.swf**". Make a note of where it's being saved to so you can play it back later. Clicking Save then opens the SWF Settings dialog. All of the options presented herein are explained in the online Help file, but here are a few particulars to be aware of:

• Not everything After Effects can do can be converted to efficient vectors for a SWF file; in fact, we've already covered most of what you can do. If you're trying to export an animation that has components that cannot be converted to vectors – known as Unsupported Features – you can use options here to Ignore them, or to Rasterize them to less efficient pixels. In this animation it's irrelevant, since we were careful

 Flash MX Mix

For more on integrating After Effects and Flash MX, including how to render animations from Flash with an alpha channel, check out the *Integration with Web Applications* chapter in *Creating Motion Graphics, Volume 2: Advanced Techniques.*

SWF Settings

Images

JPEG Quality: 5   Medium

Smaller File   Larger File

Ignore   Unsupported Features

Choose Ignore to skip all features that are not supported by the SWF format. Choose Rasterize to rasterize all frames that contain unsupported features.

☑ Audio

Sample Rate: 44.100 kHz

Channels: Stereo

Bit Rate: Auto

Options

☐ Loop Continuously
☐ Prevent Import
☐ Include Object Names
☐ Include Layer Marker Web Links
☑ Flatten Illustrator Artwork

Cancel   OK

24 The SWF Settings dialog helps After Effects decide what to do with layers it cannot convert into vectors. Flatten Illustrator Artwork affects layers with multiple shapes that are semitransparent.

Connect

For more information on topics covered in this tutorial, check out the following volumes of *Creating Motion Graphics*:

Volume 1:

A Matter of Time and Space

The Anchor Point

The Layer Essentials (markers)

All About Masking

Textacy

Volume 2:

Working with Illustrator

Audio Basics and Effects

Integration with Web Applications

not to add any unsupported features (like a Drop Shadow or Motion Blur on the title).

If you are creating what should be a pure vector-based animation, the Ignore option is a handy way to check that layers are indeed all outputting as vectors (any missing layers in your SWF file indicate an unsupported feature is being used and is thus easier to track down).

• Turn on the Audio checkbox to also export the audio. The soundtrack Carolyn West provided is CD quality, at 44.1 kHz and in stereo; if you need to keep the file size small, you can get away with a lower Sample Rate and even Mono. Leave the Bit Rate set to Auto to choose the most appropriate bit rate given the Sample Rate/Channels options you've selected.

• The only Option box that you'll want to check for the Flamingo animation is Flatten Illustrator Artwork. This will take all the individual shapes on each of the layers and flatten them so that the final animation will look like it does in After Effects.

If all the layers were set to 100% Opacity, it may not matter much whether or not you flatten. However, since the three background layers are set to 35% Opacity, if you don't flatten the artwork, each shape (not just layer) will *individually* render as 35% transparent. Export both ways and check out the difference, particularly in the palm tree leaves and shrubs. You might even prefer the effect created by not flattening the artwork.

• When you're done with the SWF Settings, click OK, and the comp will be exported post haste as both a SWF and an HTML file. Save your After Effects project at this point before exiting the program.

• Find the file **MyFlamingoR.htm** and open it in your favorite web browser. When the browser window opens, the animation will play back automatically; scroll down to see a report of the settings used. If you click on the name of the SWF file underneath the image, it will open the animation in a second window. Note that you can resize this browser window and the animation will resize – this is the beauty and power of creating vector-only SWF animations. You can also open **MyFlamingo.swf** directly in your browser or in Macromedia Flash.

Guest Artist: Kristin Harris

The concept and artwork for this tutorial were created by Kristin Harris Design; a Falls Church, Virginia studio that specializes in educational media for young children. HBO Family is currently broadcasting 40 interstitials created by the studio. The most recent series, *I Want To Be*, looks at the world of work from the point of view of small children. The studio is currently developing an environmental science/astronomy series of shorts and a DVD about animals for preschool children.

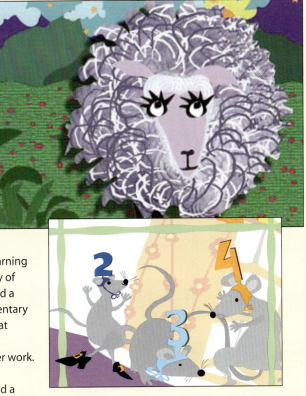

Kristin Harris combines her skills in visual learning with a profound respect for the innate curiosity of young children. Her background in fine arts and a 25-year involvement with preschool and elementary education merge to create a voice and style that speaks to children.

Kristin has received numerous awards for her work. The studio received a Gold Award at the 2002 Kalamazoo Animation Festival International and a Peer Award from ITVA-DC. Her short films have been included in the Chicago International Children's Film Festival, the Museum of Radio and Television Children's Film Festival, and the East Lansing Children's Film Festival. Kristin has served on the Board of Directors of Women in Film and Video Washington DC, and is a member of the National Association for the Education of Young Children, ASIFA, and Women in Animation.

About the Musician

To create music for this tutorial, Harris enlisted composer Carolyn West. After earning her Master of Music in Studio Composition and Production at The University of Miami in 1983, she has gone on to produce original music for film, TV, video, and electronic multimedia, with extensive experience scoring and conducting orchestral sessions with live players as well as making the most of her MIDI-based home studio. West has earned a reputation of musical inventiveness and detail in music scoring, with sensitivity to style and appropriateness. Some of her clients include the A&E *Biography* series, more than 200 segments of *America's Most Wanted*, The National Park Service, Bell Atlantic, The Smithsonian Institution, Fox Television, Marriott International, and Narada Productions.

Contact:

Kristin Harris Design, Inc.
3035 Hazelton Street
Falls Church, VA 22044
Tel: (703) 536-9594
Fax: (703) 241-7463
www.kristinharrisdesign.com

Carolyn West
1761 Honey Trail
Annapolis, MD 21401
Tel: (410) 849-2511
Email: cwestmusic@aol.com

The Diecks Group : ESPNDeportes.com

Swarming boxes chase and frame video clips plus web pages in this high-energy spot.

The Diecks Group in New York were approached by ESPN International to help it launch ESPNDeportes.com, a new Spanish-language web site targeted to the Hispanic/Latin American market in the United States. ESPNDeportes.com is a separate entity from ESPN.com, with original content, original artwork, original events, and original programming. The challenge was to convey the appropriate "Latin flavor" while avoiding both web commercial and Latin clichés.

One of the most popular sports for this market is soccer. A desire to abstract the organized chaos of soccer players running up and down the playing field led to the concept of colored boxes blinking, dashing, darting, and sliding rhythmically to a high-energy music track. These boxes frame images of sports and of the web site content.

An ever-changing window, bordered by a complement of constantly morphing boxes, reveals web pages and sports videos while the logo peeks from behind.

Exploring the Spot

Copy the folder for the Diecks Group case study from this book's DVD to your hard drive. Inside the **Final Movie** folder, double-click **Diecks_ ESPNDeportes.mov** to preview it in QuickTime Player. This is a special version of the spot using ESPN X Games footage, as it was impractical to clear all the original sports teams' rights for this book. Then open the project **Diecks_ESPNDeportes_ref.aep**, and look at the composition [**01_Diecks_ESPNDeportes**] where you can RAM Preview (0 on the keypad) or single-step (Page Up/Down) through the spot. Here are some details to note as you use the comp markers in After Effects:

Marking Time

Comp markers are used to mark specific frames in the animation. Press the numbers 0–9 on your keyboard (not the keypad) to jump to these marked frames.

1 ESPN has a very strong brand, so The Diecks Group sprinkled the text ESPNDEPORTES.COM throughout the spot. They chose the typeface Xenotron because they felt it had an international quality.

2 At this marker, the flowing matte opens up to reveal sports footage behind. This matte was created and animated using a clever arrangement of mask shapes timed to the music. The frame around it is derived from multiple variations on this central shape.

3 Web pages were sprinkled between the video clips, tilted in 3D to add excitement to what would otherwise be a still image.

4 & **5** Over 30 sports clips and web pages appear inside of 25 seconds. In some cases – such as between these two markers – clips are stutter-cut to create more excitement.

Some clips were stutter-cut to create additional excitement from an otherwise linear piece of action.

6 The video was originally cut as a full-frame sequence, then adjusted to taste on a shot-by-shot basis to better fit inside the framing presented by the animated matte. The process of editing and treating the video is one of the subjects we will cover in detail later.

7 In addition to the swarming boxes derived from the original animated matte, additional colored boxes were added to help fill the frame – especially at the conclusion of the commercial, when the video closes to make room for the ending tags.

The commercial ends with the name of the web site, the ESPN logo, and a scrolling list of featured sports.

8 The commercial ends with the ESPN logo partially hidden by animating boxes, and a list of sports. Notice how this list accordions together, then continues to scroll up the screen.

Style frames The Diecks Group created for the ESPNDeportes spot.

Artistic Overview

How do you avoid the pitfall of promoting a sports entertainment and news web site through the use of the television media, without resorting to showing full-frame views of web pages? To The Diecks Group, it seemed natural to profile the sports that the web site would be built upon. These sports would then provide the paint for the canvas that was the web pages. This decision led to an approach of intertwining sports footage with these pages.

The Diecks Group decided early on that the music and color palette would dictate the spirit and energy of the spots. As noted earlier, they wanted to appropriately reflect the target Hispanic/Latin American market, but not fall back on clichés. For example, it would be typical for the chosen music to head off in a fiery salsa direction. Instead, Diecks chose a hyperkinetic "drum and bass" style soundtrack from the Gravity library, represented by Who Did That Music? The upfront percussion and exhausting tempo was intended to reflect the energy of soccer players running up and down the playing field, reacting to sudden changes in the direction of the ball and game.

This tempo and its analogy of soccer players running up and down the playing field then led to the concept that the boxes which appear in the final spot should blink, dash, dart, and slide rhythmically to the drum beats. This in turn allowed the boxes to maintain a fast and furious visual pace, even if the image being shown inside the boxes was that of a relatively static web page.

Latin America has a color palette that tends to be hotter and more vibrant than what is commonly seen in North America or Europe. Members of The Diecks Group drew on their previous visits to Mexico City, from which they remembered colors such as fiery brick red, plum purple, electric blue, sunflower yellow, pumpkin orange, hot pink, and ochre green. With this in mind, they started pulling color swatches from Pantone books and spreading them out on their conference room table until they could begin to visualize the spirit they were after. These colors were then re-created by eye on the computer.

Execution

The centerpieces of the ESPNDeportes spot are the dashing, darting boxes, and the imagery they frame. These are the two main areas we will discuss, as they illustrate a great example of creative problem-solving when you're faced with an otherwise extremely labor-intensive task. Other items worth noting are the web pages, and the scrolling list of sports that end the spot.

Swarming Boxes

The video segments are revealed through a track matte that was originally constructed out of five white solids. To make this "window" constantly evolve, each solid had its own animated mask that changed shape in time with the music. A mixture of linear and hold keyframes were used, which allow the shape to stutter and turn on a dime.

To see this matte in action, open the composition [02_box examples] in the accompanying project. You can either Option+double-click on Mac (Alt+double-click on Windows) the layer **DG_videomatte.mov** and play it back, or RAM Preview the comp, making sure only the third and fourth layers (**DG_videomatte.mov** and the audio portion of **Diecks_ESPNDeportes.mov**) are enabled.

When the original style frames were presented to Erik van der Wilden, then the Director of Editorial and Animation at The Diecks Group, the element that concerned him most was the colored boxes that surrounded the video. The style frames contained an average of 100 boxes that were supposed to change constantly. Given the tight deadline he was working under, it would not have been feasible to realize this by animating 100 solids over 900 frames (30 seconds) conventionally.

His first thoughts were to create an enlarged outline shape from the video matte with a plug-in such as Matte Tools>Simple Choker or Channel>Minimax, then find a way to hollow out the center. In the end, van der Wilden used two copies of the video matte layer – one

The video matte was a composite of five white solids. Each solid had an animated mask that changed shape in time to the soundtrack.

scaled slightly larger than normal, and one slightly smaller – with the blending mode Silhouette Alpha so the smaller one would cut a hole out of the larger.

The next trick was finding a way to animate the shape of this frame so that it constantly evolved. The solution van der Wilden hit upon was to offset the copies of the matte from each other, both in time and position. By doing this, the portion being cut out would have a different form than the outside shape, but the two would always be related, as they came from the same source. The result was a swarming, chasing effect that's very engaging.

A smaller version of the video matte, in Silhouette Alpha mode, cuts the center out of a larger version of the matte.

Ten variations of this animated mask frame were rendered, each using a different combination of offsets in scale, position, and time. To see one of these frames in action, in the comp [**02_box examples**] turn on the layer **DG_boxbase.mov**. Move the time marker to different points in the timeline, and turn this layer on and off to compare it with the underlying **DG_videomatte.mov** it came from.

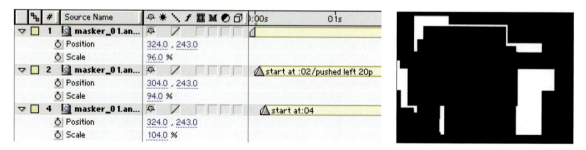

The layers that make up the frame are offset in time and position from each other (left), resulting in a broken shape (right) that evolves over time as it chases the video matte.

The original video matte layer was used to mask the edited video. However, the frame still looked somewhat whole, if slightly fractured. In contrast, the style frames employed a large number of smaller boxes and fragments that made up the overall frame shape.

To create smaller boxes from the larger frames, multiple rectangular masks were created at random. The result was that only fragments of each remained; these more closely resembled a series of overlapping, animating boxes than a carefully constructed frame. To observe this, turn on the layer **DG_boxresult.mov** in the comp [**02_box examples**]. Again, move to different points along the timeline and audition the various layers to see how the matte (layer 3) became the frame (layer 2), which in turn became a set of fragmented boxes (layer 1).

The animated, fragmented frame that remained was then tinted a color from the target palette. A blending mode was applied to make the frame merge with the video and solid-colored background in a more interesting, semitransparent fashion. Several more of the variation frames were layered on top of this, adding more boxes and interest. Between 10 and 25 of these layers could appear at any one time. If the final image became unbalanced, additional tinted solids were created to fill the blank areas.

Open the comp [**03.1_videomatte example**] to see a simple version of this stack. In this example, **DG_videomatte.mov** is used as a matte for an edited video subcomp. Instances of **DG_boxbase.mov** and **DG_boxresult.mov** are used as mattes for color layers, which are then applied with modes. These layers were also offset in time and position. RAM Preview the section between markers 1 and 4 to see the result.

A series of random rectangular masks over the animated frame creates a fragmented series of shapes (above). The final stack (below) included several variations of the masked animating frames, plus additional color solids to help fill excessive open areas. Different modes and opacity settings create a semitransparent, overlapping mix.

Close to the Edit

Another strong feature of this commercial is the way the video fits so well inside the evolving matte. This is a result of both planning ahead and of making adjustments after the fact.

The first pass at the video edit was executed before the boxes were created. It was executed with a Media 100 nonlinear editing system,

using the soundtrack and a working copy of the voice-over as guides. The voiceover gave a general idea of which visual subject should be presented when in the original multisport version of this spot; the soundtrack suggested where to place specific cuts. A secondary edit of alternate clips was created to allow more flexibility during the times the video matte would close down and re-open. This second edit wasn't as sport-specific; instead, it was intended to provide interesting fills when only a small portion of the frame would be revealed.

These Media 100 projects were then imported into After Effects as compositions. The advantage to this approach, rather than rendering out the Media 100's timeline and importing it as a single linear clip, was that the resulting compositions contained the entire original clips with their handles. This allowed The Diecks Group to tweak the edits inside After Effects without having to make a trip back to the Media 100.

Much of the original video source material was provided on VHS, and would require enhancing to bring up to typical "sexy-looking commercial" standards.

When the animated matte was created, some consideration was given to the video content, but the greater focus was on how it articulated to the music. The video clips were then scaled and repositioned as needed to better fit into the matte's openings. A simple form of this is demonstrated in [**03.2_video edit precomp**], particularly in the way the position of the second video clip animates across the frame to better align the skateboarder with the matte opening (turn layer 1 on and off to compare).

The comp [**03.2_video edit precomp**] gives a simple example of how individual video clips can be repositioned to better fit the matte openings. Skateboarding footage courtesy of Creative License.

The next task involved enhancing the source footage. Many of the clips provided came from VHS dubs of live sporting events – not exactly your ideal shot-for-commercials footage. Raw Media 100 clips also exist in the 16–235 luminance range, compared with the 0–255 luminance range After Effects works in. The result was a lot of washed-out imagery.

Each clip was duplicated, with a blending mode such as Overlay applied to the copy on top. Opacity was varied to control the blend. This is a great technique to increase the apparent richness of an image. Effects such as Adjust>Levels and Adjust>Curves were also applied to bend the color closer to the vibrant, Latin palette desired for the spots.

Text Elements

Although most of our focus in this case study has been on the video and the colored boxes that swarm around it, text elements also play important roles in this spot. In addition to the web site address mentioned earlier, there are sample web pages throughout, and the spot ends with a list of some of the sports to be covered (reinforcing that soccer would not be the only sport covered).

The web pages were not frame-grabbed from the site, but instead painstakingly re-created, then imported into After Effects. As this project was originally executed before After Effects directly supported 3D space, the pages were tilted and moved in 3D using Effect>Simulation>Shatter. As you probably noticed, these layers did not shatter apart in the final spot; however, The Diecks Group personally found the 3D positioning controls in this plug-in more responsive than the other 3D effects available to them at the time. (To have Shatter not blow up a layer, set its Radius parameter to 0.)

These tilted pages were then masked by the animated matte, just as the video clips were. Since these were stills being animated inside After Effects rather than having preordained

The Comp window shows how individual clips were animated to center inside the animated matte. Clips were duplicated and a blend mode applied to the copy on top; Levels and Curves were applied for additional color correction.

Web pages were re-created, then tilted using the 3D controls in the Shatter effect. (The image in this window was blurred for rights clearance reasons.)

These animated pages were then treated the same as the other video elements, masked and ringed with the swarming boxes.

motion, it was easier to choreograph their movements to better fit the music and matte. A good example of this is after comp marker 3 in [**01_Diecks_ESPNDeportes**], where two of these pages appear back to back, tilted at different angles.

While still in the comp [**01_Diecks_ESPNDeportes**], go to comp marker 8 and step or RAM Preview from here to the end, keeping an eye on the list of sports in the upper right corner. Notice that it "accordions" together, while continuing to scroll off the top of the frame – a trick that is hard to accomplish with the typical Adobe Illustrator file often used for text elements in After Effects.

This spot was created before After Effects had a native text engine. Therefore, The Diecks Group employed the plug-in Text>Basic Text using the font Helvetica Neue 43 Light Extended. The accordion effect was created by animating Basic Text's Line Spacing parameter; normal Position was animated to continue the scrolling action. To fade the bottom of the list, a gradient was created using the Render>Ramp plug-in applied to a solid, which was then used as a luminance matte.

The text list at the end was made to accordion together by animating its Line Spacing parameter, then scrolled by animating its position (right). A gradient created with Ramp was then used as a luminance matte to fade it off at the bottom (left).

Postscript

Three different voiceovers were created for each of these spots: in Spanish, Portuguese, and English. In the original composition [**01_Diecks_ESPNDeportes**], turn off the Audio switch for the layer **Diecks_ESPNDeportes.mov**, turn on this switch for the layer **DG_voiceover_english.mov**, and preview the comp again.

Creative Director Brian Diecks notes "Spanish and Portuguese have so much more spirit and zest than English. In my opinion, the English version of the spots is weaker than the other versions – the tonality in the English version is all 'used car salesman' where the Spanish and Portuguese are full of life, energy, and excitement."

The Diecks Group, Inc.

Opened in 1993, The Diecks Group was a creative development and branding agency for the entertainment industry. The multi-disciplinary firm offered marketing, strategy, and brand building as well as design, editorial, live action production, and visual effects for clients involved in various media: broadcast, advertising, interactive and convergent media, and print.

In their 10 years in the industry, The Diecks Group won numerous awards from organizations such as AIGA, International Monitor Awards, New York Festivals, Promax/BDA, and the Type Directors Club. Their clients included ABC, Discovery Kids, ESPN, Fox Cable Networks, HBO, The Independent Film Channel, Leo Burnett/USA, Lifetime, McCann Erikson/Detroit, Media 100, Mullen Advertising, National Hockey League, PentaMark, Sci-Fi Channel, Showtime, Tribeca Films, Turner Network Television, and Young & Rubicam.

Brian Diecks – who founded The Diecks Group – is now Executive Creative Director of DZP Marketing Communications. Erik van der Wilden has gone on to co-found the studio nailgun*.

Contact:

DZP Marketing Communications
(212) 226-7336
www.dzpusa.com

nailgun*
(212) 785-5885
www.nailgun.tv

Belief : Alive

Crafting a flexible, international image using fluids and silhouettes.

Belief has developed a name for themselves in branding multinational networks. Their success is partly due to their ability to cross cultures with suggestive yet abstract imagery. For the Hong Kong-based Alive travel network, Belief used water to depict landscapes, and silhouettes to depict people of many nations enjoying themselves. In addition to creating beautiful designs, Belief also created projects that would be easy for affiliates to localize and personalize.

In this case study, we'll look at how the human and liquid elements were captured, processed, and blended into final frames. Equally important, we'll discuss some of Belief's concepts behind creating a look that translates across cultures and languages, and projects that local affiliates can further customize to their needs.

Common themes throughout the Alive package include silhouettes of people, water movements as landscapes, 3D universal travel icons, graphical sunbursts of rays, and curves everywhere.

Exploring the Spot

Open the project **Belief_Alive_ref.aep**, locate the **Sources** folder, and play back the three **Belief_Alive** movies by double-clicking them in the Project window; you can also locate these movies on the DVD and open them using QuickTime Player.

Now open the comp [**03_Belief_Alive_3**] and RAM Preview it (hit 0 on the keypad). Note the constant use of curves, including animated strokes that snake throughout the frames. Also note the gentle use of 3D. We'll be taking a look at several of these details later. Referring to the comp markers, here are a few of the highlights:

1 Curves are used to mark borders between graphical elements, to give the action something to follow, and to create a sensuous feeling overall.

1 Note the use of curved lines, as well as curved matte shapes that keep the elements separated. These shapes also give the action something to follow, such as the skier in this open.

2 Although most of the look is graphical 2D, there are subtle 3D touches that create a more tactile look. Press the spacebar to play or use Page Down to single-step forward from this marker, and note the horizontal icon bar that forms on the right.

Also note the stroked line that snakes from right to left across the screen. You can create a simple version of this using the Stylize> Write-On effect or Trapcode's 3D Stroke; to have it travel along a path, Belief had a custom plug-in written.

Marking Time

Comp markers are used to mark specific frames in the animation. Press the numbers 0–9 on your keyboard (not the keypad) to jump to these marked frames.

3 The ghosting of the water skiers, as well as other silhouettes, was the result of slowing down the original footage and using Frame Blending. You'll also note very subtle, diffuse hazes or drop shadows around many of the elements; these were created by using a drop shadow effect, setting the distance parameter to 0, and increasing its softness to very high values.

A graphical design element you will notice throughout is a series of rays that might remind you of a sunburst or spikes on a lens flare. They were created a number of ways, including starting with Illustrator artwork and using the third-party plug-in Hall of Mirrors from the Image Lounge plug-in package (distributed by Red Giant Software) to repeat the patterns and give animated control.

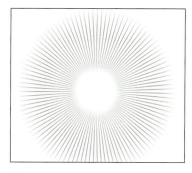

3 Other common design elements are graphical flares or rays.

4 Notice the color change from blue to orange. Belief color-coded different themes of activities for Alive: blue is "traveling," orange is "learning about," and green is "learning to do."

As you step or play forward from here, you will notice that another 3D icon bar appears. Watch how the moving colors in the bar are a reflected wash of those in the frame; we'll discuss how Belief created this later on.

5 Liquids are used throughout as stand-ins for landscapes. Here, the mountain range in the background is actually an upside-down

Real footage can be too literal. By converting scenes with people to silhouettes with abstract backgrounds, viewers can more easily project themselves into a scene, at any locale.

image of viscous fluid dripping. Later we'll reveal the original elements used for the landscape as well.

This scene includes another instance of the 3D icon bars. Note how they usually have additional small figures inside them. This sense of big and small helps add depth to the scene. We'll also be looking in more detail at the large version of the mountain climber that appears inside this particular bar.

6 The ending wipes in with a splash, which gives way to the final logo and the ink element drifting much more slowly in the background.

6 A splash wipes into the end logo for Alive, where graphic lines create the outlines of slow-moving waves.

By the way, as you step frame-by-frame through these movies, you may notice a pattern of five unique frames, with the fifth frame repeated for the sixth frame of the sequence. The Alive project was originally created at PAL frame rate and resolution, full frame without interlaced fields. These renders were then merely scaled to fit in an NTSC-size comp running at 29.97 frames per second (fps), resulting in this 5:6 sequence (the same as the ratio between 25 and 30 fps).

Artistic Overview

Just before the Alive project, Belief completed a branding campaign for Columbia-Tristar's AXN Action Network. The Singapore-based AXN airs in six languages across 42 countries. Alive saw Belief give a presentation on AXN at the Promax Asia conference in late 2000, and was interested.

Alive was based out of Hong Kong, serving the Asian region including India, Singapore, and Australia. Their plan was to focus on the moderate-income travel market: the large middle ground between youth hostels and four-star hotels. In addition to cable channels, Alive intended to move into physical stores, books, and electronic versions of information for web-access phones (WAPs) and personal digital assistants (PDAs). Belief worked closely with Alive to develop an overall brand for the entire cable network, while also taking into account how it would translate into other media.

Being Suggestive

Your first thoughts of a travel channel might be footage of exotic locations with people enjoying interesting activities such as skiing, climbing, or spending a night on the town. But aside from being too obvious, this path can also be too literal – especially when you want your brand to extend across multiple countries and cultures. The scenery you choose may not be representative of the affiliate country you're in; the ethnicity or manner of dress might not match that of your viewer. Belief was also interested in capturing the essence of travel: the sensations of relaxation and relief, the seductive quality of exotic locales, the feeling of immersing yourself in another culture.

One solution Belief came up with was using liquids. For example, the outline of water cascading can easily form the image of a cliff that's not a specific cliff. Water flowing and bubbling also has the sensuous quality Belief was looking for. To test that this idea would work, Belief shot quick tests with a still camera, and incorporated them into early storyboards.

A second solution was representing all the people in silhouette. This solved the problem of nationality, and in some cases, even masked the manner of dress, gender, or the activity. Aside from being more flexible, silhouettes let viewers more easily project themselves into the activity portrayed. It also contains a bit of a voyeuristic quality, furthering the sensuous feeling Belief wanted to promote.

Separating the people from their locations also provided more flexibility. For example, a silhouette of a water skier gliding across a graphical landscape eliminates problems such as "but wait – our lakes don't have sandy shores, and they're supposed to have mountains in the background."

To see if the idea of using liquids would work, Belief shot quick tests with a still camera and incorporated them into early storyboards.

Shooting various activities on a greenscreen stage, rather than on location, allows them to be relocated into an entirely graphical scene that could be anywhere. The result is that the viewer focuses on the activity, instead of the person or location.

Style frames Belief presented to Alive two weeks into the project. At this stage, ideas other than fluids – such as a tree branch (far right) – were still being considered as stand-ins for landscapes.

Phasing In

Belief is a strong believer in creating storyboards and style frames at early stages in a project, and in testing design and production theories at this early point. Rather than use the computer to generate stand-ins, Belief will shoot preliminary versions of ideas to make sure they will work, and to see if any unexpected results shake out before a design has already been committed to. In the case of Alive, Belief used a still-image camera to shoot a first pass at the fluids. They also shot other ideas for textures such as branches or crystals.

The graphics were created in three phases, which in many ways were three complete iterations of the entire design. The first phase consisted of basic elements: end pages, IDs, transitions. They were considered placeholders while Belief developed more complex portions of the design.

Phase 2 introduced more liquid and silhouette elements. All of these elements were custom-shot for this project on 35mm film. Alive used these earlier phases for fund-raising, as well as for internal testing: it ran the network internally for three weeks before it went on the air, to work out any kinks.

Phase 3 brought a further evolution in design, elegance, and complexity. As you look at some of the examples on these pages, you will notice some of these refinements, such as the use of more gradients, more curviness (further enhancing the sensuous, rather than technical, feel), fewer of the murkier desaturated colors, and simplifying some elements while adding others such as more bursts of graphical rays.

Examples of how the design evolved from Phase 2 (above) to Phase 3 (below). Note in particular the increase in readability, including fluid elements that are less distracting from the text. Sunburst rays are also used more to fill in areas that might have been too empty otherwise.

Whereas it might seem more work to do everything three times, Belief welcomed the chance to go back and revisit the designs. All too often, you have time to do everything only once. Although the schedule was very tight, Belief felt that working in phases allowed them to refine and further evolve the look they had developed.

Execution

We've hinted above how Belief created many of the elements used in the Alive spots. Shooting preliminary ideas at the storyboard stage helped Belief focus on refining techniques during production, rather than scramble to see if an idea would even work.

Fluid Motion

Although it's tempting to refer to the "water elements" Belief used throughout the Alive spots, in truth the water is usually what you *don't* see. Instead, a variety of fluids – typically ink, food coloring, methylcellulose, oil, and mixtures of these, as well as ice and dry ice – are dropped into water, with the results being what was captured on film. Different techniques were also used to physically animate the results, such as feeding fluids down a clear tube (which needed to be rotoscoped out later), or using a jet of compressed air.

Many fluids were shot looking through an aquarium filled with water. When the fluids needed to be shot from below, a mirror underneath reflected the image back up to the camera. For shots from above, the camera was mounted on a post, looking down, and lit from below. A video tap previewed what the camera saw. Pictured above are Mike Goedecke, Belief's creative director and live action director/cinematographer (right), and Maziar Majd, the lead designer/ animator on Alive (left).

Not all of the fluids were originally colored – many of the images started essentially as grayscale (left), then had color added during transfer or in post production. They were then composited with other elements (right).

Many of the fluid elements were shot at high speed (100 fps on up). Even with a video tap on the camera to preview what it was seeing, the short duration of the events resulted in a certain chance element: you would get the camera up to speed, drop the fluids into the water tank, and let it rip – hoping you had captured something in those brief few seconds.

Not all of the elements had color in them when they were shot; color was added to the resulting grayscales either in the film-to-video transfer at Company 3 in Los Angeles, or in After Effects using the Digital Film Tools Composite Suite plug-ins.

Belief prefers to shoot elements on 35mm film for several reasons. Besides the usual advantages of resolution, texture, and natural motion blur, film's large dynamic range of luminance and color provide the additional visual information needed to perform more extreme color corrections without yielding posterized images. This additional color information is often missing from video, especially if it has already been compressed either by the VTR or during capture into a nonlinear editing system. That said, there were still occasions when Belief needed to go back and shoot additional elements on video in the name of expediency as the deadline approached.

Dripping Spires

But Belief didn't stop at capturing and colorizing various liquids. Many of the liquid elements were inverted, masked, and warped to create more curvaceous, landscape-like shapes.

For example, look again at comp [**03_Belief_Alive_3**], previewing between comp markers 5 and 6. Notice how the tips of the mountains in the background seem to break off and float upward. In reality, this is a highly viscous fluid dripping downward.

Look again, and you'll notice that the mountain range has an undulating, rather than level, base. To create this, Belief took the dripping footage and fed it through a wave warp effect. After colorization, plus masking to create a clean horizon line, Belief had a fluid mountain range.

To create a mountain range, Belief filmed a highly viscous fluid dripping. They then inverted it to get the shape of mountain peaks, and warped it to create an undulating horizon. Belief then masked and colorized it for the final composite.

Hot Winds and Cool Ice

As you may have noticed in several of the illustrations, the liquid elements have a lot of grayscales and gradients which give them more character than simple shapes would. Belief wanted the same look for their silhouettes, to give them more depth and dimension. At one point, they even experimented with painting a person head to toe in black body makeup, hoping this would allow them to capture some lighting falloff around the body's contours.

However, this approach proved impractical, and Belief resorted to a normal greenscreen shoot. They used a large stage, with props such as walls, wind fans, and stand-off boxes as needed. Even though they planned to keep only the outlines of the people in the end, they still shot on film, liking the graininess of motion blur and its edges.

In the name of speed, Belief attempted to key the actors in real time during the telecine transfer process using a dedicated hardware Ultimatte system. Unfortunately, many shots needed to be re-done; Belief used a hardware-accelerated version of the Ultimatte keying plug-in. Belief also used the essential Composite Wizard plug-in package (also distributed by Red Giant Software) to help with automatic matte cleanup.

Ropes and Curves

Sometimes, merely keying an actor wasn't enough to create the desired final look. For example, while the rope a climber hangs onto is taut, the remaining length that falls behind is usually limp – and not aesthetically pleasing (see figures on the next page). In cases like this, Belief would hand-mask or rotoscope the undesirable elements out of a scene, then either leave a clean white plate, or replace them with stroked lines or whatever other graphical elements were appropriate.

To see the results of just such a correction, open the composition [02_Belief_Alive_2], and play or preview the frames between comp

Various actions were shot on a large greenscreen stage, with props such as fans. These were then keyed using hardware and software Ultimatte systems to create the silhouettes. Ice dropped into water, inverted, slightly warped, and colorized creates a nice abstract glacier/mountain range to composite the silhouetted dancer against.

Reality isn't always what you want. For example, in the sequence above, the rope below this climber dangles in a limp, uninteresting way. After keying, Belief hand-rotoscoped out the undesirable section of the rope, and replaced it with a more elegant stroke.

To create the cliff the climber is descending (far right), another water element (right) is positioned and non-uniformly scaled to create a thinner, taller shape. It is then rotated, warped, masked, and colorized to suit.

markers 1 and 2. Notice too that the cliff the climber is on has been created out of another water element, this time turned on its side, masked, and wave warped.

This climber element also appears in the vertical icon bar in comp [03_Belief_Alive_3] between comp markers 5 and 6. Repurposing elements in this way helped tie the look of all the promos together, without a variation seeming to be an outright copy of another version.

Bars and Cubes

The silhouettes at different sizes help give the Alive spots a sense of dimension. This is further enhanced by the subtle use of 3D in the icon bars that appear throughout.

The icon cubes were rendered in Discreet's 3ds max. Although they are simple black-with-white icons, notice how they have rounded bevels and specular hot spots as they rotate – this continues the "shades of black" idea that tempted Belief to try to shoot the silhouettes as real people in black body makeup.

These elements proved to be time consuming to create, as the icons (some of which animate) were created on the Mac, turned into texture maps for 3ds max running on a pair of Windows machines, rendered, and transferred back to the Mac. Only when it was too late to turn back did Belief get the idea of rendering just one set of blank cubes, then match-moving the icons onto them using an After Effects plug-in such as Boris Cube. Next time…

As you play the various movies, notice how the colors in the glass bars that hold these icons react to the overall frame. You would expect this reflected and refracted look to be the result of a render inside a ray-tracing 3D program. In fact, they were created inside After Effects by taking the background composition, blurring it, color correcting it, and processing it through Panopticum's third-party Lens effect. Remember, in motion graphics we are often creating impressions, not realities; giving the viewer the impression of a more complex reality is often enough to really lift a design.

Designing for Change

Unlike some cable networks that deliver 24 hours of full programming, Alive's concept was closer to a network/affiliate model, in which the main network has a core of programs, but the local affiliates that carry it fill a substantial amount of the day with their own programming. In the United States, many local stations develop their own look for their own programming.

The challenge for Belief was delivering a package of graphics that the local affiliates could easily slip their own programs into and customize as needed, without losing Alive's overall look. Beyond just swapping out layers, Belief took the approach of enabling the affiliates to swap out concepts to better tune the package to their own markets. This extended to colors (so affiliates could color-code their own programming blocks) and even speed of cuts.

The icon bars subtly enhance the sense of dimension. Note the beveled edges and specular hot spots on the black cubes as they rotate. Also note how the colors change over time in the glasslike bars: rather than 3D renders, they are actually copies of the background composition inside After Effects, blurred, color corrected, and fed through Panopticum's Lens effect.

Examples of some of the lower thirds Belief created for Alive. Since Belief delivered entire After Effects projects, it would be easier for Alive's affiliates to customize these elements for their own programming.

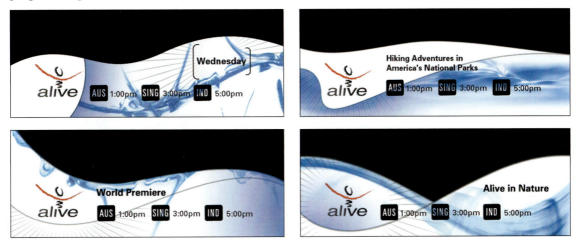

To accomplish this, Belief actually delivered a toolkit of QuickTime movies, image elements, and After Effects projects, with a guide on how to use and customize them. Belief specified the hardware and software required, so Alive could open the projects with no problems.

After Effects has several features that make delivering a project in this manner easier. For example, sources and compositions could be organized into logical folders in the Project window. Nesting compositions also make it possible to build processing chains so that an edit in one comp – say, just a text element – could then ripple through to several different final spots.

Postscript

Belief and Alive met in November; the network planned to go on the air by the end of February. Since Belief traditionally takes a company-wide vacation between Christmas and New Year's, they essentially had two months to design, film, and deliver the package. As we mentioned earlier, working in phases allowed Alive to approve the elements and execute its off-air test while Belief refined their designs and created additional elements. The time difference between Hong Kong and California also worked to an advantage: Belief worked while Alive slept; Alive approved elements while Belief slept.

The final elements were delivered via the internet. Belief had their own server on-site, making it easier to load or change elements. Although it took all weekend for Alive to download, this was still faster than any express delivery service because packages would get held up in customs in Hong Kong. Backups on FireWire drives and videotape followed later.

The Alive job also represents a bit of a visual departure for Belief. Many of their prior designs were based on light sources – glows, neons, and so on – against a black background, with many, many layers. Alive isn't nearly as dense or layered. Belief feels the design has a softness and maturity to it that they probably wouldn't have conceived even a year earlier.

Diversifying into online services was one of the keys to Alive's business plan. As a result, the internet slowdown caught up with Alive, and they ultimately ceased operations. Fortunately, Belief was able to apply many of the clever marketing and design solutions they developed for this project in their work for other clients in this region.

Water, silhouettes, subtle 3D, and key colors add up to a clear, elegant, flexible design.

Belief

Founded in 1997, Belief is a design and production studio based out of a 9,000-square-foot artist's loft in Santa Monica, California. They view modern motion graphics as a new visual language, which they harness to help deliver messages and branding for their clients.

Belief has an unusual structure: rather than run an assembly line, in which a project gets passed from specialist to specialist inside the company, virtually all of Belief's employees are multidiscipline designers. When a designer is assigned a job, he or she oversees (and often executes) every aspect of it from concept to delivery. Another important concept of Belief's is its reliance on desktop tools. This allows them to put more money "on the screen" – for example, by shooting custom film, rather than relying on video stock footage – instead of in the pockets of lease companies.

Belief has been recognized for its world-class design and production for clients including Columbia-Tristar, USA Networks, TVS Superstation, New Line Cinema, The Food Network, Universal Pictures, The Discovery Channel, The Disney Channel, Mattel, and many others. The company has designed and produced an extensive list of image campaigns, show opens, originally produced content, and stylized graphics for commercials and on-air promotions.

Belief also founded an experimental content division in 1999, known as Belief EXP. It exists to stretch the talents of its in-house designers in the arena of experimental media, fine art, and non-commercial creative content. Belief EXP projects have been showcased extensively at film festivals, museums, and galleries including The Sundance Film Festival, The Museum of Modern Art San Francisco, The Museum of Contemporary Art Los Angeles, New York VideoFest Lincoln Center, and Resfest.

Contact:

Belief
1832 Franklin Street
Santa Monica, CA 90404
Tel: (310) 998-0099
Fax: (310) 998-0066
www.belief.com

ATTIK : Adidas Performance

A dense collage of graphical layers and treated live-action footage.

Performance was originally projected at the Adidas global marketing meeting at the Sydney Opera House in March 1999. Later that year it appeared in Adidas stores in Europe and eventually as television commercials in the United States. This high-energy video quickly intercuts between highly processed images of athletes melded with graphical backgrounds and provocative type.

The creation of this spot wound a path from After Effects to 16mm film to the discreet inferno* to the Quantel Henry and back to the inferno*. By combining systems, and pushing each to their limit, directors Monica Perez and Simon Dixon of ATTIK felt they were able to achieve a spontaneous energy that would not otherwise be attainable through careful planning. We'll step through some of the individual frames, explaining some of the techniques used.

The Adidas Performance video combines filmed athletes, abstract backgrounds, heavily treated text, and other graphic elements to create a tightly wound, high-energy collage.

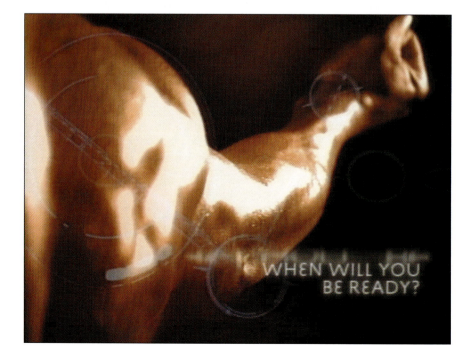

WHEN WILL YOU BE READY?

Exploring the Spot

Open the project **ATTIK_Adidas_ref.aep** on the DVD that came with this book. Play back the entire clip, **ATTIK_Adidas_Perf.mov**, by double-clicking on it in the Project window's **Sources** folder, or locating it on the DVD and using QuickTime Player. Now open the comp **[01_ATTIK_Adidas_final]**. We'll be referring to different sections of the finished piece by using composition markers – just hit the corresponding number to jump to that point. If you have a lot of RAM installed (Performance is one minute long), you can RAM Preview the entire piece by hitting 0 on the extended keypad or using the Composition> Preview>RAM Preview menu option. You can preview just sections of the comp – such as between two markers – by setting the comp's work area.

Got all that?! Good. Now, referring to the comp markers in **[01_ATTIK_Adidas_final]**:

Marking Time

Comp markers are used to mark specific frames in the animation. Press the numbers 0–9 on your keyboard (not the keypad) to jump to these marked frames.

1 A large amount of the tension in this spot is created by the way the images of the athletes flicker from frame to frame. Step forward from this marker (use the Page Down key) to get an idea for how fast these flickers occur.

2 A female athlete slowly comes into focus as graphics flicker on top.

2 Another technique is to blur the athletes in and out of focus. A lot of this was done "in camera" using manual defocusing. As you step (press page down repeatedly) or play (hit the spacebar) from here, note how the female athlete slowly comes into focus while the graphics flicker at a much faster rate on top. The combination of skittering elements with slower or more linear layers is used throughout.

3 Lending to the concept that athletic performance is a science – an appropriate message for a sporting goods company – is the regular use of technical graphics such as circles, graphs, and connecting lines over muscles and bodies. This marker shows the scene from the first image (opposite page) of circles over a well-developed arm.

4 A variety of graphic elements were constructed to overlay the live action and backgrounds, such as the modern update on da Vinci.

4 Continuing the theme, this scene plots an athlete stretching over a grid. The organic-looking background was a real backdrop that was shot at the same time as the action; the more technical elements were

7 Distorted type is used to great effect throughout the piece to echo the main message. Also note the honeycomb pattern in the background, mimicking the pattern on a real soccer ball.

overlaid later. Overall, note the cinematic switching between close-up, medium, and wide shots, such as between this full-body image and the close-up on the arm in the previous scene.

5 Another good example of the "flickering" technique is the female athlete running. This is one of the sequences we'll step through later. Note the slow motion nature of this shot as well as others; many scenes were filmed at 48 or 72 frames per second (fps), then played back at normal speed.

6 An additional example of technical overlays combined with live footage. In this scene with the basketball player, note the spinning arrow – another apt metaphor for an athlete focused on attaining a goal.

7 A recurring image is the circular icon, this time over a soccer ball. Also note the use of distorted type here and throughout the entire spot.

8 One of the "clearest" (pun intended) examples of distorted type elements. We will go into this technique in more detail later.

9 In addition to blurring and applying lighting tricks to the athletes, ATTIK also plays with sudden jumps in time, such as this extended scene of an athlete straightening to stare at the camera.

0 The spot ends with a flickering Adidas logo, an echo of which zooms toward the viewer as the final athlete walks away.

Artistic Overview

ATTIK has a reputation for having a ball-of-electricity style that pushes through conventional boundaries. Adidas knew this full-well going in, and gave ATTIK a lot of free rein, simply asking ATTIK to focus on the themes of "performance" and "never accepting second best." Their main concern was that ATTIK capture the energy and intensity of the athletes. This led ATTIK to interpret the athlete's motion and the passion behind their drive as a series of short, inspirational visual bursts.

These bursts contained frozen and active live-action shots of pivotal moments in an athlete's actions. ATTIK wanted the live action, animation, graphics, and spirit of the piece to be a natural and fluid extension of an athlete's explosive, yet controlled, inner strength.

The live-action was shot with a very textural feel, often against graphical backdrops rather than the traditional blue or green screens. This raw material provided an organic bed for ATTIK to begin building on. Using the live action as a template, typography, graphic elements, and lighting techniques were then layered and blended above the live action. Part of this layering included processing elements multiple times then re-compositing – usually pairing unlikely source footage to result in another level of texture.

Execution

The production flow for Performance more closely resembled a jam session than a carefully orchestrated symphony. ATTIK likes using this method because they are more likely to come up with fresh ideas when they spontaneously react to the different inputs than when they try to plan everything out in advance.

The general overview went this way: The live action was shot on both 16mm and 35mm film stock and transferred using several different colorization techniques such as color casting, solarization, negative transfers, and inverting certain color plates during the telecine process. The studio Realtime in San Francisco then edited together a template for the spot with varying cuts, scenes, and transitions from this footage on a Quantel Henry.

Meanwhile, the typographical elements were created in After Effects, printed out, and reshot on film (a process we'll cover in more detail below). Radium in San Francisco then scanned in and further manipulated the typographic treatments in 3D and with Sparks plug-ins on a discreet inferno*. ATTIK's directors chose Radium because they liked working with Radium's inferno* operator, Alaina Goetz.

These treated layers of text were then transferred back to the Henry to color correct and blend with the live action. This blend of footage and typography was then re-transferred back to the inferno*. This second inferno* session saw further visual effects, dimensional manipulation, color treatments, and blending.

"Overall, this produced a system of design that would have been hard to create on an individual

The live action was shot with rich lighting and projected backgrounds, rather than on an evenly lit greenscreen stage.

After the footage was shot, it was transferred using a number of colorization techniques.

Color-treated live footage layered with organically distorted type – the result of multiple processing passes on multiple systems.

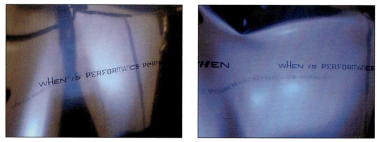

Typographic elements were printed on clear acetate, then projected on a warped reflective Mylar background, creating a multilayered effect. You can see the cameraperson reflected in the first frame of this sequence.

system," notes ATTIK. "By leveraging two post facilities working at once, we were able to create an organic way of compositing all the info, with the two styles coming together. We were reacting to each progressing pass of footage or animation, enhancing it, re-compositing, and then returning it to the original source."

Type, Project, and Capture

As mentioned above, ATTIK built the typographic elements in After Effects, with help from Photoshop and Illustrator. Stills were printed to clear acetate. A layer of reflective Mylar film was then placed behind and manipulated by hand. In some cases, different words or symbols were printed on different layers of acetate, allowing interaction such as the different elements coming in and out of focus. Additional animations were projected directly onto the Mylar. The result was a seriously warped echo of the original type.

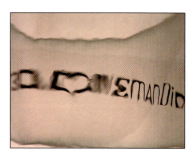

These constructs were then shot in house on 16mm film, which resulted in a grainy, slightly blurred version of the original: "Anything we can gain in camera when mixed with After Effects to create a more fluid and organic result." ATTIK also performed exposure grade changes to the footage, enhancing the depth and blackness of the film. You can see in the before and after images how this process really softened up the normally clean type.

Text elements were shot on 16mm film, resulting in a grainy, organic look (right) from the previously laser-sharp type (above).

These filmed text layers were further color-treated and processed, and blended with the live action. This particular sequence starts at comp marker 8 in the comp **[01_ATTIK_Adidas_final]**.

"The typographic elements work so well because of the combination of real and virtual elements – things shot and things created on the fly," ATTIK suggests. The spontaneity goes well beyond what most could animate with keyframes and a plug-in. To a degree this means that you have to live with what you shot and find a way to make it work, rather than composing and balancing a frame like a carefully considered painting. However, the result practically crackles with energy.

disContinuity

The energy projected in Performance is not restricted to the warping of typographic elements. ATTIK employed several techniques to make the live action flicker and jump in unexpected ways, all serving to keep the viewer's attention. Several of these sequences are illustrated below; also make sure you check out the comp [**01_ATTIK_Adidas_final**] in the project **ATTIK_Adidas_ref.aep** on the enclosed DVD to get a better idea of how these techniques work at full speed.

One is through lighting and color. A good example starts at comp marker 1, flickering the first athlete with yellow hot spots over a basic blue tonality as he slowly walks toward the camera. As you look at the sequence above, keep in mind that this does not happen as a slow crossfade; these are subsequent frames at 29.97 fps. In addition to lighting tricks and colorizations during the telecine process, ATTIK also employed several custom Sparks (inferno*-speak for plug-ins) to achieve lighting and texture effects.

Another way this energy is projected is through cuts between different versions of the same footage, varying levels of blur, colorization, even points in time. Overall, this is a linear shot, which gives continuity, but these jumps catch the eye before it has a chance to become too familiar (and therefore bored) with the shot. The images below are taken from the sequence that occurs from comp marker 5 forward,

One of the graphical text elements used in Performance. This grid-like theme appears in several scenes composited with the live action.

with the main jumpiness occurring near the beginning and end of the overall scene as bookends. Step through it to see the variety of lighting and blurs.

Jumping in time is another way to introduce these breaks. You've undoubtedly seen the technique of running footage fast, then slow (made easy with After Effects' Time Remapping feature); when pure jumps in time are applied to an otherwise slow action shot, you get this effect at its extreme – with a much more nervous result. Look closely at the sequence above (which starts after comp marker 8 in the final spot) stepping just a few frames per image: You'll also note some double exposures resulting in layering the footage with itself, offset in time.

Postscript

"There is really no specific recipe to achieve this specific look; merely excellent work flow and experimentation – pushing the box to break and crash by combining things that are not supposed to work," notes ATTIK. "Key to the process is a creative director willing to take chances and trust the process. It is only through experimentation that you can transform expectations into creative vision.

"It is a natural process for us to mix our media. We work in several different disciplines – live-action, 3D, and animation – which gave us a broad perspective upon which to draw. Flexibility and a more lateral approach open doors that ordinarily remain closed."

Another series of treated text elements used in this spot. Note how the word "enough" and the question mark are on different layers, allowing them to alternate which one is in focus.

ATTIK

ATTIK was founded in 1986 by James Sommerville and Simon Needham in Huddersfield, England. They have since grown to a network of offices in Huddersfield, London, New York, San Francisco, and Sydney.

They are a brand communications group that formulates corporate brand strategy and implements creative solutions across every medium – from print, web, and video to product design and events management. ATTIK sees their mission as one to ignite their clients' brands and to inspire their customers. To achieve this, they take on the role of advisor, partner, challenger, and brand guardian.

For over 18 years they have transformed their leading-edge design sensibility into a finely tuned, rigorous and thoroughly strategic approach. They use technology and open management structures to share creative capital across the ATTIK studio hubs: Huddersfield, London, San Francisco and New York. As a result, they note "The work we generate for our clients is always underpinned by a global vision.

"Above all, our creative and commercial experience and our international capabilities ensure that the ideas ATTIK delivers are not only innovative and beautifully executed, but also work."

Contact:

Will Travis
President
ATTIK
60 Lispenard Street
6th Floor
New York, NY 10013
Tel: (212) 334-6401
Fax: (212) 334-6279
Email: WillT@attik.com

Simon Needham
Co-Founder
Group Creative Director
ATTIK
445 Bush Street
3rd Floor
San Francisco, CA 94108
Tel: (415) 989-6401
Fax: (415) 989-6419
Email: info.sf@ATTIK.com

www.ATTIK.com

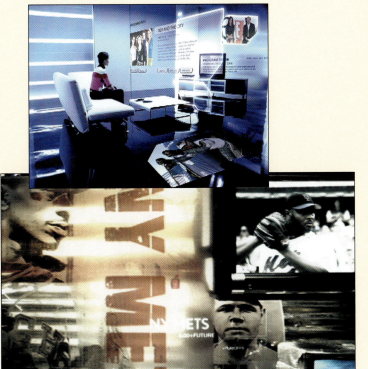

Curious Pictures : Sol

Electric pixels and wooden puppets combine to create a quirky set of beer commercials.

Ever since *The Simpsons* appeared, animated characters have been very popular. But how do you take advantage of this trend while still looking fresh and interesting? For the Mexican beer company Sol, Curious Pictures tapped the tradition of Mexican puppetry to create "Woodmation," a graphical blend of physical animation and digital compositing.

In this case study, we'll trace how these puppets were hand drawn, scanned, distressed, printed on wood veneer, filmed individually, and re-composited in a manner that makes it look like all the action took place on a puppet stage – but with the flexibility and control of digital compositing.

Exploring the Spot

Open the project **Curious_Sol_ref.aep**, locate the **Sources** folder, and play back the entire clip, **Curious_Sol_Farmer.mov** by double-clicking

For the Sol commercials, Curious Pictures constructed and filmed wooden puppets, and re-composited them in After Effects in a process they refer to as Woodmation. The result is graphical, but with textures of realism.

on it in the Project window; you can also locate it on the DVD and open it using QuickTime Player. Now open the comp [**01_Curious_Sol_final**] and hit 0 on the keypad to RAM Preview. Listen closely to the soundtrack; it's a pretty twisted little tale. Here are a few of the graphic highlights (numbers relate to Comp markers along the Timeline):

1 There are a few things to pay attention to as the beer bottle flies toward you. First is the textured flickering in the overall frame, which simulates an old-film feel; second is that the sun rays on the bottle's label are actually animating.

2 The original bottle was shot under smooth motion control; the camera shake was faked in After Effects. A clue to this is the cropped-off top of the bottle on some frames from this marker forward; this is buried outside the action safe area and is not visible during normal playback. (To check this, press the apostrophe key (') to turn the Safe Areas guides on and off.)

3 As you step forward and back between this frame and the next, notice the jump from the animated label to the puppet set with the same sun and clouds. At full speed, this is covered by the logo flying at you. The faux label was re-created in layers and matched to the real bottle inside After Effects using a combination 3D and the Final Effects (now Cycore) Cylinder plug-in. This allowed the logo to fly out separately from the rest of the label.

4 Notice the use of multiplaning as the virtual camera pans over to the farmer: the foreground elements move faster than the background

1 The flickering lighting at the start of the commercial is the result of using a blending mode to apply a sequence of paper textures over the entire frame.

Marking Time

Comp markers are used to mark specific frames in the animation. Press the numbers 0–9 on your keyboard (not the keypad) to jump to these marked frames.

ones. This is how we perceive objects at different distances in the real world. Since this puppet set was assembled inside After Effects as a series of 2D layers, Curious made sure they re-created this phenomenon in their animation.

5 To keep the commercial visually interesting while the pig tries to talk the farmer into becoming a dot-com millionaire, blinks are animated for the farmer.

4 A good example of multiplaning: the fence, which is closest, pans by more quickly than the hill with the farmer and pig on it; the sun (which is supposed to be much farther away) remains stationary.

6 In this close-up scene, the farmer's eyebrows are animated along with the blink, adding another little "surprise" element to keep the viewer's attention. To make the original puppet easier to manage, the eyebrows were animated as separate elements in After Effects.

6 The farmer's eyebrows were animated separately in After Effects to coincide with the blink, adding more interest.

7 All of the puppets were made out of wood. This is particularly apparent in this scene, where you get a chance to study the pig and the scenery behind it.

8 The signature image for Sol is the sun with its rays. The thinking-while-drinking scene transitions to the sun, which is a common thread in all the commercials Curious created for Sol.

9 Curious animated an entire supporting cast for this party scene. Note the sparkles on the bottles: rather than use a plug-in, Curious shot glitter and rhinestones on a black card through a star filter with a miniDV camera. The best flares were then composited over the bottle using blending modes in After Effects.

7 All of the puppets were really made of wood. This can be seen more clearly in the objects that are closer to wood in natural color, such as the pig.

0 The spot ends with the reverse of how it began: the set switches back to the bottle's label, which flies back into place for the final tag line.

Artistic Overview

These spots originated as a pitch by the Kirchenbaum and Bond ad agency to win Sol's North American advertising account. Curious Pictures was asked to make a 30- to 50-second animatic featuring crude, Mexican folk art-inspired characters that told a story written by Kirchenbaum and Bond.

David Kelley of Curious turned to an illustrator he had worked with for some time – Jeff Quinn – to make crude drawings in black and white. These were colored in, creating a paper cutout version of what would become the Farmer and Pig spot presented here. Sol chose this approach from a wide assortment of creative ideas pitched to the company; Kirchenbaum and Bond went back to Curious to animate three spots, refining the character's look and implementing the animation in a "wooden" style. The goal was to bring a series of twisted little fairytales to life, without looking too commercial.

The agency wanted to create a look for Sol that suggested the "roots" of being a good Mexican beer, without looking too foreign. The look decided upon was a melding of Mexican influences: Day of the Dead folk art and José Guadalupe Posada's wood-cut artwork "meets modern comic book strangeness" as Curious notes. As you look at the spots, you will notice it didn't stereotype Mexican culture using tired icons such as big sombreros. The resulting approach is more universal and current.

Execution

As Curious Pictures notes, "The beauty of After Effects is that it allows one to create animations that are a combination of animation disciplines – for example, stop motion, cel, live action, 3D computer animation, and 2D animation. When these disciplines are mixed, the results can be exhilarating. Even though some of these disciplines are mimicked in style, the final goal is to make the combinations of technique appear seamless, real, and believable."

Since Curious had to composite wooden puppets into an artificial scene in a way that made the viewers think they were witnessing a real puppet show, the company had to be mindful to avoid smooth, computer-animated looks. "Crudeness in animation is harder to mimic than one might think," notes Kelley of Curious. "There is a sort of charm in how to animate more with less; the stuttery, accidental moves; the dropped frames; sometimes a strange cut; and otherwise attempting to introduce imperfections and spontaneity."

Sol Timeline

1 week	Approval of character designs.
2 to 3 weeks	Approval of wood texture from color drawings on wood in color, and of prototype puppet design. Puppets plus some set pieces were constructed and presented at preproduction meetings with the ad firm and clients. All aspects of the script were discussed, as well as how the animation would look. Basic concerns were addressed.
3 days	All shooting was completed (with the client present), including puppet elements, set pieces, backplates, secondary plates, and motion control move on the product.
2 days	Telecine transfer including color correction and digitizing into an Avid.
2 days	Scratch voiceover and music supplied by the client were cut, and rough cuts and animatics were edited to these on the Avid.
5 weeks	Selects were digitized uncompressed with Digital Voodoo D1 Desktop on a Mac and transferred to FireWire drives. Production workflow was put into place, including naming conventions, backup protocol, deadlines, and shot priorities. Two animators did rig removal and greenscreen cleanup while another two did the compositing and animation. One animator was also assigned initially to just the product label zoom, as it required blending the live shoot with computer elements.
1 week	Client revisions, voiceover rerecorded.

The puppet sketches were printed onto wood veneer, which in turn was glued to 1/8-inch plywood and cut out.

Puppets were shot against bluescreens or greenscreens. The large green stick attached to the farmer's head can be keyed out; the wire riggings attached to his hands would need to be hand-rotoscoped.

When a character would appear small in a scene, a special "small" version with thicker outlines was created (right) so these lines would not flicker on video when they were scaled down in the final composite (far right).

Puppet Making

The characters and set pieces were first sketched in pencil, then drawn in ballpoint on white paper. These sketches were scanned into the computer. To give the objects more of labored folk-art look, each of these lines was then hatched and otherwise dirtied up in Photoshop to look more like wood cuts. The outlines were also made a dark brown instead of pure black.

Areas of the puppets were filled on separate layers from a pre-approved palette of 15 colors. The outlines were then layered on top using Multiply mode in Photoshop. By keeping the fills and outlines separate, it was relatively easy to tweak or change them if Curious or the client wasn't happy with how they printed.

These drawings were then printed directly on wood veneer using an Iris inkjet printer. This veneer was glued to a plywood backing, and the pieces cut out using a bandsaw and a jeweler's saw. Each puppet was then assembled using wire connectors the way a traditional Mexican puppet maker would have made them. They were mounted and rigged with long thin poles, and shot in front of either bluescreens or greenscreens depending on the character's colors.

Capture

Most of the puppets and major set pieces were shot solo, to be composited together later. Aside from giving total flexibility, shooting solo was physically more practical. For example, if the puppets were 15 inches tall but had to appear less than full frame, the sets would have needed to be 10 to 30 feet in size. Instead, each was shot full frame, and later sized proportionally in After Effects. Exceptions included

cases in which a puppet would be very small in the frame, such as the pig and farmer standing on the earth; special versions with thicker outlines were made so the lines would not become too thin and flicker on video when they were reduced later.

The puppeteer's actions were filmed on 35mm stock at 30 frames per second (fps), so they could be transferred frame for frame to NTSC video with no interlacing. All of the shots were then color-corrected at Manhattan Transfer in New York. Curious brought the physical product plus style frames to the session for reference. The colorist paid special attention to product color matching, like the color of the label and the beer in the bottle; the bluescreens and greenscreens were also enhanced to make them easier to key later.

Curious suggests asking for an important option during a transfer session: digital pin registration. It stabilizes any jitter or gate weave introduced by the camera – which would have made the following rotoscoping stages painful.

The puppet and product colors were checked on an NTSC monitor to make sure they would translate correctly at the final stage. This also lessened some of the worry about them during the animation stages. Everything, including some alternate color passes, was then transferred to Digital Betacam, plus a 3/4-inch or 1/2-inch viewing copy with burned-in timecode. This allowed Curious to view the dubs at home or in the office in order to start building a list of selected shots. Other elements were scanned, silhouetted, and animated inside After Effects to mimic the spontaneous movements of the live-action puppetry.

Key and Roto

All of the animation in the Sol commercials was done "on 2s" – at 15 fps. This adds a stop-motion feeling; it also halves the number of frames requiring rig removal and matte cleanup.

To create alpha channels, in most cases the puppets were masked rather than keyed out of their bluescreen backgrounds. Since their limbs and outlines didn't change shape, Curious found it was easier to create a mask in After Effects for each limb and just track the puppet's movements. The result was very clean, without the edge chatter you sometimes get from keying.

Color or difference keying was used to drop out areas too difficult to mask, such as little holes or complex shapes. The final edge cleanup was applied using the Professional edition's Matte Tools>Matte Choker plug-in. If too much edging was lost, Matte Choker was used in reverse to grow the alpha channel and reveal more edge. Another trick involved using a small amount of Perspective>Bevel Alpha to artificially reintroduce more of an edge.

Spill suppression was used to remove some of the reflections from the green or blue backgrounds. To reduce the color contamination problems resulting from natural motion blur or focus problems (blurry edges often have some of the background color mixed in), Curious tends toward camera choices that will reduce motion blur, including shooting at 30 fps instead of 24 fps. They will then fake depth of field or motion blur in After Effects.

Still Curious?

To see two other commercials Curious created for Sol, in the project **Curious_Sol_ref.aep** open the folder **Other Spots**, double-click on each movie, and play.

Since they were cut from wood, some of the puppets had rough edges and small burrs. In many cases, the puppets were masked rather than keyed to create alpha channels, since an advantage of wood is that it rarely changes shape as the puppets move.

Look closely and locate the dark spots that indicate the pivot points for the puppets' limbs, such as the farmer's arms, neck, and head, and the pig's feet and head. This is where you would place anchor points in After Effects to animate these limbs in post production.

The airplane flying was reanimated in After Effects by taking a still of the model (above), using Motion Sketch to trace out its movements, then adding or deleting keyframes to tweak the stop-motion look Curious was after (below).

Character Animation

Many of the puppet moves were executed by a puppeteer who was listening to a scratch voiceover on the set for timing. If you look closely at some of the images of the more involved puppets, you can see the swivel points for the various joints, even though the wire rigging has been rotoscoped out. Still, about 70% of the moves were modified or animated in After Effects.

There were instances when the live action footage of the puppets wasn't quite right, or when elements were added to a scene later that needed to be animated in a similar style. Simple linear keyframes for the movements would be too computer-perfect; instead, Curious used the Motion Sketch assistant in After Effects to draw out the motion it wanted.

One example of this is the airplane that flies by in the background. It was originally shot dangling from a springy wire rig over a green-screen. The puppeteer first moved the airplane horizontally across the screen from left to right while adding bumpy movements. However, the springiness of the wire made the movement too chaotic, potentially taking your focus away from the farmer and pig in the foreground.

Instead, Curious took a still image of the airplane, and set Motion Sketch to record on 2s or 3s (15 fps or 10 fps). They then moved it via the mouse while previewing the background. Afterward, they deleted keyframes that made it look too bumpy, or added new keyframes for steppiness to maintain the stop-motion flavor.

Shadowplay

Because most of the puppets and other foreground objects were shot individually, interplay between the layers such as multiplaning and shadows had to be re-created inside After Effects. One solution would be to take advantage of the 3D space and lighting After Effects offers, letting the software do the work in creating true parallax and shadows that fall correctly across multiple objects. As it so happens, Curious executed this job before those features existed in After Effects. However, even now there will still be times when you want to create these phenomena by hand to more precisely control the look you're after – even if it's not mathematically "correct."

For simpler shadows, Curious used the Perspective>Drop Shadow effect, set to a dark brown shadow color, 10% to 30% transparency, with high softness settings. When shadows fell on layers at different distances, which required different shadow sizes per object to enhance the sense of depth, Curious created their own shadows by duplicating the layers, filling them with a dark brown or maroon color, blurring them with Blur & Sharpen>Fast Blur, reducing their trans-

Parents of Characters

To perform the kind of linked character animation described in this case study, the first step is to create a layer for each limb to animate, such as hand, forearm, upper arm, and torso. You then need to align each layer's Anchor Point with the point where you want its pivot to be – in this case, the pivots on the assembled puppet were a good guide.

The trick then comes in keeping all of the limbs connected as they animate. For example, it's easy enough to rotate the hand at the wrist where it con-

nects to the forearm, but if you then wanted to rotate the elbow where the forearm connects to the upper arm, you want the hand to come along for the ride.

In the dark, earlier days of After Effects (before version 5), the only solutions for this was to either animate the Position of the hand as well, or to create separate composition for each set of limbs so they could be rotated as a group: For example, one that contained the hand and forearm, a second that contained the hand+forearm comp plus the upper arm, and

then a third that contained this second comp plus the torso.

Nowadays, the easy way is to use the Parenting feature in After Effects to build a chain of parent-child relationships. In the example here, the hand would be parented to the forearm, which in turn would be parented to the upper arm, which in turn would be parented to the torso. This keeps all the animation inside one comp. For more on this technique, make sure you check out the RoboTV and the Flamingo 4 tutorials earlier in this book.

---

parency, and compositing them using the Multiply blending mode. The combination of colored shadows and blending modes gives richer color variations inside the shadowed areas.

These shadow layers were then offset in position depending on how far (in virtual space) the shadow was to be cast onto a receiving layer behind. Layers that received shadows were then duplicated and used as track mattes for the shadow-casting layers. In this way, the shadows were automatically masked to appear just on specific layers. This procedure was repeated per layer every time a shadow needed to be cast at a different "distance" onto another layer.

This technique, combined with the multiplaning discussed earlier, allowed Curious to re-assemble a world with an interplay of light and movement that could fool the viewer into thinking all the action took place on one physical set – without the headache of trying to coordinate and shoot all the movements in one pass.

Finally, Curious created lighting mattes for the overall scene, which give the impression of a light focused on the middle of the scene, getting darker in the corners as the light's cone of illumination falls off. To do this, they masked Solids with very large feather settings (about 200 pixels or so), reduced their transparency, and used the Multiply blending mode on top. Remember that multiplying a dark object on top of another layer will darken the underlying layer.

Notice how the shadow from the bird and branch fall clearly on the pig, but are much reduced against the background. To create more realistic multidimensional shadows, Curious created multiple shadow layers, matted by the layers they would fall on. Also notice how the edges of the scene are a little darker than the center; Curious faked this lighting fall-off effect inside After Effects.

By capturing puppets and stage pieces separately so they could be animated and effected individually, Curious had more control to re-create a sense of depth inside After Effects through multiplaning and shadowplay.

The After Effects comp for the final scene. Notice in the Timeline window how many of the elements have been grouped into precomps, such as the balloons and other party revellers. The hash marks on the topmost layer mean it is playing backward; this is a great shortcut to create symmetrical animation, such as a toast in which the arm rises and then falls.

Postscript

The farmer was originally shot holding an electric carving knife. The client felt this didn't make too much sense given the otherwise rustic nature of the character. Curious made a wooden butcher knife and fork as potential alternates, with the final decision to be decided by taste and perceived violence (as you can see in the finished spot, the winner was the fork). The farmer's arm was also scanned and the fork appropriately positioned. Curious then had to rotoscope out the old arm and replace it with the new arm and carving utensil, animated in After Effects to match the live action.

Overall, Curious recommends trying to edit spots like these cinematically, varying the use of wide, medium, and close-up shots as well as cutaways. They like cut edits because they feel they add dimension to a story line, as well as reduce the amount of animation that needs to be created for each scene (since there is no need to animate overlapping handles as well). And don't be afraid to put in the work necessary to make a scene look better or more believable. As Kelley of Curious notes, "Like a painting that has been refined and retouched and polished, the hard work shows. The love and spirit comes through in unusual surprises, serendipity, and happy accidents, which all make a project all the more interesting to watch."

Curious Pictures

curious:pictures

Curious Pictures is a diversified entertainment company dedicated to creative expression in all shapes and forms. Curious creates graphically inspired live action, special effects, graphics, and animation of all types for film and television, including full-length programs such as the branded entertainment films for Mattel's line of Barbie, My Scene. Curious has developed a reputation for creating innovative animation styles. Their 30,000-square-foot facility in Noho contains a cel and a computer animation department, a shooting stage with two motion-control camera systems, a prop and model shop, and digital editing rooms.

Curious' digital division uses a combination of Mac, NT, and SGI workstations, employing After Effects for 2D compositing and graphics, and Maya plus Discreet's 3ds max for 3D animation. Digital Ink & Paint of cel animation is performed with Softimage Toonz.

Clients include numerous major global advertising agencies, Nickelodeon, Cartoon Network, and VH-1. Recent clients have included AT&T, Kraft, Wendy's, Nike, Miller, Levi's, Reebok, Sony, PBS, HBO, Mercedes, and Oxygen Network.

Credits for Sol "Farmer and Fisherman" and "Hatmaker":

Agency: Kirshenbaum Bond & Partners

Producer: Sharon Harte

Creatives: Sean LaBounty and Doug Darnell ("Farmer and Fisherman"); Megan Skelley and Chad Walker ("Hatmaker").

Creative Director: Bill Oberlander ("Farmer and Fisherman"); Stuart D'Rozario ("Hatmaker")

Production Company: Curious Pictures

Director: David Kelley

Producer: Nancy Giandomenico

Music: Gomez (original track)

Contact:

Curious Pictures
440 Lafayette Street
New York, NY 10003
Tel: (212) 674-1400
Fax: (212) 674-0081
www.curiouspictures.com

Fido : Boxman

Creating a hybrid 2D/3D cel animation Tina Turner music video with After Effects and Softimage.

Stockholm-based animation studio Fido created this series of promo spots for the Swedish Internet CD sales outlet Boxman. Each spot focused on a different artist, such as Elvis, Tina Turner, or Tom Jones, and humorously portrayed them singing a hit song by using a combination of 2D and 3D to create a final cel animation-style look.

Two recurring themes are hearts and Tina Turner's memorable lips in Fido's commercial for Boxman.

Exploring the Spot

In this case study, we'll analyze several of the animation tricks Fido employed in After Effects and Softimage to create the different scenes. Open the project **Fido_Boxman_ref.aep** and RAM Preview the comp [**01_Fido_Boxman_TinaT**] (or play the movie **Fido_Boxman_TinaT.mov** from the **Sources** folder on the DVD). This spot appears to move seamlessly between 2D and 3D realms. Fido employed some nice sleight-of-hand tricks to accomplish this, such as swapping out images on musical downbeats to cover these transitions. Referring to the comp markers, here are a few highlights to look for:

1 The O logo first morphs to a heart, then veins grow inside the heart as if they were vines.

2 Note the change from the 2D to 3D heart on a musical downbeat – you probably didn't notice it in realtime as it was masked by the musical event, but it's really obvious when you single-frame through.

3 Blood spurts as the arrows pierce the heart. Also notice how the heart reacts in shape whenever an arrow pierces it.

4 The heart cracks apart and falls.

5 Tina's face, fitted inside the logo's O, bobs around the frame and sings.

6 The scene cuts on a musical downbeat to the

Tina-face floating among 3D balloons. Note you can see her face reflected in the leftmost balloon before she even appears onscreen.

7 A balloon explodes to reveal a giant set of 3D lips singing. This sudden change masks the Tina-face slipping out of the frame on the right.

8 The lips morph back into the O logo, which later morphs back into the heart. The slogan appears inside the O heart, reinforced by the voiceover.

9 This final heart explodes, revealing the full logo.

0 Hidden again by a musical downbeat, the logo quickly cuts to an O morphing into the final CD case.

We'll discuss in more detail the veins, blood, heart cracking, singing face and lips, balloons, and final CD scenes.

Artistic Overview

Boxman hired the Bacon Advertising Agency in Stockholm to help establish its brand identity. Bacon in turn hired Fido to design and animate the spots, with the main concept of having the musical artists morph in and out of the O in Boxman's graphical red, black, and white logo.

Originally, the spots were intended only to build the brand, with broader themes such as "The Best of Rock: Elvis Presley" or "The Best of Soul: James Brown." However, there was trouble clearing songs for this broad approach; the only music they were allowed to use were songs from new releases. That meant the spots now had two jobs: to sell the brand, and to sell a specific CD.

The framework that was decided upon was to start with the O and return to it 20 seconds into each spot, add appropriate text, resolve to the full logo, then finish with a shot of the specific CD being sold.

Bacon's art director Walter Kalmaru provided Fido with the songs to use plus photos of the artists to be featured. Fido took these, watched the supporting videos (if they existed), and brainstormed a visual story to support a 20- to 30-second snippet of each song. Fido decided to capitalize on the O, using it as a common visual theme throughout to get them into and out of the scenes inspired by the song, and to tie together the various images and caricatures of the artists featured.

For Tina Turner, the song selected was *When the Heartache is Over*; the only visual guide they had were a few photos and their imaginations. They developed a list of ideas which could be used to represent the signature O in various forms, such as a heart, balloons, and Tina's famous mouth.

Fido's chief designer/director Pontus Wahlstrom drew storyboards, while the animators worked on models and motion tests. The storyboard drawings were scanned, cut up in Photoshop, and sequenced in After Effects to create a roughly timed "animatic" (animated storyboard) of the final. From here, they could divide the commercial into scenes, and decide which parts to execute in 2D versus 3D.

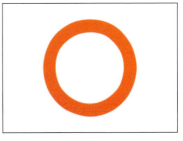

The O of the Boxman logo is a central graphical theme the spots keep coming back to.

Marking Time

Comp markers are used to mark specific frames in the animation. Press the numbers 0–9 on your keyboard (not the keypad) to jump to these marked frames.

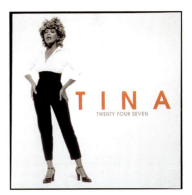

The only source materials Fido started with were a song, a few photos, and their own imaginations.

A hand-drawn storyboard was scanned in, chopped up in Photoshop, and sequenced in After Effects to get a feel for timing and scenes.

Open the comp [02_Fido_Boxman_ storyboard] to preview the storyboard Wahlstrom created for this spot. This was one of the later commercials Fido executed; they admit they were getting "a little experimental and surreal" at this stage, with throbbing hearts and huge flying lips. (One idea you'll see in the animated storyboard – Tina's head flying out of her own mouth – didn't make the final cut.)

After animation had started, Fido reports it was a normal process of showing the client the progress step by step. They found After Effects vital for this, because they could build half-finished versions quickly, render a QuickTime movie, and either email it or post it on a private web page for the client to view. Since the look of the spots was so clean and graphical, the client was able to see what was going on even with a relatively small frame size.

Execution

Overall, perhaps the most interesting aspects of the Boxman spots were deciding when to execute a scene in 2D or 3D, and how Fido transitioned between the two worlds. Here are details of some of Fido's choices.

Veins

To morph from the logo's O to a heart (above) only required animating a pair of mask shapes in After Effects (below).

Each of the spots start with the O element from the Boxman logo. Since the song chosen for Tina Turner was *When the Heartache is Over*, it was natural that the first scene was a heart. Fido created the O by using a pair of masks in After Effects, then animated the mask shapes to match the shape of the heart that appeared in the first scene.

This outline of a heart was then "pumped up" by first tracing out a series of veins, then filling the heart into a solid shape. Although the look of the final effect was 2D, Fido decided to execute it in 3D using

Softimage. Fido felt it was easier to perform the spline deformations needed to create the veins and fills inside Softimage than animating multiple mask shapes inside After Effects. Plus, the next scene would definitely be 3D; the transition was made easier by already using the same 3D model shape. Comp [03_Fido_Boxman_veins] shows a wireframe test of this animation and the final result side by side.

Harpooned Heart

The next scene – of arrows eventually causing the heart to shatter – was executed in Softimage, with a bit of sleight of hand courtesy of After Effects. Although both this scene and the prior one were rendered out of Softimage, they had very different looks: graphical 2D versus shaded 3D. When you play the spot all the way through, you probably didn't notice this transition as you were carried along by the song. Look again at comp [01_Fido_Boxman_TinaT], go to comp marker 2, and step forward a frame from there; now you'll see how abrupt the change really is. This serves as a great reminder of how much you can get away with when dealing with motion (especially coupled with sound), compared with a still image the viewer can study for a while.

In this same comp, preview the areas between comp markers 2 and 5 (refresher course: type 2 to locate to comp marker 2, press B to set the beginning of the work area, type 5 to locate to marker 5, press N to set the end of the work area, then press 0 on the numeric keypad to preview). Notice how the heart flexes each time it is hit by an arrow: a nice touch to sell the effect.

You'll also notice some drops of blood flying when one of the arrows hits; this touch adds variety to keep the scene from becoming too predictable. The blood drops were simple models following arcs plotted in Softimage.

The animation of the veins growing and the heart filling to become solid were executed by deforming splines inside Softimage. Although the final look was 2D, building the model in 3D made it easier to transition to the same shapes in the next scene, which was definitely 3D.

When the arrows pierce the heart, it is deformed briefly to give the impression of natural resistance as the arrows pass through it.

The harpooned heart set up in Softimage. The arcs leading away from the heart are the paths the drops of blood follow. Here, you see the fragmented version of the heart in Perspective view (far left) and from the Right view (left).

The transition from whole to cracked heart took place in After Effects. A mask was animated to reveal an already fully cracked version of the heart.

Making the heart crack and fall away is where After Effects came back in. Whole and fully cracked versions of the heart were rendered out of Softimage, with the whole version placed in front of the cracked version in After Effects. A mask was then animated for the whole version to reveal the cracked version behind. After the reveal was finished, the 3D cracked heart then fell away.

Floating Faces

After the heart falls off the bottom, a caricature of Tina pops down from the top and starts singing. "The design of the head was eventually decided upon after much consternation," notes Fido, and was created in Illustrator. Notice how it incorporates the signature O of the logo.

A caricature of Tina's face was created in Illustrator, keeping the signature O. These 2D splines were imported into Softimage, where a set of very 3D lips were added.

These splines were then imported into Softimage. Despite being rendered in 3D, most of the face keeps a graphical 2D look, but a shiny pair of 3D lips were added (which will appear later, larger than life). The lips were synchronized to the soundtrack; other simple animations like hair and eye movement were also added.

After Tina's singing has been established, she later floats among 3D balloons. One advantage of rendering this all in 3D is you can see her ray-traced reflection in the balloons before she even enters the scene (marker 6 in comp [**01_Fido_Boxman_TinaT**]).

Tina's head floating among balloons was animated inside Softimage. Rendering these together allowed ray-traced reflections of her head to appear in the balloons, further selling the scene.

Bursting Balloons

The relative serenity of Tina floating among the balloons is shattered – literally – by the entrance of a giant set of lips. The last frame of the balloon scene was rendered in layers so each balloon and Tina could be treated separately in After Effects. They continue to drift through the use of Position keyframes, but the real action comes in blowing them up.

Each balloon is popped by first making it grow using the Professional edition's Distort>Bulge effect, then bursting it using the Simulation>Shatter effect. Blur & Sharpen>Radial Blur is added to create a false sense of motion blur (since Shatter does not calculate motion blur). Tina's head is made to exit quickly by animating its position in After Effects; nice touches are animating its scale to make it seem to squash as it is blown off the screen, and enabling motion blur so it doesn't strobe as it moves.

For those who have the After Effects Professional edition (a tryout version is included free on this book's DVD), Fido has generously supplied a project that demonstrates this trick. Open the project **Fido_Boxman_shatter.aep** (or File>Import>Project to merge it with the current project) and step through the comp [**blowup**]. Notice that there are two copies of each balloon layer: one before the shatter, and one with the Shatter and Radial Blur effects. It is edited this way because the Shatter effect starts at the first frame of a layer.

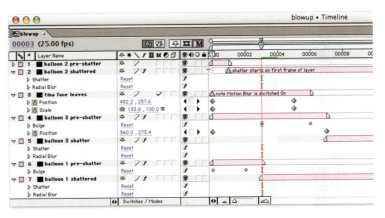

Each balloon is popped using a combination of Shatter, Radial Blur, and the Professional edition's Bulge.

Lips!

When people think of Tina Turner, they think of big voice, big hair…and big lips. For the next scene, Fido took this to the extreme by having just a large pair of lips belt out the song. Again, this was animated in Softimage.

An unexpected problem was what to do with the rest of the mouth: As you look into it from the front, you expect to see teeth and the back of the throat, but these appendages didn't look right floating around behind the lips, especially when the mouth is closed.

To cure this, Fido rendered out a separate animation with just the front of the lips turned on. The main mouth animation then borrowed this second pass as its new alpha channel using the compound effect

A giant set of lips was modeled and animated in Softimage. Notice the tooth sticking out behind the lip on the left; this and the back of the throat became a problem. A separate pass of just the front of the mouth was rendered and used as a matte to clean these up.

Channel>Set Matte, cropping the unwanted appendages. Even with this, there were still some problems with gaps in alpha channel rendered from Softimage as the lips and teeth tore at each other. The plug-in Miracle Alpha Cleaner from the Composite Wizard set (distributed by Red Giant Software) helped cure this without resorting to hand repair of the mattes.

Da Bomb

The giant lips transitioned back to the familiar O element with more sleight of hand: They were animated into a roughly circular shape, then the video cut on another musical downbeat to a graphical O in After Effects. You can see this by going to comp marker 8 in the composition [01_Fido_Boxman_TinaT] and stepping forward frame by frame (remember you can use the Page Down key for this). Again: When things are moving fast, and timed to music, it's amazing what the eye and brain will accept as continuous. The subsequent throbbing was done with simple Scale keyframes in After Effects.

A fuse constructed of a simple solid suddenly appears, progressively hidden with a mask as it burns down. The sparks on the fuse were created with Final Effects (now Cycore) Particle World. This proved faster than creating it in Softimage, and it certainly looks fine. As the fuse

The final heart is blown up in Softimage using the Explode plug-in, in order to get more depth and perspective. A soft feathered mask then reveals the Boxman logo underneath.

burns down, the masks that form the O were animated to form the recurring heart shape. The heart then suddenly contracts, which covers the switch back to a 3D heart.

This 3D heart was then blown up in Softimage using a plug-in called – appropriately enough – Explode. Fido opted for a 3D explosion this time because they felt the need for the extra depth and perspective that a real 3D package gave them. This explosion covers an animated heart-shaped mask with a large feather opening up to reveal the Boxman logo. Since they had already established the throbbing O and the heart shape as common motifs, they decided to continue to use them here for visual interest, and to help lead into the final transition.

CD Cover

Each Boxman commercial ends with the CD of the music it's promoting. The question then becomes how you transition to it. As Fido explains, "The transition to the pack shot of Tina's CD cover turned out to be more complicated than it probably should have been, but it wasn't really clear what anyone wanted until we found something which looked good, and seemed to match the music."

The heart/circle steadily grew bigger with each throb, and over the last couple of frames turned into a rectangular-ish shape. At the same time, the CD case scene – modeled and rendered in Softimage – was faded in underneath as it was morphed in shape to match using the Professional edition's Distort> Mesh Warp, which allowed the two to wipe together "as seamlessly as any two completely different things could."

The CD case was repurposed from another job Fido had done previously, which required far more detail than you get to see here. The fortunate bit was they had already figured out the lighting: Even though it looks like just one big specular hot spot, in reality myriad lights were employed to make it look like hard, cheap plastic.

The drop shadow from the CD case was a copy of the CD case, using Channel>Shift Channels to convert its alpha channel into RGB. It was then inverted, blurred, and tweaked using Channel>Levels to get the look Fido wanted.

The fuse is a simple solid; the sparks were created in After Effects using Simulation>Particle World.

The CD case was also modeled in Softimage. Notice the large number of lights around it employed to fake the look of one big light hitting cheap plastic.

A high resolution screen dump (**Fido_TinaT_finalscreen.tif**) of the final Timeline window is included in the Sources folder in the project **[Fido_Boxman_ref.aep]** for you to study. Note the adjustment layer applied on top; Edge Blur from the Composite Wizard third-party plug-in set was used to even out the antialiasing and smooth some of the sharpness resulting from using all synthetic sources.

Parting Shots

The issue of color correction was considered from the very beginning, especially since the scenes bounced between 3D rendered out of Softimage and 2D created in After Effects, and Boxman's signature red color was so distinctive. In the end Fido decided to just be careful when modeling and texturing, and leave the 3D renders largely untouched when they were later brought into After Effects. If the color shift was too great, Fido preferred to re-render the offending sequence, rather than risk posterizing the image by trying to shift it too much with color correction in After Effects. (If you have the Professional edition, this is a reason to take advantage of its 16-bit per channel mode.)

As a last step, Fido added an adjustment layer on top of the final composition, applying a small amount of CW Edge Blur from the Composite Wizard set. Because all of the images and sequences were very graphic and created digitally, Fido felt it necessary to apply a blur over the top to take away the unnaturally sharp look of all the layers, and to even up the different levels of antialiasing which were created by different programs and techniques.

Fido notes that it may seem a lot of cheats were used and corners cut, but that several factors allowed them to get away with it. One was that it was a relatively fast-paced commercial. There were lots of things going on, and new images would jump up and disappear before anyone would really have a good look at them. Another reason was that the whole job was synchronized to an obvious music track which had a strong beat to it. The mere presence of a strong beat helps propel the viewer from scene to scene, and the transitions are perceived as bridges, rather than new scenes unto themselves.

Postscript

Fido produced four spots for Boxman in a period of eight weeks, noting that this resulted in "not much time to dwell on each." As we all do, they admit they look at it now and wish they'd had more time. But the results were still effective: Within months, Boxman was one of the most visited web sites in Sweden, with 200,000 unique visitors a month (in a country of 8.5 million). The brand was known by 30% of Internet users in Sweden, and 15% of the general population.

Although everyone agreed that these spots succeeded in establishing the Boxman brand and selling CDs on a relatively modest media budget, Boxman went out of business during the Internet collapse of late 2000. The name has since been purchased by an outlet that rents DVDs by mail in Sweden, akin to Netflix in the U.S.

To see the other three spots Fido created for Boxman – Elvis, Cher, and Tom Jones – in the project **Fido_Boxman_ref.aep** open the folder **Other Spots**, double-click on each movie, and play. See if you can spot similar tricks employed by the TinaT spot as they progress from scene to scene.

Fido

In 2000, four companies merged to form Fido Film. The four companies were well established in different areas of visual and special effects – each with its own speciality. The merger resulted in a mix of diversified talents that sets Fido apart from other companies in Scandinavia. Fido uses the latest computer techniques side-by-side with plaster, clay and silicones. Fido's commissions vary from completely CGI animated characters to radio-controlled creatures and advanced make-up effects. The focus is clearly set on character design and animation. In the autumn of 2004 the movie *Håkan & Josef – double trouble* opened in cinemas across Sweden. Fido has created Josef: a tortoise and Sweden's first realistic, digital character in a feature film.

The mix of advanced techniques and artistic skills has created an environment attracting the best animators and the most interesting projects in Sweden.

Contact:

Fido Film AB
Stadsgården 17, 116 45
Stockholm, Sweden
Tel: +46 (0) 8 556 990 00
Fax: +46 (0) 8 556 990 01
www.fido.se

CyberMotion : PAX TV Promo

Filling the frame with light through a mixture of 3D rays and 2D compositing tricks.

The LePrevost Corporation was responsible for a significant redesign of PAX's on-air image. LePrevost developed a different look for daytime, primetime, and weekends. We worked with Creative Director/Designer John LePrevost of the LePrevost Corporation plus Art Director/Designer Wendy Vanguard of Manna-Design to execute the prime-time promotional graphics. The central concept was to create a feeling of wonder using radiating, prismatic lights.

Although most of the elements – such as the PAX logo – originated as print-like 2D, the overall look had to be very dimensional. This seemed to call for working in 3D. But the way individual elements were to evolve and interact went well beyond what is easy to control inside most 3D programs. Therefore, a diorama of the logos and various light effects was created in 3D, rendered a piece at a time, and reconstructed inside After Effects. In the end, these layers faded in and out over time, were blended together using modes, and even acted as mattes for each other.

Exploring the Spot

In After Effects, open the project **CyberMotion_PAX_ref.aep**. Now open the composition **[01_CyberMotion_PAX_Final]**, and RAM Preview (0 on the keypad). This is the opening bookend for the string of shows being promoted during a given evening. Since this sequence goes by very quickly, in many cases it will be easier to step through it frame by frame to see what's happening. Using the comp

The final design is the result of compositing numerous individual 3D elements – the letters, each individual light ray and beam, and even the separate surface colors and specular highlights – inside After Effects to maintain maximum control of how they blended together.

markers in After Effects (hit the numbers 1–8 on your keyboard), look for these details in particular:

1 Pieces of characters that ultimately form the PAX logo unfold as laser beams shoot through the frame. Note that these beams alter their path to always trace along the edge of these logo pieces.

2 The light rays emanating from the logo – which started as sharp search beams, streaking off to the left and right – evolve over time: They become softer rays emanating from the ends of the character pieces. This is the result of crossfading between hard-masked versions of the beams to the beams in their original form. A smaller version of the logo also starts to unfold from inside the larger logo.

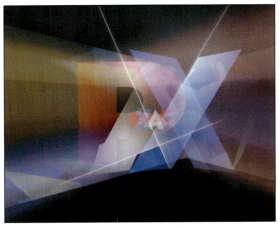

Both large and small versions of the logo unfold, while laser beams trace their edges and light rays emanate from their surfaces.

3 Both logos snap into their final shape as a set of four laser beams trace the X in the small logo. The spark in the middle of the X is created by a "scratch" plug-in from an old version of special effect wizard John Knoll's Lens Flare plug-in set, so named because the effect was originally created by scratching the film frames. (Through the generosity of Knoll's distributor Red Giant Software, a more capable version – LightFactory LE – is included on the DVD that came with this book in the **Free Plug-ins** folder.)

4 Copies of the slogan – "share the wonder" – start appearing at different angles and trajectories, while the larger logo slowly spreads apart.

5 & **6** Sprays of prismatic light shoot through the logos as the overall shape continues to evolve. Also note the colored shards tumbling inside the broader light rays. We'll discuss both of these effects in more detail below.

7 Reprising the earlier action, four lasers intersect the small X again while a spark in its center flares up. This is the motivating moment as the entire construct flies apart.

8 As the logos and slogans fly apart, a final spark is cranked up in intensity until the entire frame flares out in white. This is the transition to the promo segments of the shows that are edited in afterward, and changed as needed from week to week.

The end of the sequence reprises the beginning, where four laser beams cross the X in the small logo. After these frames, the entire construct flies apart and toward the viewer in a blaze of light.

Artistic Overview

Style frames were created for client feedback by Creative Director/Designer John LePrevost (left) and Art Director/Designer Wendy Vanguard (right) before we started the animation. Our job was to blend these ideas with the client's own, and animate them.

Before we were hired, John LePrevost and Wendy Vanguard had already worked up design ideas to present to the client. LePrevost does a lot of his work in the 3D program Electric Image, which we also use; Vanguard does most of her design work in Photoshop.

The client liked aspects of both designs. The interesting challenge to us as the project progressed was finding ways to integrate all the different bits people liked so that they flowed together cohesively. We came to the conclusion that we would not be able to do this by just building one model or set in 3D and animating it: Instead, we would be fading elements in and out, practically morphing the elements as the overall spot progressed.

One of Manna-Design's early guide storyboards for the project is shown below. At this stage, we were performing tests of how to execute the overall motion. Vanguard would then take one of our test frames, and add graphic elements on top for the client to get an idea of what the final would be like – thus her notations as to who was doing what.

We have worked with Wendy Vanguard of Manna-Design on several jobs before. She always provides us with an informal storyboard of how the elements should generally move. Sometimes this "storyboard" even takes the form of a cardboard or plastic model that Vanguard constructs so she can illustrate physically how the camera moves around a scene, or a particular element animates. In this case, she divided the characters such as the main X of the logo into pieces and rejoined them to give us an idea of how they were supposed to swivel together.

Execution

Far from being just a production job from this point forward, many of the details were left for us to fill in. A common exchange when we and Manna-Design work together is for us to ask "and how do we get from this point to the next?" and for the reply to be "Well, that's for you to figure out, isn't it?" – usually resulting in much laughter all around.

As a result, we always plan for a week or two for R&D (research and development) at the start of these projects. Manna-Design is also very open to seeing alternate ideas or interpretations, and working them into the overall design. The result is quite collaborative. Below we'll give some behind-the-scene looks at some of the R&D and problem-solving this project required.

Faux Cubist

Part of working with Manna-Design is developing a shorthand language for visual concepts, which usually ends up being a melding of our individual and shared experiences. For example, a central part of Vanguard's design included shards of glass that loosely formed a pyramid in the center of her frame. As we were studying the artist Picasso at that time, this was christened the "cubist" effect.

We were initially petrified at the idea of having to animate each of these shards by hand. Whenever trying to create a scene containing numerous semi-random objects, it's a good idea to see if there is some physics simulation engine that can help out. We turned to one inside our main 3D application at the time – Electric Image – called, appropriately enough, Mr. Nitro.

As you can guess by its name, Mr. Nitro is normally used for blowing up models into little pieces. After some experimentation, we found that if we started with simple geometry like a pyramid, kept the polygons as large as we could, and balanced off the Force, Gravity, and

The animated shards were the result of exploding a simple pyramid model in Electric Image, reducing the Force parameter so the pieces would not fly out of the frame too quickly. These example frames are from just after the explosion; the resulting pieces were allowed to fly around for a few seconds to randomize their position before they appear in the PAX spot.

Rotation parameters so the resulting pieces would tumble but otherwise not fly too far away, we ended up with a look remarkably close to what Vanguard had hand-built in her style frames.

The next challenge came in coloring these shards. Chris had read that the music group Ultravox once toured with a completely gray stage and instruments, and did all of their dramatic coloring solely through the use of lights. As a result, a lot of our 3D work starts with white or gray models, and uses lights – as opposed to surface textures – to color them.

In this case, a half dozen lights were arrayed around the Nitro'd pyramid, using colors chosen from a palette Manna-Design provided. As the pieces tumbled and faced different lights, they would reflect different colors back to the camera. The overall object was semitransparent, so you could see through individual shards to others behind. An additional three lights of different colors were positioned behind, and aimed at the virtual camera to cast multicolored light rays through the shards. The resulting surface color of the shards (known in Electric Image as the diffuse color pass), the specular highlights on them, and the light rays were all rendered separately and reblended to taste in After Effects.

The resulting cubist composite was used throughout the spot as a background element, often matted by other layers or objects. We also blurred a copy of the result to use as a fill for the text elements: We felt this was far more interesting than white text, and the resulting color washes tied in nicely with the animation already happening in the background, as they were derived from it.

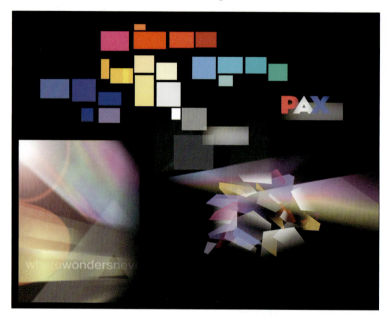

Manna-Design provided us with a color palette for the overall look (above). We used these colors as the starting points for the array of lights aimed at, and projecting rays through, the exploding pyramid (below).

In the project **CyberMotion_PAX_ref.aep**, open the comp [**02_cubist element**]. This includes a version of the final cubist/shards animation. You can RAM Preview, play, or step through this to get an idea of the overall movement. Select the layer **CM_PAX_cubist.mov** and apply a blur-type effect to it, such as Blur>Fast Blur, Channel>Minimax, or the Foundry plug-in Tinderbox-Blurs>T-LensBlur that came free on this book's DVD, and experiment with turning the image into a colorful wash. Then turn on the Video switch (the "eyeball") for the layer **Text Mask** and preview to see how your wash works as a fill for another element.

Narrow spotlights and reduced specular sizes contributed to just portions of the background logo's characters being lit, increasing the sense of mystery and wonder. Note that the P is also slightly bowed to make the light play across it in a more interesting manner.

Mysterious Text

The logos originated as simple Illustrator artwork. For the beginning of the spot, it was decided to have pieces of each character swivel into place to create an origami-like unfolding. To do this, we broke the characters down into simpler shapes in Illustrator, and converted them into 3D models using Zaxwerks' EPS Invigorator plug-in for Electric Image. A simple animation was then set up to have the pieces swivel in different dimensions as they unfolded.

To impart more of the sense of wonder the client was after, we paid attention to the surface properties and lighting applied to the logos. We used narrow spotlight cones and reduced the size of the specular hot spots to just hint at portions of the overall characters, rather than illuminate them evenly. As the pieces animated, the lights played across them. The P was also slightly bowed with a deformation to increase the amount of light play. The letters were more opaque over time to make them more substantial as the spot progressed. As with the cubist shards, surface color and specular highlights were rendered separately, so we could later decide in After Effects how they blended, including animating their intensity.

The laser beams that slash through the frame at the beginning and end of the spot were thin 3D tubes, attached to the logo pieces and textured with bright, fully self-luminescent colors. We then revealed them by animating a "clip" map quickly along their lengths.

As the pieces swiveled into place, laser beams shot across the frame, outlining the edges of the pieces. To make sure the lasers tracked the movement of these pieces, we constructed them out of very thin tubes in 3D, and attached them to the logo pieces. The surfaces of these tubes were made to be self-luminant; a clipping map was then animated along their lengths to simulate the effect of a beam shooting across the frame – when in fact it was a solid model, merely having its transparency animated.

There was a desire to make the laser beams as thin as possible. However, as we made the model pieces smaller in Electric Image, the beams started to break up into aliased lines. Our solution was to use thin tubes, but render the frames from Electric Image at double the size needed, then scale them back down in After Effects – the thin lines held up better. A combination of the Add blending mode and the Professional edition's Effect>Stylize>Glow finished the transformation from boring tubes into slashes of light.

Blending Rays

Next came the light rays that emanate from the surfaces of the logo. These were created with additional lights in Electric Image. The lights were attached to the character pieces, so they animated along with them, causing the light rays to sweep across the camera as the logo unfolded. Since the design called for a prismatic effect, we used a number of small rays of different colors, allowing them to overlap and give us prism-like gradients between the colors.

3D light rays take a very long time to render. Although we had a color palette from Manna-Design to use as a guide, we knew there was a chance the client might want the colors changed. Therefore, we "animated defensively" by rendering each ray out separately, so we could later reblend and even change colors inside After Effects.

To see this technique in action, in the project **CyberMotion_PAX_ref.aep** open the comp [**03_light rays**]. This includes a still of each ray as a separate layer – temporarily click on the Alpha swatch at the bottom of the Comp window to see their combined transparencies. Go ahead and turn individual layers on and off to get a feel for which is which. To alter the color of one of the rays, select it, and choose Effect>Adjust>**Hue/Saturation**. Change the Hue value in the Effect Controls window to get different colors.

A number of small, differently colored light rays were employed to give a prismatic effect. Each was rendered separately so we could later change their color, transparency, and blending modes to taste in After Effects.

Blending modes gave us different options in choosing how the colors in these individual beams mix. Make sure the Switches/Modes panel in the Timeline window is set to Modes (click at the bottom of the panel or use the keyboard shortcut F4 to switch between the two), select all the ray layers, and experiment by selecting different blending modes from the Mode popup menu (changing the mode for one layer will set all the selected layers). Note how these are much more interesting than using Normal. Screen mode is considered the normal way light rays would blend, and it's the look we settled on in the end; the other modes threatened to shift us away from our chosen color palette.

These rays illuminate a considerable portion of the frame. As the design evolved, it was decided we needed more black space early on, opening into more light later. We accomplished this by creating two versions of the ray composite: one with the rays in all their glory, and one masked down by a large X which animates in the background during the length of the spot. We then blended between the two over the duration of the open.

Even this X was not left unmolested. At the beginning of the spot, its center is masked out. This mask was then faded out over time to reveal a more solid X shape. The light rays were also reused as an alpha matte for the cubist layer, to prevent it from dominating the frame. These cubist layers were then given the same crossfade treatment of first being matted by the X, and then later being allowed to open up into its ray-matted version.

By using elements already contained in the animation to matte out each other, we ensured the entire animation tied together, even though disparate elements were being layered.

Different blending modes result in different blendings between the rays. Illustrated here are (left to right) the modes Normal, Screen, and Add.

To create more black space in the frame, the light ray and cubist elements were often masked by other elements in the animation. At the beginning, they are masked by a hollowed-out version of a large X that scissors open throughout the spot.

Shooting Light

A central theme for this spot was finding different ways to shoot light around the frame. In the composition [**01_CyberMotion_PAX_Final**], go to markers 5 and 6 and observe the prismatic light rays that travel quickly from the middle of the frame out through the logo. These were added to create a bit more excitement in the middle of the spot. Animating these rays to "shoot" rather than just fade on and off again required a combination of 3D and After Effects.

Vanguard's sketch of how she wanted the prismatic light rays to appear in the middle of the spot is shown above. Part of the instructions were for a spark or flare to mark their origins, distorted in a way that pointed in the direction of the beams.

Electric Image has options to create volumetric (visible) lights. These can either form a solid cone emanating from the light source, or become visible once they hit a 3D model. We used both types, rendered as separate passes. To further the sense of dimension, we composited the "from the light source" version behind the logo, and the "from the surface of the model" version on top. In both cases, these rays were used as mattes for a prismatic wash element John LePrevost had also created for the PAX daytime promo package – otherwise, we would have had to use several lights per layer or a different technique to create the desired rainbow effect.

The light rays acted as mattes to reveal the prismatic wash element Creative Director/Designer John LePrevost had created for the daytime promos he was working on.

It is possible to set and animate the overall length of rays and the size of their cone, but it is far more difficult to make them start from a particular point other than the light or the model. Therefore, half of the effect – the lengthening of the rays from their start point – was rendered from Electric Image, while the other half – shortening the back end, so the ray would appear almost as a physical object that was shot through space – was faked by animating a mask in After Effects.

The sparks the rays originated from were another application of our old friend, the old Knoll Scratch Filter. We scaled and rotated them in After Effects to elongate them into more of a beam that pointed in the direction the rays were shot. A slight problem is these plug-ins did not give us much control over the direction the various spikes extended. Therefore, we pre-rotated them using the effect Distort> Transform to alter the orientation of the spikes. We then squished and rotated them into their final shape using After Effect's normal geometric transformations.

Whiteout

This animation acted as a header that ran before previews of other shows. To make the transition, it was decided to end the open with a flare-out that ended in an all-white frame. We also provided a solo version of the ending flare as a matte, as an alternative way to dissolve on the first show to be promoted.

To realize this, we fell back on the Knoll Scratch Filter yet again. After the second crossing of the laser beams on the X of the small logo, the scratch dips in intensity, but then increases in brightness and size

Light rays were animated in Electric Image to shoot out from a point in space. They were then masked in After Effects (the thin gray lines in the top set of images) to chase the light blasts off the screen, giving the illusion that they were a physical object that was shot through the logo.

The spot ends with a flare-out to an all-white frame. By using the Add blending mode for the flare, the underlying elements appear to be overexposed, instead of just obscured.

until it engulfs the entire frame. To make sure we ended in pure white, a white solid was placed on top and also faded up over the last few frames.

The scratch was composited using the Add blending mode. Rather than just obscuring the layers underneath, this instead caused it to "expose" those layers to a brighter and brighter virtual light, which creates a nice bloom that looks like film being progressively overexposed. Even relatively transparent elements such as the large X lurking in the background are illuminated. To add to the sense of drama, some of the 3D elements were also animated to fly apart or toward the camera.

We also created a bookend animation designed to end the promo segment. It came out of an all-white frame by reversing the flare-out described above, and resolved to an exploded "cubist" version of the logo. This endcap was much simpler, leaving room for the network and its affiliates to superimpose their program line-up over the animation, and hold it for as long as necessary.

Postscript

One of the reasons we used a 3D program to render essentially flat elements is that we applied a subtle overall camera move to the entire scene, adding to the weightless feeling of the piece. If we were doing this job again today, we would import the camera move from Electric Image into After Effects to better tie together the motion of all the elements.

Why not just do the entire job in a 3D program? Flexibility, and time. The 3D elements alone took about 24 hours to render across two machines. If the spot was to be finished inside 3D, every change or tweak would require a time-consuming re-render. Instead, we could accommodate most changes by altering just the transparency or color of already rendered elements inside After Effects, or by altering the way the individual elements blended together through the use of mattes and blending modes.

Since the motion in this spot was so quick, and we wanted to create a surreal smoothness to the movements, we field-rendered the final. We rendered all the 3D elements at 60 frames per second (fps) and conformed down to 59.94 fps (the field rate) in After Effects, so we could scale and position them as needed without worrying about messing up fields rendered out of 3D. Delivery was as frame sequences, loaded into a discreet flame* for final color correction. Since no video captures were used

Manna-Design

Wendy Vanguard is Creative Director at Manna-Design, a Los Angeles-based company providing image design to the entertainment, television and corporate world.

Early in her career she designed titles for shows such as *The Rockford Files*, *The Six Million Dollar Man*, and *Planet of the Apes*. She was part of the innovative design team that worked on Charles and Ray Eames' *Powers of Ten*. Ms. Vanguard was also an Art Director for Universal Television and a Design Director for renowned broadcast designer Harry Marks during ABC Network's "Still the One" campaigns.

Afterwards, Ms. Vanguard created the award-winning broadcast design firm California Film. Clients included CBS, HBO, The Walt Disney Company, ABC Primetime Live, National Geographic, TBN, The Movie Channel, plus Australian and Canadian TV networks. She also created computer imagery for LucasFilm's *Return of the Jedi*. Most recently, Ms. Vanguard has created image campaigns and collateral marketing materials for projects including the NBC11 2003 Broadcast Package, Time Warner's The Roadrunner Group, Lifetime Cable, and The Fremont Street Experience in Las Vegas.

manna-design

Contact:

Manna-Design
Tel: (818) 789-7688
Email: wvanguard@manna-design.com
www.manna-design.com

	#	Source Name	Mode	T	TrkMat
▷	1	whiteout solid	Add		
▷	2	spark out	Add		None
▷	3	spark mid2	Screen		None
▷	4	spark mid1	Screen		None
▷	5	spark in	Screen		None
▷	6	X rayflash 2.15-> D1/60.ei	Normal		None
▷	7	Daytime 500x338.ei	Hard Light		Luma
▷	8	P rayflash 2.05-> D1/60.ei	Normal		None
▷	9	Daytime 500x338.ei	Hard Light		Luma
▷	10	slogan main 1.f D1/60.ei	Normal		None
▷	11	01.4 blurred cubist	Add		Luma
▷	12	01.1 rays composite	Add		None
▷	13	PAX sml beams v1.06 2D1/60.ei	Add		None
▷	14	PAX sml beams v1.06 2D1/60.ei	Add		None
▷	15	PAX sml spec v1.06 D1/60.ei	Screen		None
▷	16	PAX sml diff v1.06 D1/60.ei	Hard Light		None
▷	17	PAX sml diff v1.06 D1/60.ei	Hard Light		None
▷	18	Hue/Saturation adjustment layer	Normal		None
▷	19	slogan ribbon 1.f D1/60.ei	Normal		None
▷	20	01.4 blurred cubist	Overlay		Luma
▷	21	slogan ribbon 2.f D1/60.ei	Normal		None
▷	22	01.4 blurred cubist	Overlay		Luma
▷	23	PAX lrg beams v1.10 2D1/30.ei	Add		None
▷	24	PAX lrg beams v1.10 2D1/30.ei	Add		None
▷	25	slogan main 2.f D1/60.ei	Normal		None
▷	26	01.4 blurred cubist	Screen		Luma
▷	27	PAX lrg spec D1/60.ei	Screen		None
▷	28	PAX lrg diff D1/60.ei	Screen		None
▷	29	X raycone 2.15-> D1/60.ei	Normal		None
▷	30	Daytime 500x338.ei	Hard Light		Luma
▷	31	P raycone 2.05-> D1/60.ei	Normal		None
▷	32	Daytime 500x338.ei	Normal		Luma
▷	33	02.1 cubist through rays	Normal		None
▷	34	02.2 cubist through X	Normal		None

The final composite consisted of 34 layers, many of which acted as mattes for other layers. Also notice the constant use of blending modes to blend the layers together.

in the final, we were also able to re-create select frames at print resolution (3240×2430 pixels) for marketing materials.

The final composite required 34 layers, including seven sub-comps which blended additional layers such as the individual rays. Virtually all of the layers either had a blending mode applied, or were acting as mattes for other layers. The use of blending modes are what lent the highly luminescent quality to the final piece. Mattes helped ensure that no one element blotted out the others and left some black space. Using elements already in the animation to matte each other added another layer of interaction between elements which makes the final composite feel like a cohesive whole, rather than a hodgepodge of individual ideas.

Vanguard emphasizes that every successful and innovative project has been a collaboration of people with various skills and talents. She says she has especially enjoyed teaming up with CyberMotion since "they never seem to be intimidated by impressionistic ideas but find creative solutions to actually birth them into reality."

The LePrevost Corporation

The LePrevost Corporation was founded in 1975 by John C. LePrevost in Los Angeles. Considered pioneers in the industry, they were one of the first to combine graphic design with computer technology.

LePrevost has created and designed sixteen national campaign graphic packages for CBS, NBC, PBS, PAX, TCI and USA Network. Clients have included Americast, Democratic National Convention, CBS News, EMI Capitol, Greenpeace, MCA, Metromedia, Microsoft, NBC News, Paxson Communications, TBS, Travel Channel/Discovery Networks, Warner Bros. and World Cup Soccer. Their work has been honored with four Emmys, numerous gold medals from some of the world's most prestigious designs shows, the Monitor Award and an "Andy" from the Advertising Club of New York.

"We approach each client and project on an individual basis, by first understanding and evaluating their needs…then by working with them to solve problems," states LePrevost. "Our commitment to excellence in conceptual design and service enables us to create both classic and cutting edge solutions for all projects."

Contact:

The LePrevost Corporation
6781 Wildlife Road
Malibu, California 90265
Tel: (310) 457-3742
Fax: (310) 457-6142
www.leprevost.com

L e P R E V O S T

MEDIA CREDITS

*We would like to acknowledge and thank the companies and artists who provided the media we used in the illustrations and projects throughout this book. To find out more about these companies and what they have to offer, check out the **Credits and Info** folder on the DVD-ROM.*

12	**12 Inch Design**	www.12inchdesign.com
AB	**Artbeats**	www.artbeats.com
CL	**Creative License**	www.creative-license.com
DV	**Digital Vision**	www.digitalvisiononline.com
GI	**Getty Images**	www.gettyimages.com
VS	**Pixélan Software**	www.pixelan.com

Please read and understand the End User License Agreements (EULAs) included on the DVD; you are agreeing to abide by these whenever you use the content on the DVD.

Note: *Sources prefixed by* **CM** *originated at CyberMotion, www.cybmotion.com*

Thanks to Our Team

Only two names end up on the cover, but in reality, scores of people are involved in the creation of a book like this. We greatly appreciate everyone who worked with us to create *After Effects in Production*, including:

- Everyone on our team at CMP Books, including Matt Kelsey, Dorothy Cox, Paul Temme, Meg McCalmon, Gail Saari, and Sachie Jones, who gave us the tools we needed to realize the book we wanted to make.

- Guest artists Alex Lindsay and Kristin Harris, who designed two tutorials: *3D Mechanic* and *Flamingo 4*. We appreciate the variety these tutorials added to this book. Thanks as well to Carolyn West, who composed the music for Kristin's tutorial.

- All of the guest studios – ATTIK, Belief, Curious Pictures, The Diecks Group, and Fido – who willingly shared their tricks and techniques for the benefit of their fellow artists, and who dug deep into their archives to provide us with screen shots and production imagery so we could better detail their process.

- Testers extraordinaire Beth Roy and John Asbacher, whose hard work testing the first edition lives on in this edition. Additional thanks to Michael Natkin and Leila Toplic of Adobe.

- *DV Magazine*, for whom we write the monthly *Motion Graphics* column plus the occasional feature, for giving us permission to reproduce some of those articles on our DVD.

- Every one of you who bought *Creating Motion Graphics* – your positive response and support are what convinced us to write this companion volume.

- All of our motion graphics clients who have waited patiently while we immersed ourselves in yet *another* book.

- The numerous companies, studios, and artists who created the source material used throughout this book. A special thank you to Artbeats and 12 Inch Design for donating free D1 NTSC & PAL stock footage.

- And of course, the entire After Effects team, for crafting this wonderful piece of software from which we derive our livelihood. You changed the motion graphics industry, and the lives of so many people who work in it.

Production Credits

- The book layout, cover, and DVD art were designed by Trish Meyer.

- Typesetting and page layouts were performed in QuarkXpress by Stacey Kam and Trish Meyer with assistance from Dreyers Grand Light Ice Cream and Bewleys Irish tea.

- The text was copyedited by Mandy Erickson, proofread by Sam Molineaux, and indexed by Ken DellaPenta.

- The Tip, Factoid, Gotcha, and Connect icons were designed by Trevor Gilchrist.

- Printed by R. R. Donnelley, Salem, Virginia, USA.

- Whenever we created elements for these tutorials outside of After Effects, we have endeavored to explain how they were made through sidebars in their respective chapters. More info can be found in the **Credits and Info** folder on the DVD.

INDEX

Note: BT refers to Bonus Tutorial.

Example: BT8B = Bonus Tutorial from Tutorial 8.

Note: BT refers to Bonus Tutorial.
Example: BT8B = Bonus Tutorial from Tutorial 8.

Note: BT refers to Bonus Tutorial.

Example: BT8B = Bonus Tutorial from Tutorial 8.

Note: BT refers to Bonus Tutorial.

Example: BT8B = Bonus Tutorial from Tutorial 8.

CINEMA 4D

Anne Powers

Realize your artistic vision with this treasure chest of instructional projects. Each project introduces new concepts and techniques. Perfectly suited for classroom use, as well as the self-guided learner, each project is a discrete lesson complete with media supplied on the companion DVD.

$39.95, Softcover with DVD, 337 pages, ISBN 1-57820-242-6

Color Correction for Digital Video

Steve Hullfish & Jaime Fowler

Use desktop tools to improve your storytelling, deliver critical cues, and add impact to your video. Beginning with a clear, concise description of color and perception theory, this full-color book shows you how to analyze color correction problems and solve them—whatever NLE or plug-in you use. Refine your skills with tutorials that include secondary and spot corrections and stylized looks.

$49.95, 4-color softcover with CD-ROM, 202 pages, ISBN 1-57820-201-9

Designing Menus with Encore DVD

John Skidgel

Create great looking, functional menus with the latest version of Encore DVD. This full-color book guides you through all of the essential DVD authoring concepts and shows how to plan and manage projects and inter-application workflows. The companion DVD contains tutorial media, plug-ins, and templates essential to the design process.

$49.95, 4-color softcover with DVD, 257 pages, ISBN 1-57820-235-3

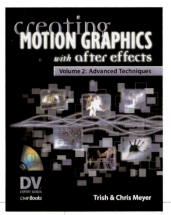

Creating Motion Graphics with After Effects, Volume 2

Trish & Chris Meyer

Refine your workflow by integrating After Effects with other programs. You'll master the vital details of preparing files for broadcast with an understanding of the technicalities of video and film, as well as tackle advanced animation techniques, expressions, color keying, and motion tracking with the Professional Edition. The CD-ROM is packed with tutorials, clips, and free plug-ins. Second edition for Version 5.5.

$59.95, 4-color softcover with CD-ROM, 403 pages, ISBN 1-57820-207-8

Instant Boris Effects

Chris Vadnais

Learn the basics of masks, splines, containers, and filters as well as the more advanced effects including rotoscoping, animating still images, text on a path, 3D extruded objects with media mapping, and clean chroma-key effects. Beginning with an interface orientation, you get detailed, step-by-step instructions on using Boris to create interesting and useful effects.

$24.95, softcover, 192 pages, ISBN 1-57820-262-0

Photoshop CS for Nonlinear Editors, Second Edition

Richard Harrington

Use Photoshop CS to generate characters, correct colors, and animate graphics for digital video. You'll grasp the fundamental concepts and master the complete range of Photoshop tools through lively discourse, full-color presentations, and hands-on tutorials. The companion DVD contains 120 minutes of video lessons, tutorial media, and plug-ins.

$54.95, 4-color softcover with DVD, 336 pages, ISBN 1-57820-237-X

Creating Motion Graphics with After Effects
Volume 1: The Essentials
3rd Edition for Version 6.5
Trish & Chris Meyer

"I can't think of anyone more qualified to show you how to get the most out of After Effects…"
– Steve Kilisky, After Effects Senior Product Manager, Adobe Systems Inc.

Trish and Chris Meyer share their years of real-world production experience in the critically acclaimed *Creating Motion Graphics with After Effects*. Learn how the program thinks as these award-winning artists share the tips and techniques they use in their own work. This full-color guide is packed with visual examples, while the accompanying DVD is loaded with projects that reinforce important skills you can apply to your own work. *Creating Motion Graphics* is divided into two volumes. *Volume 1: The Essentials* is for all users of the version 6.5 Standard Edition. It covers the core concepts and tools you need to tackle virtually every job, including keyframe animation, masking, mattes, 3D space, and over 100 plug-in effects.

The thoroughly updated third edition features new chapters to demystify the Type animation engine, as well as Animation Presets. The Effects chapter is also expanded to cover Cycore FX. The book's DVD includes free plug-ins and full-size footage.

USER LEVEL: All Levels. *Topics include:*

▶ Mastering complex animation through keyframe and velocity control

▶ Blending imagery using masks, mattes, and modes

▶ Building groups and hierarchies through parenting and nested comps

▶ Thorough coverage of 3D layers, cameras, and lights

▶ Exploring the new Type tool, as well as Text and Animation Presets

$59.95, 4-color, softcover with DVD, 496 pp, ISBN 1-57820-249-3